ISLAMOPHOBIA

ISLAMOPHOBIA

HISTORY,
CONTEXT
AND
DECONSTRUCTION

ZAFAR IQBAL

Los Angeles | London | New Delhi
Singapore | Washington DC | Melbourne

First published in 2020 by

SAGE Publications India Pvt Ltd
B1/I-1 Mohan Cooperative Industrial Area
Mathura Road, New Delhi 110 044, India
www.sagepub.in

SAGE Publications Inc
2455 Teller Road
Thousand Oaks, California 91320, USA

SAGE Publications Ltd
1 Oliver's Yard, 55 City Road
London EC1Y 1SP, United Kingdom

SAGE Publications Asia-Pacific Pte Ltd
18 Cross Street #10-10/11/12
China Square Central
Singapore 048423

Published by Vivek Mehra for SAGE Publications India Pvt Ltd. Typeset in 10.5/13 pt Berkeley by Zaza Eunice, Hosur, Tamil Nadu, India.

Library of Congress Cataloging-in-Publication Data Available

ISBN: 978-93-532-8695-8 (HB)

SAGE Team: Rajesh Dey, Ankit Verma, Madhurima Thapa and Rajinder Kaur

To my late parents

Bulk Sales

SAGE India offers special discounts
for purchase of books in bulk.
We also make available special imprints
and excerpts from our books on demand.

For orders and enquiries, write to us at

Marketing Department
SAGE Publications India Pvt Ltd
B1/I-1, Mohan Cooperative Industrial Area
Mathura Road, Post Bag 7
New Delhi 110044, India

E-mail us at **marketing@sagepub.in**

Subscribe to our mailing list
Write to **marketing@sagepub.in**

This book is also available as an e-book.

Contents

Foreword

The contemporary world sees strident globalization in ascendance. Parallel to this development is a comparable decline of democracy and closures of social and cultural groups, communities and nationalities. In the vortex of liquid existence, both familiar time and space are redefined. The canon and criteria of believing and belonging find themselves in quicksand. The emerging mentalities in inter-group relations have salient motifs of uncritical affect and unconscious bias.

In this backdrop, Professor Zafar Iqbal appropriately locates Islamophobia in the way it occurs, its scholarly representations and its examination in historical time and social space. The challenge confronts both the subject and the object of Islamophobia. After all, both representations and the subject matter of research are found in a state of continuous flux. The validity and reliability of scholarly portrayals of Islamophobia are always short-lived insofar as the object of knowledge is always ahead of what can be represented about it through social sciences. There is also the methodological problem posed by the corpus of scholarly produce on Islamophobia as it sometimes suffers from the error of misplaced concreteness. That is to say, the intellectual constructs on Islamophobia miss their focus and come to accommodate isomorphs of descriptions and representations that are not accurately the phenomena understudy. Professor Iqbal is right in saying 'how hostility, prejudice, racism, orientalism and many other cynicisms are baptised as Islamophobia'. This is complicated by the scholarly penchant, in the author's words, 'for resorting to inventive approaches to explain and theorise Islamophobia'.

Professor Iqbal opts to run a marathon in his research on Islamophobia to delve into material, both historical and sociological, where he examines the policy and practice of actors in the public sphere, as well as the real or the virtual sites where the phenomenon is represented. In sifting the substance from superfluity, Professor Iqbal clarifies Islamophobia with theoretical and empirical adequacy and moral responsibility. The depiction uses a language that initiates the reader with a vivid experience of the theme, its facets and diversities. There is also an inspirational supply of a policy vision to offer the needed correctives for the world view that fears the imagined motifs of Islam. In the process, a nuanced perspective is developed that not only enriches our understanding of Islamophobia but also clears the ground for a more inclusive world echoing Rabindranath Tagore's poem, 'Where The Mind Is Without Fear':

Where the mind is without fear and the head is held high
Where knowledge is free
Where the world has not been broken up into fragments
By narrow domestic walls
Where words come out from the depth of truth
Where tireless striving stretches its arms towards perfection
Where the clear stream of reason has not lost its way
Into the dreary desert sand of dead habit
Where the mind is led forward...
Into ever-widening thought and action....

The present intellectual pursuit paves the way for an alternative vision where phobia of Islam is sought to be defused allowing for mutually edifying transactions across the dead insularities in collective living. This helps incorporate Islam as a vital principle in the social and cultural living. The identity and solidarities of communities in this vision are leavened with a dialogue that assumes the democratic access to full citizenship and constitutional rights for everyone.

Professor Mohammad Talib
University of Oxford
Oxford, UK

Preface

For many among us, and especially for those who are least interested in history, Islamophobia is merely a media construction, the roots of which can stretch maximum to the Iranian Revolution of the late 1970s. The tragedy of 9/11, however, fuelled and crystalized the hatred and enmity towards Muslims. With this Islam also came in the limelight as an ideology and religion posing serious challenges to security and peace of the West. Hardly a few scholarly works surfaced to trace inimical relations between Islam and other religions between the First World War and 9/11. It was probably the reason that the Runnymede report on Islamophobia (1997), one of the most cited literary pieces in Islamophobia scholarship, could not go beyond 1991 in tracing the first use of the term 'Islamophobia'. Even the bestsellers such as *Clash of Civilizations* by Huntington and *Orientalism* by Edward Said did not bother tracing the roots of Islam versus West strained relations in the history. Nonetheless, even a peerless glance at history gives us huge stuff to theorize the relations between religions and provides a diagnosis of the 'problem' and prognosis for a peaceful future.

Entirety of Islam—including the religion itself, its Prophet (PBUH—peace be upon him) and the message of God (the Quran)—has been subjected to systematic denigration since its birth in the early 7th century in the deserts of Arabian Peninsula, which sent a shock wave, predominantly, to Judaism and Christianity and other religious ideologies when Islam expanded exponentially across the continents. Islam posed serious challenges to existence and persistence of dominant religions of the world due to its metastasizing growth. Followers of other religions embraced Islam in a colossal number due to one or other reasons. The message of Quran had magical appeal, which compelled people to accept it without any qualm. The Prophet (PBUH) of Islam's mesmerizing personality attracted and turned the people towards Islam. This state of affairs made elders of other religions to stop conversion of their faithful followers to Islam, accepting Quran as a message book of 'true' God and Prophet Muhammad (PBUH) as His messenger. Wars were waged to exterminate Islam and its Prophet (PBUH), which failed. Sword did not pay dividend. Then started the movement to demean Islam, prove Quran as a set of human-created poetic injunctions and the Prophet Muhammad (PBUH) as a 'magician'. The elders of other religions produced massive literature with strategic plans to impede the spread of Islam. All such literature was polemic in nature with clearly demarcated and delineated objectives.

Studying Islam and other religions in historical perspective, it can be said without any shadow of doubt that Islam enjoyed adversarial relations with other religions of the world since its inception. The nature of adversaries, however, kept on changing due to geo-politico-religious reasons. In the beginning, there was an anxiety of being disliked by Islam, which turned into fear due to its expansion. Other religions turned hostile towards it because they feared it being a competitor of Christianity and Judaism. When Islam did not stop its expansion, the hostility turned to the denigration of Islam, its prophet and followers so that people avoid embracing it, which ultimately emerged in a kind of prejudice towards Islam and Muslims in its various forms. Moreover, Muslims turned into a race of people with eternal enmity towards others and a disgusting race (indeed). Contemporarily, it has taken many other shapes like Islam as a symbol of terror, extreme fear, an orientalist 'other', an opposing political, social and religious ideology, and a threat to world peace overall. Thus, the phenomena of hatred, fear, prejudice, racism, othering, orientalists, terror and Western-opposing ideologies when combined together form Islamophobia—a corpus of phobias. Not all of them may be available at one place at a time, but in either of the forms, Islamophobia may exist. Due to its multifarious nature and antecedents, Islamophobia has been variedly defined and explained in the literature and a consensus on its definition is yet to be reached, but its manifestations are mostly common and seemingly independent of their antecedents. Essentially, Islamophobia have always been there as a phenomenon in history since the birth of Islam in the early 7th century.

The present work, nevertheless, provides an alternate way of studying the problem, more focused on providing the diagnosis of the problem and prognostic solutions to avoid further degradation of the relations between Islam, the West and the rest. Islamophobia needs to be studied scientifically to investigate the antecedents of the problem in a given social system, which might differ in various societies, but with the same set of manifestations almost everywhere. Antecedents must be identified and a solution based on those antecedents can only guarantee peace and normalcy in Islamophobia-hit societies.

This book traces Islamophobia as a phenomenon from history and attempts to break some myths prevailing in the contemporary literature. It has been assumed that Islamophobia is a corpus bundle of phobias with multiple facets/dimensions. All of its dimensions/ antecedents might not have caused anti-Islam or anti-Muslim sentiments in a society, but may be one as the primary reason coupled with some other secondarily. Anti-Islam or anti-Muslims' feelings could be because of sociocultural and economic problems emanating from Muslim populations and their ghettoization in some pockets as one of its facets. Historic prejudice and racism have also been contributing to fostering Islamophobic sentiments in some societies, especially in relation to Muslims and Islam since centuries. Similarly, civilizational clash and political threats may give birth to Islamophobia in some societies. Contemporary unrest in the Muslim world and security situations at some places might also have affected masses' feelings towards Muslims and Islam. This book covers these and some other interesting debates.

Acknowledgements

At the end of my postdoc with Professor Colin B. Grant at the University of Surrey, UK, in 2008, where I was primarily investigating Islamophobia as a mediated construction and was in process of devising a tool to measure it quantitatively, I had envisioned that this debate must take shape of a book or monograph. From what I could make out from my study of the phenomenon in the last over a decade, Islamophobia is much talked about, but least understood, construct. Much of literature on it is qualitative in nature and is seen to be produced in haste and, hence, does not provide scientific means to study the phenomenon and propose possible solutions to stop its further fostering in our societies. This book is an attempt to identify the problem in a scientific fashion by delineating on its conceivable antecedents, and ways to measure it for possible policy ramifications for the governments and policymakers.

This took me more than 10 years to reach to this stage, of course, with the help of so many scholars and scholars in the making. Professor Colin B. Grant and Professor Christopher Flood during my stay at the University of Surrey had been of great help. Professor Fazal Rahim Khan, my mentor and an ideal teacher and researcher, has always been supportive to keep me on the track during my professional endeavours. I am also thankful to Professor Diane Winston, University of Southern California, USA, who with her excellent academic knack of handling intricate phenomena related to religion and media helped and guided me during my stay with her at USC in 2013 as a postdoc fellow.

Nonetheless, Chevening Secretariat at British Commonwealth and Foreign Office was the one that made it possible for me to come up with this book. As a Chevening Fellow at the Oxford Centre for Islamic Studies (OCIS), University of Oxford, I completed most part of this book, and for that I must congratulate the Chevening programme and pay it my heartfelt gratitude. I am also grateful to the entire team of OCIS that has been extremely inspiring. Professor Mohammad Talib, my academic coordinator at the OCIS, has been a great source of inspiration for my work and me. I am also greatly indebted to Professor Dr Farhan Nizami, Director, OCIS, University of Oxford, who provided me every possible assistance during my stay at the OCIS to make this work take shape of a book. Richard Weyer, Deputy Director Academics and other colleagues at the OCIS deserve special thanks, indeed.

I have been fortunate enough to have great academic and scholastic assistance of Miss Sidra Choudhary and Mr Ali Abul Hassan for producing the chapter on civilizational dimension of Islamophobia; Miss Maria Khalid and Mr Junaid Ghouri for completing my work on otherization as a facet of Islamophobia; Mr Qamar and Miss Riffat Alam for conceiving and developing a model on political dimension of Islamophobia; Miss Ruqiya for helping me greatly on security dimension of Islamophobia and Mr Shahid Raja for helping me on the chapter covering prejudice as a facet of Islamophobia. Miss Zoya Khalid also contributed on mediated aspects of Islamophobia.

Of course, my better half and children deserve special thanks as being the ones who suffered the most during the completion of this work and my long stays abroad. I am also thankful to SAGE for its support in making this book a success in this beautiful outlook.

May Allah (SWT) bless us all and keep us protected and productive for the cause of humanity, Ameen.

Islamophobia
History, Myths and Facets

History helps us understand complex problems, but at times it makes seemingly easy-to-understand issues appear exceedingly perplex and intricate. Islamophobia is one such phenomena/construct which would get further convoluted if you attempt to develop clarity on it with the help of history; more the alacrity, more the convolutedness. Contemporary advances on the Islamophobia construct are fast paced; nonetheless, they leave more doubts than crystalizing it for a better understanding. In addition, to have a simple understanding, Islamophobia has often been associated with 'fear or hatred of Islam and Muslims'. Not only hostility, prejudice, racism, orientalism and many other cynicisms are baptized as Islamophobia, but also some of the scholars resort to inventive approaches to explain and theorize Islamophobia. The term 'Islamophobia' has been used in abundance since the release of the Runnymede report in 1997, and more so after the 9/11 tragedy. So far, a large body of literature has been produced on it in all disciplines of social sciences. Nonetheless, sustained confusions in the literature pose it to be a *literature produced in haste*.

The aim of this endeavour is to eliminate the myths plaguing the literature, which generated more misunderstandings than resolving the problems the construct and phenomenon of Islamophobia are confronted with. The following hypotheses would help us to debate on the serious issues concerning Islamophobia besides breaking some myths:

- The phenomenon of Islamophobia is historic in nature. This has been there since the birth of Islam in the early 7th century.

- Islamophobia has not been defined in a systematic and scientific fashion in literature; rather efforts have been made to include all negativities in its ambit without substantiating it with cogent rationale.
- Islamophobia is not a monolithic bloc or phenomenon, but a construct having multiple facets/dimensions.
- The literature on Islamophobia seems to have been produced in haste; hence, inundated with countless glitches.
- Orientalist's perspective on Islamophobia has mostly driven the debates and definitions of Islamophobia, which is not more than a mere fab.
- Antecedents of Islamophobia are less debated in literature; if exist, they are mostly impressionistic and not scientific.
- Islamophobia has often been discussed and debated in literature as a qualitative phenomenon. Less efforts have been made in explicating Islamophobia as a concept and making it operational for the purpose of quantitative measurement.
- In terms of its antecedents, Islamophobia at various places is not the same in nature; however, its manifestations are similar.
- Contemporary Islamophobia has genesis in its mediated construction–mediated Islamophobia.
- There are huge doubts on the first use of term Islamophobia in contemporary and most cited literature.

Additionally, there are some long-lived myths about Islamophobia, which are as follows:

- Myth 1: Islamophobia is a European hostility and is prejudice towards Arabo-Muslim people (Said, 1978).
- Myth 2: Islamophobia came into existence as a new enemy to the West after the demise of communism (Huntington 1993).
- Myth 3: Islamophobia is directed towards Muslims and not Islam.

Primarily, this attempt is qualitative in nature, but it paves a way for quantitative measurement by conceptualizing and operationalizing the various dimensions of Islamophobia. For such sensitive issues, avoiding researcher's bias is one of the most difficult tasks. At the outset, I would like to make it clear that I myself being a Muslim may fall prey to fighting to clear doubts and breaking myths in a jingoistic manner, but my efforts would be to distil the truth in a scientific fashion burying the biases deep.

Islamophobia is a complex bundle of episteme and discourses (Iqbal, 2010). Epistemology of Islamophobia propelled the scholars from various regions and backgrounds in a multiplicity of directions in at least past one century when the term was used for the first time in a doctoral dissertation in France in 1910 by Alain Quellien (Lopez, 2011). Quellien, interestingly, put up a critique on a negative posturing of the West towards Muslims and Islam and described what was it meant to be an *Islamophobe*. His pioneering perspective characterized Islamophobia as racism, prejudice and negation of Islamic civilization, and a dominant approach of labelling Muslims and Islam as an 'implacable enemy' of the Europeans. Nevertheless, Islamophobia as a phenomenon has a long intractable history. Initially, it was declared as hostility towards Muslims and the entirety of Islam. Then scholarly developments on the phenomenon of prejudice interpreted this hostility as prejudice in favour of Islam and Muslims, and lately emerged as racism, which labelled followers of a religion (Islam) as Moors—demeaning and subhuman—in some parts of the world. As the time passed by, labelling of Muslims and hostility towards Islam took different shapes and their interpretations varied; yet, it was nothing but fundamentally a negative posturing of the religion and its followers who grew manifold despite being hated in a variety of ways.

Islam since its rebirth in the early 7th century has been encountering hostility as a religion and a challenge to Judaism and Christianity alike. Rather, for the Christian world, it was an addition of another religio-sociopolitical threat besides Judaism. Followers of both—Islam and Judaism—were, then, characterized as 'people with the wrong religion' as opposed to the Christians, followers of the *right religion* (Grosfoguel & Mielants, 2006). This trend persistently sustained for centuries as even the 16th-century literature is traced with such polemics when *Broughton's Dictionary of All Religions* (1745) categorized the religions of world into two classes: 'true religions' (Christianity and Judaism) and 'false religions' (all the rest), more specifically pointed towards Islam (Dewick, 1953). Hostility of this nature was primarily unfounded and somewhat irrational, as Islam did not pose any terror or fear threat to other religions, except the voluntary mass exodus of believers of other religions and non-believers of Islam and Muslims' way of life. In fact, it was more an inability of other religions to hold their followers attached with them than Islam's promise to give them the *right direction*. Intolerance to *others*, whether religion(s), people or doctrine, has been a dominant character among all groups of people, which played an important role in mounting inimical approaches to Islam. Nevertheless, Islam was a religion of entirety of human life (unlike many other in practice); hence, it had to face an unprecedented disapproval from all corners.

Long hostility, albeit fear in traces, towards Islam and Muslims made them 'others'; consequently, the construction of prejudice as a collective attitude was the net outcome. Said (1978) labels prejudice for Islam and Muslims as Eurocentric hostility towards the Arabo-Islamic population in his widely acclaimed work *Orientalism*. Though Europe and Arabs were, of course, vital components of the phenomenon of early prejudice for Islam and Muslims, that was not all. Islam reached out of the Arabian peninsula during the Second Caliph Umar's (RA) period, and non-Arab also became part of this voyage of spreading Islam across the world. Islam reached South Asia in the early 8th century when Taif-born Arab Muhammad Bin Qasim anchored the shores of Sind in 711. Also, in the early 8th century, the Muslims, most of them newly converts, also reached Europe when a Berber Tariq Ibn Ziyad touched Gibraltar, Spain, in April 711 with around 7,000 men of his tribe and conquered most of Spain in few months (Roth, 1976). Interestingly, it has been claimed in some pieces of literature that he had quite a few Arabs with him joining the Spain invasion. A little earlier in the 7th century, the Muslims stretched to parts of Eastern Europe, which are now part of Russia, but it took them long time to get entrenched to the central Europe with Islamic flag, that is, during the 14th and 15th centuries when the Byzantine Empire was defeated by the Ottomans, while elders of other religions took such storming spread of Islam as a threat to their monarchy and stalwartness; hence, they strategized to abase Islam and Muslims by declaring Islam as 'static in time and space' (Said 1978) and its followers as barbaric, irrational, cruel and intolerant. Consequently, as claimed by Said (1978), hostility towards Muslims and Islam not only emerged in Europe during the 8th-century invasion of Spain but also in other parts of the world such as India and Eastern Europe when Muslim invaders conquered their lands. Nonetheless, except Europe, rest of the invaded regions were so poorly underdeveloped that they did not have enough to translate their hostility in literature. Europe had nation states, established institutions, so it was able to transpire its hostility in a better fashion. That's what more often reflected in the modern literature, which Said (1978) has referred to, but on a relatively large scale.

Contemporary literature on Islamophobia is riffled with mistakenly espoused perspective(s) on racism. In a way, racism has often been often translated as one of the main antecedents of hatred, since Middle Ages, towards Muslims and Islam. Racism, though, does contribute to growing Islamophobia in some parts of the world, but considering it as one of the main ingredients of Islamophobia would make the loaded construct of racism seem too simplistic. Historically, roots of hatred towards others in the garb of racism are fairly visible from the 15th-century Spain when some initiatives to mitigate the menace were launched. For instance, *La Raza* was one such effort to mix the people of difference(s) with each other to have less racial indignation among the groups and eventually a peaceful society. Vascoselos (1948) in his seminal work *La Raza Cosmica* authenticated this move, wherein an attempt was made to raise the 'Fifth Race' beyond any difference of colour, creed, race and religion, in a way of a new civilization.

Naively, Islamophobia is also labelled as a form of racism; however, it is usually termed as either cultural racism or Islamic (religious) racism (Turner, 1997). Both facets of racism need to be reconceptualized and revisited for their association with Islamophobia, which itself is a compound phenomenon, linking two complex phenomena together for a better understanding of the one call for a higher level of scholarship and interpretation of the construct from many perspectives in a coherent and holistic manner. Racism itself has been classified into many categories such as symbolic racism, biological racism, aversive racism, reversive racism, internalized racism, subtle racism and cultural racism to name a few. Almost all have to do a lot with in-group and out-group dynamics. Furthermore, racism has to be viewed for clarity as whether it is an individual-level phenomenon or systemic-level endemic. There might exist a form of racism among the people of a group against other(s), nonetheless, latent in nature. This form may be potentially dangerous for a peaceful environment and can become volcanic anytime. The form of racism with a potential to effect social order is even more catastrophic, capable of ushering legislation and offensives against the out-group at the societal level, whereas the hate or hatred against the 'others' appears normal.

Islamophobia, at places, has been contemplated as cultural racism, where Islam and Muslims are considered threat to the culture of a society, but by no mean they could take any other form. Also, whether this threat has fostered at an attitudinal level among the individuals or has set a climate of indifference and hostility towards Muslims and their religion is quite relevant for a better understanding of Islamophobia as a form of cultural racism. The worst form of racism associated with Islamophobia, nevertheless, is the biological racism, which takes a society back to the 14th- and 15th-century ecosphere. Issues related to the manifestation of such forms of racism are equally important and require a deeper understanding of the construct of racism today than ever before. Also, it is imperative to understand whether islamophobia is mere hate against Muslims or Islam as an ideology or fear of both or anyone of them, as a consequence of being affected by any form of racism. Succinctly, labelling Islamophobia as a form of racism needs scholastic underpinning of both the complex constructs and threading them in a way to develop commonalities and differences, and points of co-occurrence of the both.

Lately, orientalism has been accepted by a huge number of scholars around the world to understand Islamophobia or hatred against Muslims and Islam. The Runneymede report released in 1997 following orientalists' contours presented binary schematization between the Muslims/Islam and the West/rest. This schematization used Islam and Muslims interchangeably, though it focused more on Islam than on the

Western societies at various levels including individual, societal, polity, economics, sociocultural and religion, presenting them 'other'. Rat race following this trend in literature somewhat blurred the historical dimensions of Islamophobia, which had host of other approaches to offer. What could be viewed as the reason of this is perhaps the growing fear of communism as a threat to world peace during the 1970s and 1980s, when Said (1978)'s remarkable work surfaced. Relatively, this significant and potent danger to the world could grab more attention of the scholars. But after the demise of communism in the late 1980s and publishing of Huntington's (1993) seminal work *Clash of Civilizations* redirected the flow of literature production towards Islam and Muslims which was, of course, spiced up by the Runnymede report in 1997. Catastrophic 9/11 proved to be a watershed in this regard. Islamophobia, then, became one of the most talked about, however least understood, topics in the world media and literature.

As discussed earlier, Islamophobia, as a construct and a phenomenon, has deep and complex roots in history, archaic literature and modern disciplines of today's academic arenas. It is a complex bundle of different episteme and discourses having strong linkage with historical developments that took place between various civilizations, religions, social systems of the world, and its construct has been developed through a complex process of development before reaching its present state. Thus, it would be out of place and void to rest our understanding on any singular perspective to comprehend Islamophobia and its development process. Nonetheless, most significant would be to trace islamophobia, hatred against and hostility towards Muslims and Islam in histories that our societies have been through.

HOSTILITY TOWARDS MUSLIMS AND ISLAM: PEEPING THROUGH THE HISTORY

Just before Islam emerged as a 'new religion' in the early 7th century, Christianity was at loggerhead with Judaism with credence that the latter was the crucifier of Jesus. An anti-Semitic climate prevailed across most parts of the world, especially the areas constituting todays' Europe and Middle East. Chaos was the order of the day, wars spanned over centuries, and social fabric of almost every society was completely ravaged in the 6th-century world. As put by Ali (1949), 'Never in the history of the world was the need so great, the time so ripe, for the appearance of a deliverer' (p. xviii). And then Islam emerged on the horizon as a religion in 610 AD with Mohammad (PBUH) as the last prophet of God. Appearance of Mohammad (PBUH) as the prophet was the culmination point and the completion of Islam as a religion and the prophet hood, which started from Adam, Noah, David, Ibrahim, Moses and Jesus, and thousands more between them.

Naturally, the birth of Islam was not seen as an omen for peace and tranquillity to the already troubled world; rather, it was contemplated as another 'problem to the world' (Prideaux, 1808).[1] Denigration to Islam and its Prophet (PBUH) remained the prime objective of the church, primarily to save Christendom as the 'new religion' was spreading swiftly across the world and church's inability to clamp down Islam's growth. Misrepresentation and misinterpretation of Islamic tenets were the main tools in hands of the enemies of Islam. Thus, the Christian Byzantine, Greek monks and church elders wholeheartedly joined hands to demean Islam by calling it an 'apostasy' and not a religion but 'barbaric paganism'[2] (Payne, 1990, p. xii; Smith, 1874; von Grunebaume, 1955). Such a campaign of contempt and vilification distorted the image of Islam and its Prophet (PBUH) in the minds of non-believers, Jews and Christians alike. All means of communication including art, architecture, literature, poetry and other media were used to blackening Islam with an aim to hamper its growth in the world.

---

[1] It is also mentioned in the first edition of H. Prideaux's *The True Nature of the Imposter Fully Displayed in the Life of Mahomet* published in 1697, which the author obtained from the preserved books section of library of University of Glasgow, UK. The 4th edition of the book was published in 1708, while the 8th edition appeared in 1723. For further details, please refer to *New Cambridge Bibliography of English Literature*, Vol. 2, Volume 1660–1800, by George Watson under the Humphrey Prideaux (1648–1724) title on page no. 1705. The 10th edition of the book, published after H. Prideaux shifted to Norwich from University of Oxford, is now available online (free) at https://ia801407.us.archive.org/15/items/truenatureimpos01pridgoog/truenatureimpos01pridgoog.pdf.

[2] Originally published with title *The Holy Sword*.

Saint John of Damascus (676 AD–December 749) used gruesome measures to disparage Islam. He was a priest of the highest order of his time. His writings and sayings enjoyed a prophetic status with a huge number of followers. In his famous work *De Haeresibus* (730), he put the Prophet (PBUH) in an extremely bad light and labelled Islam a 'pagan cult' (Sardar, 1999). He rather accused the Prophet (PBUH) for writing Quran by himself to deviate people from the true religions of Christianity and Judaism, and also declared Islam as the last and greatest heresy to Christianity. (Al-Olaqi, 2010; Southern, 1962). His inscribed way of accusing Islam and its Prophet (PBUH) was followed by even the modern historians and orientalists such as Patricia Crone and Michael Cook (1980) in their widely acclaimed work *Hagarism*.

Saint John of Damascus' other writings concerning Islam and its prophet are also no less polemical than *De Haeresibus* (730). The emergence of Islam challenged his status of being the eldest of the Christendom, and the (mass) conversion of Christianity to Islam was a direct threat to his realm of supremacy. Besides, John and his family were enjoying close relations with Umayyad Caliph Yazid, as his father used to work for the Caliph administration for some time. John also suffered the allegation of his opponents in Christianity that his elders handed over Damascus to Muslims when Khalid Bin Waleed (RA) attacked his area. This made him an irreversible enemy of Islam and he never left any stone unturned to insult Islam and its followers. Furthermore, after becoming a monk and then one among the elders of the Christian fraternity, it gave him an opportunity to spew more venom against the religion of Islam and its prophet.

Islam widened its reach so quickly during the late-7th and early-8th centuries that it grasped Damascus, conquered the Tigris Valley (presently part of Turkey) and then stretched to the Black Sea, and in south it touched North Africa. In 711, Tariq Ibn Ziyad anchored at Gibraltar in Spain, and Mohammad Bin Qasim reached Sindh in Asia, while some of its gallant leaders touched parts of Eastern Europe, which now form Russia. This mesmerizing spread of Islam made the Christian and Jewish world fearful of their very existence from the map of the globe. They had to come in bizarre agreements at places with Muslims to regain their strength before sending threatening message(s) to Muslim warriors of their regions. Alternately, they had to fight with Muslim armies that were known to be exceptionally courageous and fast-moving in battlefields. Thus, declaring truce with and surrendering to Muslim warriors/armies were the ways to hold the frightening objects at a distance from them. This time was utilized to contain non-believers, polytheist, Christians and Jews from embracing Islam and adding strength to Muslims' fast-spreading population in the world. And that was done very cleverly. Muslim armies were posed as the brutal crushing forces who destroyed their lands, burnt their places of worship, cut into pieces their young men, women and infants, looted their assets and raped their women (Fernández-Morera, 2016). Peaceful acts by Muslims were posed as deceitful acts in the 8th-century literature, and surrender was labelled as surrender to the ruthless terror. In this regard, Khuddari (1955) said:

> Islam, emerging in the seventh century as a conquering nation with world domination as its ultimate aim, refused to recognize legal systems other than its own. It was willing to enter into temporary treaty relations with other states, pending consummation of its world mission. The Prophet and his successors, however, reserved the right to repudiate any treaty or arrangement, which they considered as harmful to Islam.... Although the normal relationship between Islam and non-Muslim communities is a state of hostility, it is not considered inconsistent with Islam's ultimate objective if a treaty is concluded with the enemy, whether for purposes of expediency or because Islam suffered a setback.

When Berbers and Arabs invaded Spain, Italy and Gual during the 8th century, they had to face despicable allegations at the hands of scholars from Christianity and Judaism. Saracen was the title given to Muslim invaders from Africa and Arab world and, quite disgustingly, Muslim armies were remembered as *circumcised race* in apocalyptic terms (Wallace-Hadrill, 1981). These invasions were mainly portrayed as the scourge of God and less as religious adversary till the elders of Christianity and Judaism started translating their defeats into reasons and preached their people to avoid accepting Saracens' religion and their belief system.

The 9th century's vociferous polemics included *The Apology of Al Kindy*, which was one of the filthiest literary pieces ever produced in defence of Christianity against Islam. It was written in the Court of Al Mamun in 830 AD.[3] It would not be out of context to regard the 8th and 9th centuries as the most polemical epochs of the time towards Muslims and Islam, more specifically towards the Prophet (PBUH). A massive literature was produced during the centuries to make the most sacred personality of Islam's departure from this world controversial and to attach the highest level of negativities to his burial episode. Krisztina Szilagyi[4] has put most of such pieces of literature together in her PhD dissertation (2014) at the Princeton University, New Jersey, USA. Her work was mainly driven and overseen by two notorious polemists of the modern times—Patricia Crone and Michael Cook. Reviewing this literature does not leave any shadow of doubt that the main motivational force behind this drive was hatred towards Islam. However, whatever St. John of Damascus produced, it may mainly be attributed to the fear of Islam as he being the priest with responsibility to spreading Christianity and containing the ingress of any other religious doctrine entering into his realm of ideologies, but literary artefacts produced later rest on extreme hatred towards Islam and its Prophet (PBUH). Alternatively, it could be said that they were unwilling to deprive Jesus of the status he was enjoying in Christianity by agreeing to Muhammad (PBUH) as the

[3] Its present edition can be accessed from https://www3.nd.edu/~reynolds/nehc20624/al-kindi.pdf. It was published by the University of Edinburgh in 1886 and reproduced by Sir William Muir, the then principal of Edinburgh University. Sir William Muir is the one against whose writings putting the Prophet (PBUH) of Islam in dark light, Sir Syed Ahmed Khan wrote rebuttals.

[4] Krisztina Szilagyi's PhD dissertation title was 'After the Prophet's Death: Christian–Muslims Polemic and the Images of Muhammad', which she completed under the supervision of Professor Michael Cook. In 2014, it was presented to the Department of Near Eastern Studies, Prince University for the award of PhD degree. In the acknowledgement, she owes a huge gratitude to Patricia Crone and Michael Cook for their mentorship to her thesis, and support they provided in completing the dissertation. Though extremely polemical literature she fleshed her thesis with, but she in a way hugely unveiled 8th and 9th century anti-Islam literature. Interestingly, she attempted to remove this misconception at the outset, as a result of her reviewing of archaic literature, that polemists were immensely aware of what they were writing, and by no means it was their ignorance and misunderstanding of Islam.

last and the most sacred prophet of God. Hence, demonizing everything associated with him was kept on top by the polemists of the 8th and 9th centuries, and even those who followed them until the 20th century were also greatly inspired by their literature. Contrarily, Allen (2010, p. 28) claims that there is hardly any evidence of 'substantive writings about Muhammad (PBUH)' from a European context.

The 9th century witnessed the cultural invasion of lands under Muslim control. The native Christians and followers of other religions took that horrifically, though it had nothing to do with their religion as such. However, Muslim population had their culture deeply embedded in their religion, which not only pushed its followers to adapt their lives according to Islamic festivities but also prohibited heresies of other religions. For instance, Christmas encountered prohibitions from the Muslim religious leaders, though it was a long entrenched sociocultural and religious ritual among the natives who used to celebrate it with fervour and passion. It did not stop here; rather, music, poetry, literature and other cultural artefacts put the ailing Spaniards culture at stake. The *dhimmis* (name given to non-Muslims in invaded regions as being the protected citizens) smelled danger of being at risk of losing culture in the hands of the invaders, especially when it was combined with polemics produced by the church elders who hampered the acculturation of natives through their sermons and writings. Muslims were enjoying high intellect during the century and were leading the world affairs on every front, not only militarily and politically. This was the first time when monasteries and bishops of Christianity and Judaism started cursing their youth for leaving Bible and other precious books away, and not taking any lesson from their past glories. They imbibed in their youth that their fall is not owing to Muslims' power and culture, but a punishment to their sins. The latent message was, of course, that Islam is a false religion imposed on them as being a punishment of their misdeeds and distance from Christianity. Their superior to supine status was mainly because of their distant relations with Bible and Christ, which made infidels and disgusting creatures to rule over them.

On another front during the 9th century, the production of the anti-Muslim literature reached its peak. The political and propagandistic onslaught of Islam as a religion and its Prophet (PBUH) seems unparalleled to even some of the literature produced in modern times. Primarily, it was an effort to keep Islam sweeping Christian population into its ambit. Saint Eulogius of Cordoba (Spain) (d.o.b. not known–d. 857) was one such priest and scholar of Christianity who disfigured the image of the Prophet (PBUH)—the blasphemous of all times. According to the picture he painted in his writings and sermons about Muslims, they were our servants and now ruling them, destroying their culture and religion; he also used animal metaphors such as beast and savage and said that 'Saracens (Arabs) were not human beings like us' (Tolan, 2002).

Since the 7th century, it had remained an utmost effort of scholars from other religions to pose Islam as a pagan cult, following the idolatry and caricatured Prophet (PBUH) as an idol who Muslims worship, particularly in areas far from the Arabian peninsula. It is quite in abundance in the 9th-century literature where Muslims were depicted as pagans and followers of devil. Muslims were posed as pupils of the pseudo-apostles unlike Christians and Jews (Kedar, 1984).

The 10th and 11th centuries continued with polemical writings of priests and scholars of the Christian and Jewish world. Islam became a collective enemy of both the religions that, earlier to the emergence of Islam in the 7th century, were in squabble with each other over many issues. The prominent polemists of the 9th and 10th centuries were Saint Eulogius (d.o.b. not known–d. 857), Saint Bede (672–735), *Mozarab*[5] and Iberian poet Paulus Alvarus (800–861), Asturian King Alfonso III (866–910) and John of Gorze (900–974), to name a few, who levelled the ground for the late 11th century's First Crusade (1095–1100) against the Muslim rule in the Middle East and Spain. It is commonly remembered as a crusade by Christianity versus Islam; a clash of dominant ideologies of the time; or the revival of Christianity and was acknowledged as 'militaristic pilgrimage' (Allen, 2010, p. 27) by the Vatican. Jerusalem, the holy city for all three religions—Islam, Christianity and Judaism—was scaled by the Christians and the Jews. Also, it was a revenge of the Christ followers against those who crucified the Christ.

---

[5] Term used for Iberian Christians lived under the Muslim rule in Spain.

The 12th century witnessed triumphs of crusaders over the Muslim rulers, and this was the time when common people came to know that Muslims were not the pagans or idolatries but monotheist like them; they believed in one God. Nonetheless, Saracens as pagan was the impression they carried for centuries and deviating from this would amount to an anti-Christ act; millions kept following this belief. Most important aspect of the 12th century is the translation of the Quran in various languages with an intention to translate it negatively for the Christian and Jewish world. For instance, Peter the Venerable instructed his aides to translate Quran in Latin to find out those inscriptions in it that contrast Christianity and could be transpired into anti-Christ pieces, with essentially an aim to let the people of Christ continue living with polemics against Islam and remain the enemies of Muslims. This was a time of little respite for the priests and scholars of the 12th century to reassemble their intellectual potentials and political powers to launch another offensive after the First Crusade with more power and preparation. This was his (Peter the Venerable) efforts which led Islam to continuously appear as a heresy to Christian its Prophet (PBUH) as anti-Christ.

Information about Muslims and Islam continued reaching Europe and other parts of the Christian world; hence, scholars and priests of those areas took a shift in their stance towards Islam. Yes, Islam was a monotheist religion, but they worshiped the messenger of God instead of God himself; at places, individually they pronounced 'My God', and 'they laid the idol of the Prophet (PBUH) in their places of worship like the one placed in the temple of Jerusalem', William of Malmesbury claimed (Cole, 1993). The ruler of Leon (Spain) declared the mosque situated in Toledo (Spain) as 'habitation of demons' (Tolan, 2002, p. 119), and some of them during the time pronounced that the prophet of Muslims was a self-declared prophet with other slanderous adages. Even some traces from the Spanish literature vet this notion that Islam was not a paganism, but called it a variant of Christianity, as dangerous and a devilish variant.

Earlier in the 12th century, scholars of Christianity could not find much to refute Islam and its teachings. Some of those who attempted to challenge Islam in comparison to Christianity were Comte de

Guibert, a French General and military writer; and Petrus Alphonsi, a Jewish physician and writer, using their abilities to understand Arabic, they attempted to refute some principles of Islam. Their writings were adored by Peter the Venerate and he wrote a piece where he branded Muhammad (PBUH) as a heresiarch. Later, a few more authors (mainly clerics) used other diatribes to label the most sacred personality of Islam as trickster and magician. In a way, it was submission on part of these hostile polemicists to accept the Prophet (PBUH) as the one who has great influence on people of other faiths too as they turned towards him at once on meeting him. There were mainly four or five polemicists notorious for their hostility towards Muslims, Islam and the Prophet (PBUH) during the entire century, namely Embrico of Mainz (the one who wrote biography of the Prophet [PBUH] in Latin), Gautier de Compiègne (primarily a monk), Adelphus (a bishop) and Guibert of Nogent (a French theologian and historian). Interestingly, they all were converts to the Christianity—two from Judaism and two were used to be Muslims (Tolan, 2002, p. 130).

The 12th century is generally known as century of renaissance, when Christian scholars and notables moved towards translating the celebrated scholars' work from the past and tried understanding social, political and scientific concepts to get rid of the dark times of ignorance. Aristotle's literary work and work of scientists got translated into vernacular languages. Though polemicists continued their work in their regimes, educational and academic institutions started functioning in central Europe and other parts in a bid to have their systems institutionalized and kick-start scientific developments in the Christian world. That made a difference and with a little variation in the coming centuries, it continued with a renewed vigour in the 15th century, which may be regarded as second phase of renaissance in Europe. But this was not all about the 12th century as it had the most renowned scholars such as Peter the Venerate, Gautier and Adelphus, and numerous other produced literary artefacts during this period like *Summa* and *Risalat Al-Kindi*; hence, this time period enjoys special status on the timeline of polemics against Islam and Muslims. Nonetheless, last two to three centuries' literature from Christian world clearly indicates an all-out battle against Islam and Muslims to prove religious superiority of Christianity over Islam. Though whatever efforts put in to prove Islam as Christian heresy and greying the personality of its Prophet (PBUH), it might have been more productive for Christianity if they had struggled to demonstrate the positivity of their religion in a contemporary catholic missionary style.

The 13th century takes a turn in terms of 'Christianity towards Islam'. Earlier, it was onslaught at all levels to demonize Islam, its Prophet (PBUH) and its followers. The turn was to bring the converts to Islam back to Christianity and also alluring the born-Muslims. This move, of course, was coupled with the ongoing campaign of indignation towards Islam. Disparaging Islam campaign was added with new approaches like Islam as a religion is an 'insult to God', and its followers and Prophet (PBUH) did not show that extraordinary sanctity, which is usually attached with the true messenger of God (Tolan, 2002, p. 149). Posing the prophet of Muslims in grey provided the Christian preachers an excuse to invite Muslims to Christianity, and, of course, as said by Said (1978), it also provided them with plenty of reasons to wage military and political wars against the torchbearers of Islam.

Among many others, Jaume the Conqueror (the Crown King of Aragon, north-eastern Spain, and a celebrated crusader) in a systematic manner knit a nest around Muslims and Jews (please keep in mind that during this time, anti-Semitism also grew as it used to be in the past for Christians being at ease after some successful episodes of crusade). He decreed in 1263 in favour of Jews and Muslims saying that they would not be forced to attend Christian sermons and their neighbourhood must be protected against any abuse or attack by the laymen and their religions may not be put into any dispute (Burns, 1960, 1984; Chazan, 1989). Jaume's strategy of being polemical towards Judaism and Islam is not the indicator of fervent crusader paid him dividend as many converted Jews and some Muslims got back to Christianity.

Archbishop of Toledo (central Spain) Rodrigo Jiménez de Rada (1170–1247) followed more sophisticated strategy to convert Muslims and Jews to Christianity. Unlike Jaume, Muslims took most of his attention and became foci li of his strategy. He along with some of his aides like Mark translated the Quran in Latin, where they misinterpreted most of the Quranic injunctions, and in the preface of the translated Quran, he showed the Prophet (PBUH) as a magician of highest order, without any trace of sanctity that may essentially be attributed to the prophets of God. This was a complete denial of Islam and Quran as a divine religion and main thesis of the translated work was constructed around the personality of Prophet (PBUH). Mark wrote in the preface as how Archbishop of Toledo wept tears to see the sorry state of affairs of Christians during the Muslim rule in Spain when churches were turned into mosques and instead of church bells; it was dreadful voice of Muslims' announcers calling fake faithful for prayers five times a day. For them, it was conversion of holy city of Cordoba into a filth due to Muslims and their rituals (Tolan, 2002),[6] while Reconquista was like bringing the things in political and ecclesiastical order.

Then comes Alfonso X (1252–1284), the king of Castile and León, who have always claimed himself as being 'king of three religions'—Islam, Judaism and Christianity. His interpretations of Arabic literature and Muslims were extremely polemical when he described the coloured people of other faiths, especially Muslims, as being deceitful creatures, devil and diabolical in nature. Devils were mostly interpreted in black colour and Muslims from Africa were given resemblance with the devils by Alfonso X in the literature he produced, and their religion (i.e., Islam) as the devilish religion.

Alfonso X, in true sense of the meanings, made lives of the Muslims hell during his time in 13th-century Spain. He decreed that the Muslims would not build mosques in the Christian towns, no animal sacrifices in the region, already existing mosques were declared royal properties, Muslims would enjoy lower status as citizens as compared to Christians, no legal right to appear in courts as witnesses, would not own a Christian slave, to highlight a few (Tolan, 2002). Adding insult to the injury, it was decreed that conversion to Christianity by a cousin couple would not require a divorce as cousins' marriage was considered ancestral in Christianity, and in case of one converting to Christianity from a cousin couple, divorce would be an essential act, otherwise it would be considered 'spiritual fornication'. It did not stay

---

[6] Please see chapter of the book, where John Tolan got translation of the Preface.

here, rather punishments for conversion to Islam from Christianity were even more lethal. The conversion to Islam was adjudged as an unforgivable sin, and the convert may be put to death, attaching and confiscating his properties, etc. However, if anyone who was converted and felt repentance and inclined getting back to Christianity, his status would be lower than other Christians and he would not appear in courts as a witness, would not be able to hold a public office and inherit property of any kind. Moreover, if a Muslim or Jew sleeps with Christian virgin or widow, he would be stoned to death and his partner would be deprived of her possessions. In case of a married girl, both would be stoned to death. Alfonso X was found saying that he translated and invoked Muslims law against them in a Christian state (Simon, 1987; Tolan, 2002).

Following Alfonso X, some other popes from France and Jerusalem like Innocent III also enacted similar rather more stringent rules for Muslims and Jews in their regions. In France, Muslims were not even allowed to wear the dress as the Franks do, and timings for Muslims and Jews' visit to some places of the cities were displayed (Powell, 1990). Council of Nablus from Jerusalem was on the forefront in issuing such canons and codes for Muslims and Jews in the 12th and 13th centuries. During holy weeks of Christianity, Muslims were banned entering to some of the places completely and were not even allowed to come out of their houses in parts of Spain, France and Jerusalem under the canons of Council of Nablus.

Besides such animosities in the Christians' controlled regions, some efforts are on record where the Christian elders sought Mongols' help to attack the areas under the infidels' (Muslims') control. Innocent III was hopeful that powerful Mongols would defeat Muslims in Baghdad and help him hoist the Christian flag in the heart of Muslims' dominated areas. He sent some missionaries to strike a deal with Mongols for alliance with the Christians.

The 14th century is marked with 'Divine Comedy' by Dante Alighieri, who was an Italian poet and was known as the 'supreme poet' (Hollander, 2004). 'Divine Comedy' is a long poem written by Dante that he completed in 1320, after more than a decade-long efforts on it. This is believed to be one of the masterpieces of polemics against others, primarily Muslims. Dante called it a travel through hell, and he portrayed the most holy Muslim personalities in inferno, rather in the lowest level of inferno due to his extreme hatred towards Islam and the Prophet (PBUH). Dismaying would be to know that the excerpts of this masterpiece of literature are available in various textbooks being taught to children in some parts of Europe even today. The literary significance of this artefact can hardly be denied, which was written in some specific sociocultural settings when hostility towards Islam was at its peak, but continuing to take such literary polemics as something to be transferred as an asset to future generations would do more harm than good.

Another significant episode of the 14th-century anti-Islam and anti-Muslim was meeting of Council of Vienne that took place between 1311 and 1312 AD at Vienne. One of the monumental recommendations of meeting of the Council was declaring Islam as a theological heresy at the level of morals and practice, whereby elders of the Council agreed that Muslims cannot be converted to Christianity; hence, an academic onslaught be initiated against them (Iqbal, 2010; Sardar, 1999). One of the elders of the Council of Vienne, Pope Clement V, decreed that *adhan* at mosques and Muslims pilgrimage be stopped at once, and he urged upon the rulers of Christian world to stop this infidelity in their areas, which displeases the Christ. The members of the Council demonstrated extreme displeasure on calls from mosques while discussing the matter in greater detail to see how it could be avoided. Some of the elders indicated that death penalty as a punishment for the call from mosque even did not prove to be detrimental in putting it at halt (Constable, 2010). To many of angry priests at the Council, the call from mosque was not just a religious duty but public announcement of faith and a challenge to Christianity in a way. Owing to this state of affairs, the Council resolved to launch an avalanche of diplomacy, legislation and compromises to 'Muslim religious noise' (Harvey, 2005).

Literary contributions of some of the scholars of the 14th century are noticeable. For instance, Ramon Llull (1232–1315 AD), a philosopher and writer, authored *Vita Coaetanea*, which is viewed as one of the best books available on errors of infidels (primarily, the Muslims), convincing the elders of the time to eradicate them from earth to appease the Christ (Tolan, 2002). He was found to be saying this to his friends that he had been given the task of converting the Saracens to Christianity by the Christ himself; his book was a revelation—a God revealed art. His work includes around 250 literary artefacts and his main argument was 'not against the faith, but through the fate' (Grautoff, 2000).

Rise of the Ottoman Empire during the 15th century sent a wave of fear of Islam and Muslims across the Europe. Earlier, successions by Muslims altered the Western culture and social life immensely, of which backlash majority of Muslim minorities in whole across the world suffered. New tide of wars by Muslims under Ottoman rulers made them reach Balkan states, Mediterranean states, North England and Ireland. Constantinople (today's Istanbul) came under Ottoman control where indigenous population consisting of Christians and Jews left with hardly any option except to live as subjugated population on their lands. Nonetheless, Spain was a reverse example where last area, the Granada, went out of Muslims hands. This was the time when Columbus anchored on America's shores in 1492 and Muslims lost their last lands in Spain in the hands of Christian rulers. In a way, the world became divided among the powerful rulers, where subjugated populations were the main losers and their lost rulers.

Giovanni da Modena was an Italian painter who translated Dante's poem into fresco committing extreme blasphemy against the Prophet (PBUH) in 1420–1421. Dante's poem has already been discussed earlier, which was an imaginary visit to hell. The painting is available in a basilica in Northern Italy. According to some news reports, the basilica was allegedly conspired to be blown up in 2002 due to the presence of this blasphemous painting by some people connected with Al-Qaeda.

Luca Signorelli (1450–1523), again from Italy, painted blasphemous images of the angels and Muslims in his art. *The Damned Cast into Hell* is one of his most popular frescos where demons and devils are punishing men and women, posed to be Muslims mainly. One of his paintings, now available in the National Gallery in Washington, DC, portrays Muslim soldiers in their traditional dress surrounding the cross of Jesus hoisting flags with Turkish (Ottoman) symbols. Such images illustrate the hatred and prejudice for Muslims and Islam. Not only this, English plays of the 14th century, such as, *Alexander the Great*, *Julius Caesar* and *Pontius Pilate* are shown swearing by 'Mohound'—used to vilify the Prophet (PBUH) (Bray, 1984).

When Ottoman captured Constantinople around mid-15th century, Christian elders started cultivating fear of Muslims and Islam among the Europeans, especially Roman population in order to prepare them for any possible crusade against the Turks. They employed influential preachers to do the job. Roberto da Lecce was among them who had immense control over peoples' pulse through his sermons, which he delivered for decades. He used all the polemical literature produced in the last centuries against Muslims and Islam (Thompson & Mallett, 2013). Earlier, it was not widely read literature, but Roberto made it public through his sermons, which multiplied the fear of and hostility towards Muslims and Islam.

End of the 15th century is also remembered as an end of religious tolerance by some writers when sketching the state of lives of Muslims and Jews in Europe. Portugal is one of such examples, which persecuted Muslims and Jews alike in the late 15th century. Some of the measures taken were identical to what Muslims and Jews were already accustomed to in the past in various parts of Europe, but severity of these measures was renewed in the late 15th-century Portugal. For instance, death punishment for Muslims found having sexual relations with the Christian girls, wearing of distinctive badges on the Muslims clothes like those of slaves, controlled religious festivities, prohibition of religious sacrifices, etc. (Soyer, 2007).

Fresh wave of anti-Muslim atrocities started in the wee years of the 16th-century Spain when Muslims were compelled to convert to Christianity or leave the country, and the same was followed by Isabel of Castile's grandson Charles V who decreed conversion of all Muslims living in the territories of Crown of Aragon. This was the time when a new term was coined for those who did not accept the order and they were named as Moriscos (Harvey, 2005). Crypto-Muslims was another term, which was in use for those Muslims who have posed themselves as converted Christians, but at heart they were still Muslims and were spuriously following the teachings of Islam. Moriscos, through another royal edict, were ordered not to wear clothes of their past to retain any memory of the previous life. Interestingly, even Christian women were prohibited wearing veils like Muslims, which was nothing but a symbol of sheer hatred towards anything that may relate to Muslims. Interestingly, etymology of word moors (word used for Muslims in narrow and derogative sense) might have some link with the term Moriscos. So much so, when Columbus got back discovering the Americas, he came with some native people from the newly discovered lands, which to some of the scholars resembled with African Muslims in their ways of life and faith, and hence were named as mestizo (Mignolo, 2006). Mestizo, Moriscos and moors do not carry dissimilar meanings and connotation except people from different regions and status in the 16th-century Spain. All these pessimisms are now assembled in one word in modern literature, that is, moors (carrying negative connotation for any individual).

Muslims in Europe, in general, and in Spain, in particular, had to face systematic expulsion from various kingdoms of Spain. There are hardly any concrete estimates of Muslims' population in parts of Spain; however, some historians rely on data of coerced expulsions and claim that there were around 300,000 to one million Muslims natives of Spain during the 16th century (Harvey, 2005). But due to increasingly difficult life in various kingdoms of Spain, the Moriscos were moving to nearby areas like Morocco, etc. Their culture was being evaporated in an orderly fashion; for example, in 1525, an edict was issued to stop people speaking Arabic in public, and Arabic literature was swept out from the libraries and other public places. Many earlier edicts like non-veiling of women, etc., continued in the 16th-century Spain. Some more stringent measures were introduced, such as Muslims were not allowed to use bathrooms for a fear of having *wuzu* for prayers and were ordered to keep the doors of their houses open during Fridays and Sundays. This order vested enormous powers in authorities to have unwarranted raids to ensure that no one is offering Friday prayers at home, and they were doing like others on Sundays.

Adding insult to injuries, an edict in 1567 banned Muslim parents to name their children with Muslims/Islamic names.

Granada and Valencia had the greatest number of Muslims in the 16th century. Extrapolating a chance of reaction, the authorities used extreme coercive measures to avert any rebellion on part of Muslims. Hence, many Muslims immigrated to other places in huge number like 80,000 to 90,000 to avoid restrictions and coercion.

Most interesting piece of the 16th-century polemics against Islam and Muslims has been when priests bowed to God to seek his assistance to defend Christianity and save them from the wrath of infidels on every Wednesday and Fridays in common prayers. The prayer said (Foxe, 1838):[7]

> O lord of God of hosts, grant to thy church strength and victory against the malicious fury of these Turks, Saracens, Tartarians, against Gog and Magog, and all the malignant rabble of anti-Christ, enemies to thy Son Jesus, out Lord and Saviour. Prevent their devices, overthrow their power, and dissolve their kingdom.

Sixteenth-century Muslims in all across Europe suffered almost the same plight everywhere. They kept on moving to various locations for the sake of safety and food for centuries, their culture was completely destroyed, they were accorded less than a subhuman social status and were forced to live in ghettos, etc. What seems to be the most significant reason for all this was a fear of Islam and Muslims. Christian world was extremely scared of them to be holding any social position and power in the system. Christendom believed that allowing Muslims to hold important social positions would mean wielding Islam to subvert Christianity. Fear of Muslims and Islam as being an expanding force did not let them flourish in Europe, but they were also fearful of Judaism. Jews had to face almost same fate by the hands of Christianity, and anti-Semitism was hallmark of the Middle Ages. However, Jews due to less in numbers were not as such the direct target and they did not have much in their past to hold reigns of worlds. For them, it

---

[7] Retrieved from the online sources of Bodleian Libraries, University of Oxford, UK on 13 November 2017.

was merely a religious animosity as being the people of religion that crucified the Christ. While Muslims had done both—alleged to be the crucifiers and invaders to the Christian world; hence, they deserved more severe backlash of their past in the Middle Ages.

Reviewing it in retrospect, relations between Islam and Christianity can best be described as 'Christianity was Western, Islam was Eastern, and between two there could only be war' (Matar, 2009). Seventeenth-century affairs are just another episode in the continuity.

Thomas Mills was a polemist of the 17th century who authored *The History of the Holy War* in 1685. He said, 'God willeth it, God willeth it' (Mills, 1685).[8] He rather prophesied that by 1701, this world would be a Christian world after having total destruction of Islam, and whole lot of Muslims would be converted to Christianity. This kind of manifestation of extreme hatred towards Islam is unending while Muslims were also conceptually associated with animals like beasts, scorpions, etc., and a race bent upon circumcising Christians, while Jews suffered in a different way as hate mongers associated them with an 'odour' (Matar, 2009). Metaphors used for both the hated groups demonstrate clearly that this world was meant for Christendom only. Matar (2009) cites a good number of archaic and contemporary authentic sources of literature from *The Fairie Queene* to *Paradise Lost*, which are famous literary pieces of English, wherein Muslims, Islam and Jews have been depicted as objects of extreme hate and displeasure. At some of the places, the Prophet (PBUH) had been shown in grey and dark light. These literary resources are widely and freely available in even present-day commercial world. The main object of such acts is nothing but demeaning the Muslims and Islam, and making them appear as objectionable creatures.

Why such portrayal of Muslims and Islam was essential in the 17th century? Though it is all in continuity of what used to be the past, but Europe, at that time, had less to offer to its inhabitants in terms of food, security, employment, social security and 'liberty of conscience'

---

[8] Viewed the book in soft as member of the Bodleian Libraries, University of Oxford on 13 November 2017.

(Robinson, 1643),[9] etc. Hence, there were a huge number of people who were migrating to the countries under Ottoman Empire. This trend should have essentially been reduced and for that, scholars, priests and elders of the Christianity had to come to rescue their societies. Not only people were migrating to locations under Ottoman Empire, discovery of the Americas was also posing the world another promising place for security, wealth and food. This trend made the migration appeared mass exodus from mainlands of Europe to Americas and Ottoman Empire. On this, Henry March said in 1663, 'we are defeated and got no victories.... We have a God most great, most good, but alienated from us' (Marsh, 1663).[10]

Matar (2009) narrates in a convincing fashion the reasons for European prejudice for Islam and Muslim, when he says that it was Christians' inability to fight back and compete with Muslims in many spheres, they then turned to 'denunciation, invective and invention' and prejudice which got multiplied over time (p. 223). Nonetheless, Marsh (1663) insisted that Christians were technologically advanced and were enjoying higher mental potentials and were gifted with good institutions, but remained laggards when compared with Muslims due to their fear of infidels and devils (Muslims), and their failure was that of moral, religious, not of intellectual and technological advancement. Cribbing on the situation of Christians during the 17th century, it was pronounced that 'despite God being English, He was unable to protect His English people against the "Mahometans"' (Malik, 2012, pp. 16–17).

The 17th-century famous poet and playwright William Percy (1574–1648) also denigrated the most sacred personality of Islam in his plays as a result of extreme prejudice for Islam. The Prophet (PBUH) was shown in Madina in an insulting posture in his play

---

[9] According to the University of Oxford library sources, this book is usually attributed to Henry Robinson, but sometimes attributed to William Walwyn; this attribution was rejected by McMichael and Taft.

[10] Interestingly, multiple versions are available in Bodleian Library, University of Oxford, for this book. No controversy of the authorship and title of the book, but caricatures made on Ottoman emperors are in variety. At least different versions of the book can be found.

Mohamet and His Heaven, and despite the fact he knew it that Islam is a monotheist religion, he showed the prophet as a pagan unfortunately (Al-Olaqi, 2017). His accusations, though, have been dispelled by many scholars and polemists in the past, but he was hellbound to make his play as a masterpiece of art. More than that was probably his lust to remain part of the group highly appreciated at large as being polemicists in the history, hence depicted the Prophet (PBUH) in a compromising manner with the Angel Gabriel, and a God in Himself. Even coffee, introduced in Turkey in the 1650s, when reached Europe, was declared as 'Mahometan Berry' capable of converting English to Islam with its spurious effects (Matar, 2004).

A complex mixture of prejudice, hatred and fear is evident in literature of the 17th century against the Prophet (PBUH) and Islam as a religion. Quran was translated in a non-serious fashion and was ridiculed by some authors, such as Alexander Ross (1688), as being the most renowned, orientalized and demonized Islam. Not only he, Islam was depicted grey in some literary artefacts like *Arabian Nights*, and then popular revolutionists like Voltaire also misrepresented Islam and its Prophet (PBUH) in their masterpieces. Succinctly, Islam in totality was remained a target and victim of misrepresentation and misinterpretation due to utter hatred, prejudice, fear and orientalist approaches towards it.

The 18th century started with Humphrey Prideaux saying that Islam is a 'problem'[11] to the world (Crone & Cook, 1977; Fahlbusch et al., 2001; Hamilton, 1985; Prideaux, 1697; Southern, 1962) and is 'a punishment to the sins of Christians'. Humphrey Prideaux's posture towards Islam is based on his hostility towards it and being the Doctor of Divinity, his writings and sayings were considered no less than prophetic. His style of hostility and hatred towards Islam has

---

[11] It is mentioned in the first edition of H. Prideaux's *Mahomet: The True Nature of the Imposter Fully Displayed in the Life of Mahomet* published in 1697, which the author obtained from the preserved books section of library of University of Glasgow, UK. The 4th edition of book was published in 1708, while 8th edition appeared in 1723. For further details, please refer to *New Cambridge Bibliography of English Literature*, Vol. 2, 1660–1800 by George Watson under the Humphrey Prideaux (1648–1724) title on page no. 1705.

been followed for centuries, and even modern literature like that of Patricia Crone and Michael Cook seems to be following his footprints. Peter Heylyn, Prideaux's contemporary, in *Cosmographie* (Heylyn, 1682) and A. Ross[12] in *Pansebeia* demonstrated their hatred towards Islam without any fear of being out of logic to condemn and demean a religion, which had followers in billions. Such authoritative writers being polemicists hardly left others with any option except to continue following their line of arguments against Islam. That could be observed even in *Broughton's Dictionary of All Religions* (1745), which categorized the religions of world into two classes: 'true religions' (Christianity and Judaism) and 'false religions' (all the rest; Dewick, 1953, pp. 117–118).

The works, cited and discussed so far on the timeline, plainly indicate that scholars by large were inclined towards giving a biased view of Islam. Majority of the scholastic efforts were from those who were bent upon belittling Islam, its prophet and its followers. Character assassination of the Prophet (PBUH), denigration of the Islam and proving Muslims as subhuman, brutal forces, barbaric, bunch of beasts and fifth columns were the main characteristics of the literature produced. John of Segovia's imprints aiming at character assassination of the Prophet (PBUH) in the 15th century seems heavily followed till contemporary times, wherein he intends launching intellectual assault on the prophet. This becomes quite evident when *Bibliotheque Orientale* of Barthelemy d'Herbelot (1625–1695) was written to disparage the Prophet (PBUH) in the 18th century. The polemical work got huge applaud from the Western scholars and got reprinted multiple times after its first print in 1697.

George Sale in 1734 translated Quran in English after having spent some 25 years in Arab lands to learn Arabic and their culture for better understanding of Quran and its injunctions, translating the book with its proper cultural contexts (Sale, 1734). He was a lawyer by profession, orientalist and had mastery on linguistic discourses. This made him misrepresent Quran in a systematic manner, wherein he found it difficult to place Islam equal to Christianity. He did not stop here in

---

[12] Retrieved from http://www.jstor.org/sici?sici=0013-8304(193709)4%3A3%3C180%3ATECOPL%3E2.0.CO%3B2-H.

his polemics; rather he rudely criticized the personality of the Prophet (PBUH). Dismaying would be to learn that first Muslim to the US Congress Keith Ellison took oath on a copy of Sale's translated Quran (which is commonly known as *Alcoran*) which got published in 1764, which was nothing but a pack of diatribes.

Voltaire, a French enlightenment writer, philosopher and historian, was one of the most vocal polemists of the 18th century. He wrote worst of its kind about the Prophet (PBUH) by saying that he was ambiguously cruel and great man at the same time. He described the Prophet (PBUH) as 'a fictional and historically inaccurate fanatic character, to whom accuracy is also devoid of interest' (Daniel, 1960). According to Daniel (1960), he tried to soften his stance towards the Prophet (PBUH) in his later writings, but he never changed his mind and continued disgracing Islam and its prophet.

The 19th-century fear and hostility towards Islam and Muslims was joined by the US scholars, priests and academicians alongside the thousands of year's old enmity and prejudice of the European West. Primary reason for this hostility, fear and prejudice in the USA was migration of millions of Muslims from Africa and Middle East to a new land of opportunities, who on getting settled there started building their places of worship and congregational seats. According to Sally Howell, first mosque in the USA was built in 1893 in Chicago (Howell, 2014). Five times a day call from mosque was an unexpected ritual for Christians and Jews, and Muslims gathering on Fridays created a sense of insecurity among the natives of the land, that too the Muslims usually in their traditional dresses, somewhat dissimilar to what they were usually found wearing during the weekdays. Additionally, Muslims were initially brought to the USA as slaves and Islam was, in way, a subordinate religion in the USA in its early days. There was a great variety of Muslims brought to the USA from various regions of the world, so was the case with their languages, ethnicities, economic and social backgrounds and religious rituals due to variety of Islamic identities. But these differences faded away over time and they got mixed with each other and appeared as a Muslim community, the size of which reached to around 3 million in North and South America (Turner, 2003). High minaret of mosque in Cairo Street of Chicago sending a call for Muslims five times a day and Friday congregations sent a wave of fear among the people from other religions, as the USA was promised to be a state of no-religion or at least respecting no religion as per its constitution.

Till the beginning of the 19th century, the world had emerged differently following the imprints of imperialism and nationalism (Said, 1978), and Muslims had appeared to be a contending power in the realm of international affairs. The image of Islam, on the other hand, was crystalized as an obscurant, archaic and despotic religion capable of posing serious threats to world peace. Conversion of Muslims to Christianity and avoiding non-Muslims to embracing Islam did not remain the main target of hatred towards Islam in the 19th century, but the image of Muslims as competing superpower in the world was also not blurred at all. Thus, it changed the whole set of hostilities towards Muslims and Islam, wherein prejudice and racism were the main predictors of anti-Muslim and anti-Islam sentiments. In a way, hostility towards Islam and Muslims consolidated into few refined terms having no obscured meanings attached. Nevertheless, it was not an end to what had been in practice since centuries such as misrepresentation, misinterpretation and misunderstanding of Islam.

One of the most renowned polemicists of the 19th century includes William Muir (1819–1905) from Scotland who authored many books demeaning Islam. *The Life of Muhammad*, published in 1861 having four volumes, was one of his most celebrated works. Muir's (1861) thesis rests upon Islam as being a static religion, incapable of reforming itself, and the Prophet (PBUH) of Islam was not worth allegiance. *Time* magazine in its November 1883 issue called it a 'propagandist writing' having enough Christian bias in it (Powell, 2010). Criticizing his work *The Life of Muhammad* and *The Caliphate*, Said (1978) pronounced that his work is an 'impressive antipathy to the Orient, Islam and the Arabs' while quoting Muir he said that 'the sword of Muhammed, and the Koran, are the most stubborn enemies of Civilisation, Liberty, and the Truth which the world has yet known' (p. 151). Sir Syed Ahmed Khan in his famous writing *Al Khutbat Al-Ahmediay* (1870) was a detailed response to anti-Islam writing of Muir, while Ali (1949) declared Muir as 'Islam's avowed enemy' (p. 211). *The Rise and Decline of Islam* by Muir (1884) is another bundle of lies and orientalist's bias against Islam; however, it could not get much popularity.

Winston Churchill in his book *The River War* published in 1899 criticized Islam as being a fanatical frenzy and anti-women religion and a proselytizing force against the Christians (Churchill, 1899). He said that Islam is 'as dangerous in a man, as hydrophobia in a dog' (p. 248). However, later some authors saw him changing his views about Islam, wherein he was found admiring the marshal aspects of Islam and was aspiring to adopt them to expand British Empire across the world. So much so, according to Patrick Sawer who wrote in *The Telegraph* on 28 December 2014,[13] Churchill's family feared him converting to Islam due to his liking of military successes of Islam. This is, somehow, again anti-Islam tendency in him where he saw Islam as being a religion expanded with sword and militancy.

Philip Schaff (1819–1893) also saw Islam as a source of fanaticism and violence, and he said that Islam left nothing but chaos and insecurity wherever it reached. He was a church historian who wrote *The History of Church* in eight volumes (Schaff, 1960), a widely read and referred source of church history of modern times. In Volume IV of his book, he ruthlessly criticized the holy book of Muslims as being a pack of poetic beauty but mixed with absurdities, bombast, unmeaning images and low sensuality. John Mason Neale (1818–1866), a priest and scholar of Christianity, also followed almost the same lines what Schaff did, and he criticized the Prophet (PBUH) as the one who fooled his people by promising them heaven having countless sensual delights and was making mockery of people while showing his connection with Angel of God (Neale, 1847). *Vindicia Christian* by J. Alley may not be missed out as a piece of polemical literature of the 20th century, which says that Islam is a 'perpetual falsehood, pernicious and extravagant'. All conclusive statement, however, was given by a French writer Jules-Hippolyte Percher (1857–1895), when he said that 'Muslim is the natural irreconcilable enemy of the Christian' in 1891 (Lopez, 2011).

---

[13] Retrieved from http://www.telegraph.co.uk/news/religion/11314580/Sir-Winston-Churchill-s-family-feared-he-might-convert-to-Islam.html.

In the beginning of the 20th century, we encounter a French explorer Louis-Gustave Binger (1856–1936) who in his work *Islam and Muslims as a Threat* (*Le Peril de l'Islam*) declared Islam a historical and living threat for the world, especially for the French. His entire work is devoted in creating binary differences between Muslims and Christians, and possible areas of threat that might emanate from Islam and Muslims for the West and their way of life. Continuing this trend in polemics, O'Leary (1923) also affirmed Muslims and Islam to be a constant threat and called the Balkan War of 1912–1913 as the 'Crusade against Islam'. The most significant aspect of this narrative was its wide publicity as O'Leary used mainstream print media to create anti-Islam sentiments among the people. On the other side, the Holy Quran's disgrace continued unabated by the scholars from other religions. Encyclopaedias have also been used to give misinterpretation of Quranic verses and injunctions, for instance, the *Jewish Encyclopedia* of 1901–1906 non-sensically disapproved many Quranic verses and declared some of the injunctions as factual inaccuracies.[14] Later, the Holy Quran was also declared as redaction of other scriptures from Judaism and Christianity (Wansbrough, 2004), Bernard Lewis argued that Quran is a 'Judaizing heresy' (Lewis, 2014).

Some events from the 20th century unmistakeably demonstrate increasing Islamophobia among the non-Muslims. During the First World War when General Henri Gouraud reached the Middle East, he ironically moved to the Umayyad Mosque on reaching Damascus in July 1920, and while standing at the tomb of the great warrior Salahuddin Ayubi, who died in 1193, he said, 'Behold, Saladin, we have returned' (Meer, 2014). Richardson writes that he further added that 'my presence here consecrates the Cross over the Crescent'[15] (Ali, 2002, p. 42). Although scholars from the Muslim world glamourized the triumphs by Salahuddin Ayubi in a remarkable fashion, proving it to be the triumph of Islam over Christianity when he succeeded in taking control of major parts of Palestine, but literature on Muslims'

---

[14] Jewish Encyclopaedia can be accessed online through http://www.jewishencyclo-pedia.com/search?utf8=%E2%9C%93&keywords=koran&commit=search. This site indicates its polemics against Quran while putting 'Kuran' in the search box.

[15] Retrieved from http://www.insted.co.uk/anti-muslim-racism.pdf.

hoodwinking to defeat their enemies in an inimical and polemical manner is also available in abundance. This mutual hostility resulted in perpetuating the enmity between the warring factions. From Muslims' side, the acts and moves of their 'eternal enemy' is more often taken as a manifestation of Islamophobia; while from Christians' point of view, it were the Muslims who destroyed the world peace as being barbaric, cruel, the others and an enemy race, which had given births to many ills of today's world such as racism, prejudice and threat perceptions.

As French had to face tough resistance to their expansionist desires from African countries, most of the writings by the French scholars considered hampering of usurpation efforts by the French forces a result of Islamic doctrine. Besides Louis Binger and O'Leary, Andre Servier also saw Islam as an Arab-adapted version of Christianity. He argued that Islamic laws are Roman codes revised by the Muslims, while Greek architecture was redesigned to appear as Islamic art and architecture. Muslims, to him, did not come up with any novelty to science, arts, philosophy and law, but adapted the best out of others for their benefit and named them as Islamic (Servier, 1924). His conclusion about Muslims and Islam argued that Islam is a destructive force, which mutilated and dissipated the established systems of peaceful world. Earlier to Sevier, Burton criticized the monotheism of Islam despite being a missionary of Christianity—again a monotheist religion. He took sovereignty of God in Islam as denial of human freedoms and fundamental rights, eventually paralyzing human creativity (Burton, 1918). According to him, monotheism stagnates the civilizations against time and causes backwardness. G. K. Chesterton (1925) refined Seveir's argument by arguing that Islam was a parody of Christianity in his famous book *The Everlasting Man*. He said:

> Islam was a product of Christianity; even if it was a by-product; even if it was a bad product. It was a heresy or parody emulating and therefore imitating the Church...Islam, historically speaking, is the greatest of the Eastern heresies. It owed something to the quite isolated and unique individuality of Israel; but it owed more to Byzantium and the theological enthusiasm of Christendom. It owed something even to the Crusades.[16]

---

[16] Its online version can be retrieved from http://gutenberg.net.au/ebooks01/0100311.txt.

The early 20th-century negativity against Muslims and Islam was also on the rise in the Indian subcontinent where Hindus and Muslims were fighting against the imperial rule of the British Empire. Mahatma Gandhi, the torchbearer of non-violence, also did not stop speaking against Islam and Muslims. He once said that 'thirteen hundred years of imperialistic expansion has made the Muslims fighters as a body', and hence they have become 'aggressive', and 'bullying is the natural excrescence of an aggressive spirit' (Jahanbegloo, 2013). On the other hand, he said that Hinduism is an age-old civilization and essentially non-violent (McDonough, 1994). The first Prime Minister (PM) of India, Jawaharlal Nehru, toed Gandhi's line when it came to Muslims and Islam. His statement on Islam is on record when he said that Islam is a faith fit for military conquers and not for conquering human minds. His views towards the followers of Islam also did not sound very different when he said Muslims did not bring anything new to India, and they were also class-bound individuals of the feudal mindset like most Indians (Srivastava, 2004).

In the late 20th century, movement against Islam and Muslims got world's attention when Salman Rushdie's *Satanic Verses* (Rushdie, 1988) and Taslima Nasreen's *Lajja* (Shame) (Nasrin, 1993) appeared on the international media scene. Earlier to them, Miller's (1976) work where he stated that 'Islam is Satan's most brilliant and effective invention for leading men astray' created unrest in the Muslim world while protesting his polemics. Laffin (1988) also condemned the Islamic concept of Jihad and provoked the world to rise against the infidels who pose danger to the world at large.

Owing to many reasons, the 20th- and 21st-century literature against Islam, Muslims and the Holy Prophet (PBUH) got wider publicity, acceptance and reaction. It could have been due to these being happening in the mediated world where anything can get an instant response. Also, after the demise of communism, Islam appeared as the most dangerous and probably the only enemy of the developed West that is potentially harmful for peace and order of the world. Hence, some new dimensions to polemics against Islam and Muslims added and continued polemicity of the religion, like Islam as a threat to the world peace, a set of codes for the secret society of the world aimed at fighting for eternity against the world, a prejudice fostering religion against all others combined, and Muslims as a bunch of most irrational creatures that may appear to be democratic, liberal and enlightened but when do they convert to be radicalized and barbaric individuals, you would never know.

As we have found that the archaic literature is abound with cynicism against Islam and its followers, the modern one seems to concretizing it rather filling the gaps in hostility towards Islam in a way. At some points, it gives an impression that contemporary writings on Islam and Muslims attempt to explore and find new dimensions to move with the historic hostility against the religion. Grasping the subject of hostility with epistemological augmentation from various disciplines of social sciences and humanities seems to have provided new ways of waging hostility on the religion and exploring the ways to integrate the societies and religions of the world for a better coexistence unlike the past. Ontological dimensions of Islamophobia or Islamofascism have helped the world of literature to play with new branches of knowledge like *orientalism*, which had hardly been a subject assisting to study the sensitive issues such as prejudice and racism, rather it had more to do with fictions and fables in the past; unlike what it does now to study Islam and its relations with other civilizations (Sardar, 1999).

In the late 1980s, Edward Said's work entitled *Orientalism* substantiates the narratives built in the earlier pages that anti-Islam and anti-Muslim prejudice and hostility is historic in nature; however, he was bent upon calling it merely Eurocentric and against Arabo-Islamic people (Said, 1978), while it seems much bigger than this and has multifaceted strands. His imaginative configuration of the Orients (or Muslims) being static in time and place, incapable of refining and redefining themselves with the fast-changing realities of life and the Occidents (developed West) as being dynamic and expanding are remarkable. According to him, this binary schematization has legitimized the Western supremacy and colonization of the underdeveloped nations, including Muslims (Turner, 1989).

Norman Daniel's work take precedence on 20th-century renowned writers like Edward Said or Samuel Huntington and is a widely referred source for tracing historic Christian hostility towards Muslims and Islam. Daniel (1960) crystalized historic cleavage between the 'orient' and the 'occident' in an interesting and scholastic manner. As per Kritzeck and Daniel (1961) and Poole (2002), while referring to Daniel (1960), anti-Islam discourse in the history was generated to jeopardize the status of Islam and Muslims in the West and to restrain the pervasive growth of Islam as being a 'threatening other' to the West. It has also been the argument of John Esposito (1992) that he pronounced in his work entitled *The Islamic Threat: Myth or Reality?* As said by French writer Jules-Hippolyte Percher (1857–1895) that Islam is an irreconcilable enemy of the Christians (Lopez, 2011), Esposito also followed his line by asking, 'are Islam and the West on an inevitable collision course?' (Esposito, 1992, p. 3). Like Herman and Chomsky (1988), Esposito believed that political Islam, in fact, has replaced communism as the main enemy of the West after 1989.

Understandably a refinement in the work of Said (1978) and Huntington (1993), Homi K. Bhabha (1994) developed overlapping binary positions like centre–margin, civilized–savage, enlightened–ignorant, etc., between the West and other cultures (Bhabha, 1994), and his trail of arguments also remained the same as enunciated earlier that this schematization pushed the West to colonize, expand and make 'other cultures' subordinate to the West. The works of Hall (1992) and Huntington (1993), however, overturned these rather hostile schematization by making culture as the basis of hostilities among civilizations. It is generally criticized that Huntington's thesis is just the replacement of biological notion of race by Hall with cultural racism associated with ethnicity as the main antecedent of racism. One noticeable point in Huntington's work is that his original piece appeared in 1993 in *Foreign Affairs* entitled 'Clash of Civilization?' However, in his expanded work on the thesis, he removed the question mark (?). Apparently, it sounds like he got sure of existence of clash of civilization just after a few years of its publication.

All these celebrated scholars at least collide at one point that Islam and the West (not as a geographic area in this case, but a distinct cultural and civilizational identity) are at odd binary strands in their history, culture, ideologies, outlook, destinations and religions. Hence, their integration is a remote possibility, but not the coexistence. In this wake of hostilities, Fred Halliday (1999, 2003) stands distinguished whose rhetoric temps, which does not link contemporary antagonism (might he meant contemporary Islamophobia!) to Muslims with long history of conflict between Islam and the West.

Even some of the renowned journalists from the West fan the flare of Islamophobia in their writing affecting millions of people in days. For instance, Oriana Fallaci, a famous and influential Italian journalist who once interviewed Zulfiqar Ali Bhutto (PM of Pakistan during the 1970s), wrote an extremely blasphemous article in the backdrop of 9/11 that later appeared in shape of book *The Rage and the Pride* and painted Muslims as follows (Marranci, 2004):

> I consider them [the terrorists] people who want to show off and nothing more. And, in the case of those who pray to Allah, [they want] a place in the Paradise of which the Koran speaks: the paradise in which heroes f**ck....
> I say: Wake up, people, wake up! ...you don't understand, or don't want to understand, that what's under way here is a reverse crusade. Do you want to understand or do you not want to understand that what's under way here is a religious war? A war that they call Jihad. A Holy War. A war that doesn't want the conquest of our territories, perhaps, but certainly wants to conquer our souls. ...They will feel authorized to kill you and your children because you drink wine or beer, because you don't wear a long beard or a chador, because you go to the theatre and cinemas, because you listen to music and sing songs....

Summarily, this historical tracing of Islam–Christianity or Islamo-Christo-Judo relations reveal a few interesting realities, such as Christo-Judo relations due to crucification of Jesus were at extreme adversary before the birth of Islam in the early 7th century; emergence of Islam challenged the dominance of Christianity and Judaism, and appeared as third contending force in the realm of religions; mass conversion of Christians, Jews and atheists to Islam jeopardized the future of other religions seriously; establishment and then fast-paced expansion of an Islamic state (IS) was considered dreadful; economy came largely under Muslims' control; church establishment lost its control over regional and world affairs; Judo-Christian adversaries reduced to fight off Islam as a common enemy and Islam as a symbol of all problems of the world.

Studying Islam and other religions in historical perspective, it can without any shadow of doubt be said that Islam enjoyed adversarial relations with other religions of the world since its birth. The nature of adversaries, however, kept on changing due to geo-politico-religio reasons. There was an adversary of being dislike to Islam in the beginning, which turned into fear due to expansion of Islam; and then it turned to hostility towards it due to Islam being a religion in competition with Christianity and Judaism; and when Islam did not stop its expansion the hostility turned into the denigration of Islam, its prophet and followers to avoid people embracing Islam, which ultimately emerged in a kind of prejudice for Islam and Muslims in variety of its forms; and Muslims turned into a race of people with eternal enmity towards others and a disgusting race (indeed) and, contemporarily, it has taken many other shapes like Islam as a symbol of terror, extreme fear, an orientalist 'other', an opposing political, social and religious ideology and a threat to world peace overall. Thus, the phenomena of hatred, fear, prejudice, racism, othering, orientalists, terror and Western opposing ideologies when combined together form Islamophobia—a corpus of phobias. Not all of them may be available at one place at a time, but in either of the forms, Islamophobia may exist. Due to its multifarious nature and antecedents, Islamophobia has been variedly defined and explained in literature and a consensus on its definition is yet to be reached, but its manifestations are mostly common and independent of their antecedents. Essentially, Islamophobia has always been there as a phenomenon in history since the birth of Islam in the early 7th century. This necessitates having a look at variety of definitions of Islamophobia contemporarily available in literature.

ORIGIN OF ISLAMOPHOBIA

Origin of the term *Islamophobia* does not seem to be well researched in contemporary literature; hence, there are huge confusions on its first use. However, the term is in common use since the release of Runnymede report titled 'Islamophobia: A Challenge for Us All' in

November 1997. The report says that the term Islamophobia came in print for the first time in February 1991 in a report published by weekly *Insight*.[17] Tamdgidi (2006) claims its first use in the 1980s, though he did not specifically refer to where did it get published. Probably, he was referring to Edward Said's use of term Islamophobia in 1985 in his famous article 'Orientalism Reconsidered' (Said, 1985). Said (1985) used Islamophobia in the light of his thesis of orientalism—orients and occidents. According to him, more crystalized and intriguing the differences between orients and occidents, more visible and stringent would be Islamophobic feelings. Or Tamdgidi (2006) might have been reflecting upon Christopher Harrison's *France and Islam in West Africa, 1860–1960*, wherein he was referring to 'new dimension to traditional European Islamophobia' in the backdrop of growing radicalization in the Egyptian nationalists (Harrison, 1988, p. 29).

Interestingly, Lopez (2011) claims in one of his writings that the term Islamophobia was used by Americo Castro, a Spanish historian, in 1968. The Spanish historian, according to Lopez, was comparing anti-Semitism with Islamophobia when he used the term, which makes sense, and his focus was to see the influences of Jews and Muslims on the history of Spain. Islamophobia in Spanish is pronounced almost the same way as in English and there is hardly any difference in letters also like *Islamofobia* (in Spanish); hence, there is less doubt in use of the term in Americo Castro's work as the term's usage in English. Now we will discuss whether it was used in the same context as Islamophobia in terms of its meaning in the modern literature. Apparently, there does not seem to be a significant deviation from contemporary meanings of the term as it talks about the influences of anti-Semitism and Islamophobia in the backdrop of Jews and Muslims' influences on the Spanish society.

Not only this, Lopez (2011) cites Hichem Djait (from France) who in his book wrote in 1978 that Islamophobia is being replaced by Arabophobia. This interesting comment by Hichem Djait makes this

---

[17] The report by Runnymede says that Islamophobia appeared first time in a report by *Insight* on 4 February 1991 (p. 37), wherein its exact usage was: 'Islamophobia also accounts for Moscow's reluctance to relinquish its position in Afghanistan, despite the estimated $300 million a month it take to keep the Kabil regime going'.

claim further weak that Islamophobia as a term was used by Edward Said for the first time in 1985. Looking at the perspective and context under which the term Islamophobia was used, it seems evident that fear of Islam as an ideology was being replaced by the fear of Arab as an ethnic group. Hichem Djait's understanding of this fear was the consequence of growing tension in the Middle East in the 1960s. Nonetheless, some scholars naively, by taking a turn from their claim, say that Edward Said's use of Islamophobia in 1985's article 'Orientalism Reconsidered' is, in fact, the first use of Islamophobia in English literature.

Interestingly, *Oxford English Dictionary* (online)[18] divulges the first use of the term Islamophobia in 1923 in *Journal of Theological Studies*, however, without any proper citation. Deeper search revealed that English version of the term Islamophobia was used in an article entitled 'The History of Religions' by Stanley A. Cook in *The Journal of Theological Studies* (Cook, 1923).[19] Also, the term was used in English in 1976 in another article entitled 'Dialogue with Gustave E. Von Grunebaum' in *International Journal of Middle East Studies* (Anawati, 1976). These two resources clearly endorse our hypothesis, mentioned earlier, that Islamophobia literature seems to be a *literature produced in haste*. If it had not been like that, these important sources might not have been missed out.

Furthermore, the term Islamophobia was, as per Allen (2010) and others, used by Dinet and Ibrahim (1925) in their work entitled *L'Orient vu de l'Occident* (French). Allen (2010) claims that the essence of term used was somewhat dissimilar to its contemporaneous usage—rather a fear of Islam by the liberal and modernist Muslims, and not by the non-Muslims. *Islamophobie* was the term actually used by Dinet and Ibrahim, which means Islamophobia in the modern French language; however, according to some scholars, it carries the same meanings like Islamophobia—feelings against Islam, but not as such present-day

---

[18] Retrieved from http://www.oed.com/view/Entry/248449.

[19] The journal can be retrieved from https://academic.oup.com/jts/search-results?rg_IssuePublicationDate=01%2F01%2F1923+TO+12%2F31%2F1923&&f_JournalDisplayName=The%20Journal%20of%20Theological%20Studies.

Islamophobia (which has multiple facets; hence a bundle of phobias). Modern English to French dictionaries, nonetheless, give Islamophobia as the English translation of French *Islamophobie*. Strangely enough, even that was also not the first use of the term Islamophobia in any of the modern languages. As per Lopez (2011), an article by a French, Maurice Delafosse, entitled *létat actuel de lafrique occidentale francaise* (trans. The Current State of French West Africa) published in *Revue Du Monde Musualman* (trans. *Review of the Muslim World*) in 1910 used the term Islamophobia in its recommendations for the colonial French authorities as how to fight of Islam (Delafosse, 1910). Continuing on this, Lopez (2011) argued that Marty (1921) (in French), Cook (1923) (in English), as mentioned earlier, and Bernard (1927) (in French) also used the term Islamophobia and tried to conceptualize it.

The controversy on the first use of the term does not end here. Robin Richardson, the co-director of Insted Consultancy who had a role in launching the Runnymede report in 1997, claimed in his paper that the first use of *Islamophie* (in French) appeared in a book entitled *La Politique Musulmane Dans l'Afrique Occidentale Francaise* in 1910, the reference of which Alain Quellien made in his PhD dissertation.[20]

The earlier discussion clearly demonstrates that neither the term Islamophobia in English nor in any other language is quite new to the modern literature or a neologism as claimed in some studies. The first use of Islamophobia (the term) in English has been found in 1923 in *The Journal of Theological Studies* and its first use in any other language has been traced in French in 1910, again in a journal of research and in a PhD dissertation (Quellien, 1910). The probable reason for Islam and Muslims as being the less focused object from the early 20th century until the late 1980s was Communophobia—communism remained the biggest threat to the Western world during this period.

---

[20] This source has been retrieved from http://www.insted.co.uk/anti-muslim-racism.pdf. Also, Quellien (1910), as per a doctoral thesis submitted to the Faculty of Law of the University of Paris on 25 May 1910.

DEFINITIONS OF ISLAMOPHOBIA

The construct of Islamophobia, as explained earlier, is a complex bundle of episteme with a long history and has varied dimensions as a phenomenon; hence, presenting a composite definition covering all aspects is a cumbrous task. Scholars with variety of backgrounds, experience and their understanding of the construct have defined and conceptualized it, nevertheless, with more confusions and less clarity. Any holistic and agreed upon definition is yet to surface. The only common aspect of all definitions of Islamophobia is that it speaks about something negative against Muslims or Islam, or both of them. At some place, the construct is shown as a cultural or religious racism (Modood, 1997) or 'new racism' (Barker, 1981) directed towards Muslims or Islam; and at some other place, it is pronounced as prejudice for Muslims and Islam. Other negativities typically associated with the construct are fear, hostility, terror, others, orients, hatred, threat, violent religion, dislike, to name a few, or anti-Muslims/anti-Islam. On the other hand, some dismissal of the construct, having either an institutionalized outlook or the phenomenon having long historical roots, have also joined the discussion on Islamophobia lately, like Halliday (1999). Even some of the definitions following a linear root to conceptualize the construct considering it as a contemporary concept emerged after the release of the Runnymede report and flashed after 9/11 on the world media scene. The most interesting comment in this regard, however, was that the term was 'invented by the Islamists to condemn any criticism of Islam' (Lopez, 2011).

Let's have surgery of some of the definitions of Islamophobia in a bid to reach to some consensus. For simplicity of our understanding, we would not divide the definitions into broad or narrow and close or open spectrums; rather the focus of definition would be kept in view like whether a definition emphasizes fear, prejudice, hostility or any other disapproval of Muslims/Islam, etc.

Fear of missing out any aspect that Islamophobia might stand for, the scholars have attempted to present multiple factors in their definitions of the construct. This, itself, demonstrates the confused state of affairs in the process of defining and conceptualizing Islamophobia.

And, of course, the construct being so obscure and complex in nature allows every kind of negativity to become part of its explanation, and then history is also generous enough to offer all sorts of negativities to substantiate any negative element in its ambit. This interesting situation has facilitated the scholars to propose bundles of definitions in various dimensions with cogent reasons to believe. On the other hand, critique on the given definitions has also become easy. Allen (2010) considering this problem says that Islamophobia is a 'fluid, protean, and largely inconsistent' and 'ambiguous phenomenon' (p. 102). Thus, Islamophobia may be taken as an umbrella term, which has the potential of covering all negative concepts like fear of racism and prejudice in favour of Muslims and Islam. For instance, when French writer Jules-Hippolyte Percher (1857–1895) said that '(a) Muslim is the natural irreconcilable enemy of the Christian', he was in fact explaining Islamophobia in 1891 without of course coining the term itself.

Alain Quellien, quoting Jules-Hippolyte Percher and other Islamophobes, said (Lopez 2011):

> Prejudice against Islam has always been widespread among the people of Western and Christian civilization and still is.... For some, the Muslim is the natural and irreconcilable enemy of the Christian and the European; Islam is the negation of civilization, and barbarism, bad faith and cruelty are the best one can expect from the Mohammedans.

Using the term Islamophobia for the first time in 1910, Quellien attempted to explain and define it. This loosely structured definition of Islamophobia opened up ways for others who followed him using this term with some explanation about it. Here, prejudice and hostility aimed at Muslims and Islam are the main components of the explanation of the term. Interestingly, Muslims and Islam both, independent of each other, are explained as an 'irreconcilable enemy of the Christian(s)' and a 'negation of civilization', respectively. Not only this, but the use of word 'Mohammadans' also indicates hatred towards the Prophet (PBUH) of Islam. Probably, it has been the reason that when Islamophobia as a term was used for the first time by Cook (1923) in English, he used the same argument referring to some authors who put Mohammad (PBUH) in the bad light in their discussions. His argument(s) for Islamophobia, which he used just once in his article (p. 101), rest on hatred aimed at the prophet of Islam. Other elements include Islam as a *violent religion* in the earlier explanation.

Fear is one of the earliest ingredients of Islamophobia, as it is usually described phobia of anything as fear. Phobia of Islam and Muslims was taken as an important component part in many definitions of Islamophobia. *The First Observatory Report of the Organisation of Islamic Conference* (OIC)[21] gave a simplistic definition of Islamophobia wherein 'an irrational or powerful fear or dislike of Islam' has been referred to as Islamophobia. Of course, fear generates feelings of hatred and dislike, and can incite to violence too. But Shryock (2010) notes that Islamophobia is not just fear or hate, but also the designation of enmity to a group of people or a society is also quite essential to convert a fear into phobia. He further argues that people may have the fear of Al-Qaeda as a group of dangerous people, but it may not encompass the whole Muslims and Islam unless it is done systematically against a community/group of people. Robin Richardson[22] confirms it when he defines Islamophobia as 'feelings of anxiety, fear, hostility and rejection towards Muslims'. Similarly, Lee, Gibbons, Thomson, and Timani (2009) also define it in an absolute fashion as 'fear of Muslims and the Islamic faith', without taking another element in the Islamophobia domain unlike many others. Abbas (2004) and Zuquete (2008) also use 'fear' as the single most important component of Islamophobia; however, the latter considers fear as an antecedent of the blanket judgement of Islam as an enemy, 'other', monolithic bloc and a natural hostility to the Westerners.

It was probably the pushing fear of Muslims that made the Australian authorities to think of deleting multiculturalism from its immigration services, which earlier was the Department of Immigration and Multicultural Affairs and Indigenous Affairs (DIMIA) and later

---

[21] The report may be retrieved from http://ww1.oic-oci.org/uploads/file/Islamphobia/islamphobia_rep_may_07_08.pdf.

[22] This source has been retrieved from http://www.insted.co.uk/anti-muslim-racism.pdf.

the nomenclature was changed to Department of Immigration and Citizenship (DIAC; Morgan & Poynting, 2012). Australia, indeed, is hit badly by media-constructed Islamophobia, suffering from huge surge in Islamophobic attacks on Muslims lately. While leaving 'multiculturalism' as an official slogan might have brought some adverse consequences for the government authorities, it also indicates that immigration is extended to people coming across the continents, but no rights are embedded with grant of citizenship to foreigners to put the Australian culture on change. Not essentially, it could be taken as an act influenced by Islamophobic feelings, but its denial is also hard as Muslims in Australia are already suffering from increasing racial attacks. The UK also suffers from the same trauma where Islam as a religion is racialized and gendered identity of educated Muslims, especially females, is particularly examined, more often for their ethnic identity, with fear when employed for any task. A recent study confirms this phenomenon indicating Islamophobia to people from Pakistan is changing into Pakophobia in the backdrop of terrorism discourses in media, workplaces and among the peer groups (Saeed, 2016). Uenal (2016) also confirms Islamophobia as 'an irrational or exaggerated fear of Islam as a religion' (p. 68).

Prejudice component of Islamophobia's definition has also been covered heavily in contemporary and archaic literature. Alain Quellien's explanation of Islamophobia also referred to widespread prejudice against Islam, which was there in the past and is still there, said over one century ago (Lopez, 2011). His explanation about enmity of Islam and negation of its civilization and Islam as a bad faith and barbaric rests on prejudice for the religion. Said (1975) is also one of the proponents who considers prejudice of Islam and Muslims as Eurocentric hostility in his famous work *Orientalism*. Tolan (2002), throughout his work, highlighted numerous occasions where prejudice became instrumental in waging hostility against Muslims and Islam. Hatred and hostility against Muslims and Islam are a few manifestations, among others, of extreme prejudice. Fairness and Accuracy in Reporting (FAIR), a US-based think tank destined to monitor reporting of Muslims and Islam, defines Islamophobia as a 'term refers to hostility towards Islam and Muslims that tends to dehumanize an entire faith, portraying it as fundamentally alien and attributing to it an inherent, essential set of negative traits such as irrationality, intolerance and violence' (Hollar & Naureckas, 2008). Toeing the same line, the United Nation Human Rights Council (UNHRC) also defines Islamophobia as 'a baseless hostility and fear vis-à-vis Islam, and as a result a fear of and aversion towards all Muslims or the majority of them' (Blitt, 2011). Discrimination, prejudices and unequal treatment of Muslims are treated as manifestations of hostility, the UNHRC report says, unlike many other scholars. Blitt (2011) declared Islamophobia as a 'defamation of the religion' (p. 149).

Islamophobia has also been defined as racism by some quarters— cultural racism or religious racism or both. Anti-Muslim racism is Islamophobia, Massari (2006) in Tyrer (2013) notes. Interestingly, her definition of Islamophobia centres on Muslims, excluding Islam as a religion being the target of hate by Islamophobes; besides, she also claims that Muslims' places of worship are not targeted. Geisser (2003) calls it religiophobia, while some others, interestingly, declare Islamophobia as race–religion mix (Nieuwkerk, 2004; Werbner, 2005). Halliday (2003) also believes that 'Islamophobia is a term that has been applied more frequently to the practical hatred of Muslims than to the psychological fear of Islam'. However, data about vandalism and arson of mosques in recent media reports from the USA, the UK, Canada, France and Germany depict a different picture.

In another publication, Tyrer (2010) argues that Muslims are racialized on the basis of their 'degree of difference from the white', which agrees to the older discourse of racism (p. 104). Saeed (2007), in the same way, locates Muslims as a race of indeterminate people, which the Westerns believe is their enemy and are trying to conquer the West. Contrarily, Sayyid's (2010) argument draws our attention to a different understanding of Islamophobia in the sociopolitical Western context focusing on racialized groups not essentially biological but, at the same time, religion, culture and territories may also be used to fabricate the racialized social groups. This context may not be ignored altogether as Arabophobia and Pakophobia like terms are also on sale on the basis of fear or hatred towards people from certain territories/regions. Even yellow racism, fear of Chinese and Japanese, due to the economic overpowering of the Western markets is gaining momentum. The Turkish representative Umut Topcuoglu, in Human Dimension Implementation Meeting of Organization for Security and Co-operation in Europe (OSCE) held in 2013 in Poland, argued that Islamophobia is a contemporary form of racism, of which manifestations are intolerance, discrimination and adverse public discourse against Muslims and Islam.[23]

Omi and Winant (1994), interestingly, associate race with culture while studying the evolution of modern racism. They say:

> [T]he emergence of a modern conception of race does not occur until the rise of Europe and the arrival of Europeans in the Americas. Even the hostility and suspicion with which Christian Europe viewed its two significant non-Christian 'others'—the Muslims and the Jews—cannot be viewed as more than a rehearsal for racial formation, since these antagonisms, for all their bloodletting and chauvinism, were always and everywhere religiously interpreted.

This point of reference ushers an interesting debate when race is linked with culture. Taking Muslims as a distinct race, it is obvious that Muslims' culture is greatly influenced by their religion, that is, Islam. Though culture is more dynamic in nature and multiple elements like history of society, geography, weathers, the degree of modernism, etc., contribute to develop a culture, while Islam and Muslims enjoy different cultures as being from various geographical regions such as Arab Muslims, Middle Eastern Muslims, African Muslims and Asian Muslims. Despite being different in many cultural traits, there are so many commonalities in their culture due to Islam as the religion playing an important role in lives of Muslims from various regions. In this case, race may be associated with religion at secondary level as being the main predictor of Muslims' culture from various regions. Winant (2001) in his illustrious work *The World is a Ghetto* confirms the relation of race with religious ideologies. This would, of course, make a point that Islamophobia is religious racism, while wars and anarchy in the Muslim world further with this notion where Muslims all across the world appear to be a singular race. Succinctly, Islamophobia may

[23] The report has been retrieved from http://www.osce.org/odihr/106577?download=true.

be referred to as racism on the basis of religion, culture or both, which has roots in history and was labelled as such over a century ago; nevertheless, as Sajid (2006) aptly remarked, it was nothing but 'a new word for an old fear'.

Sayyid (2014) defines Islamophobia as 'a form of racialized governmentality...more than prejudice...a series of interventions and classifications' about the Muslims (p. 19). His definition does not refer to Islam at all but considers only Muslims as a class, of which well-being is affected by Islamophobia. Most interesting aspect, which he raised in his article, is that 'ontic approaches to Islamophobia cannot do justice to the concept' (p. 22). Indeed, not always one can present empirical evidence to support that Islamophobia as a phenomenon does occur, primarily, due to subtle nature of pluralities that might constitute the construct. While earlier, Sayyid and Vakil (2010) pointed out that religion is 'raced', and Muslims are racialized (p. 276). Probably, Sayyid (2014) revisited his approach towards Islamophobia in his late publication with Vakil, excluding Islam from explanation of the construct by making it more focused on Muslims only.

While shedding light on various shades of definition and explanation of Islamophobia, it would not be out of place to discuss Runnymede Trust's report and the way it deliberates on the construct. The report defines Islamophobia as anti-Muslim racism and prejudice, and 'a shorthand way of referring to dread or hatred of Islam—and, therefore, to fear or dislike of all or most Muslims'. It hardly refers to its historic formulations and depth making the term appeared as a neology, inspired by the contingencies of race relations in Britain only (Sayyid, 2014). The report draws upon eight questions about Islam while attempting to explain Islamophobia as a construct, which are as follows (Conway & Richardson, 1997, p. 4):

1. Whether Islam is seen as monolithic and static, or as diverse and dynamic?
2. Whether Islam is seen as 'other' and separate, or as similar and interdependent?
3. Whether Islam is seen as inferior, or as different but equal?

4. Whether Islam is seen as an aggressive enemy or as a cooperative partner?
5. Whether Muslims are seen as manipulative or as sincere?
6. Whether Muslim criticisms of 'the West' are rejected or debated?
7. Whether discriminatory behavior against Muslims is defended or opposed?
8. Whether anti-Muslim discourse is seen as natural or problematic?

This interesting binary schematization of Islamophobia entered the definitional debate into a new phase, where prejudice and racism have been accepted as the minimum negative posturing to Islam and Muslims. Interestingly, the eight questions are equally divided between Islam as a religion and Muslims as its followers to distinguish whether Islamophobia is towards Islam or Muslims, as our earlier discussions undertake this aspect. Second, open and close views are addressed in this definition in multiple dimensions, which makes it evident that Islamophobia may not be taken as monolithic and linear construct, but multidimensional and dynamic in nature.

On the basis of these questions, the Runnymede report crystalized the binary positions in open and close views of Islam and Muslims with major dimensions of these oppositions. The following table would help to understand it more clearly (Conway & Richardson, 1997, p. 5).

#	Dimensions	Closed View of Islam	Open View of Islam
1	Monolithic/ diverse	Islam seen as a single monolithic bloc, static and unresponsive to new realities.	Islam seen as diverse and progressive, with internal differences, debates and development.
2	Separate/ interacting	Islam seen as separate and other: (a) not having any aims or values in common with other cultures, (b) not affected by them and (c) not influencing them.	Islam seen as interdependent with other faiths and cultures: (a) having certain shared values and aims, (b) affected by them and (c) enriching them.
3	Inferior/ different	Islam seen as inferior to the West: barbaric, irrational, primitive, sexist.	Islam seen as distinctively different, but not deficient, and as equally worthy of respect.

#	Dimensions	Closed View of Islam	Open View of Islam
4	Enemy/partner	Islam seen as violent, aggressive, threatening, supportive of terrorism, engaged in 'a clash of civilizations'.	Islam seen as an actual or potential partner in joint cooperative enterprises and in the solution of shared problems.
5	Manipulative/sincere	Islam seen as a political ideology used for political or military advantage.	Islam seen as a genuine religious faith practised sincerely by its adherents.
6	Criticism of West rejected/considered	Criticisms made by Islam of 'the West' rejected out of hand.	Criticisms of 'the West' and other cultures are considered and debated.
7	Discrimination defended/criticized	Hostility towards Islam used to justify discriminatory practices towards Muslims and exclusion of Muslims from mainstream society.	Debates and disagreements with Islam do not diminish efforts to combat discrimination and exclusion.
8	Islamophobia seen as natural/problematic	Anti-Muslim hostility accepted as natural and 'normal'.	Critical views of Islam are themselves subjected to critique, lest they be inaccurate and unfair.

This schematization has been developed in the orientalist perspective; however, Islam and Muslims are compared with themselves wherein the close view matches with the orient category as proposed by Said (1978). Although the open view of Islam and Muslims is probably the one which is acceptable for the West with no or minimal chances of occurrence of Islamophobia, it means that the positioning of Islam would determine how it should be treated by the West. This table solemnly justifies West's response to Islam and Muslims on any of the views on the spectrum and seldom on Muslims and Islam as independent identities. Furthermore, all negativities, possibly associated with Islam and Muslims, are listed in the closed views, regardless of colour, race, creed, territory of Muslims and factions of Islam as a religion. Publishing of this report helped generate a debate on the issue and clear dust from many of the complex areas related to the understanding of Islamophobia; nonetheless, it has unconsciously institutionalized the menace of Islamophobia, though in a subtle fashion.

There are hardly any ills left to be associated with the term Islamophobia, hugely explained with cogent reasons in the contemporary and archaic scholastic literature. However, we assume that some of the dimensions of Islamophobia have become clearer through this debate and are helpful in drawing some fundamental assumptions about the construct. These assumptions are as follows:

- First and the foremost assumption is that Islamophobia is not monolithic and linear in nature, but a multidimensional and dynamic construct.
- Islamophobia may not be singularly associated with Islam or Muslims, independent of each other, but it is holistic in nature taking both the entities in its ambit.
- Islamophobia may not be directed at people of any particular colour, creed, caste, territory, but to all those who follow Islam as a religion.
- Islamophobia may not only be fostered at the attitudinal level among the individuals of a society, but it may also exist in the social order capable of affecting everyone in a social system.
- Islamophobia is not just a contemporary phenomenon, but it also has traceable roots in the history.
- Islamophobia may not only occur in Western or non-Muslim societies, but it may also exist in Muslim societies, though mostly in its radicalized form.
- Manifestations of Islamophobia are mostly common and are independent of its antecedents.
- Not all antecedents/dimensions of Islamophobia essentially constitute to make it occur at one point in time in a society; rather, societies have different singular reasons to be Islamophobic.
- Thresholds of Islamophobia's manifestations vary from society to society; hence, there is no critical point for manifestations to be visually determined.
- Islamophobia is a complex bundle of episteme and discourses, and it has multiple facets/dimensions; hence, it may be termed as Islamophobias.

On the basis of our understanding of the construct, the following tree diagram would help us understand Islamophobia having multiple dimensionalities and strands.

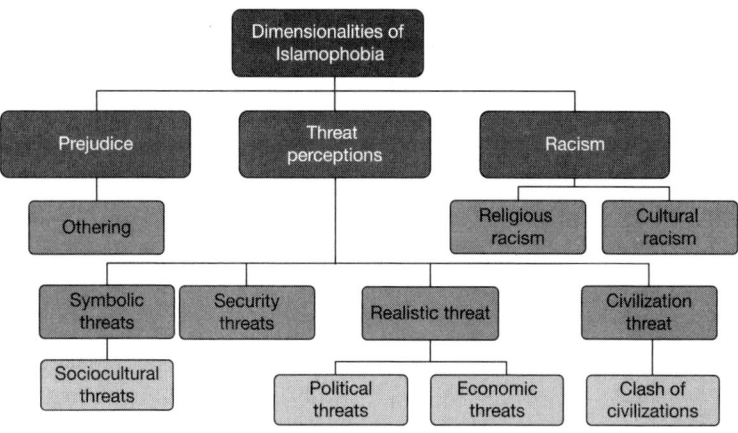

Islamophobia is the negative posturing to Islam and Muslims; it mainly refers to prejudice, threat perceptions and racism and is independent of each other or otherwise, where prejudice may be characterized as 'othering'; threat perceptions may have four sub-dimensions, namely symbolic threat (or sociocultural threats), security threats, realistic threats (either as political or economic threats or both), civilization threat (in clash of civilization perspective) and racism with two possible sub-dimensions, that is, religious and cultural. These epistemic dimensions of Islamophobia may not have a single antecedent, but numerous factors may contribute in cultivating Islamophobia at individual level or as a social order in a society. Some of the antecedents, in this case, remain constant, while some other may vary due to sociopolitical and security reasons. Thus, Islamophobia is essentially not a stagnant construct in time and space, and rather bears great ramifications of the situations where it fosters. For instance, after 9/11, the US society confronted with huge surge in Islamophobic incidents due to precarious security situations and maddening media bashing of Muslims and Islam. On the same analogy, this should not appear to be surprising to observe media criticism of Muslims or Islam when acts of obvious terrorism are witnessed in the streets of London or Paris. Nonetheless, intensity of Islamophobia as a menace to the society may vary in different times due to the degree of historic antagonism and social alienation of Muslims in any particular period.

History of prejudice and racism as antecedents of Islamophobia is predominantly constant in various regions of the world with varying degrees of course. Centuries-old enmity and demeaning clichés (like Moors) that emerged in hundreds of years of (combative) interaction between Muslims and non-Muslims, and the nature of relationship between Muslims/Islam and others whether as friends, enemies, 'other', subjugators, usurpers or as a racialized group of people are the main determinants of Islamophobia or Islamophobic sentiments. Contemporary Islamophobia, thus, carries a huge load of the past and is manifested in multiple ways. Fear and hatred are not Islamophobia as such, in this context, but are some of its manifestations. Others may include the exclusion of Muslims, dislike of all or most of Muslims and/or Islam, feelings of disgust, etc. However, reasons for three main dimensions of the construct, namely prejudice, threat perceptions and racism, might differ in nature from each other as antecedents of Islamophobia.

Islamophobia at the epistemic level (prejudice, threat perceptions and racism) and its antecedents can be studied and correlated with each other either in a logistic or point-to-point fashion for a better understanding of the problem. Similarly, the collection of empirical data on the episteme and antecedents of Islamophobia after having them adequately operationalized could lead to resolving problems of serious nature amicably.

Sociocultural Dimensions of Fear of Islam and Muslims

Threats emanating from the phenomenon of Islamophobia generally fall in security and terror domains. Prejudice and racism towards Muslims and Islam are some other antecedents or outcomes of Islamophobia, profoundly discussed and deliberated in talks and literature related with the construct. Continued historic dislike of Muslims and fear of Islam as a subjugator or destroyer of other cultures and religions more often than not diminish the significance of debates on sociocultural and economic domains of Islamophobia, which are relatively more practical threats in some countries of the world, but are not exclusively limited to Muslims only. Growing Muslim population in Europe alone could send deafening alarm to those who value their sociocultural norms and traditions, and they, with a great sense of insecurity, are watching the indicators/developments that could indulge them into severe economic impasses. Let us take a view of Muslims in Europe.[1]

Over 25 million Muslims are residing in 28 countries of the European Union (EU), making it 4.9 per cent of the total population, and around 46 million (about 6%) all across Europe. This estimate does not include those who are seeking asylum in various countries of Europe. Only in Germany and France, as per the Pew Research Report, more than 320,000 and 140,000 Muslims, respectively, are waiting for their legal status to be determined yet. France, Germany, the UK and Italy are among the most thickly Muslim (as minority) populated countries. The increasing trend in Muslim population is quite visible

---

[1] Please see complete report on Muslims in Europe by the Pew Research Center (http://www.pewresearch.org/fact-tank/2017/11/29/5-facts-about-the-muslim-population-in-europe/).

as the number surged from 3.8 million in 2010 to 4.9 million in 2016 in the EU. Surprisingly, out of 4.9 million Muslims living in the EU, the majority are young with an average age of 30 years—13 years lesser than the average age (43) for the Europeans. If the increasing trend continues along the timeline, the EU would have over 14 per cent of Muslims in its 28 countries by 2050, even if immigration level is brought to zero in the EU (which is a mere hypothetical proposition), still the population would amount to 7.4 per cent by 2050. Nonetheless, some parts of Europe are hot spots for Muslim immigration, such as the UK, France, Germany and Italy, especially for immigrants from Syria, Afghanistan, Iraq and Somalia. On the other hand, views of Europeans about Muslims are increasingly negative in most parts of Europe. Taking both the scenarios into consideration—growing Muslim population and increased negative perceptions towards them—a grim picture develpos of the future of Muslims in Europe alone, and thus increased Islamophobia. But what essentially makes this happen?

Mosques are seen with suspicion in Europe. For many, they are home to fundamentalism and terrorism on their lands. At community level, mosques are the bone of contention at various places across Europe. The mosques got media flashing during 2009 when some people in Switzerland reacted to raising the minarets of a mosque. This steered the 'banning minaret movement' in Switzerland, which is home to about 450,000 Muslims and has more than 150 mosques, Islam being the second largest religion after Christianity in the country. The country, being multicultural and a world tourist resort, caught the attention of world leaders and media on the banning of minaret movement. Majority of the population (about 57%) voted in favour of the ban on minaret of mosques in Switzerland that are great attraction for the globetrotters; this was followed by another ban, on burqa. People's reaction to mosques in Switzerland provided the impetus to enchant slogans against the Muslims and spread of Islam in Europe, and minarets of mosques were viewed as 'symbol of Islamic power'.[2] According to Allievi (2010), there are about 11,000 mosques

---

[2] Retrieved from http://www.independent.co.uk/news/world/europe/swiss-move-to-ban-minarets-as-symbols-of-islamic-power-1771879.html.

in around 15 major countries of Europe including the UK, Germany, France, Italy, Switzerland, Denmark, Norway, Sweden, Belgium, Greece, Netherlands, etc. However, at some of the places, quite a less number of mosques are available for relatively large Muslim populations; for instance, Italy has only eight mosques for 1.6 million Muslim population, while France has more than 2,100 registered mosques for about 6.5 million Muslims, as per 2010 data (Allievi, 2010). In general, views about Muslims in the European countries are mostly negative, as the following map indicates.[3]

What about the USA? According to the Pew Research Report 2017, Muslims constitute slightly more than 1.1 per cent of the US population—about 3.45 million. Despite being less in number, visibility of Muslims in the entire USA is fairly high, primarily due to their sociocultural outlook. That may include a number of mosques in the USA, a conspicuous symbol of Muslims presence. For instance, 1,209 mosques were found in the year 2000 in the USA, which rose to 2,106 in the year 2010—74 per cent increase in one decade. According to somewhat fresh estimates, there are more than 3,186 mosques in the USA with California having the highest number with more than 525 mosques[4]; interestingly, only 0.7 per cent of total Muslim population (3.45 millions) dwells in California, while highest concentration of Muslims is found in Illinois (2.8%), Virginia (2.7%), New York (2%), New Jersey and Texas (1.8%). New York is placed second with 507 mosques.

Initially, Muslims were brought to the USA as slaves from Africa. Later, immigrants from Middle Eastern countries and Ottoman Empire landed in the Americas for better employment opportunities, food security and to experience a new life in a newly explored world. Apparently, Muslims are seen as a singular unit in the USA, but they are extremely divergent groups associated with different religious factions and are divided on their ethnic, linguistic and

---

[3] Retrieved from http://www.pewresearch.org/fact-tank/2017/08/09/muslims-and-islam-key-findings-in-the-u-s-and-around-the-world/.

[4] Retrieved from http://islamthreat.com/distribution_of_mosques_in_usa_2015.html.

regional affiliations. Nonetheless, Islam under its ideological umbrella makes them identify as a singularity. This creates uncertainty about Muslims among the westerners, which may fall under the 'fear threat perception' domain. Pew Research Survey 2017 indicates all negativities strongly linked with Muslims, with high percentage of people perceiving them as the threatening other, violent, extremists, anti-US and anti-democracy. The survey shows that about 41 per cent of the Americans perceive that Islam is a religion that encourages violence against non-Muslims; 35 per cent of survey respondents have been found to be taking Muslims as a bunch of dangerous extremists; 25 per cent people say that Muslims in the USA are anti-US despite being Muslim Americans; 50 per cent people believe that Islam is not and can never be a part of the US society; while 44 per cent conceive Islam and democracy are inherently in conflict with each other. The catastrophic event of 9/11 is one of the main sources of development of such negative perceptions among the US citizens, which got greatly fortified by the political and civil unrest in nearly entire Arab world, including wars against Talibanization in Afghanistan and Pakistan. Whether such hostilities against Muslims and Islam are primarily due to security threat perceptions among the US citizens or sociocultural, political and economic domains also play any role, are some of the important questions that need to be seriously investigated.

Australia is another good example to quote as a country where Muslims surged extraordinarily in the last decade. There were 341,000 Muslims in 2006, which soared to 604,000 (about 2.6% of the population) in 2016[5] as per the census, making Islam as the second largest religion in Australia. Among them, 36 per cent of Muslims are Australian born, with an average age of 24 years; and unlike general impressions, they are diverse in their culture, religious following and regional affiliation.[6] It is interesting to note that 30 per cent of

---

[5] Retrieved from http://www.dailymail.co.uk/news/article-4641728/Number-Muslims-Australia-soars-Census-2016.html.

[6] Retrieved from https://www.aph.gov.au/About_Parliament/Parliamentary_Departments/Parliamentary_Library/Publications_Archive/archive/Muslim Australians.

Australian population is registered having no religion at all; hence, doubling of followers of Islam in just one decade appears to be a serious question for many bigot and right-wing associates. On the other hand, unfortunately, Australia is badly hit by religion-related racial crimes against Muslims as per Human Rights and Equal Opportunity Commission (HREOC). The problems Muslims face in Australia mainly include discrimination, racial vilification, threats of violence and actual violence. Women and children are direct target of such racial offences at public places, schools and in their residential areas. This fear has forced parents to send their children to religious centres of learning instead of sending them to public schools; not because they want their children to learn religion but because of the growing security threats.

Nowhere else but in Australia in August 2017 it happened when Senator Pauline Hanson entered the Australian parliament wearing a black burqa[7] to ridicule Muslim women and enforce burqa ban in Australia. 'I am very much against the *Burqa*…it is not a religious requirement….it is oppressing women',[8] she said after burqa-wearing drama in an extreme bid to get her message heard across the parliament for banning of burqa in Australia, as it looks more like bandits looting a bank, she furthered.

Do Muslims pose serious sociocultural and economic threats to the Western societies and can deprive them of their social capital and economic resources? Does Islam play any role in fortifying these threats or Islam itself as a religion is a sociocultural threat to the West? In what ways, do Muslims or Islam, or both threaten the social and cultural settings of the Western societies? What are the dominant threat perceptions—whether it is a threat to the Western cultural values, social system/order, art and craft, way of life, economy or centuries-old traditions or all of them? Or Islam as an ideology is a

---

[7] Burqa is a traditional veiling style for women in most part of the Arab world, Pakistan, India and Bangladesh.

[8] Retrieved from https://www.theguardian.com/australia-news/2017/aug/17/pauline-hanson-wears-burqa-in-australian-senate-while-calling-for-ban.

threat to sociocultural ideologies of the West? Also, whether media or elite political discourses have any role to play in flaring up the sociocultural threats from Muslims and Islam. These and some other significant issues would essentially be undertaken while debating on Islamophobia as a sociocultural and economic threat. This piece of literature would also attempt to conceptualize and operationalize sociocultural threats for possible collection of empirical data on this dimension of Islamophobia. This would, indeed, help understand the phenomenon in a holistic manner, which may be used to identify the problem itself, its antecedents and possible ways to address it in a systematic fashion. But it would be apposite to understand as what do we mean by sociocultural values or factors before exploring and explicating Islamophobia in sociocultural perspective.

WHAT DO WE MEAN BY SOCIOCULTURAL FACTORS?

Understandably, sociocultural factors are customs, lifestyles and values that characterize a society (Ajami & Goddard, 2018). Explicating it further would mean two broad spectrums—social and cultural systems of a society. A social system is a relatively wider umbrella that may have many sub-social systems or cultures operating under it. But a sub-social system, which may be called culture of a specific group, does essentially have some common strands with the umbrella social system under which it functions; hence, a micro sub-social system or cultural system has more clearly defined and operationalized values/cultural artefacts at some functional level. These sociocultural systems, then, affect the thought process at individual level, govern peoples' behaviour, define mores and taboos, provide socio-psychological recognition to individual and social actions, develop individuals' attitudes, may become a cognitive evaluative framework for every aspect of human life and eventually form commonness among the individuals by extending shared values and meanings to social products.

For every society, there are predominantly four main elements of their sociocultural settings, namely language, customs and traditions, art and craft, and dressing styles or attires. Some sociologists suggest religion as an integral component of a social system besides the other four. Religion plays a fairly stronger role in closed societies, while its influence on social deeds is usually weak in open or cosmopolitan social systems. In a way, the relationship between religion of a social system and society's level of modernity is more often inverse in nature—more the modernity, less the influence of religion and vice versa. Nonetheless, these five important components of every social or sub-social system are crucial in understanding how a society would look like.

Muslims, whether living in a larger Muslim society or as a subgroup in somewhat contrasting social system, enjoy special peculiarities in some of their aforementioned components of social system. Not all ingredients of their subcultural system are functional at equal level in every subgroup of Muslims, rather significance of some traits of their sociocultural value system overwhelms under some kind of circumstances. For instance, during their religious festivities, most of the Muslims prefer wearing their traditional attires regardless of the set-up they live in. During special religious days like Eid or month of Ramadan, every Muslim would appear to be much different than he/she is usually seen otherwise. It is somewhat true in marriage ceremonies or other special social occasions. Adaptation to the umbrella cultural value system, if it is in contrast, recedes drastically without any consideration for the larger groups. It would not be out of the way if pronounced that Muslims imprison themselves in their cultural cocoons on certain religio-cultural occasions.

Such a state may give birth to sociocultural conflict(s) between sub-sociocultural system and macro-level sociocultural system, especially when there are weak common strands between them. This appears to be true in case of Muslims living in a ghettoization fashion in the Western societies. Things may worsen if there exists historical cultural estrangement between them or macro-level social system is equally dominating and socially coercive. Sociocultural conflict is then the natural outcome and extremely unavoidable. Tolerance and adaptation at sociocultural level are the only conflict mitigating factors; in their absence, clash is inevitable. This sort of clash in the West may be termed as Islamophobia.

ISLAMOPHOBIA DEFINED IN
SOCIOCULTURAL THREAT PERSPECTIVE

The Western societies view Muslims as a community and a group of people with unique sociocultural outlook or somewhat unlike their social values. While Islam as a religion also enjoys almost the same status, orientalist's perspective helps the developed West to define and draw lines between 'us' and 'them', mostly on sociocultural lines, where growing unrest in the Muslim countries added the element of terror in the game. The socially constructed notion of Muslims as 'problematic' in the contemporary Western world also has a long history of dislike and hatred of Muslims and Islam (Miah, 2017). The Iranian Revolution in 1979, Oklahoma bombing in 1993, Rushdie affair in 1988 and last few big nails in the coffin were 9/11 and 7/7 bombing episodes; all contributed in furthering with the Western notion of Muslims and Islam as a problematic religion and group of people on the planet earth. Coupled with such fear perceptions, sociocultural, political and economic differences and issues helped pose Muslims and Islam as threatening other with huge dangers for Western societies from within, unlike what it used to be historically. Realizing that to save their values, norms and customs from being overwhelmed by historically alien 'others', the sociocultural and economic threats from Muslims and Islam in mainlands of Europe, North America and Australia are aggrandized.

Islam is against Western civilization and Muslims are different in terms of their values and norms (Allen, 2010, p. 37), capable of changing their neighbouring social orders with least chances of adjusting to its macro-social system; that is how Islam and Muslims are generally perceived in the West. To avoid Westerners becoming victim of Islamic sociocultural norm and values, Islam was represented as irrational, backward, barbaric, dogmatic and repressive by the global media and literature. This domain, sociocultural threats from Muslims and Islam, of Islamophobia has remained least researched in contemporary literature; probably due to abundant evidence of Islam and Muslims as threatening and terrorizing others. On the contrary, some factional elders of Islam, Khomeini as being the most popular among them, are fearful of 'Westoxification' of Islam (p. 38) and hence urged upon Muslims to return to fundamentals of the religion to avoid adulteration of Islam.

The first connection of Islam with other religions, more prominently Christianity and Judaism, has often been perceived as threat; however, diverging views exist on what kind of threat was it. Was it the threat of Islam as the subjugator and eliminator of other religions, which seems somewhat more justified from outward social perspective, or Islam was a threat to sociocultural values of other religions in a macro-social system scenario? The latter perspective seemingly talks about sociocultural dimensions of Islamophobia. Evidence from history supports this perspective that even during the colonialization period, reforming Islam in its sociocultural context did not pay much dividend. Failing efforts left the colonial powers with no other option but resort to debase Islam as a retrogressive and inferior religion; impossible to be subordinated, and hence its followers are 'a civilization doomed to barbarism and backwardness for ever' (Ahmed, 1999, p. 60). Some of the contemporary scholars like Halliday (2003) do not agree to see Islam and Muslims as historically tracked enemies, but a problem of modern world where ideological warfare may determine the fate of societies in the days to come. He traces Islam as a competing ideology, a direct and potent challenge to the West, while peeping through the Iranian Revolution, and foresees Christian Europe overthrown by Islam and London as a Sharia state in 2050 (Allen, 2010, p. 40). This fear essentially demonstrates Islam as a coercive social ideology aimed at reforming the sociocultural mechanisms of a society in accordance with its Holy book Quran and *Sunnah*—teachings and deeds of Holy Prophet (PBUH). How could that be possible—a question arises—maybe through increasing Muslim population in the Western societies, building of more mosques, spreading of religious education through their religious institutions in the West and, more importantly, the tendency of Muslims to appear to be a distinct creed and unassimilable sub-social systems within Western macro-social systems.

Islam and Muslims pose serious and strong resistance to Western values and cultural system in many ways; hence, they are regarded as the most transruptive culture and religion. On this, Marranci (2004) writes:

> Islam is, among many others, a *transruptive* culture, and religion in Europe. But today in the West, Islam is seen as the most *transruptive*, the culture/civilisation that resists (although through it different and variegated national and cultural expressions) to Western values, challenges the Western concept of democracy, refuses to acknowledge the European exclusive Judaeo-Christian heritage. In other words, Islam becomes the culture/civilisation that 'never the less refuses to be repressed'.

This refers to one of the most visible fears in the Western world that Muslims are hard to be integrated into their values, which in a way denies the multiculturalism enchantment in the hands of cultural bigotry. Muslims' ghettoization in urban and suburban centres in Europe and other Western countries is not seen with respect. Building of their places of worship, 'halal' shops for meat and other groceries do get noticed by the natives with some degree of fear and repugnance. Probably, such a fear pushed Angela Merkel, German Chancellor, to warn Muslim refugees from Syria that 'integration is a must… want to settle in Germany? Then learn the language, get accustomed to Western values and find a job'.[9] She emphasized by saying, 'We say it clearly. We have learned from the past'. Her reference to past also demonstrates Germans' understanding of Muslims and Islam's sociocultural norms and values, which probably have been found to be transruptive in nature. Crown Prince Charles from the UK also remarked in almost the same rather a little harsh tone while addressing Muslims that 'if you live in our country, you must abide by our values'.[10] The French also did not lag in expressing their sentiments towards Muslims and Islam. In February 2011, the then PM of France Nicolas Sarkozy vehemently declared that 'If you come to France, you have to melt in a single community, which is the national community. If you don't accept this, you cannot be welcomed in France' (Sunar, 2017, p. 60). Later developments in most of the European countries are even more startling. Such frightening

---

[9] Retrieved from https://www.politico.eu/article/angela-merkel-to-refugees-integration-is-a-must-germany/.

[10] Retrieved from https://www.express.co.uk/news/uk/556880/Prince-Charles-tells-UK-Muslims-abide-British-values-start-tour-Middle-East.

statements by the elders in the West underline the emergence of sociocultural phobias that might have link with the past and are becoming fault lines for future confrontational politics within and across the Western societies.

Many scholars while tracing Islam's enmity with Christianity view Islamophobia as a sociocultural divergence between Islam and others. For instance, Watt (2004) explores a great effect that Islam had on the social and cultural value system of Europe in the medieval time on almost every aspect of European lives. The European languages, sociocultural values and artefacts, due to Muslims dominance in parts of Europe, were vulnerable to change. Hobson (2004) went to the extent of tracing the Western civilization's root from the East in his famous work *The Eastern Origins of Western Civilizations*. For them, Islamophobia symbolizes the takeover of Western civilization by the Muslims and Islam. 'The enemy within' narrative primarily considers Muslims and Islam as one of the greatest threat that the West is facing since centuries and has grown manifold in present-day terror manufactured environment of the West. The reality is that Muslims are an inalienable part of Western societies believing them to be the most dangerous creature on the planet earth. Terror and security threats from Muslims are the product of 9/11 or 7/7 episodes, while Muslims and Islam as threatening sociocultural entities are centuries old.

Noticing the effects of Muslims and other civilizations on Americans and their religion, Huntington (2004) stressed that the US citizens should now re-establish themselves along their sociocultural and religious lines following Christianity and declared the US elite as dead souls who have become increasingly denationalized. On the other side, Muslims, visibility of their religion and their control of sociocultural artefacts are on rampant, giving the scholars like Huntington enough substance to awake American elite from deep slumber over their waning culture and social systems in the name of multiculturalism. Such oppositional moves by the scholars of time definitely have potential to invoke 'cultural racism', which essentially prevails due to the colonial past and is legitimizing 'white supremacy over inferior cultures such as Jews, Arabs or everyone who was described as people from the wrong religion' (Grosfoguel & Mielants, 2006; Sunar, 2017). They (Muslims and Jews) are considered contra-political, but cultural and religious entities; the notion is strongly supported by the history and 'the others' who represent a menace to the civilized and modern Western world (Ulger & Benitez, 2017). Rather, they are, more specifically Islam, interpreted as 'anti-thesis of modernity' (p. 55), which is a hallmark of the Western civilization.

Moreover, it is significant to understand that cultural racism, as the modern form of racism and eventually a form of Islamophobia, makes sufficient space available for the racists to avoid being caught under the stringent racism laws. They, the racists, mainly aim at establishing the cultural inferiority of a group of people associated with some particular religion, area, ideology or culture. Usually, the people, supposedly the victim of cultural racism, are symbolized with unacceptable and strong social taboos using modern sophisticated theoretical propositions (like symbolic interactionism).[11] This leaves the victims of cultural racism at the mercy of 'superior cultural groups' whose authoritarian treatment of the subjugated people appears normal over time. Thus, symbolic interactionism through associating culturally inferior groups with social taboos such as barbarism, uncivilized creatures, bunch of savages, primitive and terrorists or potential terrorists paves the way for cultural racism.

Islamophobia in sociocultural context has to do a lot with visibility of cultural traits of Muslims. This may include veiling of women in the form of hijab or headscarf, halal meat shops, garments covering whole women bodies, turban or cap on men's head, mosques, prayer call (*Azaan*) from mosques five times a day, Friday prayer congregations, variety of cultural dresses from various regions including Middle East, Fareast Asia and Asia. Contemporarily, this visibility has increased in Western societies, which may be regarded as the revolting and rebelling acts owing to the mounting criticism by the West of Muslims' sociocultural values or West's fear of Muslims and Islam as the dominating culture or maybe because of a media construction that more

---

[11] Symbolic interactionism, formulated by Blumer (1969) is the process of interaction in the formation of meanings for individuals. The inspiration for this theory came from Dewey (1981), which believed that human beings are best understood in a practical, interactive relation to their environment.

often portrays them negatively. Whatever could be the most significant reason, such visibilities have pushed politicians and other notables to suggest their governments and Muslim communities to 'adopt discretion in the visibility of their religion', and reclaim and rename their sociocultural actualities to avoid criticism of the Westerners or, in a way, reduce sociocultural Islamophobia, such as declaring halal meats as vegan, banning burqa in Europe and avoiding the use of hijab or headscarf in public places (Ulger & Benitez, 2017).

Sociocultural context of Islamophobia, which is deeply embedded with civilizational aspects, overwhelms the contemporary debates on the construct. Both entities, Muslims and Islam, are equally central to these debates, which at times take Islam as a discursive religion inciting Islamism—a discursive construct that completely rejects the West and modernism. Labelling a religion having billion of followers across the whole world as a discursive religion itself is an Islamophobic discourse and manifestation. Moreover, the author could not substantiate its premise of Islam as a discursive religion with compelling evidence. Nonetheless, Islamism is relatively a contested phenomenon engaging scholars from all shades of opinion. Here, Muslim scholars have been found to be more piquant in commenting on Islamization of every aspect of society without valuing the sociocultural values of a given system. This radicalized view has hardly been appreciated in any part of the world including the Muslim societies. On the other hand, Western scholars contextualize Islamism and the process of Islamization of societies as one of the important predictors of clash of civilization with a demonstrated possibility of irreconcilability of the Islamic values with Western cultures (Schiffer, 2011) and hence the natural rise of Islamophobia.

Rise of Islamophobia in most parts of Europe, the USA and Australian continent is primarily a 'social anxiety of the west towards Islam and Muslims' (Gottschalk & Greenberg, 2008, p. 5). The main cause of anxiety may have roots in history, but Muslims' reluctance to toe the Western cultural lines in toto and unloosened bonds with their religion are some of the main sources of this anxiety. Long prevalence of such socio-psychological anxiety in a wider social order results in horrendous corollaries like, and ultimately as Bleich (2012, p. 10) puts it, absolute 'rejection of religious referent', wherein Islam is taken 'as an irreducible identity' and a 'marker between Us and Them'. Once such lines are drawn clearly in socio-religio-cultural realm, as seen obvious in most of the cases of Islamophobic manifestation, then rejection of a religion and its socio-cultural values become normal and go unnoticed. Some sociocultural and religious peculiarities, in such a state of affairs, consequently become special target of hate and objection. Veiling and usage of headscarf by the women in most parts of Europe, especially France, are considered traits of Muslims culture worth hatred, and Gallup polls often reject them completely (Bleich, 2012). Not only this, in a vow to liberate women from the so-called religious oppression, France enacted laws in 2004 and 2010 to prohibit women from wearing veils and hiding their faces in educational institutions, transport and hospitals, and the use of religious symbols in schools (Ulger & Benitez, 2017). Denmark also followed French footprints regarding Muslim women veiling in public spaces. When seen in a wider religious perspective in a scholastic manner, such moves in fact are nothing but representation of Islam as a sexist religion that believes in violence against women as a religious ritual.

Sociocultural threats dimension of Islamophobia is quite broad and diverse in nature. It brings into its ambit both Islam and Muslims posing serious threats to the Western way of life and their value system. If taken in two broad domains, these threats are characterized as tangible and intangible sociocultural menaces to the West. Tangible sociocultural threats may include building of mosques, distinct dressing of Muslims on their religious rituals or prayers or otherwise, veiling of women and their dressing, religious literature, etc., while intangible artefacts that may pose sociocultural menaces include Muslims' sociocultural values, customs and traditions, way of life, religiosity, Muslims' views towards their religion and sacred personalities of Islam and their views towards other religions, etc. In a way, strong sociocultural identities of Muslims impede their way to integration with the macro-culture of the West, which is always seen with suspicion. Contrarily, Westerners' strong in-group identity promotes lack of tolerance towards micro-groups in a wider social system, resultantly thin cultural lines between social groups start swelling, further degenerating multiculturalism and making the societies sick and somewhat non-functional in certain aspects, wherein Islamophobia is one of them. Hence, in broader terms, Islamophobia in sociocultural perspective may be regarded as the process of degeneration of basic precepts of multiculturalism, particularly towards Muslims as an out-group and Islam as an inassimilable ideology, mainly due to the West's strong in-group affiliation.

CONSTRUCTION OF ISLAMOPHOBIA IN SOCIOCULTURAL PERSPECTIVE

Sociocultural indicators generally deal with issues related to development of human well-being in a given social system (OECD, 1976), ranging from inequality, employment and unemployment of people, educational attainment to life expectancy, etc. Nonetheless, this study does not aim at exploring and explicating hard-core sociocultural development indicators available for Muslims in the Western countries. Rather, it would attempt to conceptualize and operationalize the sociocultural conditions of Muslims and acceptance of Islam as a religion in the West, which, once jeopardized, might lead to a threatening state for the potential victims (Muslims), primarily due to the majority's fear of the minority's affiliation with its religion and culture. Commonly known sociocultural indicators are manifold in nature, but broadly they are classified into objective and subjective sociocultural indicators. Objective sociocultural indicators are more often easy to measure like poverty rate, unemployment rate, living conditions, etc., while subjective sociocultural indicators may include confidence, trust and attitude towards a minority group of people by the majority group, degree of self-respect, respect to minority group's language, attire, religion, way of doing things, their places of worship, colour, creed, etc. Objective sociocultural indicators for Muslims living in the West might have multiplicity of explanations and may not directly be linked with Islam as a religion; however, the fear of Islam as a pernicious religion and Muslims as potentially dangerous creatures might affect subjective sociocultural indicators. Hence, our focus would remain on them while discussing and unpacking Islamophobia as a construct in sociocultural perspective.

As enunciated earlier, Islamophobia in sociocultural perspective is the process of degeneration of basic precepts of multiculturalism, particularly towards Muslims as an out-group and Islam as an inassimilable ideology, mainly due to the West's strong in-group affiliation. Bringing the phenomenon down from the ladder of abstraction to some observable measures, the definition has fundamentally two main strands: (a) epistemic dimension, which may embrace multiplicity of sociocultural indicators and (b) antecedent(s) dimension that explains the potential roots and routes of the degeneration process including the catalytic variable(s), if any. Epistemic dimension of Islamophobia construction in sociocultural perspective may have four major components, namely social, cultural, language and religion. Indicators for social component or sub-dimension may comprise, but not limited to, anti-to-West way of life, anti-to-West social values and customs, social discrimination, social marginalization, social distance, social violence of subtle nature (like gazing), colour, creed and visible geographic positioning/affiliation, etc. Cultural indicators may include women veiling (burqa, headscarf), marriage ceremonies, cultural festivities, cultural or regional attires, in-group social activities, foods and cultural fads. Third component encompasses written and spoken languages of Muslim countries, especially Arabic, Urdu, Persian, Pashto and Hindi coupled with the colour and guise of the speakers. Fourth and the most significant component is religion. The indicators for religious component may include visibility of mosques, conduct of religious rituals in mosques like Eid prayer, Friday prayer congregations, prayer calls from mosques, recitation of Holy Quran, visibility of written Quranic verses (particularly in Arabic), typical wearing of cap for prayers, long bearded men, women with hijab, religious festivities, peculiar religious gear such as *tasbeeh, miswaak* and *uba'a* (dress usually worn by the imams of mosques). The following diagram dilates and elucidates the epistemic dimensions of Islamophobia in sociocultural perspective.

Muslims Make up 4.9% of Europe's Population in 2016

Estimated % of Muslims among Total Population in Each Country

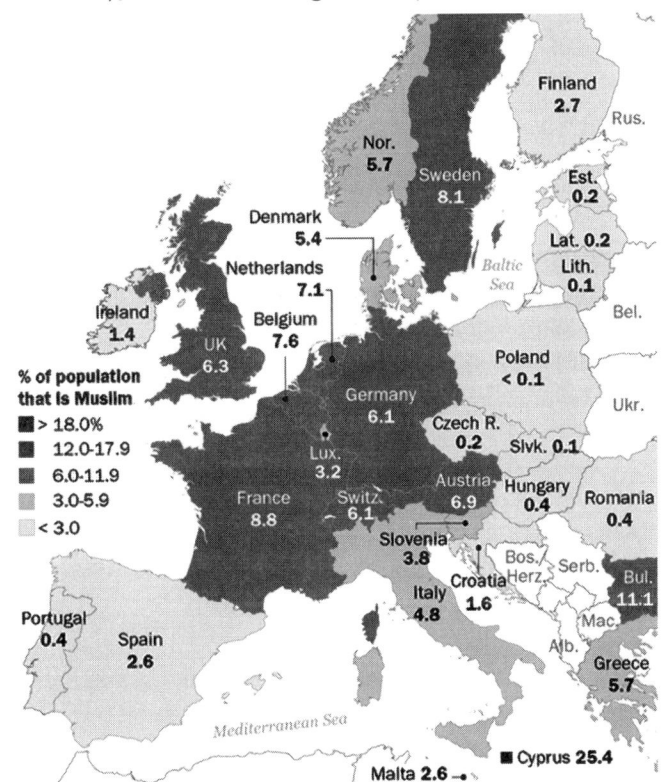

Source: Pew Research Center.

Note: This figure is not to scale. It does not represent any authentic national or international boundaries and is used for illustrative purposes only.

In antecedent dimension, Social Identity Theory (SIT), as a predictor of in-group identity, seems to be providing theoretical foundation to investigate the cultivation of Islamophobia in sociocultural perspective. Tajfel and Turner (1986) developed SIT in 1979 with an aim to identify minimal conditions under which an individual discriminates the out-group in favour of the in-group (Iqbal, 2010). This prejudice takes birth when an individual attempts to strongly correlate himself with the group he belongs to. Usually, 'significant others' for individuals (i.e., parents, peer group, teachers, etc.) and their experiences shape an individual's behaviour towards the out-group—'the others' (Hogg, 2002, pp. 353–354). The following SIT model may help us understand it well.

Views of Muslims More Negative in Eastern and Southern Europe
Unfavourable View of Mulims in Our Country

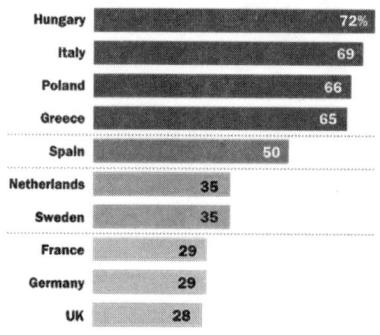
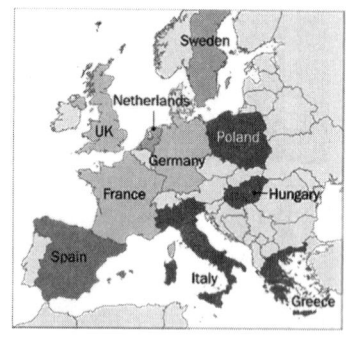

Source: Pew Research Center.[12]

Stronger in-group (us) identity at macro-level more often affects the social order with a clear potential of institutionalizing the 'othering' process against the out-group (them). Eventually, it becomes easier for the people from dominant group to identify themselves and 'others' mainly due to the reason as Grant (2007, p. 84) explains while quoting Habermas and Lohmann (1972) that every society tends to reduce and simplify the complexities of subtle and complex phenomena. Such simplification, in the case of Islamophobia in sociocultural perspective, may reflect in the manner explained in the preceded paras in four main sub-domains: social, cultural, language and religion. Inherited crystalized differences between the in-group and out-group in these four components help the macro-level dominant groups marginalize

---

[12] Retrieved from http://www.pewresearch.org/fact-tank/2017/08/09/muslims-and-islam-key-findings-in-the-u-s-and-around-the-world/.

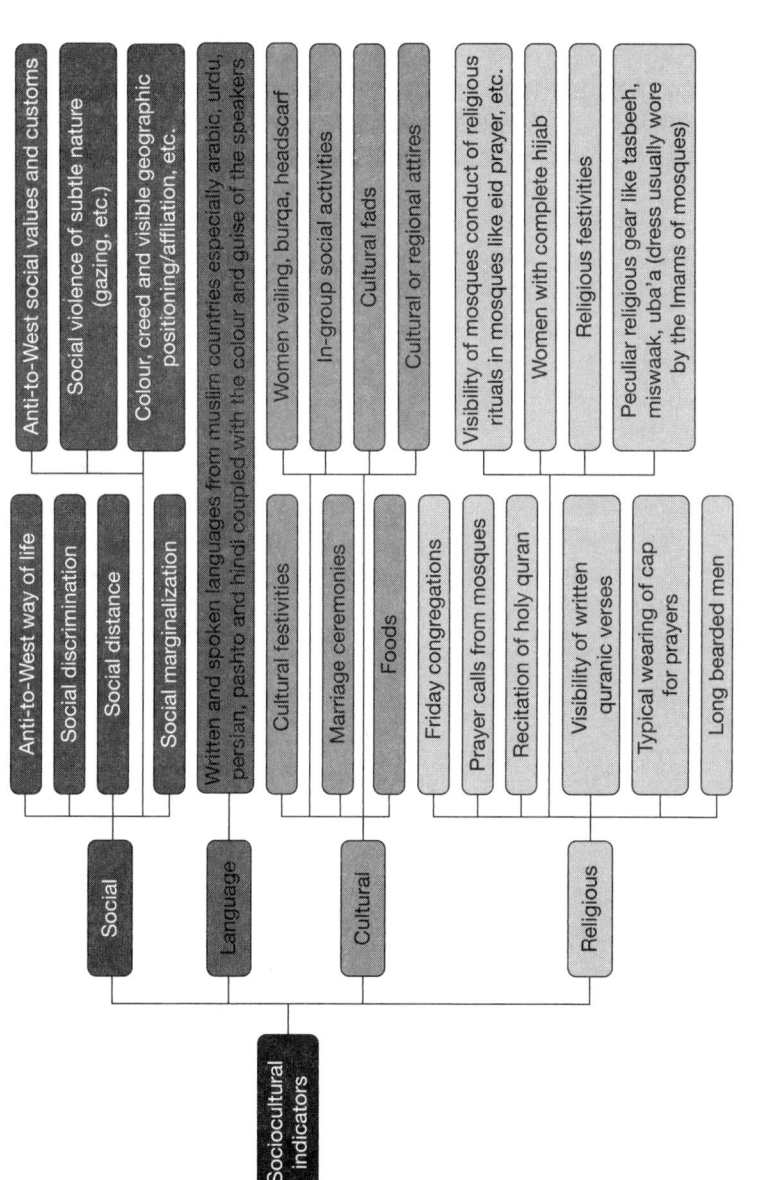

Sociocultural indicators

Social
- Anti-to-West way of life
- Social discrimination
- Social distance
- Social marginalization
  - Anti-to-West social values and customs
  - Social violence of subtle nature (gazing, etc.)
  - Colour, creed and visible geographic positioning/affiliation, etc.

Language
- Written and spoken languages from muslim countries especially arabic, urdu, persian, pashto and hindi coupled with the colour and guise of the speakers

Cultural
- Cultural festivities
- Marriage ceremonies
- Foods
  - Women veiling, burqa, headscarf
  - In-group social activities
  - Cultural fads
  - Cultural or regional attires

Religious
- Friday congregations
- Prayer calls from mosques
- Recitation of holy quran
- Visibility of written quranic verses
- Typical wearing of cap for prayers
- Long bearded men
  - Visibility of mosques conduct of religious rituals in mosques like eid prayer, etc.
  - Women with complete hijab
  - Religious festivities
  - Peculiar religious gear like tasbeeh, miswaak, uba'a (dress usually wore by the Imams of mosques)

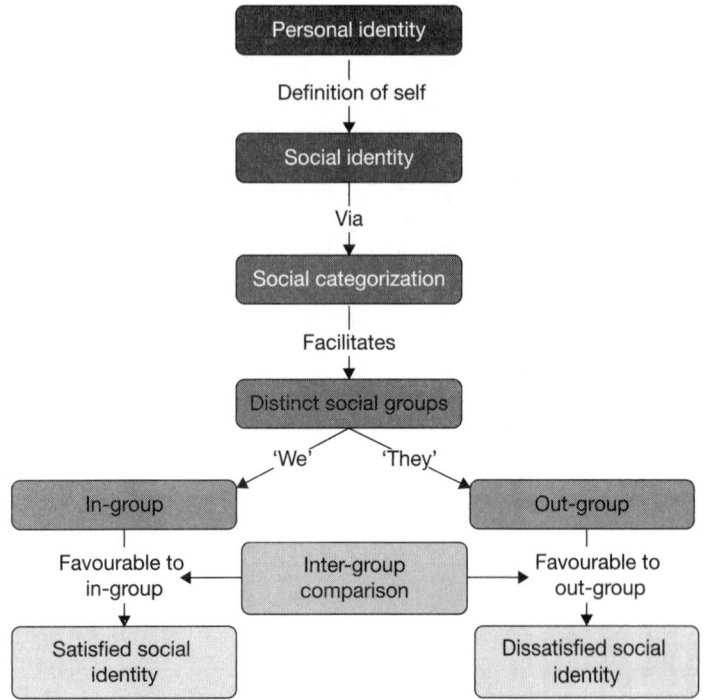

Source: Tajfel and Turner (1986).

the minority group(s). In this scenario, Muslims belong to the minority group.

Mass media representation of Muslims and Islam as 'others' is another significant antecedent of Islamophobia construction in sociocultural perspective. This fact can hardly be overemphasized that mainstream media images, representations and discourses about Islam and Muslims are clearly negative and hostile (Poole & Richardson, 2006). Mainly, this hostility is depicted in events of extremism and terrorism, but even the images in sociocultural domain are also not objectives and mostly embedded with a tinge of negativity in them. Combined picture of terror, extremism and sociocultural distinction add insult to the injury, wherein Muslims and Islam in entirety appear to be as absolute 'others' and a potential danger to the solidarity and safety of dominant in-group. Moreover, polemical representation of

Muslims and Islam also provides a huge amount of substance for political and social discourses to people in the public spheres, which help them fortify, solidify and multiply their individual and social attitudes towards Muslims and Islam. This process perpetuates gradually due to overwhelming influence of media on its target audience and eventually concludes in the construction of a social reality 'in a predictable and patterned' fashion (McQuail, 1994, p. 331); nonetheless, it is not a reality based on objective social realities but a mediated reality. This is, indeed, one of the most significant factors in developing Islamophobia in almost all its facets.

Historical prejudice and hostility towards Muslims and Islam, of course, is a constant, not variable in most of the cases, and an intervening factor in the process of Islamophobia development. The nature of history of hostility as a constant factor is mainly due to the reason that Islam and Muslims have not been an equal impediment in the Christian Zionism movement everywhere in the world. That is why, Islamophobia in the UK may be different from Islamophobia in Spain, France or Italy. It is primarily due to the fact that historical interaction and experience between Muslims/Islam and the Spaniards, French, Italians and Britons varied in their nature and intensity of negativity, if any. Hence, history of prejudice and hostility do play its role in cultivating Islamophobic feelings in sociocultural domains, but this is fundamentally an intervening one and not primary in nature.

COMPARING ISLAMOPHOBIA WITH ANTI-SEMITISM

Generally, religious discourses rooted deep in prejudice, racism, hostility and intolerance are similar in nature. That is why Islamophobia is often known as another form of anti-Semitism, but towards Muslims and Islam. Religious intolerance is an umbrella term, which covers Islamophobia and anti-Semitism alike and poses serious challenges to the goals of peace, normalcy and multiculturalism.

Anti-Semitism is to Jews and Judaism what Islamophobia is to Muslims and Islam. Both faces of religious intolerance, as phenomena, are found in abundance in history, mainly inflicted upon them by the Christian Zionism. Nonetheless, the term was first coined by Wilhelm Marr in 1873 in his famous work *The Victory of Judaism over Germanism* (Marr, 1879). He discerned that Jews would soon take over the German government and run the state of affairs due to their extreme abilities to conspire and seduce the events; hence, they must be isolated and be deprived of the citizen rights. This approach, he termed as anti-Semitism, the traces of which can be found in thousands of years' history like the *Protocols of the Elders of Zion*—a secret plan of the Jews to control the world. The Holocaust was the ultimate of its kind against Jews, which the Vatican itself repented in 1998 in the following manner (Yallop, 2007).

> This century has witnessed an unspeakable tragedy, which can never be forgotten—the attempt by the Nazi regime to exterminate the Jewish people, with the consequent killing of millions of Jews. Women and men, old and young, children and infants, for the sole reason of their Jewish origin, were persecuted and deported. Some were killed immediately, while others were degraded, ill-treated, tortured and utterly robbed of their human dignity, and then murdered. Very few of those who entered the [concentration] camps survived, and those who did remained scarred for life. This was the Shoah.

It is of no significance that Jews square measure passed through distressing times in Europe on occasions with same frequency and intensity as did the Muslims. The list of European cities is not short where Jews have of late been attacked, and the range of anti-Semitic uttering or violation of Judaic graves could not take place, even in the recent past. No speculate Jews in Europe may raise queries that they were banished long ago; like, is it safe to wear a kippa (skullcap), or send their youngsters to Judaic faculties or attend synagogue? Several observers question the new skin tone of the new anti-Semitism rising, contemporarily. Whether or not we tend to face a comeback of the previous kind of 'brown' racist anti-Semitism, or whether or not what we have got at the instant square measure, essentially Muslim attacks against Jews and leftist liberals' bashing of Israel and Zionism? As Wistrich (2005) remarks, 'once well thought out the safeguard of backward-looking clerics, standard nationalists, fascist bigots, and ultra-radical leftists, Judeophobia has undergone a basic alteration in current years' (p. 1). It has become a problem for the liberal left and it's the banishing of Israel by all its interpretations and manifestations.

The image of Europe and entire West as multicultural, liberal and tolerant bunch of countries does not match its tyrannies of the past towards Muslims and Jews, which contemporarily emerged into Islamophobia and anti-Semitism. Hardly much is found on the pages of history substantiating today's portrayal of multiculturalism by the Europeans, which has yet to pass through the test of time. Prejudice, racism and hostilities are the products of European bashing of 'others'. Contrarily, Islamic civilization took birth in a multicultural, multiethnic and multireligious society; hence, tolerance to 'others' seems to have crept into its genes even on its own lands. In the process of expansion to other regions, Islamic civilization presented special laws to prevent its people to pose any dangers to people from other civilizations, sometimes in the shape of *dhimmi* laws and at other times public clemency for the people of other faiths. Nevertheless, it is quite logical and legitimate to condemn and criticize the Muslim countries engaged in violation of human rights, women rights and promoting or unable to resist extremism on their lands, and it also merits to condemn the maltreatment of people from other faiths in Muslim countries, but by no way these acts make it legitimate to resort to and return such atrocities in shape of Islamophobia in the West.

As explained in detail the rudimentary components of Islamophobia earlier, which include racism, prejudice, hostility towards Muslims and Islam, perceived threats of sociocultural, political and economic nature from Muslims and Islam, anti-Semitism as a phenomenon also carries almost the same traits. However, historic reasons for all these components differ grossly. For Judaism, the birth of Christianity was a 'problem' and Christendom declared Jews as the crucifiers of the Christ; thus, an extreme state of religious conflict rose that took shape of anti-Semitism, while Islam emerged as a 'problem' for the Christianity and its expansion dreaded it the most to the level of extinction, which caused Islamophobia that is still active with all its disparaging facets. Interestingly, for better or worse, Christendom is the common face and inventor of the both—whether Islamophobia or anti-Semitism.

MASS MEDIA AS A SOURCE OF SOCIOCULTURAL ISLAMOPHOBIA

Contemporary Islamophobia is in fact mediated Islamophobia, whereby global media is the main source of its dissemination and a force to foster it with gigantic effects on masses across the globe. Mass media report the incidents of terrorism when involving Islamic identity, though a terrorist should not be tagged with any religious identity, in such a way that further engenders Islamophobia with an increased potential to exponentiate similar or graver events by sending the feelings of fears across the board to victims and the perpetrators. Reckless and irresponsible reporting, in this regard, have adversely contributed in worsening the already worsened situation. Media have lately used extremely dehumanizing metaphors, especially for Muslims involved in terrorist activities in the USA, Canada, Europe and Australia. Global media invariably employed metaphors such as rats and cockroaches for Muslims; Islam is a cancer, a barbaric ideology, a false religion and an inalienable enemy of the West. Such dehumanizing and demeaning metaphors often broadcast or published unabatedly on media, especially when used in popular political elite discourse, having powerful and systematic impact on the way masses perceive, think and discuss Muslims and Islam in their public spheres. Then Islamophobia becomes normal as people over time develop a potent cognitive framework to assess events of terror without brooding much on how information is poured on them by stripping off the humanity and sanctity of religions of peace.

'Enemy within' is the first impression of hostile attitudes by masses in the societies where Muslims are in minority. Successive opinion polls and reports by non-governmental organizations speak volumes on the negative attitudes of the Westerners towards Muslims and Islam. Exclusion and marginalization of minority Muslims, workplace harassment, bullying of females and kids at schools and institutions, arson of mosques, racial attacks, etc., have become quite common and are considered normal. In short, sociocultural Islamophobia is the net outcome of mediated Islamophobia or polemical construction of Islam and Muslims in the global media. To comprehend this in a little detail, it would prove to be prudent to evaluate as how do media from main parts of the world such as the North America, Europe and Australia cultivate sociocultural Islamophobia. Also, let us have a peerless glance on social media construction of Islam and Muslims too, which is increasingly influencing our way of looking at the world, in general, and Muslims and Islam, in particular.

The following lines from media, in ditto, shed some light on the polemical and negative construction of Islam and Muslims in the US media using negative frames, hostile languageand so on:

- The Islamic Cultural Center of Fresno and three other mosques in California received the letter on Monday, which calls the recipients 'children of Satan' and 'vile and filthy people'. The letter also threatened that President-elect Donald Trump is 'going to cleanse America and make it shine again' and will 'do to you Muslims what Hitler did to the Jews'.[13]
- During his campaign, Donald Trump told CNN, 'I think Islam hates us' and said it's difficult to separate 'radical' Islam from Islam itself. Since winning the election, he has continued to call for a registry of immigrants and visitors from Muslim countries and a ban on others from entering.[14]
- Another letter stated, 'There's a new sheriff in town—President Donald Trump' and tells Muslims to 'pack your bags and get out of Dodge'.[15]
- Fuchigami said, 'If something happens like 9/11, what are they going to do? Take all the Muslims and put them into camps like

---

[13] *The San Francisco Chronicle*, 30 Nov 2016; *Inland Valley Daily Bulletin*, Ontario, Canada, 29 November 2016; *Redlands Daily Facts*, California, 29 November 2016; *Long Island City—Astoria Journal & Jackson Heights News*, New York, 29 November 2016; *Daily Breeze*, California, 29 November 2016; *Fresno Bee*, California, 28 November 2016; *The Davis Enterprise*, California, 2 December 2016 Friday; *Telegram & Gazette*, Massachusetts, 20 January 2017; *Redmond Reporter*, Washington, 19 May 2017.

[14] *Fresno Bee*, California, 28 November 2016; CNN International, 16 November 2016.

[15] *Fresno Bee*, California, 28 November 2016.

we were put into concentration camps?' and recalls the infamous ABC system used to track Japanese Americans during the Second World War era. 'When you start to make lists, it's sort of like the first step towards doing things like that'.[16]

- A Muslim woman narrated that she was wearing a hijab as she shopped in her favourite Wichita store when a woman stepped close to her. 'Bye', the woman said to the Muslim woman, waving her hand. 'You need to go home ... pack up and leave'.[17]

- American civil rights organizations and faith leaders said that they were disturbed by Trump's appointment of retired Lieutenant General Michael T. Flynn to be his top national security adviser. Flynn, a former head of the Defense Intelligence Agency, has repeatedly referred to Islam as 'a cancer' and claimed that a 'fear of Muslims is rational' and warned—despite a lack of evidence—that Sharia or Islamic law is spreading throughout the USA. Flynn joined the board of ACT! for America, an activist group that has helped introduce bills to ban Islamic Sharia law in nearly two dozen US states, shortly after he joined the Trump campaign. ACT! for America's founder, Brigitte Gabriel, has assailed a 'cancer called Islamofascism' that permeates a Muslim world in which 'extreme is mainstream'. Hooper said, 'Why it's okay to be an anti-Muslim bigot and have a powerful post in the administration is a mystery'. Of Flynn, whom Hooper described as 'beyond the pale', he said, 'He should not be in public office. We can only imagine what policies will flow from the fact that he believes Islam is a cancer, and that he's been at war with Islam'.[18]

- Basatneh

> You know, in the past, twelve years of wearing my headscarf, I occasionally get the 'go back to your country' or 'you're a terrorist', something like that, on the streets, and I'd ignore it. But for someone

---

[16] *The Denver Post*, 27 November 2016.

[17] *The Wichita Eagle*, Kansas, 22 November 2016; *Daily News*, New York, 6 December 2016.

[18] *The Washington Post*, 20 November 2016; *CNN, SHOW: CNN NEWSROOM*, 19 November 2016; *Los Angeles Daily News*, 19 November 2016; *Herald Democrat*, Texas, 30 December 2016; *Telegram & Gazette*, Massachusetts, 20 January 2017.

to pull out a weapon in a safe place, which was a hospital, and set it next to me, and I was waiting to be stabbed, that just escalated to a whole new level.[19]

- Mr de Maizière said, 'The translations of the Quran are being distributed along with messages of hatred and unconstitutional ideologies', 'Teenagers are being radicalized with conspiracy theories'.[20]
- 'This is absolute madness! Islam is incompatible with western civilization!' Rodne wrote on Facebook. 'In the interim, Americans [sic], arm yourselves!!!!!'[21]
- When Elsokary intervened, the man called her an 'ISIS (expletive)' and threatened, 'I will cut your throat. Go back to your country!' police said.[22]
- Gastelum did not respond to requests for comment. When confronted on Facebook about use of the #SubhumanMonsters hashtag, he replied, 'I'm trying to think of a different way, but what do you call people that treat women like secondhand citizens, stone them to death, honor killings, etc., throw homosexuals from the roof'.[23]
- Saturday's event provided a contrast to a campus speech in January by Milo Yiannopoulos, a right-wing provocateur who has said Muslims are prone to 'gang rape'. His Spanos Theatre speech drew a crowd of about 500, as well as protests outside.[24]
- Mosque's imam received a text message carrying a death threat: 'In case someone in your family dies, I have a coffin for you—and more than one, if necessary'.[25]

---

[19] CNN NEWS, 16 November 2016.

[20] The New York Times, 16 November 2016.

[21] The Seattle Times, 7 December 2016.

[22] Daily News, New York, 5 December 2016; Daily News, New York, 3 December 2016.

[23] Los Angeles Times, 27 February 2017.

[24] The Tribune, California, 29 April 2017.

[25] The Salt Lake Tribune, 10 April 2017.

- 'Sorry no room for Muslims in our government', wrote Chris Siemers.[26]
- Sieting previously defended his First Amendment right to publish whatever he wants on his Facebook page, including numerous anti-Muslim and other controversial posts. One post he shared made a call to 'Kill every last Muslim'.[27]
- Center officials point to its founder, Brigitte Gabriel, who has said that Muslims who follow the teachings of the Quran cannot be loyal citizens of the USA.[28]
- I'm the farthest thing from 'flesh-eating bacteria'. The closest I've ever been to a death cult was the last time I was at a Black Friday sale. I'm not 'destructive to society'.[29]
- The Southern Poverty Law Center (SPLC) calls Perkin's Family Research Council 'a hate group'. Perkins denies that Islam is a religion and regularly rails against gays and warns that LGBT citizens plan to round up the Christians in 'boxcars'. His Vice President, William 'Jerry' Boykin, Jr., claims that Islam is 'pure evil' and should not be protected under the First Amendment. Boykin has threatened to physically attack anyone not using the bathroom that he thinks they should use.[30]
- As she left the store with a friend, Nereim allegedly told the woman to 'go back to where you came from', called her a 'dangerous terrorist' and at some point referred to her as a 'Muslim (expletive) bitch'.[31]
- Vanessa Gera and Karel Janicek, The Associated Press reporters, write in their story published in *Seattle Times* on 8 October that 'Islam wants to destroy Europe', and 'They want to turn us away from Christianity'. 'Today Islam is flooding us, and we are afraid

[26] *The Washington Post*, 21 July 2017.

[27] *Traverse City*, Michigan, 20 July 2017.

[28] *The Virginian-Pilot*, Norfolk, VA, 20 July 2017.

[29] *Detroit Free Press*, Michigan, 16 July 2017.

[30] *The Charlotte Post*, 19 October 2017.

[31] *The Seattle Times*, 19 October 2017.

of this too', they added. 'We are afraid of terrorist threats and we are afraid of people departing from the faith'.[32]

It would be interesting to see how Australian media in general discuss and generate discourses on Islam and Muslims. Australia is preoccupied with a particular minority strand of Islam, which does not represent the Muslims in compatibility with democracy or modernity (Harding, 2017). Islam remains in media spotlight, with anti-Muslims and anti-Islamic rallies being held around Australia. It is presented as the religion that fails to integrate into the modernity. It seems that the only remedy is the construction of a 'Western Islamic' identity (Milani, 2015). Hardly a day goes by in Australia without some egregious media attacks on Islam and Muslims, and Australian politicians add fuel to the flame.

Senator Pauline Hanson said, 'Now we are in danger of being swamped by Muslims' (Reilly, 2016). 'It (Islam) is purporting to be a religion but I (Pauline) believe it is a political ideology who (Muslims) want to impose their Sharia law and impose their way of life and their thoughts, processes, on the rest of our society', she said. She claimed, 'They (Muslims) hate Western society. They want to change us. Do you want to be changed? Would you be happy under Islam?' (Gartrell, 2017). Special Broadcasting Service (SBS) News reported her saying that 'Muslims were planning to take over the government by lying', and 'people had told her Muslims were threatening people and trying to force them to leave their homes'. She furthered, 'it's to blend into a society until the numbers grow and then they will actually then impose their will on the people'.[33]

The Age writes that 'the main schools of traditional Islam have always embraced a theology of politics that recognizes the proper use of force in the name of religion. It is a distinctive feature of Islam that it is inherently, not just incidentally, political' (Shumack, 2017).

---

[32] *The Seattle Times*, 8 October 2017.

[33] Retrieved from https://www.sbs.com.au/news/which-is-the-good-one-you-can-t-tell-a-good-muslim-from-a-bad-one-hanson.

Another paper writes, 'the links between Islam and political violence are now so obvious—and demonstrated so bloodily often—that they cannot be denied'. Muslims are, after all, followers of a faith established by a man who conquered by the sword, slaughtering Jews and even singing girls who mocked or defied him. The paper claims that 'up to 15 per cent of Muslims worldwide are militant, radical, extreme and potentially active in violent forms' (Bolt, 2017). *Mail Online* writes, 'there is a threat behind the ideology of Islam against the Western nations and there's a threat to dominate and take away our freedoms' and 'Australia will have to submit to Islam. That's coming out of the Lakemba mosque'.[34]

A blinkered report[35] shared on social media exposes trashy standards of Australian media reporting. It claims:

[T]here was a plan to increase the population of Muslims in Australia, to buy real estate, and give the streets Islamic names. And those Islamic names would be in memory of those who 'massacred and killed people'. And then they'll ban drinking and anything 'un-Islamic', it'll be a small Islamic country within Sydney.

Comments elicited in the report include 'Deport this scum now'. Or

Like a cancer cells it can spread unless you go through chemotherapy or radiation or surgical removal. They may be small in number, but they can grow exponentially. Australia right now is in level 2 cancer. Pin hole surgery should be able to remove the cancerous tumour. (Gartrell, 2017)

There is a widespread tendency in Australian media to confuse the culture and traditions with religion. A newspaper writes that one is free to choose and to change one's religion in liberal societies; however, 'Koran and Muslim tradition punish these things with death sentences' (Monk, 2017). Senator Pauline accused Muslims of seeking out potential child brides in Australian schools and said that there were

[34] Retrieved from http://www.dailymail.co.uk/news/article-4353194/Elderly-lady-Q-worried-Islam-Australia.html.

[35] Retrieved from https://www.facebook.com/AustraliaLoveItOrLeave.I/videos/1416488331726945/.

child brides under Islam. She further said that if we don't think 'it's happening here, we're fools' (Clark, 2017). About women's rights, an Australian newspaper mentioned that girls in a strict Muslim family are often beaten, shamed, isolated, forced into marriage, forced to wear burqa and subjected to all kinds of physical, psychological and even sexual abuses for their violations. Burqa or other veils are presented as hard-core Sharia or political Islam. 'We should no more want to see it imported into Australia than we should want to see wife-beating legalised', the newspapers assert (Ali, 2017).

Representing the history, a paper writes:

> Islamist ideology poses a danger to women, as seen in the bloody civil war in Algeria, the revolution in Iran, the hijacking of the Arab Spring and, more recently, Islamic State. The threat of this ideology also underlies Western concerns and confusion about the veil, which has evolved into a banner to promote the cause and recruit adherents to the Islamist struggle to become mainstream.[36]

The veil represents female disempowerment, but today, it has come to symbolize a new purpose that serves the Islamist movement and its view on the importance of veiling (Lichter, 2017). *The Australian* writes, 'Sharia law recommends the stoning of women for infidelity and permits the honour killing of the victims of rape'[37] (Mitchell, 2017). *The Australian's* polemics does not stop here, rather it writes on another occasion that 'there's no elevation of women in Islam ... of course women are downtrodden, this is something nobody can deny'[38] (Edwards, 2017). *The Sydney Morning Herald* writes that the ideas of freedom, of tolerance, of equality, of free enterprise are 'superior to the ideas of total submission to a god who demands that of forcing women to completely submit to men, the intolerance towards people

[36] Retrieved from http://www.theaustralian.com.au/news/inquirer/veiled-agents-of-political-islam-burka-hijab-have-new-meanings/news-story/80ca102fc455b56 8c6d09e2309699cf8.

[37] Retrieved from www.theaustralian.com.au/business/.../597250f6f536b7d3b3 4bad737a866715.

[38] Retrieved from www.theaustralian.com.au/news/...a.../9d737c12f2ec059f4b 601164d7547c96.

of other religions, the homicidal attitude to homosexuals. This is what Sharia law, what Islamic law, advocates'[39] (McIlroy, 2017).

Marcus (2017) says that simply mention the words 'Muslim' and 'terrorist' in the same sentence and even after all these attacks, all these senseless deaths, you will still likely to find yourself denounced as an Islamophobe. According to Dean (2017), Islamophobia is used to admonish any who dare criticize Sharia and barbaric Islamic practices, such as throwing gays off rooftops, treating women as personal property or threatening to blow Israel off the face of the earth.

Social Media Construction

It is now over a decade that social media has developed as a new form of media that helped its users to participate in socio-religio-political debates in a new fashion such as uploading, sharing, tagging and liking. Social media is self-regulatory form of media, which has drastically changed the nature of communication in contemporary tech-savvy world. Unlike other forms of the mainstream media, there is no concept of gatekeeping on social media. Free flow of communication phenomenon seems operative in social media dominated regime only; earlier it was just a fancy phrase without any reality in it. That is why social media has become a hot topic of debate due to its role and effectiveness in creating awareness and giving the sense of motivation to its users to participate in social, political, economic and religious discussions. On the other hand, available content on social media has also opened up new vistas of discussion along with many new problems due to its unauthentic and unreliable information. As long as Islam and Muslims are concerned, various organizations, individuals and social media activists are using this hot source for spreading anti-Islam sentiments among their audience.

There are few threats which have been found commonly under heated discussion on social media, especially on Facebook pages, for

---

[39] Retrieved from http://www.smh.com.au/federal-politics/political-news/ayaan-hirsi-ali-australia-needs-programs-to-assimilate-muslim-migrants-20170404-gvdu91.html.

example, suicide bombings, security of churches and Christians in Muslim majority countries, attacking, bombing, hijacking and beheading, slitting of throats, honour killings, gang rapes, Islamic caliphate, mass execution, women veiling, forced acceptance of Islam, kidnapping, building mosques, halal slaughtering and death for apostasy, etc. Not only on mainstream media, the concept of radical Islam has also emerged among the top trends on social media platforms. Muslims are posed to be the biggest threat to the world peace and normality. Jihad is the name given to global terrorism and extremism. Halal food chains are thought to be supporting the Islamic jihad, which has resulted in activation of campaigns to boycott the halal food in Europe by the right-wing activists. Muslims living in Western countries are promoting jihad and giving training to the citizens of their respective countries. The statements of many Western scholars and leaders on social media depict Muslims as a serious threat to their peace and stability. It is commonly thought that Muslims are very brutal, and violent, barbaric, cruel, heartless and inhuman are commonly used metaphors. The gory pictures of brutal incidents, such as cutting heads, slaughtering humans, mass execution, marriage with underage girls, attacks on common people, violence against innocent citizens are posted on social media to portray Muslims having no sympathy for mankind. Burqa (women veiling) is also considered a security risk, which can be used for any malicious activity. All the activities in this context are attached with Muslims and Islam. Meanwhile, Muslims are also considered to be the threat to the Western lifestyle.

Muslims are looked at as a threat to the Western civilization, and Islamic culture is propagated negatively for posing a threat to Western culture in which building of mosques, Sharia law, Islamic punishments are the main components of denigration. Quran is also one of the hot discourses on social media. Westerners are made to think that the teachings of the Quran are the actual reason of extremism and terrorism, wherein Quran spreads hate speech and promotes jihad with non-believers.

The most common discourses on Facebook related to Islam and Muslims are: halal meet, Sharia law, Quran as an evil book, intolerance to other religions, Muslims as terrorists, suicide bombers, stoning of men and women, hijacking, kidnapping, Muslims' brutality and violence, subjugation and jihad, hijab and niqab, threats from radicals, force marriages, Islamic punishment, apostasy, marriage with little girls, imposition of Sharia law, building mosques, animal slaughtering, jihadi camps and training, adultery, cultural invasion, attacks on churches, Quran as a tool of war, hate towards Jews and Christians, anti-Israel ideology, gun culture, protection of prostitutes, Muslims' lifestyle in a derogatory fashion, etc., to include a few. The discussions on these issues on social media are mostly done in epistemic style where information-pegged comments and posts are placed on the media. All news about terrorism, global jihad, various types of threats and most other discourses are reflection of mainstream media discourses. The crux of all such stories is same as they are discussed in broadcast or other form of media. However, attitude of the individuals participating in discussion is quite negative and misleading. Muslims are shown to be inferior to the Western societies as being inhuman, barbaric and dangerous creatures. The usage of specific adjectives, negative terms and heavy words for describing the negative impression is commonly prevalent. Mostly, Islam, Quran, burqa, mosques and Sharia law have been discussed metaphorically. Quran has been called as an evil book, a tool of war and a hate speech. Islam has been given the name of cult, virus, rabies, cancer, problem, bigot, etc., similarly Muslim women while wearing burqa are called 'bullies' and 'a potato sack'.

Pictures and shared links are mostly common on all these anti-Islamic pages, few website and blogs are the hot sources which generate the material to fuel the fire against Islam and Muslims, and all other sources use this material to spread hate and prejudice against Islam and Muslims. English Defence League (EDL) and many other pages are strongly linked with each other, especially in the USA. All Islamophobic actors have their strong association with one another and are heavily contributing in this anti-Islam campaign on social media, such as Jewish Internet Defense Force, Jihad Watch, Militant Islam Monitor, Politically Incorrect, Atlas Shrugs, Bare Naked Islam, Bay People, Creeping Sharia, Infidel Bloggers Alliance, Islam Exposed, Walid Shoebat, FrontPage Magazine and Britain First. These sources are heavily generating and uploading material on these social networking sites not only on daily basis but almost after every hour. Few sources, which are very active, especially on Facebook include ACT! for America, Bare Naked Islam, Anti-Islam Alliance, Sharia Free and Islam Exposed. On the other hand, there are many individual actors like Brigitte Gabriel, Robert Spencer, Frank Gaffney, John Marsh, Mark A. Gabriel, Peter T. King, Pamela Geller, P. David Gaubatz, Terry Jones (Pastor), etc., who are running NGOs and organizations, have their own accounts on Facebook and social media and are constructing the negative messages to share them on their individual and collective walls and accounts.

Some 40 Facebook pages were selected to see as how they construct Muslims and Islam, and what metaphors do they use for them. The metaphors used repeatedly for Muslims were Islamic suicide bombers, Islamic terrorists, Islamic radicals, Islamic militants, Muslim murderers, Islamic jihadists, Sharia adherent jihadist, civilizational jihad, Islamic fundamentalists, etc. There are few sentences or phrases which are mostly used about Islam in various posts and paragraphs, like Islam is a problem, Islam is not a religion of peace, Islam is a religion of bigot, Islam is a religion of cult, destroy Islam save humanity, ban burqa, ban Islam, jihad is a political act, say no to Islam, ban the burqa, etc. The selected pages have been found following a tendency in the favour of Israel, and Islam is also considered as a threat for Christianity and Judaism.

INCIDENTS OF SOCIOCULTURAL ISLAMOPHOBIA

Let us have a look at the incidents of sociocultural Islamophobia which took place in various parts of the world including North America, EU, Scandinavian Europe and Australia.

The USA

Islamophobia is not new to the American society. It got a spike with the fall of twin towers in New York in 2001, increasing anti-Muslim hate incidents immediately all across the USA. However, George W. Bush's rhetoric declaring 'Islam is peace' and 'the face of terror is not the true faith of Islam' brought down the hate crimes against Muslims in the aftermath of 9/11. Political rhetoric followed by overwhelming coverage of mass media created social and public consent of hate, especially towards the groups of people who do not interact frequently. However, Donald Trump reversed the game by declaring that 'Islam hates us' and accused American Muslims of protecting terrorists. He did not realize that Islamophobic political rhetoric may have devastating consequences and increased Islamophobic reporting by the media may heighten anti-Muslims sentiments among the US citizens.

'A total and complete shutdown of Muslims entering the United States' was Trump's slogan during the elections, and, on 27 January 2017, he made it possible. *The New York Times*, in its 28 January 2017 edition, wrote 'Islam itself as a problem' in the light of actions being taken by the US administration. Some independent think tanks declared 2016 as a 'Banner year for hate'. FBI reports 67 per cent increase in crimes against Muslims but independent research organizations claim it to be 89 per cent in 2016 and 2017. Such a remorse positioning of Islam and Muslims in the Western media reminds us the time of Prophet Muhammad (PBUH) when the birth of Islam was considered a 'problem' and a punishment to the unscrupulous sins of other religions and their followers.

Donald Trump is surrounded by anti-Islam advisers and strategists in the White House such as George Flynn and Steve Bannon. Bannon, a polemical filmmaker and Internet bomb thrower, calls the contemporary position of the US against Muslims as a new political order in his e-mail to *The Washington Post*. He proudly calls himself to be like Lenin who was eager to bring everything crashing down and destroy all of today's establishment.[40]

Hatemongers in the USA are taking great advantage of the situation and are creating havoc for Muslims in the entire Western world. More than 892 hate groups are operating only in the USA and media are giving them huge time and space, wherein they are claiming that 'We must secure the existence of our people and a future for White

---

[40] Retrieved from http://www.newsbeat.me/news/is-steve-bannon-the-most-powerful-man-in-the-world/605ce727-ce41-3df0-a753-f537c880fbe9.html.

Children. It isn't Islamophobia when they really are trying to kill you! Take our country back!'[41] On the other hand, Britain's most vocal Brexit figure, Nigel Farage, welcomed Trump's executive order. Farage told the BBC:

> He was elected to get tough. He was elected to say he would do everything in his power to protect America from infiltration by ISIS terrorists. There are seven countries on that list. He is entitled to do this. He was voted in on this.[42]

Australian PM Malcolm Turnbull said, 'It is vital that every nation is able to control who comes across its borders'.[43] He is one of the few leaders to openly show support for the ban.

Rising Islamophobia has posed two main dangers: a rise in socio-cultural nature of the hate crimes and anti-Islamic legislation. In the last year, in most parts of the USA including Florida, there has been a 500 per cent increase in hate crimes against Muslims. Mosques have been vandalized and there have been many bomb threats towards Islamic groups. Florida's government is even trying to ban school books from making any references to Islam in history. Since 2013, the country has seen a rise in the number of bills or amendments—about 81—designed to 'vilify Islamic religious practices', 80 of which were introduced to state legislatures by Republicans.[44]

Places of worship, hospitals and educational institutions enjoy special protection even in bloody wars. But religious centres, especially mosques, are under extreme threat in the USA where Islamophobia industry is working day and night to fuel anti-Islam and Muslims sentiments among the non-Muslims. A great number of mosques in

---

[41] Speech by the US President can be retrieved from https://www.nbcnews.com/video/trump-tells-iowans-were-going-to-take-our-country-back-613821507604. Also, the text can be retrieved from https://www.theguardian.com/commentisfree/2016/jun/20/take-our-country-back-consequences-poison-politics.

[42] Retrieved from http://edition.cnn.com/2017/01/30/politics/trump-travel-ban-world-reaction/index.html.

[43] Retrieved from http://www.bbc.co.uk/news/world-australia-38792411.

[44] Retrieved from http://www.aljazeera.com/indepth/features/2016/06/report-islamophobia-multi-million-dollar-industry-160623144006495.html.

the USA and other parts of the world are hit by Islamophobes. On 7 January 2017, the Islamic Center of Lake Travis in Austin, Texas, was burnt. A week later, on 14 January, the Islamic Center of Eastside in Bellevue, Washington, was also burned. CNN affiliate said firefighters spotted 40-foot flames on the back side of the building. 'Crews were able to save half of the building',[45] CNN reported. 'We have confirmed it was arson, but do not know a motive', Bellevue Police Chief Steve Mylett said.

Two weeks after that, on 28 January, several hours after President Donald Trump signed an executive order banning immigrants from seven Muslim-majority countries, a fire destroyed the Islamic Center of Victoria in Texas. Someone intentionally set fire to the Islamic Center of Victoria in Texas in the middle of the night, according to investigators. The blaze caused more than $500,000 in damage and completely destroyed the 16-year-old mosque, shaking the Muslim American community in South Texas.[46] Sadly enough, the Victoria Islamic Center in Texas torched on 28 January was burgled a few days earlier to this event. The religious centre was also the subject of hate graffiti in 2013.

Then, on 24 February 2017, a blaze broke out at the front entrance of the Daarus Salaam Mosque near Tampa. The fire at the Daarus Salaam Mosque in Thonotosassa, Florida, was at least the third time in seven months that a mosque in the Tampa area had been set on fire, following incidents at the Islamic Education Center in July and the Omar Mosque in August. Besides burning of mosques, many Islamic centers received intimidating messages including a bomb threat saying, 'death is waiting for you and your kind', prompting calls for increasing security at Muslim facilities.[47]

[45] Retrieved from http://edition.cnn.com/2017/01/15/us/washington-mosque-arson/index.html.

[46] Retrieved from https://www.nytimes.com/2017/01/28/us/fire-destroys-mosque-in-texas-in-early-hours.html.

[47] Retrieved from https://www.khaleejtimes.com/international/americas/five-mosques-in-us-receive-death-and-bomb-threat.

Another mosque in Lexington, Kentucky, beefed up its security when it received a bomb threat in March 2017. The bomb threat against Lexington's Masjid Bilal was received through the mail traced to be originating from Sheffield, England, Council on American-Islamic Relations (CAIR) said in a Facebook post. The letter contained a green index card wrapped in a blank sheet of paper with the words: 'An explosive device will be placed at your mosque very soon!'[48] Similarly, a New Jersey City mosque reported that it received a threatening letter calling for violence against Muslims in the rash of bias incidents targeting Islamic institutions. The letter, sent to the Masjid Al-Iman, stated: 'You and your filthy kind will be beheaded' and featured an illustration with the words 'MUSLIM SLAYER'.[49] It was also postmarked in Sheffield, UK. Three other mosques received identical e-mails threatening widespread attacks against American Muslims on 15 March 2017. The Greenview Madani Center, a mosque in Lawrenceville, received a mailed handwritten letter from a 'Muslim slayer' with the message, 'Death is waiting for you and your kind'[50] along with a crudely drawn picture of a decapitated person.

Masjid Omar bin Abdul Aziz in Norcross, Al-Farooq Masjid and another Atlanta-area mosque received a threatening e-mail on 18 February 2017. The e-mails, with the subject line 'your one warning' stated in part, '... Muslims, Mexicans, blacks will (be) hunted nationwide until (they) are dead and gone ... Plan to run or die, this is a kindness that we give you all warning, take it and go'.[51] Two mosques in Maryland in the USA also received threatening letters calling for the

---

[48] Retrieved from https://www.cair.com/press-center/press-releases/14167-cair-kentucky-calls-for-hate-crime-probe-of-bomb-threat-to-mosque.html.

[49] Retrieved from https://www.usnews.com/news/best-states/new-jersey/articles/2017-03-03/group-seeks-probe-of-threat-mailed-to-new-jersey-mosque.

[50] Retrieved from http://edition.cnn.com/2017/03/06/us/atlanta-mosques-threatened/index.html.

[51] Retrieved from https://www.ndtv.com/world-news/us-mosques-get-intimidating-messages-including-a-bomb-threat-1667672.

'slaughter of Muslims'.[52] Furthermore, several mosques in Atlanta and Georgia have also received bomb threats in the past.

The number of reported anti-Muslim hate crimes had already been on the rise before; however, President Donald Trump's anti-Muslim stance picked up the steam from late 2016. According to a report by the CAIR, there were 79 instances of mosques being targeted—counting arson, vandalism and other destruction—in 2015. By comparison, 2014 saw just 20 such incidents. A report released last year by Georgetown University's Prince Alwaleed bin Talal Center for Muslim-Christian Understanding found that in 2015 there were eight instances of arson that targeted mosques, businesses or homes associated with Muslims. FBI data also show that the number of reported anti-Muslim hate crimes surged by 67 per cent from 2014 to 2015. Hate groups destined to cultivate Islamophobic sentiments among the non-Muslims are spending millions of dollars to make the Islamophobia industry work day and night.

According to the most recent CAIR report, which appeared on Monday, 24 July 2017, there were more than 940 reports of potential bias incidents involving the targeting of Muslims between April and June 2017. Of those, the organization determined 451 stemmed from anti-Muslim bias, which contributed to a 91 per cent increase in anti-Muslim hate crimes during the first half of the year as compared to the same time period in 2016. Non-violent and non-threatening instances of harassment accounted for 16 per cent of the incidents involving Muslims between 1 April and 30 June, while outright hate crimes—in which violence or a physical altercation was involved—accounted for 15 per cent. Incidents in which Muslims were inappropriately targeted by the FBI made up 12 per cent of cases.[53] People were targeted at their places of residence in 17 per cent of the reports, while 14 per cent involved Muslims who were on streets or driving their cars. Another 13 per cent faced anti-Muslim bias while flying or traveling by bus or

---

[52] Retrieved from https://www.ndtv.com/world-news/us-mosques-get-intimidating-messages-including-a-bomb-threat-1667672.

[53] Retrieved from http://www.newsweek.com/hate-crime-america-muslims-trump-638000.

train. About 33 per cent of incidents took place at a mosque or Islamic centre, and 9 per cent occurred at schools.

Of the incidents reported, CAIR identified triggering factors for 358, including a victim's ethnicity or national origin (32 per cent) and preconceived notions of a victim being a Muslim (20 per cent). Fifteen per cent of incidents were triggered by the presence of a headscarf or hijab. Forty-six per cent of the people targeted were from Middle Eastern and North African countries. Even the Muslims who are sacrificing and have sacrificed their lives to protect the USA are not far from discrimination and marginalization. They fought for America in every major conflict the USA got engaged in including Afghan and Iraq wars. More than 15,000 Arab Americans fought for the allies during the Second World War and hundreds have served in diplomatic positions or as translators for the US troops since then.[54]

A report from 2011 showed that 6,024 Muslims have fought honourably in the US military since 9/11, a number that is undoubtedly higher today. One of the highest ranking Muslim was Marine Colonel Douglas Burpee, who spent more than 20 years in the military.[55] But, in response, Muslims have to pay the price of their loyalty and patriotism. On 18 March 2016, a 20-year-old Muslim Marine recruit, Raheel Siddiqui, jumped three stories to his death after suffering repeated abuse by officers at the Parris Island base in South Carolina. Siddiqui's death is one of the dozens of cases of officer abuse that have emerged at Parris Island alone.[56] Across the USA, officers of the various branches of the US armed forces systematically abuse young recruits, the overwhelming majority of whom, like Siddiqui, come from working-class families.

According to a media report, a Muslim Marine was called a terrorist and ordered to enter into an industrial clothes dryer multiple times by

---

[54] Retrieved from http://www.dailymail.co.uk/news/article-3715233/Faces-American-Muslims-died-fighting-country-9-11-revealed-fallen-soldier-s-father-tells-Trump-sacrificed-no-one.html.

[55] Retrieved from http://americanmuslim.info/index.php/directory/item/sample2.html.

[56] Retrieved from https://www.wsws.org/en/articles/2016/09/12/offi-s12.html.

a drill instructor who then turned it on, burning him. The investigation, later, described the abuse of recruits at the service's training centre at Parris Island, South Carolina. 'You're going to kill us all the first chance you get aren't you, terrorist?' The drill instructor thundered at the recruit, the new Marine alleged according to *The Washington Post*.[57]

Canada

A report by Statistics Canada says that hate crimes against Muslims in Canada increased by 253 per cent between 2012 and 2015. In 2012, police reported only 45 hate crimes against Muslims. By 2015, the number shot up to 159. According to the report, these hate crimes in Canada were increased due to 'incidents targeting certain religious and ethno-cultural groups, specifically the Muslim population and Arabs or West Asians'.[58] While many have focused on the growing Islamophobia in Canada's southern neighbour, the USA, particularly under the administration of President Donald Trump, Canadian Muslims are pointing out that their country has its own problem to deal with. 'The media narrative has focused more on the religion aspect and also this sort of American political thing', Chelby Marie Daigle, the editor-in-chief of *Muslim Link*, an Ottawa community newspaper told the Global News.[59]

Islamophobia has been a big political issue in Canada quite recently. In March 2017, the Canadian government overwhelmingly passed a motion calling on the government to 'condemn Islamophobia and all forms of systemic racism and religious discrimination'.[60] The motion, which was introduced by liberal Muslim lawmaker Iqra Khalid, also

---

[57] Retrieved from https://www.washingtonpost.com/news/checkpoint/wp/2016/09/13/drill-instructor-accused-of-repeatedly-running-a-clothes-dryer-with-a-muslim-marine-inside/?utm_term=.6cca41490c16.

[58] Retrieved from https://www.statcan.gc.ca/daily-quotidien/170613/dq170613b-eng.htm.

[59] Retrieved from https://globalnews.ca/news/3523535/hate-crimes-canada-muslim/.

[60] Retrieved from https://globalnews.ca/news/3751731/house-of-commons-islamophobia/.

calls on the government to study and better document the hate crimes in Canada. The action by Canada's parliament unleashed a torrent of anti-Muslim hatred. Khalid reportedly received 50,000 e-mails about the motion, many of which she said were direct threats. Commentator Sabreena Ghaffar-Siddiqui wrote in the National Observer[61]:

Given the alarming rise in attacks against Muslims, it appears that Muslims are being singled out. Hate crimes have decreased overall, yet hate crimes against the Muslim community have doubled. One in four Muslims reports having encountered difficulties crossing borders. And Muslim youth are the least optimistic about the next generation facing less discrimination than them.

VICE Canada published a story on the rise of US-style paramilitary anti-Muslim groups in the Canadian province of Alberta. Mack Lamoureux, who infiltrated the group, writes[62]:

Anti-Islam sentiment is the beating heart of Alberta. This worldview unites the group online and has been assuredly the driving force of recruitment. In the closed group, posts have been made about wiping all the Muslims off the earth, and there is frequent use of dehumanising terms like 'goat f**ker' to describe the religious group. Another post by a member, referring to a debunked story about Syrian youths in a Red Deer high school, indicated that they should round up Syrian children 'like animals'.

The next blow to any rose-tinted images of Canada as a multicultural idyll came via a video of a racist rant by a mother at a clinic in Toronto, calling for a 'White doctor' for her child. In the video, already watched more than 100,000 times on YouTube, she repeatedly asks to see a doctor who 'doesn't have brown teeth' and 'speaks English'. In the most recent anti-Muslim hate crimes, a woman who came to visit her family in Manitoba this summer was shocked by the racist verbal attack. In an exchange captured on a video, a man who described himself as a 'Nazi' told Calgary teacher Kaniz Fatima to take her 'head

[61] Retrieved from https://www.nationalobserver.com/2017/03/10/opinion/you-know-theres-problem-when-you-get-50000-anti-muslim-emails-your-inbox.

[62] Retrieved from https://www.vice.com/en_ca/article/new9wd/the-birth-of-canadas-armed-anti-islamic-patriot-group.

towel off because it 'supports Muslims'. He also told her to 'go back to your country'.[63]

The bitter reality of Islamophobia in Canada became all too real in January 2017, when a White supremacist terrorist attacked a mosque in Quebec during prayer time. Six worshipers were left dead following the attack and 19 were wounded. Alexandre Bissonnette, the 27-year-old terrorist, was arrested and charged with six counts of first-degree murder and five of attempted murder. In response to the senseless violence, Canada's PM Justin Trudeau called it 'an act of terror committed against Canada, and against all Canadians'.[64] Thousands of Canadians, including Trudeau, attended a public funeral for three of the victims, showing the world what solidarity with Muslims looks like. 'Our country was united', Trudeau said at the funeral. 'It is an entire country that is joining the families of the victims. Together, we will rise from this darkness stronger, more unified, than ever before'.[65]

On the other hand, the Canadian media have been criticized for their role in perpetrating Islamophobia. Canadian professor of journalism asserts that in the post-9/11 era, an 'Islamic peril' has replaced the 'Soviet threat' of the Cold War years in Canada. After comparing Canadian mainstream media coverage of religious minority communities in Canada, a research concludes that the Canadian media commonly apply the frames of dehumanization, extremism, fanaticism, inequality and islamophobia to Muslims.

The stereotypes of Muslims, Arabs and Middle Easterners are: terrorists, savage and a fifth column. These stereotypes are then said to fuel suspicion for Muslims in general, which then results in hate crimes against them. Nevertheless, some other scholars argue that Canadian media is relatively balanced and objective in its coverage of Muslims

---

[63] Retrieved from http://www.cbc.ca/news/canada/manitoba/racism-against-calgary-woman-1.4259853.

[64] Retrieved from https://www.washingtonpost.com/news/morning-mix/wp/2017/01/29/multiple-people-reported-shot-by-gunmen-at-quebec-city-mosque/?utm_term=.2c545b3b5be7.

[65] Retrieved from https://www.thestar.com/news/canada/2017/02/02/funeral-service-for-3-quebec-mosque-victims-to-be-held-today-in-montreal.html.

than that of the UK, the USA and Australia. They cited many cases of terrorism where the suspects were on the fringe of the Muslim community and Canadian media gave coverage to Muslim leaders, allowing them to present a more peaceful side of Islam, unlike media in the USA and Australia.

However, one of the most disturbing moment was when in a meeting held by Peel District School Board in Mississauga, Ontario, in March 2017, an anti-Islam protester torn the pages of Quran in huge gathering of parents. The spokesman from the school board, Brian Woodland, told the media that about 80 people attended the meeting and shouted some 'fairly horrific' Islamophobic comments. 'I was actually deeply shaken by what I heard. I'm not sure I've ever in my life seen this level of hatred', he said. The video of the event was later posted on social media, which disturbed the Muslims across the whole world where the protester is clearly seen shouting, 'Islam will kill you'.[66]

The United Kingdom

Xenophobia has long been an overt feature of right-wing nationalism in the UK; in recent years, Islamophobia, too, has come to play a central part in nationalist rhetoric. The debate that surrounded Brexit revealed that these twin hatreds have also become prominent props in mainstream political discourse. That does not bode well for the relationship between the UK's government and its Muslim population. Far-right and fascist organizations in the UK step up Islamophobic and anti-EU activities in the wake of terror attacks in Paris and Brussels as well as attempting to take advantage of a possible British withdrawal from Europe in the June 2016 referendum.

The ideology of the British right-wing political groups is pretty much the same: British nationalism, Euroscepticism, anti-immigration and anti-Islam. The tactics to get to their ideal state are also the same; they are contesting various elections in order to be able to influence

[66] Retrieved from http://www.huffingtonpost.ca/2017/03/23/ontario-schools-muslim-prayers_n_15568254.html.

the political picture of the country, and with an occasional march or a rally they are trying to get their message heard without much violence. However, there are also more extreme right groups present and functioning in Britain that seem to have no interest in contesting the elections but are guided by extreme violence and hatred.

In the UK, the extreme right is fractured, leaderless, confused and dispirited. It is also highly unpredictable and, on occasions, violent. Rather than one party or group—such as the British National Party (BNP) or the EDL—dominating the stage, a couple of dozen smaller groups contend for attention. The groups favour so-called direct action, such as picketing mosques, invading halal slaughterhouses and harassing staff at Muslim-owned restaurants. On the other hand, Islam and Muslims are no longer welcomed in Europe. The decision by the European Court of Justice to allow employers to ban staff from wearing the headscarf seems certain to only further marginalize and push Muslim women out of public life. Economic marginalization is of course not the only obstacle that women must face due to decisions like the one made. There are much more dire consequences for the average woman on the streets of London or Paris. It is evident from the reports of a woman in hijab being dragged along the streets of London and another woman attacked and bitten for wearing hijab in Vienna.

In the following lines, some events of extremism and terrorism and their backlash for Muslims in Europe including the UK, France, Germany, Italy, Norway, Sweden, Switzerland and Denmark are discussed in the sociocultural Islamophobia perspective.

On 3 June 2017, three attackers killed 7 and injured more than 48 after striking pedestrians on the London Bridge and stabbing people in a market near London Bridge. In a similar event in March 2017, 5 people were killed in a car and knife attack near Parliament in London, and two weeks earlier 22 people died in a suicide bombing at a concert in Manchester. In an interesting move, the Islamic State militants claimed responsibility for the London Bridge attacks. The terror group, which had been hailing the carnage throughout the day on its online accounts and anonymous message boards, said its fighters carried out the rampage, according to the SITE Intelligence

Group, which tracks the web activity of jihadist organizations.[67] One of the kinds included the iconic image of the Royal Air Force bomb with 'Love from Manchester'[68] written on it—referring to the attack on the Ariana Grande concert and adding that the weapon 'is your merchandise, and tonight we responded'.[69] The attack on London came just a few hours after Islamic State's Nashir News Agency called for followers to 'Kill the civilians of the Crusaders'[70] with guns, knives and trucks, according to *The Independent* and *The Telegraph*.

Mayor of London Mr Sadiq Khan and British PM Theresa May issued responsible statements on media to mitigate the effects of tensed situation in the UK. However, the US media and politicians including President Donald Trump remained aggressive and issued sentiment flaring statements. For instance, Clay Higgins, Republican representative of Louisiana's third congressional district and volunteer law enforcement officer, said in a social media post on Sunday, 'free world ... all of Christendom ... is at war'[71] with 'radicalized Islamic suspect[s]'. He said, 'Not a single radicalized Islamic suspect should be granted any measure of quarter'. 'Their intended entry to the American homeland should be summarily denied. Every conceivable measure should be engaged to hunt them down. Hunt them, identify them, and kill them. Kill them all. For the sake of all that is good and righteous. Kill them all', he finished the post with 'Kill them all'.[72] Higgins' statement—which has been shared more than 2,500 times and spawned 3,600 comments (as of 31 December 2017)—was

---

[67] Retrieved from https://nypost.com/2017/06/04/isis-claims-responsibility-for-london-bridge-attacks-extremist-watchdog/.

[68] Retrieved from http://www.mirror.co.uk/news/uk-news/london-bridge-terror-attack-was-10560009.

[69] Retrieved from http://www.telegraph.co.uk/news/2017/06/04/pro-islamic-state-social-media-users-claim-london-attack-revenge/.

[70] Retrieved from http://www.independent.co.uk/news/world/middle-east/isis-london-bridge-terror-attack-ramadan-greater-reward-terrorism-a7774061.html.

[71] Retrieved from https://www.facebook.com/captclayhiggins/posts/997878010315211:0.

[72] Retrieved from https://www.washingtonpost.com/b50617e7-bc7e-4bfc-a3d4-2e637d7cbd3e.

released hours after three men using knives and a vehicle killed seven people during a bloody rampage in central London.

The US media said that London is 'reeling', but Londoners beg to differ. Londoners today are standing up for the capital after a leading US newspaper said the country was still 'reeling' from the Manchester bombing. *The New York Times* tweeted that Saturday's terror attack at London Bridge hit a nation 'still reeling from the shock of the bombing in Manchester'[73] two weeks earlier. Not all Londoners agreed and one, seen making sure his pint was safe while fleeing the scene, has become a symbol of the capital's spirit. While Will Straw, founder of the political website Left Foot Forward, added, 'The UK is mourning, angry and defiant but we're not reeling'.

In the wake of the London Bridge attack, American media described the city as 'under siege' in a country still 'reeling' from the Manchester attack in May 2017. However, people and British media have denied this impression and negativity on part of the US media. Rather some of the luminaries have slammed the US media for insulting coverage of the London attack. However, social media is generating huge discussions on the London attack and new terminologies are being coined like Trump Effect on the analogy of a political communication theory CNN Effects, indicating how tweets and statements by the US president are viewed and discussed by the people at large. It seems that insane and senseless statements by the US president are becoming vehicles of US media discussions.

Such mediated anger makes lunatics further furious and provide justifications for terrorist attack on Muslims. Ploughing van into a crowd of Muslims coming out of a mosque in Finsbury Park, London, on 19 June 2017 that killed one and seriously injured 11 was nothing but a consequence of anger-filled media messages and the statements by the political hatemongers. The victims were all Muslims and the incident was declared a terror attack on the Muslim population by the local police. However, the perpetrator was saved from wrath of angry crowd by the imam of mosque and other men, who have been

---

[73] Retrieved from https://www.nytimes.com/2017/06/03/world/europe/london-bridge-van.html.

credited with saving his life. The perpetrator was Darren Osborne, 47-year-old UK national, resident of Cardiff, Wales. Police called it a premediated attack and not a spontaneous decision. The Scotland Yard declared him as 'self-radicalized' individual. The attacker once caught said loudly, 'I did my bit, you deserve it'.[74] As said earlier, there have been some responsible statements like the one by British PM Theresa May, who said,

> [T]his was an attack on Muslims near their place of worship and, like all terrorism in whatever form, it shares the same fundamental goal. It seeks to drive us apart and to break the precious bonds of solidarity and citizenship which we share in this country.[75]

The Archbishop of Canterbury, Justin Welby, also said, 'The appalling attack on Muslims in Finsbury Park is an attack on us all and on the culture and values of our country'.[76]

More recently, there are acid attacks on Muslims as a symbol of extreme Islamophobia, which have left some Muslim residents of the UK afraid to leave their homes. Fears heightened when a 21-year-old aspiring model Resham Khan and her cousin Jameel Mukhtar, 37, suffered horrific injuries when an attacker squirted acid through their car window in Newham, East London, on 21 June 2017. Resham Khan and Jameel Mukhtar were attacked while celebrating Khan's 21st birthday. A man poured acid through their car window as they waited at traffic lights in London. Police, who named John Tomlin as a suspect, was not initially treating the attack as a hate crime. But later reclassified it as a hate crime, after Mr Mukhtar resisted on media that Islamophobia was involved, and after posts expressing sympathy for the far-right were allegedly found on the Facebook page of John Tomlin, 24. A post on Tomlin's Facebook page featured a crusader with drawn sword held aloft and a roaring lion and reads:

---

[74] Retrieved from http://edition.cnn.com/2017/06/18/europe/urgent—london-vehicle-collision/index.html.

[75] Retrieved from http://www.telegraph.co.uk/news/2017/06/19/finsbury-park-mosque-latest-terror-attack-london-live/.

[76] Retrieved from http://www.archbishopofcanterbury.org/articles.php/5877/archbishop-condemns-attack-on-muslims-in-finsbury-park.

A sleeping lion can only be provoked so much before it wakes up and attacks...and so will us British. We will stand & we will fight. We will reclaim what is rightfully ours. We will not surrender. Out of ordinary Brits, heroes will arise, champions will be made & we will make Britain great again.[77]

There were also social media reports of two other attacks in London—one involving a woman being partially burned on her doorstep by someone pretending to be a delivery man, and the other of a woman being targeted by moped-driving acid attackers in the Plashet Grove area.

There was a rise in acid attacks in 2016 also. According to figures from the Metropolitan Police Service, the number of acid attacks has risen from 261 in 2015 to 454 in 2017. In March 2017, a Freedom of Information request to the Metropolitan Police suggested Newham was the London borough with the most recorded acid attacks, with 398 incidents between 2011 and 2016. Tower Hamlets had the third highest number of acid attacks, with 84 incidents recorded in 2011 and 2016. The figures also showed a sharp rise in acid attacks across London as a whole, with 431 incidents in the capital in 2016, compared to 261 in 2015. But while most of the recent reports appear to show attackers targeting Muslims, one case involved a Chinese couple and their 2-year-old child, who were approached by a man in Islington, north London, shortly before he threw acid at them. The UK PM Theresa May has openly blamed the recent terror attacks an 'evil Islamist extremism' in the wake of rising anti-Muslim hate crimes across the UK.

Furthermore, in an arson attack, a Manchester mosque was set ablaze on 16 July 2017. Media footage showed flames and smoke engulfing the Manchester Nasfat Islamic Centre in Newton Heath. The mosque's worship area, three classrooms and the kitchen were damaged. The people on the occasion said that we tried hard to integrate with the community, we had regular meetings with non-Muslims to

---

[77] Retrieved from http://www.independent.co.uk/news/uk/crime/muslim-man-acid-attack-victim-why-not-terror-attack-east-london-jameel-muhktar-resham-khan-21st-a7816331.html.

demonstrate that we are peace-loving people; we do not know why this keeps happening. There had been two other arson attacks at the centre in the past three years. Not only this, there had also been other incidents in the past, including pigs' heads being thrown into the building, people urinating outside and verbal abuse.

The head of Tell MAMA, an anti-Islamophobia group, said that anti-Muslim hate crime in the UK has increased noticeably after the terror attacks in Manchester and London. However, the right-wing extremists have responded to the Finsbury Park terror attack by urging the UK citizens to 'rise up and cast Islam out of their country'. Extremists also sought to defend the attack by saying 'This is war... We have the right to fight back'. The social media posts were shown to *The Independent* amid anxieties that the British authorities are 'way behind' the increasingly sophisticated tactics used by the right-wing extremists to radicalize followers online. Tell MAMA said that extremists are now covering their tracks by using untraceable mobile phones and (virtual private network) services that conceal their computer's location, leaving the police unable to find them.[78]

In recent terror attacks in the UK, most of the culprits were Muslims; however, they were British Muslims and were nourished and nurtured on the land they attacked. Also, they were somewhat lunatic in their behaviour as their past record indicated. It is now over 18 years to 9/11, and all those years are witnessing a clear rise in the Islamophobic tendencies in the Western world. Media have contributed significantly in fanning the flames of extremism among the Muslims and against Muslims. On the other hand, hate groups invested huge sums of money to ignite hatred against Muslims and declaring Islam as a religion supporting terrorism, violence and extremism, and a danger to Western way of life. In the last decade, there have been hundreds of such events proving the allegations of hatemongers. On the other hand, Muslim scholars took a long time to forward with a collective stance towards these radicalized and betrayed Muslims who committed acts of violence across the world. Although a response

---

[78] Retrieved from http://www.independent.co.uk/news/uk/home-news/finsbury-park-attack-muslims-islam-right-wing-extremists-response-uk-a7799901.html.

has come to declare them terrorist who have nothing to do with the peaceful teachings of Islam, but the time they responded, the water had passed beneath the bridges. What is happening now is the aftermath of what happened in the last 18 years after 9/11. Innocent people got killed by the extremists from both sides, racial hatred is on the rampant, feelings of insecurity at unknown places is increasing and, in a nutshell, the world has become increasingly polarized on religious and ethnic lines. It is important to note that once these lines are drawn, it is hard to wipe them out even with centuries-long sincere efforts.

France

France is home to the largest Western Muslim minority yet has managed to become the laboratory for Islamophobia by inspiring other Western countries with debates on religious neutrality in public space, adopting discriminatory laws and justifying the social death sentence of Muslim women wearing headscarves who are excluded from schools, work and potentially from universities. With a deeply rooted, yet ignored colonial past, French elites have been manufacturing the Muslims problem for decades with mainstream media confining the French Muslim community to the position of a 'foreign body within the nation'[79] and a justice system that fails to meet Islamophobic attacks with proper sanctions (Thiara, Condon, & Schrottle, 2011).

The French at the state level have excluded and exploited Muslims for decades. The jihadist attacks in Paris, Nice and Rouen in 2016 have sent it to fever pitch. Of the 3,500 raids conducted since the start of that period, only six have led to investigations. In December 2016, authorities in Eure et Loire admitted that they were targeting Muslims on a purely 'preventive' basis without any specific evidence against them. Children have watched as their parents are handcuffed or dragged from their beds by heavily armed police. In the first three months of the state of emergency enacted after 2017's Bataclan attack, 274 people were placed under house arrest, the vast

---

[79] Retrieved from https://www.versobooks.com/blogs/2823-etienne-balibar-laicite-or-identity. ˙

majority of them were Muslims.[80] Racial profiling is on the rampant in modern France. Mosques have also been violently ransacked by the police. Worshippers are humiliated and degraded, including through the use of police dogs. Political organizations with Muslim links have also been threatened with closure; demonstrations, including pro-Palestinian ones, have been banned; the BDS Movement, which stands for Boycott, Divestment and Sanctions, to end international support for Israel's suppression of Palestine has been outlawed. Muslims appealing for asylum find themselves even more vulnerable than residents. The government delivers anti-Islamic broadsides while destroying refugee camps in Calais and elsewhere. In pursuing these policies, French politicians have knowingly ignored the fact that long-standing and state-sponsored Islamophobia, combined with military activity in Muslim countries, could only encourage extremism. The political classes have refused to recognize how their economic and social policies fuel the alienation that drives people to join groups like ISIS.

Islamophobia has become the very ground on which the organizational and ideological future of the French right is most directly played out. But when it comes to defending the rights of France's Muslim population, the Left, including much of the radical left, has been missing in action. Reluctance to defend religious freedom seriously undermines the Left's solidarity with Muslim refugees. As a result, Islamophobia strikes at the heart of one of the most urgent political projects for European radicals. France National Human Rights Commission (CNCDH) recently released a report on the fight against racism in France. The Commission reported 429 anti-Muslim threats and attacks in 2016—a striking 223 per cent increase from the previous year.[81]

Anti-Muslim incidents in France have seen a marked increase since the attacks at French satirical magazine *Charlie Hebdo*. These

---

[80] Retrieved from https://www.ft.com/content/f5309ff8-a521-11e7-9e4f-7f5e6a7c98a2.

[81] Retrieved from https://www.humanrightsfirst.org/blog/new-french-report-shows-rise-attacks-muslims-sustained-targeting-jews.

include attacks on mosques and Muslim businesses, arson, hate speech, racist graffiti, vandalism, discrimination, physical assault, threats with firearms and the murder of Muslims like Mohamad al-Maquli, who was stabbed to death in his own home. 'The attacks in Paris occurred in a very Islamophobic and racist context in France',[82] said Elsa Ray, spokesperson for the Collective Against Islamophobia in France (CCIF), an advocacy group that has recorded reports of over 66 anti-Muslim attacks. The number (of anti-Muslim attacks) has been increasing over the past few years because hate speech and stigmatizing discourse on Muslims have been a global trend and the French government has done nothing to counter this problem, to counter discrimination and violence towards Muslims, the CCIF spokesman furthered.

In France, this claim that 'Islamophobia is the new anti-Semitism' is taken to convey the idea, presumably, that Islamophobia has taken over from anti-Semitism as Western civilization's most pernicious and intractable form of bigotry. However, an Arab is usually perceived as a terrorist, and seeing a woman wearing the veil, the people feel themselves attacked, and they reject her. Such an increasingly anti-Muslim sentiment in France has also forced changes in behaviour. Since the *Charlie Hebdo* attacks, the es-Salam mosque on the neighbouring Bellefontaine housing estate in Toulouse has had to be closed between prayer times. Video cameras watch over the site, unlike what used to be in the past. A recent Human Rights Watch report substantiated such individuals' feelings. It accused France of using its state of emergency law, brought in after the Paris attacks in November 2016, to carry out 'abusive and discriminatory raids and house arrests against Muslims'.[83]

It was in the early 1980s that the French government began to blame Islam for the nation's social distress. Amid a global recession

[82] Retrieved from https://www.nbcnews.com/news/asian-america/increase-anti-muslim-incidents-france-post-shooting-n290781.

[83] Retrieved from https://www.hrw.org/news/2016/02/03/france-abuses-under-state-emergency.

and with a left-wing government implementing austerity, a strike movement took off in the car industry, in which approximately half of the employees were migrant workers from former French colonies. The Socialist PM blamed the religion of the strikers. Soon, popular media like *Le Figaro* were asking about French Muslims: 'Will we still be French in 30 years?' (Perry, 1997, p. 162). In 1989 and 1990, a series of schools began to target Muslim girls for wearing the hijab, supposedly a sign of their refusal to integrate—a controversy that gained momentum with the French state's intervention in Algeria's Civil War against the Islamists. Later, with the 'war on terror' in full swing, President Jacques Chirac proposed a 'veil law' banning the wearing of all religious symbols in French schools. In 2011, the state passed a further law banning the right of Muslim women to wear any face-covering material in public. The result was to effectively place those Muslim women who prefer niqab or burqa under house arrest. Today, most French people consider Islam to be 'incompatible' with French values. Leading journalists like Claude Imbert of the respected conservative magazine *Le Point* proudly claim to be Islamophobe. A recent cover of the magazine featuring an image of a Muslim woman wearing a niqab bore the headline: 'Brazen Islam ... in school cafeterias, hospitals, and swimming pools'.[84]

The culture of war against Muslims is a war with teeth. France is a country where around 70 per cent of the prison population is Muslim. It is a country in which there is systematic racist brutality on the part of police. The French government has also made it extremely difficult for Muslims to protest. In 2012, when the satirical magazine *Charlie Hebdo* published a series of Islamophobic cartoons, the government banned planned protests against the publication. In 2016, when activists sought to protest against Israeli attacks on Gaza, the government used exaggerated reports of anti-Semitism among Muslim protesters to impose bans.

---

[84] Retrieved from http://www.independent.co.uk/voices/comment/when-did-islamophobic-attacks-become-the-norm-for-the-french-media-8294053.html.

Patriotic Europeans against the Islamization of the West: The German Face of Islamophobia

Patriotic Europeans against the Islamization of the West is abbreviated as PEGIDA in German. It took birth in October 2014 in Germany. Lutz Bachmann who owns a public relations agency in Dresden founded this movement initially on social media to vent his venom against Muslims and Islam. PEGIDA now has become a far-right political movement that aims to resist what it sees as a threat posed by Islamic extremism, Islamization and its calling for stringent laws to curb immigration particularly from Muslim countries.

A moment that was initially started in an urban city of Dresden, Germany, has now emerged as a strong anti-Muslim resistance moment in whole of Europe. PEGIDA has spawned a number of smaller offshoots across Germany, such as Legida in Leipzig, Sugida in Sudthuringen, Kagida in Kassel, Wugida in Wurzburg, Bogida in Bonn, Dugida in Dusseldorf and Fragida in Frankfurt. Not only this, it has reached its neighbouring and far-flung countries too such as the UK, Poland, France, the USA, Belgium and Scandinavian lands.

PEGIDA and its offshoots at various places in Europe and other parts of the world organize anti-Muslim protests regularly to create hatred against Islam and its followers. They usually start their disgusting slogans with immigrants swallowing Western resources and a burden on us and then turn to vilify Muslims and Islam posing them a threat to world peace and European way of life. At PEGIDA's anniversary event on 19 October 2015, keynote speaker Akif Pirinçci named the Muslim refugees as invaders, with Germany becoming a 'Muslim garbage dump'.[85] Pirinçci said that politicians were acting like 'Nazis against their own people', as they wanted critics of Germany's refugee policy to leave the country. Addressing the crowd shouting 'Resistance!', he claimed that the majority of Germans were held in contempt by the political class and that politicians wished that there

---

[85] Retrieved from http://foreignpolicy.com/2015/10/22/nothing-can-take-down-angela-merkel-except-800000-refugees-germany-cdu-pegida/.

were 'other alternatives [to fight PEGIDA supporters]—but the concentration camps are unfortunately out of order at the moment'.[86]

On 21 January 2015, Bachmann resigned from his position with PEGIDA after coming under fire for a number of Facebook posts. Excerpts from a closed Facebook conversation incriminated Bachmann as having designated immigrants as 'animals', 'scumbags' and 'trash', classified as hate speech in Germany. He was also quoted commenting that extra security was needed at the welfare office 'to protect employees from the animals'.[87] A self-portrait of Bachmann allegedly posing as a reincarnation of Adolf Hitler, titled 'He's back!' went viral on social media and was printed on title pages worldwide.

Media across Europe are giving huge coverage to processions of PEGIDA's anti-Muslimism onslaught. The processions too, on the other hand, are increasing in number. Only in Germany, the birth place of PEGIDA, there were 208 rallies in the last quarter of 2015, while only 95 rallies were there a year earlier, Interior Ministry's data showed. Years 2016 and 2017 have seen further surge in PEGIDA processions against Muslim immigrants. In Poland too, hundreds of people waved Polish flags and chanted 'England and France are in tears, that's how tolerance ends'. 'We're demonstrating against the Islamization of Europe, we're demonstrating against immigration, against an invasion',[88] Robert Winnicki, leader of Poland's far-right National Movement Ruch Narodowy, told the demonstrators. The Czech Republic, Slovakia, Hungary and Poland have together taken a tough stance on migration and have been largely opposed to taking in significant numbers of refugees coming from Muslim countries. Similarly, demonstrators at the largest pro-PEGIDA rally on 5 January 2017 in the UK were heard chanting 'we are the people' with one man telling the BBC 'we don't want Mosques in Europe'.

[86] Retrieved from https://www.rt.com/news/362965-pegida-dresden-anniversary-rally/.

[87] Retrieved from https://uk.reuters.com/article/uk-germany-islam-pegida/german-pegida-leader-resigns-after-hitler-pose-prompts-investigation-idUKK-BN0KU1SA20150121.

[88] Retrieved from http://america.aljazeera.com/articles/2016/2/6/anti-islam-protests-in-dresden-prague-and-other-european-cities1.html.

The hate groups in Europe too like the USA are mustering financial resources and using social media, which help gather huge number of people in their processions to construct a negative image of Muslims and Islam. Although there have been isolated events of anti-PEGIDA like campaigns in parts of Europe and some popular leaders also denied the claims made in the anti-Muslim campaigns, hardly any concrete steps are visible demonstrating their will to fight off anti-Islam sloganeering in the West. Hate speech laws are not seen in action despite the fact that these campaigns are clearly hate speech against the religion of Islam and its followers who are part of their societies.

Spain

Since the twin attacks in August 2017 in Barcelona and seaside resort Cambrils claimed by the Islamic State group, the Muslim community in central Barcelona's neighbourhood fears an anti-Islam backlash. At least 100 were wounded when a white van ploughed into a crowd in one of the Spanish city's busiest tourist districts. The aforementioned attack, which was claimed by the Islamic State of Iraq and the Levant also known as ISIS, occurred in the bustling Las Ramblas area, a 1.2 km stretch of shops and restaurants usually crowded with tourists. Some media reported that the suspected ringleader of the recent attack, Moroccan Imam Abdelbaki Es Satty, spent at least three months in Vilvoorde—a Brussels suburb noted for its links to radical Islamism.[89]

Although the presence of the far-right in Spain remains small compared with other European countries, there has been a 500 per cent increase in the number of reported hate crimes against Muslims, according to a campaign group the Citizens' Platform Against Islamophobia.[90] An editorial in a right-wing newspaper, *La Razon*, claimed Catalonia was 'a nest of radical Islamists' and claimed Qatar

---

[89] Retrieved from http://www.independent.co.uk/news/world/europe/barcelona-attack-spain-cambrils-isis-latest-imam-abdelbaki-es-satty-madrid-bombings-belgium-a7903966.html.

[90] Retrieved from http://www.independent.co.uk/news/world/europe/barcelona-attack-muslim-catalan-city-isis-not-in-my-name-terrorism-islamists-a7904116.html.

businessmen were 'funding indoctrination' in the region's mosques.[91] So-called

> Islamic terrorism is not new to Spain. In March 2004, an al Qaeda group bombed 4 commuter trains, killing some 200 people and wounded more than 1,400 in rush hour Madrid. In April 2005, a cell of 41 al-Qaeda operatives in Spain that assisted the 9/11 attacks on the US was tried in Madrid. In Jan 2008, 14 Pakistani Taliban terrorists were stopped just before they blew themselves up in Barcelona's subway. Many other terrorists who planned attacks or funded terrorism were arrested in Spain over the years.[92]

The recent string of attacks in Europe has sparked a rise in hate incidents. The number of recorded cases jumped from just 48 in 2014 to 534 in 2015, according to a campaign group, the Citizens' Platform Against Islamophobia.[93] Thousands of local Muslims marched down La Rambla following the day of attack, the scenic, treelined boulevard where the first of two coordinated attacks took place. Young and old, men and women, many of whom were veiled, the demonstrators chanted in unison: 'I am Muslim! Not a terrorist!' Non-Muslims lined the sidewalks, clapping and crying. Some stepped forward to hug demonstrators as they passed.

Immediately following these brutal attacks in August 2017 in Barcelona and Cambrils, leaders worldwide, as well as thousands of people online, condemned the incident. Here are some reactions:

Spanish PM Mariano Rajoy called the killings a 'savage terrorist attack' and said Spaniards 'are not just united in mourning, but especially in the firm determination to beat those who want to rob us of our values and way of life'. He announced three days of mourning.[94] French President Emmanuel Macron expressed France's solidarity after what

---

[91] Retrieved from https://www.europebreakingnews.net/2017/08/spanish-muslims-just-marched-on-las-ramblas-against-isis/.

[92] Retrieved from http://acdemocracy.org/jihad-does-not-stop-in-spain/.

[93] Retrieved from http://www.independent.co.uk/news/world/europe/barcelona-attack-muslim-catalan-city-isis-not-in-my-name-terrorism-islamists-a7904116.html.

[94] Retrieved from https://www.cbsnews.com/news/barcelona-terror-attack-latest-updates/.

he termed a 'tragic attack'.[95] In Germany, Chancellor Angela Merkel described the incident as a 'revolting attack', according to a statement by her office. Merkel's spokesman Steffen Seibert tweeted that Germany was 'thinking with profound sadness of the victims ... [and] with solidarity and friendship alongside the Spanish people'.[96] British PM Theresa May called the attack 'terrible' and said the UK 'stands with Spain against terror'.[97] London Mayor Sadiq Khan said: 'London stands with Barcelona against the evil of terrorism'.[98] Dutch PM Mark Rutte condemned what he called the 'cowardly attack against innocent people', adding that Thursday is a 'black day at a place where so many people around the world gather'.[99] In Belgium, Foreign Minister Didier Reynders sent his condolences to the family of the Belgian national who was among the victims. PM Charles Michel added on Twitter that 'no barbaric act will undermine the power and resilience of our ally'.[100] European Commission President Jean-Claude Juncker expressed his 'profound sorrow and anguish'.[101] In Australia, PM Malcolm Turnbull condemned the attack saying on Twitter his country is 'resolute with Spain in the fight to defeat terrorism' and 'love and prayers are with the victims'.[102] The US President Donald Trump also condemned the attack on Twitter, saying the USA 'will do whatever is necessary to

[95] Retrieved from http://www.telegraph.co.uk/news/2017/08/17/world-reacted-barcelona-terror-attack/.

[96] Retrieved from http://www.aljazeera.com/news/2017/08/act-world-reacts-barcelona-attack-170818060019131.html.

[97] Retrieved from http://www.dailymail.co.uk/news/article-4800384/Theresa-condemnS-terrible-attack-Barcelona.html.

[98] Retrieved from https://www.standard.co.uk/news/world/london-stands-with-barcelona-against-evil-of-terrorism-sadiq-khan-says-a3614406.html.

[99] Retrieved from http://www.daily-sun.com/printversion/details/248790/World-leaders-condemn-Barcelona-terror-attack.

[100] Retrieved from https://twitter.com/i/moments/898244109047132161?lang=en.

[101] Retrieved from http://europa.eu/rapid/press-release_STATEMENT-17-2642_en.htm.

[102] Retrieved from http://www.aljazeera.com/news/2017/08/act-world-reacts-barcelona-attack-170818060019131.html.

help'.[103] Secretary of State Rex Tillerson offered US assistance to Spanish authorities. Russian President Vladimir Putin called for the world to unite in an 'uncompromising battle against the forces of terror'. 'What happened once again confirms the need for a genuine unification of efforts by the entire world community in an uncompromising battle with the forces of terror', Putin said in a telegram of condolences to Spanish King Felipe VI, describing the incident as a 'cruel and cynical crime'.[104] Pope Francis expressed 'great concern', according to a statement from his office, which added he is praying for the victims. The OIC also denounced the criminal attack and considered this barbaric act as shocking and brutal. The OIC Secretary General, Dr Yusuf Bin Ahmed Al Uthaymeen, expressed profound distress at this atrocious terrorist crime. Al Uthaymeen underlined that terrorism has no religion, nationality or race; and that the perpetrators are an affront to humanity and all moral and human values and called for bringing them to justice.

Switzerland

The Swiss political system encourages citizens' participation through direct democratic means and media play an important role in changing public perceptions in this regard. The Swiss constitution guarantees the freedom of press in Article 17, while Article 93 states the independence of broadcast media; the penal code prohibits racial hatred, discrimination, spreading racist ideology and denying crimes against humanity. The state-owned Swiss Broadcasting Corporation dominates the media market. Since the 1980s, controversial questions relating to Islamism, jihadism and Muslim immigrants have dominated the Swiss media debates and news headlines.

There has been an increase in Islamophobic tweets and attacks against foreigners on Facebook, blogs, TV and in posters. There are also Islamophobic statements highlighted by politicians in Switzerland,

---

[103] Retrieved from https://twitter.com/realdonaldtrump/status/8982432701695 63136?lang=en.

[104] Retrieved from https://dailytimes.com.pk/120311/putin-urges-global-fight-against-terror-after-barcelona-attack/.

mainly those from the right-wing Swiss People's Party. The Bern regional tribunal found the Secretary General of Swiss People's Party Martin Baltisser and his substitute Silvia Bar guilty of racism on 30 April 2015 for using slogan 'Kosovars Stab Swiss' (Bayrakli & Hafez, 2016, p. 552). According to the eighth OIC observatory report on Islamophobia, the focus of media on the heinous acts of Daesh and other extremist groups worldwide has been associated with Islamic values and jurisprudence; the acts of such groups against Western civilians have been used to manipulate the perception of Islam.[105] Such portrayal by the media, due to a 'fear' of Islam, resulted in impression that all religious Muslims were radicals and extremists.

Swiss media reported the alleged radicalization of Muslims in the city of Winterthur and Geneva, where mosques are alleged to have been responsible for radicalizing the youth, thus increasing the fear of Islam in the region. This fear has increased studies in Muslim radicalization and extremism, as shown by the study conducted by Miryam Eser Davolio, who headed the study of the radicalization of young Swiss people for Zurich University of Applied Sciences.[106] She points out that certain areas within the constituencies of Geneva and Ticino were more likely to develop radicalization tendencies due to the presence of unemployed Muslim youth in these areas.

In the Freedom of the Press 2015 Report, Switzerland, it was reported that Christoph Blocher, the right-wing politician of Swiss People's Party planned to invest in *Neue Zurcher Zeitung* (NZZ), the country's leading newspaper, which plays an important role in influencing the public opinion to right-wing policies to create anti-Muslim and anti-Islam environment. One of the problems with the Swiss anti-jihadi strategy and the media's role is that it does not address Islamophobia. Researchers claim in their studies regarding

---

[105] The report can be retrieved from https://www.oic-oci.org/upload/islamophobia/2015/en/reports/8th_Ob_Rep_Islamophobia_Final.pdf.

[106] Complete report in PDF can be retrieved from https://www.zhaw.ch/storage/shared/sozialearbeit/Forschung/Deliquenz_Kriminalpraevention/Jugendkriminalitaet_Jugendgewalt/Schlussbericht-Jihadismus-EN.pdf.

radicalization of Swiss young people that it is very important to address Islamophobia; the presence of people who are afraid of Muslims and do not approve of them enhances the theory that Muslims are being stigmatized and humiliated while also facing exclusion in different sections of society.

The public debate about Islam in Switzerland is structured around issues that are not the product of Swiss society, rather are influenced by the larger European debate on Islam. Islam became an important part of the national discourse in Swiss media and politics due to issues like the ban on minarets, headscarf issues, veiled Muslim girls being exempted from swimming lessons, the question of Muslim cemeteries and halal food; all of these raised the crucial question of integration in Swiss society. These issues are also some of the consequences of the immigration that has taken place since the 1960s, mainly from Muslim countries. The new wave of immigration in Europe, the result of civil wars in the Middle East, particularly after the crises in Iraq and Syria, and poverty in Africa, has created the greatest influx of refugees in 2015 since the end of the Second World War. According to the United Nations and International Organization for Migration (IOM), almost 102,000 immigrants arrived in Europe in 2015. Among these immigrants, half were Syrians, 20 per cent were Afghans and 7 per cent were Iraqis (Bayrakli & Hafez, 2016).

Recent images of the women and children coming from Syria to Europe via the Mediterranean resulted in the acceptance of immigrants on a humanitarian basis; however, after the Paris terror attacks, this influx was halted due to fear of further terrorist attacks and as part of a strict policy towards migration. Switzerland was no exception to the fear of terror attacks. The Swiss arm of PEGIDA and Stop Islamisation of Europe (SIOE) also stand against asylum seekers and immigrants. PEGIDA is an anti-Islam political organization that was established in Germany in 2014; it calls for more restrictive immigration policies against Muslims. It planned an anti-Islam protest on 15 January 2015, a date that was soon after the *Charlie Hebdo* attacks; this protest was banned by the Swiss police.

At the same time, the head of the Swiss Federal Commission Against Racism, Martin Graf, termed such proposed immigration policies as discriminatory as they would lead to an increased atmosphere of hate. The Human Rights Watch World Report published in 2016 states that the fear of an influx of asylum seekers to Europe, particularly after the crisis in Syria, has led Europe to close its gates for immigrants, particularly Muslims. The fear of the politicians and the governments is related to terror attacks; Muslim refugees have become the scapegoats. The polarizing us-versus-them narrative, Islamophobia and the demonizing of refugees has now entered in mainstream politics and has led many governments to curtail rights solely on the basis of xenophobic attitudes.

The current influx of refugees is the greatest since the Second World War; almost 1 million asylum seekers have now fled to Europe, with 60 million others being displaced. The result is a public discourse filled with hatred against Muslims; due to the nexus of refugees and terrorism in the media, Muslims now face discrimination.

Norway

On 22 July 2011, two terror attacks in Norway were perpetrated by a white Norwegian right-wing extremist Anders Breivik. His stated motivation was to eradicate the Muslim presence in Norway and Europe by massacring Norwegian social democrats he believed to be responsible for allowing Muslim immigration to Norway since the 1960s. Seventy-seven people died that day, most of them teenagers. The terror attacks came at the end of a decade in which Islamophobic ideas had become increasingly mainstream in Norwegian politics. Norway has a population of 5.1 million of whom an estimated 4.2 per cent are of Muslim background. It has a coalition government consisting of the liberal–conservative Conservative Party (CP) and the populist right-wing Progress Party (PP) since the parliamentary elections of September 2013.

In 2015, number of marches in Oslo were seen in support of the German anti-Muslim and anti-immigrant PEGIDA movement organized by Norwegian far-right activists affiliated with the Norwegian

Defence League (NDL), and Stop Islamisation of Norway (SIAN).[107] Some authentic surveys in Norway document that Muslims, according to social distance scales, are among the least desired citizens in Norway, after the Romans. Since 2000, the Norwegian Prosecutor General has asked local police districts to prioritize hate crimes, but until recently, efforts in this field can at best be described as limited in scope and efficiency. So much so that Norwegian Muslims interviewed for a newspaper report about this issue asserted that 'Muslims do not report hate crimes' since they allegedly 'have no confidence in the police taking it seriously'. Civil society activists as well as legal experts in this field also indicate that there is a significant under-reporting of such cases, for reasons which include a lack of confidence in the local police, a lack of knowledge of existent laws and their applicability in hate speech cases, etc.

The Norwegian mainstream media has also continued its long-standing and established practice of referring to even far-right civil society activists who regularly engage in both racist, discriminatory and Islamophobic rhetoric targeted at Muslims as 'critics of Islam', thereby implying that what organizations such as SIAN and the Human Rights Service are involved in is part of a venerable Enlightenment tradition of 'critique of religion', rather than in advocacy for stigmatization, exclusion and discrimination against Norwegian Muslims. In the media blitz, which surrounded the publication of Hege Storhaug's self-published popular book *Islam—The Eleventh Plague of the Nation* (*Islam—Den Ellevte Landeplage*), which is a replete with distortions and fabrications, Storhaug not only called for prohibitions against mosques in Norway but also insinuated on the basis of non-existent empirical data that some 'thirty to forty per cent of Norwegian Muslims could be characterized as fundamentalist' (Bayrakli & Hafez, 2016).

Central nodes for the propagation of Islamophobia in Norway are websites at present. Some notorious Islamophobes operating in Scandinavian countries include Hans Rustad; and the right-wing extremist blogger Peder Are Nostvold Jensen, believed to be living in Copenhagen, Denmark, where he is closely aligned with Lars

---

[107] Retrieved from https://www.youtube.com/watch?v=mCJSLE1fkEQ.

Hedegaard of the Danish Free Press Society, who also serves as a node for dissemination of Islamophobia in Norway and Scandinavia through his writings on various far-right websites. Rita Karlsen of the Human Rights Service is the most central and influential person in current Norwegian Islamophobia networks due to her extensive links to the governing PP, extensive state funding and long-standing links with Lars Hedegaard, Helle Merete Brix, Hege Storhaug, etc.

Many Muslims see today's welfare state in Norway as closer to the Muslim ideal state than many countries in the Muslim world, and Norwegian Muslims want to keep the Norwegian state as it is. However, public debates in Norway are no less influenced by anti-Islamic sentiments than other European countries. European Commission against Racism and Intolerance strongly recommended 'that the Norwegian authorities monitor the situation as concerns Islamophobia in Norway and take swift action to counter any such manifestations as necessary' (Neilsen, 2009). Civil society organizations such as the Norwegian Centre against Racism (ARS), Organization Against Public Discrimination (OMOD) and other organizations have continued their long-standing work of countering racist and discriminatory attitudes and ideas, but have not had the resources available to launch new initiatives and campaigns in this field. The Lutheran State Church in Norway, through its interreligious dialogue and involvement in national and international ecumenical bodies, has continued its work for interreligious tolerance, also in extensive formalized contacts with the Islamic Council Norway (IRN).

Denmark

With a history of freedom of speech that spans back to the 18th century, Denmark prides itself in its egalitarian media. The Danish media exemplify a focused interest on the differences between Muslims and Danish people rather than an all-encompassing media that treats religions and ethnicities equally. The negative portrayal of Islam in Danish media stems from the deeply engrained, politicized nature of the topic. The media is intimately tied to both the existing government and varying political parties. The depiction of Islam in the media generally follows political trends, including the Islamophobic rhetoric of the Danish PP.

Negative portrayals of Muslim–Danish relations may be a permanent staple of Danish media rather than a fluid issue dependent on an oppositional right. This is best exemplified by the 2005–2006 cartoon crisis, which occurred during a right-wing government with left-wing opposition. The crisis, which has been deemed the worst catastrophe to hit Denmark since the Second World War, took over Danish media and plagues Muslim–Danish relations to this day.

In 2005, the media got hold of a new and captivating story. Writer and journalist Kåre Bluitgen was unable to find an illustrator for his children's book on the story of the Prophet Muhammad (PBUH). Once he found an illustrator, he/she wished to remain anonymous in fear of backlash from the Muslim community. The Danish media was hooked on the story that pitted freedom of speech against Islamic beliefs. Flemming Rose, cultural editor of the most popular Danish newspaper, *Jyllands-Posten*, responded by asking Danish cartoonists to submit cartoons depicting the Prophet Muhammad (PBUH) 'as they see him'. Many cartoonists ignored the request, but on 30 September 2005, 12 extremely negative cartoons were published. The Danish–Muslim community was outraged at what they saw as an example of systemic negative portrayals of Islam in Danish media.

On 30 October 2005, the Danish PM Anders Fogh Rasmussen refused to meet with 11 ambassadors hoping to discuss Islamophobia in Danish media. Members of the Danish–Muslim community then took their grievances to the international arena and rioting ensued throughout the Muslim world. By March 2006, the crisis had left 139 people dead, over 800 injured and over 10,000 unemployed because of embargoes and destroyed buildings. In Flemming Rose's article, 'Why I Published Those Cartoons?' he depicts himself as a defender of freedom of speech in the wake of a destructive stream of political correctness. He begins with examples of self-censorship responding to fears of Muslim backlashes. He then argues that by satirizing Islam, the cartoons incorporate Muslims into Danish humour, and by extension, Danish culture. Lastly, he blames 'radical imams' for misinforming rioters in the Middle East.

In the eyes of most of the Danish population, the crisis demonstrates the incompatibility of Islam with Western liberal ideals and the Danish imams are to be blamed for setting fire to the conflict. In December 2005, a Danish imam supposedly went to the Middle East with a 43-page folder of cartoons and drawings. Some experts concluded that Danish imams did not spread false information, but simply displayed drawings that were part of the hate material sent to Muslim organizations in the aftermath of the 2005 cartoons. In 2008, a scholar Peter Hervik conducted focus group interviews with Danish people undergoing higher education. Most of them described Muslims as irrational and dangerous people. They also blamed Danish imams, Danish Muslims and Islam as a whole for the crisis. He argued that the crisis is an example of Islamophobia within the Danish media that spans decades. Like him, a small portion of the Danish population argues that the cartoons were in fact a 'cartoon crisis' rather than a sacred religious personality crisis between two conflicting cultures that pit an 'enlightened' view of media against a 'barbaric' religious view. The 'cartoon crisis' argument stems from years of right-wing populist rhetoric against immigrants in Danish media and a history of newspaper–political party affiliations.

'Cartoon Crisis' suggests that Christians in Denmark differ from Muslims because they allow the satirization of their own religion. However, *The Guardian* was contacted by a Danish cartoonist in 2006 to leak a story in which *Jyllands-Posten* refused to publish his cartoons with Jesus on the basis that they would be too offensive. *Jyllands-Posten* responded by stating 'in the Muslims prophet (peace be upon him) drawings case, we asked the illustrators to do it. I did not ask for the Jesus cartoons. That's the difference'.[108]

Of the 12 cartoonists, 4 who drew the cartoons were directly employed or previously employed by *Jyllands-Posten*. Those four cartoons are the most controversial of the group. *Jyllands-Posten* is a right-wing in its way of prioritizing journalistic stories. Therefore, it may not come as a surprise that *Jyllands-Posten* supported the premiership

---

[108] Retrieved from https://www.theguardian.com/world/2015/jan/10/drawing-prophet-islam-muhammad-images.

of Anders Fogh Rasmussen, the leader of the right-wing Liberal Party. Anders Fogh Rasmussen launched his political strategy, 'culture war', which was quickly joined by *Jyllands-Posten* with their 'culture war' strategy that would focus on the maintenance of Danish culture. The tabloid papers, *Ekstra Bladet* and *B.T.*, were also the strongest supporters of both *Jyllands-Posten* and the government. During the cartoon crisis, Fogh Rasmussen set a political precedent for many other media outlets. On 17 February 2008, following the uncovering of a murder plot against one of the cartoonists, 17 Danish newspapers, even those with a political history connected to the left wing, republished the 12 cartoons as a statement of 'freedom of expression' and in solidarity with *Jyllands-Posten*'s cartoonist.

Criticism of right-wing populist influence in Danish politics is not seen or heard in everyday media outlets. The inability to assimilate Muslims in Danish society is still a popular headline that guarantees mass viewership. Muslims are still portrayed in an 'us versus them' paradigm.

Sweden

Historically, Sweden was one of the most welcoming nations for refugees, but this norm is slowly shifting due to increased xenophobia. Although the Swedes continue to perceive themselves as an open and tolerant society, recent attacks and discriminatory rhetoric towards Muslims and immigrants reveal structural racism. Muslims are often viewed negatively. Many Swedes view Islamic and European values as incompatible, a sentiment prominent in other parts of Europe. In 2014, 35 per cent of Swedes saw Islam as a threat, while one half believed it is incompatible with the Western world. More recently, in 2015, 41 per cent said the country granted too many asylum requests. Even more recently, in 2016, 35 per cent saw Muslims in a negative light, 57 per cent feared refugees compromised national security and 32 per cent indicated that they would take jobs and social benefits (Bayrakli & Hafez, 2016).

Hate crimes against Muslims are on the rise in contemporary Sweden. For instance, in 2013, there were approximately

300 reported anti-Muslim hate crimes. While between 2010 and 2014, anti-Muslim attacks in Sweden increased by 81 per cent. However, hate crimes remain under-reported for a variety of reasons including persistent scepticism that authorities will not pursue appropriate action. Significantly, most hate crimes target women who are conspicuously Muslim (i.e., practising hijab). Anti-Muslim bias offences also targeted communal property, like mosques. In fact, in 2016, 66 per cent of mosques were subject to vandalism, arson or bomb threats, a 26 per cent increase from 2011 when approximately 40 per cent of mosques suffered such attacks. During a one-month period, immediately prior to the 2015 attack against *Charlie Hebdo*, a number of Swedish mosques were targeted in a series of highly publicized hate crimes. The violence has resulted in dozens of Swedish Muslims sustaining injuries. Mosques and Muslim prayer facilities throughout Sweden have also faced violence that has Islamophobic motivation. They have been vandalized or been subject to arson and these attacks are an ongoing trend.

More domestically, issues relating to the burning of mosques, the burning of refugee camps and the school attack in Trollhattan in October 2015 show direct or indirect connections to racism and Islamophobia. In January 2017 alone, the Gothenburg Mosque received a bomb threat, a mosque in Uppsala was attacked with a firebomb, a mosque in the small town of Jarva was threatened by mail, including pornographic images and a masjid in Mariestad was attacked with canned pork.

In a most recent attack on mosque on 1 May 2017, Sweden's largest Shia mosque has been partially destroyed by fire in what police are treating as an arson attack. Such attacks have been increasing, including 112 fires last year, most of them were arson. Discrimination in the job and labour market has also been researched in Sweden for some time. Research has indicated that employers tend to refrain from hiring those who are perceived to be non-European or Muslim. Moreover, according to mandatory directives by the National Education Agency as issued in 2003, schools are allowed to prohibit the burqa and niqab, provided that they do so in a spirit of dialogue on the common values of equality of the sexes and respect for the democratic principle.

Researchers found an explicit and implicit prejudice towards Muslim men. Their studies concluded that 49 per cent of employers had explicit and 94 per cent had implicit prejudice towards Muslim men. These prejudices are believed to have an impact upon employers' decisions to hire.[109] A politically significant development is the right-wing populist Sweden Democrats (SD) becoming the third largest party in Sweden since 2014, winning almost 13 per cent of the votes and 30 new parliamentary seats. Despite having anti-immigrant policies (often with a significant anti-Islam/Muslim focus) as their foremost agenda, the party has denied accusations of racism or xenophobia. However, history of SD and its prominent members reveals incidents of clear racist or discriminatory contents, and some less explicit, but nonetheless suspicious activities. One of the examples includes when the party secretary stated: 'Just like Nazism was overturned, so does Islam need to be overturned....'[110]

On the other hand, Swedish media is not leaving any stone unturned to insult the injuries. The studies show that minority ethnicities are presented in Swedish media quite negatively. Muslims in particular face serious negative representations as the 'other' and are described with stereotypes often connected to violent behaviour. Islamophobic contents can also be seen on the Internet, web pages and social media. According to scholars, the Internet and social media have had a hand in spreading and accelerating prejudice towards Islam and Muslims. The Living History Forum, a Swedish government body that works on discrimination, tolerance and human rights, writes that 'perhaps the biggest problem when it comes to spreading anti-Semitism and Islamophobia happens through internet and social media'. According to the Forum, the Islamophobic contents found on online pages often present stereotypes as facts.

Some studies have found that the contents on such websites present a picture of a warlike struggle between 'Islam' and 'Sweden'. Blogs often frame racist or xenophobic standpoints as a question of freedom

---

[109] Complete report can be retrieved from http://www.osce.org/chairmanship/3 33661?download=true.

[110] Please refer to footnote 80.

of speech and a critique against religious extremism. The mapping of anti-Muslim, anti-Islamic sentiment in cyberspace has been less direct, focusing more on racism and xenophobia in general. The terror attacks have been used as a catalyst to spread hate and as a source of collective blame on Muslims. An example is the spreading of Facebook comments supposedly celebrating the *Charlie Hebdo* attack by Muslims; calling for an end of all public Islamic practices in Sweden, saying that Islam is a 'direct threat to' Sweden. Someone has written in a popular blog wondering if the time has come to close all avenues for Muslims to organize themselves, including shutting down mosques and ending any financial aid to Muslim organizations. Facebook and other social media outlets have also been part of spreading Islamophobia. An example is a fake video of Muslims celebrating the attacks in Paris that was spread on social media, while the video was, in fact, the Pakistani fans celebrating a victory in cricket.

Australia

Islamophobia has become a momentous problem across the Western world. The emergence of far-right groups and a political environment that allows anti-Islamic discourse has created an increasingly unwelcome environment for Muslims, even though multiculturalism has long been a fundamental marker of Australian daily life. The rise of Islamophobia has been damaging for Australia. Islamophobia is not only breaking the bond between Muslim youth and Australian society, it is also polarizing relations within Australian Muslim communities. The rise of anti-immigration far-right parties, coupled with a political environment that is increasingly permissive of anti-Islamic expressions, has put considerable strain on Australian multiculturalism.

The Australian political landscape has turned increasingly to the right over the past two decades, especially in relation to the place of Muslims in the country. This has been spurred by the political dominance of Australia's conservative Liberal Party, which has governed for 14 of the past 20 years, as well as the ascendance of far-right parties. Although Australia is no stranger to far-right organizations, having long been home to the Australian League of Rights, the Christian

Democratic Party and the Citizens Electoral Council, a new generation of parties has emerged that directly targets immigration and Islam.

This includes parties such as One Nation, and more recently, Rise Up Australia and the Australian Liberty Alliance (ALA). One Nation party took a famously strong line on immigration and multiculturalism in the 1990s with former politician and party leader Pauline Hanson calling for a radical review of the immigration policy and the abolition of multiculturalism. Hansen's initial target was Asia, more recently she has sought to capitalize on anti-Islam sentiments, promising to provide 'absolute opposition to any more Mosques, Sharia Law, Halal Certification & Muslim Refugees' (Akbarzadeh, 2016). She has joined the anti-Islam chorus by stating 'What Islam stands for is not compatible with our country … let Muslim countries take them' (Akbarzadeh, 2016).

Daniel Nalliah, a prominent evangelist and the president of the Rise Up Australia Party expressed similar ideas, declaring that 'I strongly condemn the teachings of Islam … The attacks that have been taking place are not lone wolf attacks or people gone crazy. No, rather this is Islam 101' (Akbarzadeh, 2016). In 2016, Rise Up Australia slammed calls for greater Muslim inclusion in the Australian military by declaring that 'the Australian Defence Force [ADF] is one step away from adopting Sharia lawlessness!' The ALA is the newest addition to the stable of far-right parties in Australia. Registered in August 2015, one of the group's directors declared that Islam is a dangerous ideology that's definitely not compatible with Western culture and society … There is no moderate version of Islam … there may be people who don't follow it to the letter, but there is no moderate version, so it's dangerous. It's dangerous for our society. The ALA is the political wing of the Q Society, which is an anti-Islam organization that has been operating in Australia since 2010. The parent organization describes itself as having 'formed in response to growing concerns about the discrimination, violence and other anti-democratic practices linked to Islam' (Akbarzadeh, 2016).

The Q Society and ALA conceive Muslims to pose a direct and deliberate threat to the Australian value system. In its published Manifesto, the ALA lists 'stopping the Islamization of Australia' under its 'values and core policies' and states that Islam is not merely a religion, it is a totalitarian ideology with global aspirations. Islam uses the religious element as a means to project itself onto non-Islamic societies, which is manifested in the historical and ongoing expansion of Islam. It is our core policy that all attempts to impose Islam's theocracy and Sharia law on our liberal society must be stopped by democratic means, before the demographic, economic and sociopolitical realities make a peaceful solution impossible.

The group argues that the threat of 'Islamization' can be overcome by instituting a religious filter in immigration policy to prevent Muslims from immigrating to Australia. The term 'Islamization' is used widely in far-right statements and effectively refers to anything that relates to Muslims. This includes a female wearing the hijab, halal products on supermarket shelves, the opening of new mosques and marriage counselling by community and religious leaders. Each of these practices has been variously interpreted as aspects of the imposition of Sharia law in Australia. At times, these sentiments have infiltrated the political debate with even the country's mainstream political leadership drawing on them. This was evident particularly in reference to ISIS, which former PM Tony Abbott routinely described as a 'death cult'. Although Abbott took care to differentiate between ISIS and the broader Muslim community, it is revealed that for the 40 times that Abbott publicly mentioned Muslims between September 2013 and November 2014, Muslims were only mentioned in relation to terrorism.

Abbott's position on Muslims became even less nuanced over time. In February 2015, he declared, 'I've often heard Western leaders describe Islam as a "religion of peace". I wish more Muslim leaders would say that more often, and mean it'. Three months after leaving office, Abbott controversially added, 'all cultures are not equal and, frankly, a culture that believes in decency and tolerance is much to be preferred to one which thinks that you can kill in the name of God'.[111]

---

[111] Retrieved from https://www.theguardian.com/australia-news/2015/feb/23/muslim-leaders-outraged-by-tony-abbotts-admonishment-over-extremism.

Islamophobic expressions have been expressed even more overtly by junior government figures. The most prominent of these individuals is the Liberal Senator for South Australia, Cory Bernardi, who declared that Islam itself is the problem ... Islam is a totalitarian, political and religious ideology ... It has not moved on since it was founded and there are these extremists that want to see fundamentalist Islamic rule implemented in this country.[112] They are continually trying to change our laws. They are seeking special accommodations. Others repeated this message, including junior minister and Liberal Party rising parliamentary star Josh Frydenberg, who declared that terrorism reflected 'a problem within Islam'.

There is a positive correlation between the rise of far-right groups and the presence of anti-Islamic sentiments in the political mainstream. At times, far-right agendas have directly set the parameters for mainstream politics, most clearly in relation to the refugee intake and the high-profile 2015 parliamentary inquiry into the Third Party Certification of Food (dubbed the Halal food inquiry). Indeed, the sentiments surrounding ALA's call for a moratorium on immigration from OIC countries was recently highlighted in the discussion surrounding asylum seekers from Syria and Iraq. Senate Leader Eric Abetz publicly called for Australia to prioritize Christian refugees. These patterns have been amplified during times of international or domestic political stress, translating into more than 30 attacks on Muslims—mostly on women wearing the hijab—in the three weeks following police counterterrorism raids in September 2014. Furthermore, after extensive community consultation in 2015, the Australian Human Rights Commission noted that the Australian government's decision to raise the official terror alert level to 'high' in August 2014 'made many Australian Muslims feel a sense of "us versus them"'.

[112] Excerpt from a PhD dissertation by Mohammad Hadi Sohrabi Haghighat entitled Australian Muslim Leaders, Normalization and Social Integration submitted to Swinburne University, Victoria, Australia in 2013. It can be retrieved from file:///C:/Users/lenovo/Downloads/Mohammad%20Hadi%20Sohrabi%20Haghighat%20Thesis.pdf.

CONCLUSION

Sociocultural facet of Islamophobia has much wider canvass than the way it is explained. All three aspects—epistemic dimensions, antecedents and catalytic dimension—may accommodate more variables to make the whole scenario appear comprehensive and composite. Essentially, the set of variables in all three dimensions may or may not suit every social system. While considering to operationalize Islamophobia in sociocultural perspective, the Western system hugely influenced the researcher in his endeavour. The picture may get more complicated or appear much different if the model is applied in a Muslim society, where radicalized Islamophobia in sociocultural perspective is measured or investigated.

Furthermore, challenging the dominant approaches in the system while explicating any construct or explaining any phenomenon is always an unwieldy task. It becomes even more difficult if the axiological dimensions of the researcher also intervene to plague the process of measurement. Both the challenges are equally significant and demand highest level of scholarship and literature review to destroy one's own impressions of the phenomenon to reach to any scholastic conclusion, besides not being under the heavy influence of historic and contemporary approaches towards the construct/phenomenon.

This is understandable that mass media have contemplated contemporary Islamophobia mainly in sociocultural dimension; hence, it took much larger portion of the chapter than it was originally conceived in the beginning. More important, nonetheless, in this regard is to understand and investigate as how do mass media cultivate Islamophobia in terror domain, which is separately dealt with.

Prejudice

An Antecedent or Manifestation of Islamophobia?

INTRODUCTION

Islamophobia has not been and should not be examined in singularity, initially as a phenomenon and then as a construct. It is, rather, a complex bundle of episteme and an umbrella term used invariably for multifaceted problems mainly in the West and primarily directed at the Muslims and Islam. Allen (2010) rightly describes it as a 'fluid, protean and largely inconsistent' concept (p. 102) of which imprecision and 'ambiguity' have been recognized by many scholars like Field (2012, p. 147). The literature produced on the construct more often mixes its manifestations and antecedents, and eventually presents a complex mix of terms associated with it. Racism, prejudice, hostility towards and fear of Muslims and Islam are some of the commonly used interpretations of Islamophobia. Alain Quellien who coined the term Islamophobia in 1910 summed it up by saying that it is 'prejudice against Islam' that 'has always been widespread among the people of Western and Christian civilization' (Lopez, 2011). According to Quellien, prejudice becomes quite natural when Islam is declared as 'negation of civilization' and 'Muslims as irreconcilable enemy of the Christians and the Europeans' (Lopez, 2011). Zick et al. (2008) also call Islamophobia as a group-focused enmity towards Islam and Muslims, which they later describe as prejudice towards Muslims and Islam. Uenal (2016) furthers with conflating prejudice with enmity against Islam and Muslims.

Hence, the significance of studying prejudice as a construct and a facet of Islamophobia can hardly be exaggerated. This chapter would shed some light on the literature produced on prejudice as a phenomenon and then as a construct; and what makes it appear as a facet of

Islamophobia. How Muslims are prejudiced under the phenomenon of Islamophobia in the West contemporarily and may a religion, an ideology, or a region be prejudiced, or is it mere a construct directed at some specific group of people are some of the conundrums which essentially need to be unpacked for better understanding of Islamophobia as a composite construct. How prejudice could be measured as a facet of Islamophobia and what different forms it may take in its explication in the process of conceptualization and operationalization would also be investigated in this chapter.

PREJUDICE

Prejudice[1] mainly relates to basic needs of human beings, that is, process of categorization (being sine qua non of prejudice) and the capacity to think. So any 'being' capable of thinking can possess and experience prejudice. Nonetheless, prejudice is one among the much talked about, but least understood terms, which still looks towards academic scholarship for its explication. It has generally been expressed as a narrow term, relating to prejudgement, where an individual is viewed in relation to a group for being its member or having affiliation with or simply put 'cumulative negative attitude toward a group or its individuals' (Weiten 2017, p. 449). Even, Gordon W. Allport (famous American social psychologist on the subject) gave a simplistic definition of prejudice as 'an antipathy based upon a faulty and inflexible generalization' (Allport, 1954, p. 9). He termed it as an entirely 'normal' categorization or a categorization process which is innate to all human beings. The construct is basically a convoluted term with

---

[1] Dictionary.com defines 'prejudice' as 'an unfavorable opinion or feeling formed beforehand or without knowledge, thought, or reason, any preconceived opinion or feeling, either favorable or unfavorable, unreasonable feelings, opinions, or attitudes, especially of a hostile nature, regarding an ethnic, racial, social, or religious group'. While talking of one type of religious prejudice, the Oxford Dictionary defines 'Islamophobia' as 'dislike of or prejudice against Islam or Muslims, especially as a political force'. The Webster's online dictionary defines it as 'prejudice against Muslims'. Here, Merriam-Webster offers the following definition: 'irrational fear of, aversion to, or discrimination against Islam or people who practice Islam'. Another definition is 'A judgement or opinion formed beforehand or without due examination' (Chambers English Dictionary, 1988).

different hidden aspects and factors, of which only few could have been understood while others are still in the process. Researchers have variedly defined prejudice. As referred earlier, Allport (1954) defines prejudice as 'an antipathy based upon a faulty and inflexible generalization. It may be felt or expressed. It may be directed toward a group as a whole or toward an individual because he is a member of that group' (p. 9). Here, Allport could only cover the racial and ethnic dimensions of the concept and neglected the gender aspect, which was not an important issue in the 1950s as such when anti-Semitism had huge visibility and was a much talked about subject. Nuances in the definition were crystalized later, after the 1950s, due to ideological and religious differences in world politics and rise of racism in parts of the globe.

Jones (1972) described prejudice as 'the prior negative judgement of the members of a race or religion or the occupants of any other significant social role, held in disregard of the facts that contradict it' (p. 61). Here, race and religion have been identified as the dimensions of prejudice and shaded as negative, which somewhat makes it appear lacking neutrality in it or a definition radicalized in nature. Later, some researches pointed towards the positive nature of prejudice (for own group) and was considered neutral dimension of its definition. Worchel and Cooper (1988) defined prejudice as 'an unjustified negative attitude toward an individual based solely on that individual's membership in a group' (p. 449). This explanation leads to the question of context relatedness of the held prejudice, which could only be relevant for a particular time and space or related to sociocultural aspects. Stereotypes of the time are not a constant feature and can change. Brown (1995) comes with a relatively broader definition of prejudice, wherein he says that it is 'the holding of derogatory social attitudes or cognitive beliefs, the expression of negative affect, or the display of hostile or discriminatory behaviour, towards members of a group on account of their membership of that group' (p. 8). This definition brings in its ambit the latent and manifested aspects of prejudice, which most of the definitions lack, besides viewing prejudice construction as attitudinal and social order levels. However, own-group prejudice has been neglected (in the definition) at the cost of prejudice towards the out-group, which is essentially a negative posturing directed at some group. The behavioural aspect of hostility or aggression has been explained as prejudice, from perception to action.

These definitions, though appropriate for some specific time or context, lack focus on some of the considerable features of the construct. First, it is not always the generalized negative attitude, which is taken as being only against a group in general (covering mostly religious and ethnic dimension) and that too in extreme form (like anti-Semitism to Jews then and the Holocaust in the 1930s until 1950s or like Islamophobia to present-day Muslims and Islam). However, it may persist in more subtle forms and dimensions. The target of prejudice may also not necessarily be a social group; rather it could be an individual or other entity. Second, the antipathy, discrimination or negativity to a prejudiced group can have questionable concerns for their accuracy, as they cannot be based solely on 'faulty generalization' for the prejudiced group/individual being different to prejudicing group or an individual. Third, prejudice is not absolutely inflexible phenomenon and is, in fact, related to social context, which can change over time. Finally, the real issue is of the role presumably given to a group or a segment of the society, which is expected to be congruous to the expectations or past role of the group. It is the incongruity of this specified role that potentially produces prejudice.

Contemporary literature, though plenteous, hardly seems to be addressing the nuances of definitional problems of the construct of prejudice, rather being approach specific. Mostly, it starts with individual's complex thought process, takes its shape in a cultural or religious context and influences the action of a group in shape of power struggle of individuals and groups. In viewing it from this perspective, three major theoretical approaches to prejudice surface, namely personality-centred approach, cultural-based approach and power-conflict approach. The current study will fundamentally rest on the first approach as being the initiating point of prejudice and basic in understanding the construct. Precisely, we need to understand that prejudice is a compound and complex phenomenon with numerous dimensions and facets. It is also more widespread than anticipated or believed and is affected by many dimensions while affecting many others in the process. Therefore, the pronounced definitions do not seem to be doing justice with this complex construct having multiple dimensions, which are necessary for understanding prejudice at cognitive level. These basic dimensions are discussed in the following text.

Cognitive Process and Normality

Psychological behaviourism and Freudian analytical approach (of childhood experiences shaping the unconscious and personality) dominated the earlier prejudice literature; however, the later cognitive approach (of conscious mental activities such as attitudes, beliefs and memory processing) emerged with more detailed and dominant explanations. Further, it was also understood that prejudice as being irrational is very natural for a human being and people do experience or undertake it for many social organisms. Humans have a natural propensity towards prejudgement, categorization (of us and them) and generating generalization. Least effort principle of Gordon Allport identifies these categorizations and generalization as mental shortcuts.

Ambivalence, Negativity and Change

In inter-group relations, the prejudice can be ambivalent and not a continuously hostile feature, with altogether and outright negativity. The prejudice, in this case, can exist in an elusive form; might have been through changes in its formation or is still changing progressively over time. The example of Blacks and Muslims in the USA may be quoted, wherein prejudice towards black folks has been through the reduction process, while towards Muslims, it is on the rise due to some national and international factors and context. These groups, according to Brewer (1999), have in fact failed to get a positive social evaluation and are not the case of strong negative evaluation either. Many celebrated scholars such as Mummendey et al. (1992) and Tajfel and Turner (1986) rightly point out that the issue is of outgroup identification and not of permanent hostility, where in-group is preferred by an individual.

Paternalism

According to Jackman (1994), the paternalism despite its visible affection to subordinates groups is a form of dominance by the 'dominant advantaged classes'. This paternalism was clearly visible in development paradigm of the 20th century when it was given as a reason for colonization and was commonly called 'Whiteman's burden'. Prejudice can also exist in the form where visible sympathy is the driving force instead of antipathy for the dominated group or its individuals. The dominant class(es) wants to help the dominated, but places them on subhuman level on the basis of its own standards. Contemporarily, the Muslims (in general) are viewed as a less developed and less advanced group in the modern world and need help for modernization (from orthodoxy). They are believed to be stuck in the past and it is the duty of the West to help them identify their problems, destinies, educate them and define them eventually. This perception leads to prejudgement of the group and the individuals. Runnymede Trust's definition of Islamophobia and orientalist's perspective towards Muslims and Islam, primarily, demonstrates this kind of prejudice.

Sexism/Feminism

A complete discipline of prejudice against women is also not included in the aforementioned definitions of prejudice. A considerable huge work has been done in this field but intentionally not taken up in this study as being a little irrelevant.

Stereotypes and Social Roles

Prejudice occurs mostly due to the discordance in stereotypes held by an individual (in his mind/psychologically) and the social/cultural role expected from the target person in a given social system. The perceiver feels that subject person does not possess the characteristics or attributes of the role he/she is being evaluated for and is inferior or from an inferior group. In a workplace environment, 'lack of fit model' by Heilman (1983) fits this approach, whereby occupational sex bias does not allow the same 'performance expectations' from female roles. However, in case of a female holding higher social status, the prejudice may be 'less positive' than being negative (e.g., a Muslim female doctor in the West may be less prejudiced in comparison to a common Muslim female who undertakes normal social chores and the stereotypes attached with her). Personal/affiliated qualities or the attributes of an individual despite being positive can also become a hindrance (in selection of that person in a recruitment process), if the role requirement is opposite to it.

Frame/Context of Prejudice

The variation in role expectation puts a frame of prejudice with which the prejudiced person sees individuals/groups and is contextual or can be general in nature (not being individual specific). Here, the context can be social or cultural (Blair, 2002) or current which guides the prejudice (e.g., an Asian may be easily viewed as an informant but not as an agent/official of the secret agencies in the West).

Levels of Stereotype— Role Inconsistency or Mismatch

There are different levels of inconsistency (with stereotypes) and the corresponding prejudice (from mild to moderate and to extreme). Moderate level produces subtle prejudices capable to channel the members into role sub-types, which are somewhat different from the main role type while remaining inside it, as identified by the American Medical Association (2000). This issue appears more of suitability for a role than the actual prejudice. The level of inconsistency produces corresponding level of prejudice while keeping other factors constant.

Change of Circumstances (Social, Political or Economic)

Change of circumstances leads to an opportunity for the discredited individual or group to get or gain access to the restricted/

non-traditional role(s); and if large number of prejudiced individuals try to do the same, then prejudice becomes a 'recognized social issue' in that particular society. Here, the path-breakers of this group are bitterly opposed than the rest. There may be some element of justification or rationality towards the stereotypically structured roles for the prejudiced (class) as being constructed so socially due to long socialization process making them appear fit for the typical roles (Hall, 1999). This rationality is traditionally aided by the perception (psychological) and motivation (defence of in-group) of the perceivers.

Prejudice Is a Social Problem

This stereotypical evaluation of perceiver restricts the perceived from assuming the aspired social roles for which they could be otherwise qualified (Diekman, 2005). In a society during its social stability, the prejudice remains latent but heterogeneity and 'upward movement urge' (of prejudiced groups) incite the dominant group subsequently, making it a challenge for the status quo of society. Nonetheless, societies with an urge to move upward socially, politically and economically suffer from this kind of challenge to supremacy of the dominant group, wherein prejudiced group(s) attempt to break the social barriers in the wake of upward social mobility.

Long-Term Accuracy

There is an issue of long-time accuracy of faulty generalizations as the generalization/stereotype can change over time, thus raising doubts about the old stereotype on which prejudice was initially based. The path-breakers (seeking social change) are mostly different from the rest of the group and mostly accused of having changed (Willie, 1975) as there is more often a rising tension in the group during the group's mobility. Recent research has also questioned the issue of inflexibility as stereotypes/beliefs are subject to context and dynamic in nature (Eagly, 2000). The new role becomes common or the 'new normal' and the prejudice dissipates after a large number joins the new role. The social system itself can contribute to social change (Allport, 1954).

Aggression Feeds on Itself/Feedback Model

Gordon Allport also proposed that aggression directed against out-group does not serve a cathartic function (like that in psychodynamic steam boiler model of aggression and catharsis). Instead, he believed that aggression feeds on itself, resulting in even worse relationships between the two groups (Pettigrew, 1999). This concept is also pertinent in scapegoat theory (scapegoat mechanism of philosopher Kenneth Burke).

In a nutshell, aim of the discussion is not only to provide an insight into the complexity of the construct but also to shed some light on the definitional issues and highlight latest research in the field. Nevertheless, still this concept needs to be explicated in the context of religion (or modern-day Islamophobia).

RELIGION AND PREJUDICE

Religious prejudice is one of the forms of prejudice and traces its origin from the day religions started interacting with each other. Historically, the conflict between religions may be witnessed in archaic religious literature and from the extremes of wars or battles fought for the domination of one religion or religious group over the other (like the crusades). The current omnipresence of anti-Islam prejudice (Islamophobia) though has the multiplication effect of ubiquitous media to it, it is nothing but a continuation. Current scholarship has also realized this quantum leap and defined Islamophobia as 'composite and multi-dimensional construct with its epistemic/symbolic dimensions having different connotations, the meaning of which needs to be distilled through its explication into less abstract dimensions' (Iqbal, 2010), where prejudice has a strong role to play. Many view present surge in anti-Islam and anti-Muslims sentiments merely as a heavily mediated construct; of which some believe that it has not much to do with the religion of Islam, but Muslims only (Halliday, 1999). This is because of the power of the media in conveying, explaining and articulating specific discourses that help represent or misrepresent a social group or minority on the basis of the interests involved. These media critics also argue that media misrepresentation has been influential in the spread of Islamophobia in the West, especially the recent outpouring of polemical sentiments against Muslims. Now the media has developed anti-Islamic prejudice and related stereotypes by putting a frame of the general attributes of a community or individual. All this has been done in a systematic manner when 'enemies' have been redefined after the end of the Cold War. Taking religious prejudice as a sub-type of the larger or general concept 'prejudice' (where at the base of the prejudice lays the religious orientation of the perceiver or the perceived), the current victims are the Muslims, who are also facing persecution of varying nature as a by-product. The current actions against Islam point out to the fact that orientation/belief system can at times override the individual and social categorization in vogue. This is visible when given a choice a White person prefers a coloured person of the same belief/religion over a White person of a different belief system, for example, the recent genocide/killing in Burma of Rohingya Muslims by the community who had previously been living with each other. The relation of religion with prejudice is a complex one and needs detailed understanding. Current work on belief system/religion points towards a relationship, which has rightly been put in words by Allport (1954) when he says, 'Religion makes Prejudice and it unmakes Prejudice' (p. 444).

Generally, most religions of the world have a basic or common distinction of liberal or conservative, wherein conservative dimension believes it to be the only true religion and its followers are the chosen ones to follow the religion by God Himself (Dewick, 1953). This self-selectiveness not only enhances the self or group self-esteem of followers but also justifies the proclaimed system of their superiority over others, which subsequently creates prejudice (like in-group prejudice or positive prejudice of own group). All these religions have a core 'doctrinal level' which is mostly the same or universal (love for all humanity and other positive features); however, the other level commonly known as 'teaching level' can be different for different religions (mostly in practical dimensions). These teachings can be internalized differently by individuals on the basis of three dimensions of religiousness in them—these are 'extrinsic', which is related to political or social aspects where religion is a means to different interests; 'intrinsic' on the other hand is related to personalization, commitment and devotion to the religion and finally the 'quest' dimension, which relates to finding of deeper reality or final truth of a religion. In this case, for example, if teachings of 'universal compassion/love for all humanity' are internalized by an individual, this will un-make prejudice in him/her, whereas if teachings of God's chosen of own superior group are heavily internalized by an individual, it will ultimately create prejudice in him/her. Here, the committed form of intrinsic religion relates to reducing prejudice but paradoxically this esteem/motivation may also create a sense of privileged status that tends to increase the animosity/prejudice towards others' religions or out-group. Hence, the line of division becomes quite complex and thin at times.

The contemporary research has reached this current understanding through evolution of the concept on historical timeline. Early researchers (taking the prevalent extreme end of Western interpretation of religion as 'a highly personal matter'; Kelle, 2007, p. 302) divided the religion into two broad categories, which could simply be named as 'teachings and practical'. Historically, every religion teaches tolerance, whereas, in practice, it seems to be the most violated religious trait in almost every religion of the world.

For ease of understanding/identification of the two divisions and their relation to prejudice, they are presented in the following table as conceived by the renowned scholars.

Theodore Adorno Identification	Allport's Early Identification	Allport's Next Identification	Allport's Final Identification	Relation to Prejudice
Neutralized	Immature	Institutionalized (political/social ends)	Extrinsic (as a mean)	Creates/ increases prejudice
Internalized (real religion)	Mature (universalistic teachings)	Interiorized (commitment and devotion)	Intrinsic (as an end)	Decreases/ no prejudice

Without understanding Allport's intrinsic–extrinsic religious distinction, it would be quite difficult to grasp the subtleties attached with the prejudice construct. The earlier table follows two distinct lines: intrinsic and extrinsic; wherein extrinsic line, the prejudice towards other religions is either created or increased due to increased institutionalization towards political and social ends mainly provided by the religion in practical dimension. On the other hand, increased maturity to the teachings of religion makes one less prejudiced or not prejudiced at all. Allport's assumption, if put in a simplistic fashion, denotes that maturity in understanding the religion is greatly associated with the measures of prejudice. Hypothetical proposition would then be: more the measures of maturity (intrinsic), less the measures of prejudice; and less the measures of maturity (extrinsic), more the measures of prejudice. In this way, intrinsic propensities help one take religion as an end, whereas with extrinsic propensities, one takes religion as a means to reach an end, which may create prejudice towards 'others'.

Taking a lead from this, Ross and Allport identified that both (intrinsic and extrinsic) are not the opposite ends of the same scale/continuum, but are independent of each other (Ross, 1967). Gorsuch (1972) further developed this in a 'three-step frequency of involvement model' giving out three levels of religiousness as follows (Gorsuch, 1972):

Involvement in Religious Activities	Religiousness
No/low	Non-religious
Moderate	Extrinsically religious
High	Intrinsically religious

Later, Batson and Schoenrade (1993) while reviewing studies on prejudice during the period 1949–1990 taking samples from the USA also substantiated the earlier distinction. They also redefined the earlier division/distinction as follows:

Old Dimensions of Religion	Redefined
Extrinsic	Religion as a means
Intrinsic	Religion as an end
	Religion as a *quest* (a new dimension of personal religious concerns—degree to which one seeks to face religious issues such as final truth and reality)

In case of Islam, it is presented as a *deen*[2] where unquestionable sovereignty belongs to Allah. Theoretically, there is only one definition of Islam; however, practically there are different interpretations while remaining within the cardinal beliefs. Like other religions, aforementioned definition may also be found true in case of Islam in practice, and prejudice prevails against other religions.

DEFINITION AND REVISION OF RELATIONSHIP BETWEEN RELIGION AND PREJUDICE

Foregoing discussion leads to further revision in definition of prejudice in 'proscribed' and 'non-proscribed' dimensions of the religion. Here, proscribed means not permitted or explicitly opposed commissions or omissions, whereas non-proscribed means permitted or implicitly encouraged acts by a religion (Herek, 1987). Along with that (according to methods of measurement or observation), prejudice was also defined as overt (self-reported by an individual) and covert (existing subtle form of prejudice in a person) omission or commission of an act. The new juxtapositioning of three dimensions of religion (intrinsic, extrinsic and quest) against two types of prejudice (overt and covert) and the way they could be presented is as follows:

---

[2] *Deen* is a composite set of rules and laws that are universal in nature and are for all times and are not for one society or group of people, but for the whole humanity; unlike the religion, which is primarily spiritual in nature and provides specific guidelines for its followers.

PROSCRIBED PREJUDICES

Method of Measurement/ Observation	Relations with Three Dimensions of Religion		
	Extrinsic	Intrinsic	Quest
Overt	Increased prejudice (+)	Decreased prejudice (−)	Decreased prejudice (−)
Covert	Increased prejudice (+)	Increased prejudice (+)	Decreased prejudice (−)

The relation of intrinsic propensity with overt and covert observations is further explained. A change has often been observed in intrinsic propensity in religion where when asked overtly, the respondent claims or reports decreased prejudice, whereas, in fact, it is an increase, according to different tests.

NON-PROSCRIBED PREJUDICES

Method of Measurement/ Observation	Relation with Three Dimensions of Religion		
	Extrinsic	Intrinsic	Quest
Overt	No relation	Increased prejudice (+)	Decreased prejudice (−)
Covert	No relation	Increased prejudice (+)	Decreased prejudice (−)

To sum up, it can be stated that the relation of religion with prejudice is a complex one and further research may answer the remaining questions. However, it can be identified that the context is extremely important in this relationship. Context can outrightly change the dimension from being positive to negative and vice versa. The second important factor is the understanding of the religion by a person and his related interests, which can create or reduce prejudice in him. Here, the religion attains a neutral position and real issue is of how it is used by a person or a group. Consequently, the prejudice (phobia) against Islam stands on weak grounds.

HISTORY OF PREJUDICE AGAINST MUSLIMS/ISLAM

Historically, the relations between Muslims and followers of Christianity and Judaism have always been adversarial since the birth of Islam in the early 7th century. Islam was taken as an enemy religion; born to exterminate other religions as being different from them ideologically and culturally. This state of enmity turned into a struggle for domination of ideologies, which is still continued and has taken many shapes before reaching the present state. This also included cultural warfare and struggle to have control over the common holy places among Muslims, Christians and Judaists on which manifestation can be seen on the issue of Jerusalem today. This historical adversary has resulted in Muslims appearing as eternal enemy to their opponents with stereotyping them as inferior, culturally, religiously and somewhat racially. As said earlier, this conflict began soon after the rise of Islam in the 7th century when Arab Muslims clashed with the Roman Empire, which used to control most of the Middle East. As a result, the Roman Empire was defeated at the hands of gallant Muslim warriors and forced out of the region by a rising Muslim power. Few centuries after the defeat, European Christendom waged crusade/war (11th–14th centuries) and occupied large regions of the Middle East, especially the Holy Land of Jerusalem. It took Muslims about four centuries to drive the crusaders out. Towards the end of the crusade, the Ottoman Muslim Empire (1299–1923) was established. Within a few centuries, the Ottomans controlled most of the Middle East, North Africa, Central Asia and Southeast Europe. Ottomans' rule over large parts of Europe fuelled European's resentment and increased their hostility towards the Ottomans, in particular, and Muslims, in general. From 18th to 20th centuries, Europeans rebounded and colonized almost all the Muslim lands in the Middle East and North Africa. Conflict peaked in the 20th century with fight for independence from the colonization in various parts of the world by the Muslims and non-Muslim countries alike. Other conflicts include the establishment of Israel with the unwavering support by the West, Arab Israeli War in the 1960s, Iraq War in 1990, 11 September 2001 attack on twin towers in New York, Afghan War, the Second Iraq War and the ongoing war on terror. Hence, with every passing day, the centuries-old misunderstanding, mistrust, cultural clash and military conflict increased, which took many shapes in the realm of history, of which prejudice towards Muslims and Islam is one of the most visible.

In the US history, the existence of prejudice remained more centric to racial prejudice against the minorities (mainly Afro-Americans/Blacks) and was quite persistent as compared to that of Europe. The racial segregation had legal backstopping till 1954 when in a case (*Brown v. Board of Education of Topeka, Kansas*) it was ruled that segregation in public schools is unconstitutional. In 1955, a Black woman Rosa Parks refused to give up her seat at the front of the 'coloured section' of a bus to a White passenger, which led to protest/boycott till these buses were desegregated a year later through the efforts of Reverend Martin Luther King, Jr In 1957, nine Black students were blocked from entering the school on the orders of Governor Orval Faubus till the intervention of National Guard. In 1965, Malcolm X (Afro-American Unity) was shot dead for allegedly abandoning Blacks in favour of Islam, and in 1968 Martin Luther King, Jr. working for Black rights was killed. It can be inferred from these instances that the contemporary history identified further augmentation of prejudice; however, this time the means were different for the old ends. At the end of the Cold War in December 1991, the 'communist boogey man' of the USSR was finally disintegrated by the US efforts (overt/covert) and with it went the theory of 'Red Scare' null and void. However, till that time, the (needed) fear of communism guided the policies of governments (and correspondingly the public) of the USA. This state-sponsored fear had created enough panic and prejudice against communism till then, but now a policy was needed to shift the target posts to a new fear/prejudice. At that time came the article of Samuel P. Huntington in 1993 titled 'The Clash of Civilizations' as an extremely important foreign policy document in the new unipolar world. Huntington (1993) saw the primary drivers of conflicts moving from princes to nations, to ideologies and now finally to civilizations (or simply cultural). The contemporary legacy of this article is drawn not so much because of its 'correctness' or 'rightness' but rather its influence due to the precise way in which it captured the zeitgeist of the post-Cold War world and also because of the powerful statement it had made about globalization, capturing both the hopes and fears present in the West (Haynes, 2013). This clash had already been identified by Lewis (1990) stating, 'This is no less than a clash of civilizations—the perhaps irrational but surely historic reaction of an ancient rival against our Judeo-Christian heritage, our secular present and worldwide expansion of both'. Resultantly, over the later historical episodes, the perception of individual Muslims as 'violent' entity led to an association of Muslims in general with violence and threat, and the perception of Muslim communities (also in Western countries) as a 'fifth column' working for a globally threatening and aggressive Islam (Roland & Julia, 2012). As per Iranian origin Professor Arshin Adib-Moghaddam, this theory of clash of cultures seems to have taken the form of an ideology, which now perpetuates the narratives of 'us' versus 'them' (Moghaddam, 2008). One of its reinvigoration was through the infamous words of President Bush in 2001, 'Either you are with us, or you are with the terrorists', which again reconstituted the 'us and them' structure; obviously indicating 'them' as terrorists, albeit particularly towards political Islam.

THE FIRST VICTIM OF PREJUDICE

Religious prejudice started from the birth of first religion and the most talked about group prejudice was against the Jews. It is now (since the 19th century) being called anti-Semitism (people who spoke old Semitic language or the Jews and Arabs) and is related to race and religion. This prejudice has mutated over history from ethnic to religious and to race while maintaining the basic theme of protecting the community. Throughout history, persecution has been the obvious result of this prejudice where different historical events were linked to it. Notable instances of persecution include the Rhineland massacres preceding the First Crusade in 1096, the Edict of Expulsion from England in 1290, the massacres of Spanish Jews in 1391, the persecutions of the Spanish Inquisition, the expulsion from Spain in 1492, the Cossack massacres in Ukraine from 1648 to 1657, various anti-Jewish pogroms in the Russian Empire between 1821 and 1906, the 1894–1906 Dreyfus affair in France, the Holocaust in German-occupied Europe, official Soviet anti-Jewish policies, and Arab and Muslim involvement in the Jewish exodus from Arab and Muslim countries. However, in the recent history, the bounce back of Jewish community had been more violent and counterproductive. It can be easily said that here religion has constructed the prejudice, while it was also the reason of earlier unmaking.

THE CONTEMPORARY PREJUDICE

According to global political history, the recent anti-Muslim antipathy (as a phenomenon) can be traced back to major events like Arab–Israel Wars of 1967–1973, the Iranian Islamic Revolution of 1979, Salman Rushdie's or Taslima Nasrin's publications of 1988–1993 or the Gulf War of 1991 or Iraqi Invasion of 2003. Nonetheless, the incident that provided impetus was violent attacks on the World Trade Center at the hands of self-proclaimed Islamic terrorists on 11 September 2001, which made several researchers to warn a dramatic rise of Islamophobia and the wariness and concerns about Islam and Muslims. It is worth mentioning that just a few days before 9/11, the UN had formally recognized Islamophobia, thereby establishing anti-Muslim and anti-Islamic prejudice, discrimination and hatred, and placing it alongside other equally discriminatory and exclusionary phenomena, like anti-Semitism (Allen, 2010).

PREJUDICE IN LITERATURE

Archaic Literature

Antagonism towards Islam was even evident in the 7th and 8th centuries, when, along with blasphemous contents, Islam had been termed as mere 'apostasy' and a sort of 'barbaric paganism of the time' by a Christian scholar John of Damascus in the Umayyad period. Later, the split of Greek Orthodox Church (Eastern) and Roman Catholic Church (Western) in 1054 forced Pope Urban II to ask for unity of Byzantine and Rome for a common enemy (Islam) under the famous crusades. For nearly 200 years, between 1095 and 1291, the forces of Christendom tried to wrest control of the Holy Land (Jerusalem) at the eastern end of the Mediterranean from the Islamic forces (which controlled it then). Later, history repeated itself when this fear was envisaged about the military expansions of Turks/Muslims in the 16th century. Although, at this time, it was also substantiated by Sultan Suleiman's campaigns in Europe (he reached Vienna in 1529 then capturing vast regions). This was primarily the reason why Islam was taken as a prelude to the Ottoman Onslaught that was never liked. The most popular 16th-century book *Acts and Monuments* (1563) of John Foxe was then full of prayers (for the Christians) and prejudice against the Muslims. Later, antipathy to Muslims dominated every branch of post-Reformation writings. In 1649, Alexander Ross published the Quran in English with a blasphemous/humorous tone. Although the military momentum declined in the last quarter of the 16th century, the retreat started after the defeat of Vienna in 1683. Shortly after the initial period of denial by the end of the 17th century, scholars like John Locke called for inclusion of Muslims in the mainstream. Although this had an effect, the prejudice persistently continued in literature/writings. *Broughton's Dictionary of All Religions* (1745) categorized the world religions into two types of religions the 'true religions' (Christianity and Judaism) and 'false religions' (all other religions, including Islam; Dewick, 1953). In the 18th, 19th and 20th centuries, due to repeat rebounding of the West against the Ottoman Empire, the tone of the prejudice of the West increased manifold. The Balkan War of 1912–1913 was even termed by British press as a 'Crusade against Islam' (O'Leary, 1923). Colonialism was a practical manifestation of the Western prejudice reaching its peak in the 20th century. The 21st century has now become the harbinger of 'shock and awe' for the Muslims and Islam. Presence of anti-Muslim prejudice in early modern Europe was identified by different researchers like Matar (2009). In the writings then, there were two views about Muslims (negative and positive) based on absence or presence of direct contact with them (the first was generated by literary and theological writers whose depictions were predominantly negative and stereotypical, whereas the positive was of diplomats and traders who have had direct interaction with Muslims). In those days, people like John Lock were an exception. This also had an effect on art and paintings of that time, where Muslims were shown to be complicit in the crucifixion of Jesus. The Crucifixion by the Umbrian painter Luca Signorelli (now in the National Gallery in Washington, DC) shows soldiers surrounding the cross of Jesus with banners flying the Turkish symbol of the crescent. The Crucifixion by the workshop of the German painter Hans Mielich (also in the National Gallery) shows a soldier wearing a Muslim turban. The altarpiece by an unknown Flemish artist (now in the Philadelphia Museum of Art) shows Turks and other turbaned horsemen at the foot of the cross, carrying spears. On altarpieces and in paintings and tapestries (wall hangings), from Spain to Italy and Malta, Muslims were depicted as the crucifiers of Christ and the enemies of Christianity.

MODERN LITERATURE

Since the publication of Edward Said's *Orientalism* in the late 1970s (Said, 1978), it has been widely accepted that 'the West' has associated Islam with negative stereotypes. He substantiated the 'subtle and persistent Eurocentric prejudice against Arabic-Islamic people and their culture'; nonetheless, this claim of him is challenged in the earlier chapters. He focused on European prejudice towards 'others', particularly Islam and Muslims, which the Occident considers as 'static in both time and place, and incapable of defining themselves' in comparison to Western culture which is claimed to be a 'dynamic, innovative and expanding culture'. He divided the world geographically into two disproportionate parts known as 'Western world' called 'the Occident' (or the West) and the outsized and 'different' one called 'the Orient' (the East). He noted that this notion of 'the Occident' as opposed to 'the Orient' covertly provides legitimization of Western supremacy and colonial power over the other. This was also substantiated by Homi K. Bhabha in the form of overlapping binary oppositions (Bhabha, 1994). Fred Halliday while agreeing to this attempted to break the confrontational myth between the East and the West. He, however, agreed with Huntington's centrality of culture for future conflicts.

Antagonism towards Islam spanning over centuries has led to the emergence of anti-Islamic and anti-Muslim racial and cultural sentiments in contemporary times. The racial dimension has resurged once again due to expansion and rapid conversions to Islam contemporarily, which swiftly challenges the West on theological, political and cultural grounds. Usage of word 'crusades' by George W. Bush may not be taken as a coincidence, nor is the common collocation of words like Islamic jihadists and others (Love, 2013/2014). Termed as 'neologism' and translated as 'fear of Islam', Islamophobia is considered the most dangerous form of prejudice and discrimination against individuals on the basis of their religious belief like Islam (Allen, 2007).

CURRENT SITUATION

Rise of the right-wing populist parties in mainstream European politics since the start of this century is a clear indication of the public mood or the sentiments there (for instance, Alternative for Germany [AfD] in Germany, Jobbik[3] in Hungary, Front National in France, Golden Dawn in Greece, Freedom Party of Austria [FPO][4] in Austria, True Finns in Finland, Party for Freedom [PVV][5] in Netherlands, Lega Nord[6] in Italy, SD and Danish People Party). Prejudice is also quite evident in their undertakings and policy statements. For example, AfD changed its slogan to 'Islam is not a part of Germany' in its Spring Conference 2016. However, on this, Doctor Ruth Wodak gave a different view while pointing out that this rise of populist parties across Europe has different reasons in different countries, and only in the Netherlands, Denmark, Poland, Sweden and Switzerland, the focus is primarily on a perceived threat from Islam. In Austria, Hungary, Italy, Romania and France, it is relationship with fascist and Nazi pasts; while in Hungary, Greece, Italy and the UK, it is a perceived threat to their national identities from ethnic minorities and finally in Poland, Romania and Bulgaria, it is a fundamentalist Christian's conservative–reactionary agenda (Wodak, 2014).

---

[3] Jobbik is a Movement for a Better Hungary and is a Hungarian political party with radical and nationalist roots.

[4] FPO is a right-wing populist and non-conservative political party.

[5] Dutch: *Partij voor de Vrijheid*.

[6] Lega Nord stands for North League.

In the USA, Republicans under Donald Trump are far more anti-Islam/Muslims than its ally the 'Tea Party Movement'[7] and the organization like 'Stop the Islamization of America' (Townsend, 2014). Tea Party Movement has links with English Defence League of the UK and the Canadian Jewish Defense League, Danish Defence League, the NDL and so on (for anti-Islam prejudice and activities). Various recent polls (Pew and Gallup) also point towards the wariness of the West towards Islam and Muslims, especially in the backdrop of terrorist-related incidents and the resurging propaganda related to it. Pervasive global media of the time is playing an instigator role in augmenting the divide as before.

However, the situation is not as bleak as it appears to be and a considerable work has been done in other direction. A good example to quote is the Forum Against Islamophobia & Racism (FAIR), which is a charitable organization based in the UK, founded in 2001 with the aim to eliminate Islamophobia and racism from the British society. FAIR recognizes Islamophobia as a form of racism and believes that the construct has many similarities with 'anti-Semitism'. It observes the manifestation of Islamophobia in the form of verbal or written abuse, discrimination at schools and workplaces, harassment and outright violent attacks on mosques and individuals. On the other side, the CAIR is an American organization, which fights against Islamophobia. CAIR was created in June 1994 with the aim to develop understanding of Islam and fight for the rights of American Muslims. It defines Islamophobia as the 'unfounded fear of and hostility towards Islam'. In its view, the growing Islamophobia is the real cause of the acts of violence against Muslims.

IS ISLAMOPHOBIA A FACET OF PREJUDICE?

Linguistically, Islamophobia is a vague term or word, which is basically a construct of two words, that is, Islam and phobia. Meaning of Islam is widely understood, whereas the definition of phobia provided by

---

[7] This is a movement by the conservationists in the USA, who associate it with the Tea Party Movement started from Boston in 1773 considered to be one of the most important movements that caused American Revolution.

the American Psychiatric Association states that it is 'an anxiety disorder which is defined by a persistent fear of an object, class of objects, organism or a situation'.[8] It is a mental representation, which is not expected to match the world reality (of the external world) of what the phobia is about. For example, we may talk about social phobia or people having a mental representation of what the crowd is, so that they are scared to go there; but more often, there is nothing wrong with the crowd, unless it is orgy or emotionally charged. We may also hear about claustrophobia (again a mental disorder), which is about a fear of being enclosed in an inside or closed space. Phobia is in fact a medical term that refers to one type of deep-seated mental illness (mental disorder) and should only be used in medical contexts and by the medical experts. If people are undertaking or experiencing it, they are, in literal terms, patients and need medical help. Phobia also implies ignorance and fear (of unknown) that projects an element of negativity in the one who fosters it among the potential victims. Here, Muslims may not like it to be attributed to Islam, reflecting negative connotation of the wording towards their religion. On the other hand, if one is to claim that people are being Islamophobes, he has to prove that this stems from irrational and extreme fear, which cannot be a prejudice itself but a cause of it.

In a language, when a word is incorporated in its usage, there are two aspects of it: first, what is being offered through the word and second, what that word has inherently in it, and if there is a gap/distance between the two, complications in its comprehension are quite natural. Resultantly, the word or construct might need some degree of social conditioning along with its original meanings. When we take a word, we take the concept, and we become conditioned by its definition socially and become capable of understanding its meanings, because meanings are in the minds and not in words, which are produced through social conditioning associated with the word/construct. Here, on its presentation, one may ask to change the definition of words 'Islam' and 'phobia' for its detailed/comprehensive interpretation, which linguistically presents a weak case. A word should also be

---

[8] Retrieved from https://www.psychiatry.org/patients-families/anxiety-disorders/what-are-anxiety-disorders.

the best to describe the current situation or what it is meant for (here, 'anti-Islam prejudice' seems more appropriate than Islamophobia). The suffix (connoting 'irrationality') can exonerate those whose hostility is cold and calculated, bearing no relation to the irrational aspect at all. The words such as 'bigotry' and 'grudge' best define the deep-rooted feelings of animosity towards Muslims and Islam.

Islam is an ideology and as per universal liberal principles and the human rights dictates, the people (Muslims) need to be protected instead of an ideology (Islam). Hence, anti-Muslim prejudice is a more victim-centred terminology than the ideology as it sounds. Even if the implication of the same is desired, there remains a need of disentangling both the words/concepts (Muslim and Islam) as both have a different meaning and use. Historically, the word came before its definition (in the literature), leaving the phenomenon of Islamophobia aside, which has, in fact, created problems for its interpretations. Ignorance of Islam is yet another aspect; rather, it is one of the major reasons for the antipathy against Islam, and the same has not been represented in the term (Islamophobia). Prejudice is quite a human feeling and is described as an unfair and unreasonable opinion or feelings formed without enough thought or knowledge. So it represents the concept well. According to the concept of freedom of academic lexical creation, any word can be created by people for use even if it does not represent the concept. Nevertheless, if the word is persistently held in vogue, the time factor can ultimately provide substantiality to it. Another aspect is of the relation of the word with the phenomenon it represents. Ideally it should be strong, but we see many words in use have a weak link to the phenomenon they represent, but still they are being used and understood.

The Runnymede report released in 1997 titled 'Islamophobia: A Challenge for Us All', offering two analytic frameworks of 'open/closed' views of Islam and ways in which Islamophobia is manifested in British society, ushered an exhaustive debate on Islamophobia. A follow-up report was also released lately in November 2017 claiming that the phenomenon of Islamophobia has now become more complex and entrenched with ideological and intellectual justification or rationalizing the stereotype or bigotry towards Muslims and Islam.

The Runnymede report also acknowledged the shortcomings of this term in this report stating:

> It must be acknowledged that the term 'Islamophobia' has itself led to some confusions and 'The definition therefore is not simply what Runnymede thinks is the best analytical account of what Islamophobia is'… Runnymede believes the focus on ideas (or 'ideologies') has obscured what instead should be a focus on people… Too many criticisms of Islamophobia suffer from bad-faith literalism and more than the suffix 'phobia', the first part 'Islam' has generated greater and deeper challenges. Many have argued that Islam as a religion is a system of beliefs, and so can and should be subject to criticism…An increasingly common argument is that Islam is a set of ideas and so there is no more a concept of Islamophobia than there is a concept of 'Communismphobia' or 'Christophobia'. Proponents of this view typically argue they are being rebuked for criticism of ideas, and many further argue that the term 'Islamophobia' itself is dishonestly used to shut down debate.

Taking advantage of confusion encircling the term, *The Guardian* columnist Polly Toynbee wrote, 'I am an Islamophobe, and proud of it' (Aly, 2011), while *The Sunday Times* columnist Rod Liddle rhetorically asks in the title of a speech, 'count me in'.[9] They took the claim that it was based on distrust of a religious ideology and not hatred of Muslims as a group and following the liberal religious orientation they have the right to object to any religion they want (Jones, 2008). However, the question still stays whether 'Can they be so candid for anti-Semitism or not?' A counterargument is that this all has been done systematically to problematize the term at the outset, so that little attention is directed to the phenomenon the term is pointing to.

Academicians working on the subject have considered prejudice to be one of the most significant elements of Islamophobia, covering both racism and ideological backdrop of the religion. It is also a researched fact that initial prejudices had their origination from the prejudices against 'others' (the non-White races) as 'This is not to deny that Islamophobia primarily originated from prejudices against a "non-white" race' (Garth, 1925). In sum, most of the scholars contend that no definition of the phenomenon is generally agreed upon, while

---

[9] Retrieved from http://www.telegraph.co.uk/comment/personal-view/3644280/It-is-proper-to-challenge-Islam.html.

different dimensions of Islamophobia have been essayed in various definitions covering cognitive, affective and conative posturing (Zafar, 2010). Complete understanding of any phenomenon is only possible if we take account of the mix of historical, political, economic and social structural forces at work in any given context. Here, historical repetition of the construct (Islamophobia) points towards the assertion that this contemporary term is though presently a new one, the problem which it identifies is quite old (the prejudice against Muslims). The politics/political process includes policies or legislation (like basic civil rights and immigration policies), which directly affect the lives of minority Muslim community or groups who live in different parts of the world. These also contribute to the ideological frameworks of various other ethnic groups as to how they are valued differentially in a society.

Economic factors may also play an important role in governing relations between groups in any particular society. When one group has the means and is willing to capture territory from another, for the purposes of economic exploitation (examples of British colonization/Imperialism and the current US hegemony), the religious and racist beliefs are often developed in justification. At the social level, there are two dimensions of the composite, one being the 'individual as individual' and the other as 'individual being the member of a group'. In the case of contemporary prejudice, the realization has come and the link/relation is more towards the second kind, especially in the overt dimension.

At the end, it can be stated that prejudice against Muslims has been given a unique identification or has been named Islamophobia. Its old name was prejudice against Muslims but now has been further described as Islamophobia. The literary criticism or the anti-Muslim prejudice (following the political orientation of religion in the West) has been divided into two main facets. First, the actual prejudice/bigotry against the Muslims/Islam and second, the legitimate/secular criticism of Islam/Muslims as a religion/practice (Imhoff & Recker, 2012). Imhoff and Recker (2012) also criticized the term Islamophobia as an expandable neologism of prejudice/discrimination against Muslim immigrants (in the form of racism) and is a discursive weapon to silence the well-motivated criticism of Islam and its practices (he has stated that it conceals more than it illuminates). He proposed to refer to this prejudiced views against Islam/Muslims with a term 'Islamo-prejudice' rather than Islamophobia stating, 'To support the usefulness of this concept it needs to be shown that it is an internally consistent concept, has any incremental value above and beyond existing prejudice scales, and that it is not just a denunciatory term for a secular critique of Islam'.[10] The term Islamophobia was also criticized by Halliday (1999) on the same by claiming that real enemy is the people and not the faith or culture. He also stated that

> [T]he term Islamophobia also challenged the possibility of dialogue based on universal principles as it suggested 'that the solution lies in greater dialogue, bridge-building, respect for the other community' while running the risk of 'denying the right, or possibility, of criticisms of the practices of those with whom one is having the dialogue'. (Halliday, 2001)

Brown (1995) sums up the whole argument when he terms Islamophobia as a specific case of prejudice. He says:

> I believe it is more useful to regard these as special cases of the more general phenomenon of prejudice. In this way we do not exclude from our discussion important intergroup prejudices such as some forms of religious bigotry which do not have any obvious biological component. (p. 8)

Inferences from the discussion help us conceive the term Islamophobia as pointing towards the fact that it can be interchanged with Islamo-prejudice or Muslimo-prejudice as they represent the same phenomenon for one being the sub-type of other. The term is in use despite the criticism for being true representative or not of the phenomenon. But it is believed that there are problems with the term Islamophobia and the need is high to formulate a workable term and the foregoing discussion might help in this regard. Gary Goertz (a political scientist) has developed an analysis of social scientific concepts that focuses on their multilevel and multidimensional nature. He breaks the term into

---

[10] Retrieved from https://www.academia.edu/545302/Differentiating_Islamophobia_Introducing_a_new_scale_to_measure_Islamoprejudice_and_Secular_Islam_Critique, accepted for publication in *Political Psychology*.

three core levels: the basic level, the secondary level and the indicator level, which is more akin to the process of operationalizing a concept (Goertz, 2005). However, the earlier discussion hardly leaves any room to challenge prejudice and Islamophobia as not being inter-related directly.

CONCLUSION

Islam and Muslims (though not a monolithic entity) have been experiencing the waves of history with ups and downs of the times. Just like the history of prejudice and Islamophobia, it is also evident that the current time is not among the cherished ones. The examples of inner conflicts and disunity can easily be observed in the Middle Eastern theatre of the world. The divide between East and West (or South and North) is at its extreme in all its facets (economics, political, cultural and social, etc.). The responsibilities of both ends of the continuum have ever increased while warranting a more resolute response for mutual coexistence. Both ends should search for commonalities (than fissures/differences) as we have only one world to live in.

Current waves of terror termed as Islamophobia in the Western world, and especially Europe, warrant an in-depth and more detailed or elaborate effort on the complex relation of religion and prejudice. Unexplored dimensions are to be seen under the new scenarios where prejudice is increasing progressively. Winning of elections or emergence of populist right-wing parties in the West, which are predominantly anti-Islamic or anti-Muslim in their agenda, is also a point of concern now. As more research has been done by the West, being one-sided and from the position of strength, a multidimensional research is needed on core factors of motivation and psychological propensities (than the automatic processes of categorization, stereotyping, prejudgement and misperception). These deficient factors, which need to be addressed, are simplification and overgeneralization, resistance to getting further information, the common defensiveness and rationalization, the leading biased decisions that served psychological functions of the concerned and the role played in life of an individual in current times (current religious prejudices and the leading gruesome acts). The xenophobia (phobia of people from other countries) against the backdrop of 9/11 catastrophe, and other related religious prejudices, need to be seen in unbiased fashion covering both dimensions of motivation and personality in the present context.

In relation between religion and prejudice, there is also a need to integrate psychological dimension/personality perspective with the social domain (social identity perspective/group membership) as both are important and have consequential interlinkage/effects on each other (in both directions, namely between individual and group religions or personality–social structures). The intrinsic religion can overcome in-group biases/ethnocentrism of (membership biased) institutionalized religion, and the devotion to religious teachings of universal tolerance/compassion can create a personality whose master motive (motive of life) of integration will dissolve categorization and barriers (Allport, 1954). The decrease of overt form of prejudice in the world and increase of covert prejudice also needs to be analysed under current scenario along with different new categorizations (symbolic racism, modern racism, aversive racism, subtle prejudice, modern sexism, neo-sexism and ambivalent sexism, etc.).

Allport (1954) argued that 'aggression feeds on itself'. It means that acting out of aggression, rather than leading to catharsis and less aggression, actually increases the probability that further aggression will be expressed (Allen, 2010). On this, he advocates for government policies, which should reduce the levels of prejudice. He also proposed inter-group contact as people who frequently interact with people across their cultural are pruned to prejudice or fear from them. Many earlier writers believed that less or no contact between groups is dangerous and is likely to lead to enhanced prejudice and conflict. He, however, asserted that contact alone only sets the scene for change; what mattered most is the situational conditions for the inter-group interaction (in other words, four situational conditions lead to reduced prejudice, which may include equal status of the groups in the situation, common goals, no inter-group competition and authority sanction; Pettigrew, 2011).

Cultural and Religious Racism

HISTORICAL PERSPECTIVE OF RACISM AND RELIGIOUS RACISM

The 'blood libels' against Jews that started in the medieval times were established with a conviction that blood could pass on holy or mysterious properties. The idea, verifiable in these allegations, that Christian blood contrasted from Jewish was unmistakably attested in the 16th-century Spanish notion of *limpieza de sangre*.[1] In any case, the way that distinctive assortments of creatures of similar species could interbreed, as could all people, implied that such pre-current hereditarianism did not debilitate the universal confidence in the fundamental solidarity of mankind. In the 17th and 18th centuries and the past, the expression 'race' or its proportionate was additionally as often as possible used to allude to countries or communities—as in 'races whether it is French race or white race?' Whenever and wherever it was utilized, in any case, the term inferred that 'races' had stable and probably unchangeable attributes (Smedley & Smedley, 2012).

The notion that Jews, overall and genetically, were the most conceivable awful human creatures was an effective motivating force for their persecution. If it was considered true, then the revile fell on Jews in such a way that they would never be exculpated of it; racism would probably be an appropriate term to define the partiality against them. Nonetheless, the doctrine, as explained by Saint Augustine and others, that the change of the Jews was a Christian obligation and basic to the salvation of the world, implied that the immense hereditary sin

---

[1] *limpieza de sangre* means 'blood purity' in English.

was not a permanent and unrealistic wellspring of distinction. Anti-Judaism move, towards becoming a discrimination against Jews, transformed into a devouring disdain that made disposing of Jews appear to be desirable; in an attempt to change them, discrimination against Jews progressed towards becoming prejudice when the conviction grabbed hold that Jews were characteristically and naturally abhorrent as opposed to only having false convictions and wrong manners (D'Souza, 1995; Fredrickson, 1998).

The concept based on 'White' or 'European race' was slightly slow to evolve and until the 18th century, this could not solidify. The previous experiences associated with Africans witness mindful hate, which was commonly understood as based on religious affiliations and national identity, while it did not rest merely on national identity but some particularly acquired characteristics. When social disparity on the basis of colour was simply the general run among Europeans, shading coded bigotry had little extension for self-governing improvement. In the new world, where European pigmentation could be promptly contrasted with that of dark slaves or copper-coloured Indians, shading soon ended up completely and got replaced with a single notable character. In the North American states, dark colour is still contrasted with the terms 'Christian, free, English, and white were for a long time utilized indiscriminately as metonyms' (Peters & Wemheuer-Vogelaar, 2016).

To imagine racism as a characteristic and for all intents and almost inescapable human reaction to experience with strangers is to take the subject outside of history and into the domain of psychology or sociobiology. However, if we keep on thinking of it as an authentic development related with the ascent of innovation and with particular national or global settings, we need to presume that it worked out as expected in the 20th century. Its two most tireless and harmful appearances—the colour-coded or White racial oppressor assortment and discrimination against Jews in its naturalistic or common shape—achieved their sensible extremes. Racial domination achieved its fullest ideological and institutional advancement in the Southern United States between 1890 and 1950, and in South Africa between 1910 and 1980, particularly after 1948 (Fredrickson, 2015). Cell's (1982) origin of American and South African isolation as the 'most noteworthy phase of white domination attracts regard for the connection amongst modernization and legitimize racism' (Kousser, 1983).

It is broadly trusted that racism remains a noteworthy worldwide issue at the beginning of the 21st century. The term is in use in few countries and in a few circles to depict antagonistic vibe and discrimination against a group for any reason; at times, utterly inexplicable. The French, for instance, some of the time use the term to depict biases established on sexual orientation, sex or age. Generally, at times, the demonstration of racializing the alternate seizes upon differential that are 'ethnic' in some sense (Banton, 1983; Horowitz, 1985).

Approaches to present-day racism or prejudice, ostensibly its first genuine expectation, were the treatment of Jewish believers by the Christianity in the 15th- and 16th-century Spain. *Conversos* were distinguished and victimized in view of the conviction held by a few Christians that the debasement of their blood made them unequipped for encountering a genuine transformation. In the 12th and 13th centuries, Spain was, by medieval principles, a tolerant plural society in which Christians, Muslims and Jews existed together in relative congruity under Christian rulers who concurred a considerable level of self-government to every religious group (Fredrickson, 1987).

In September 2001, the United Nations sponsored a World Conference against Racism, Racial Discrimination, Xenophobia and Related Intolerance in Durban, South Africa. The use of numerous words in conference title proposes that uncertainty may have existed in the matter as whether the sole expression of 'racism' without much scholastic input was adequate to mean the dangers and persecutions, and would concern the conferees. As a prologue to this chapter, efforts are exerted to make refinements among prejudice, xenophobia, racial and religious narrow-mindedness. Xenophobia (truly the dread of outsiders) is a primitive and virtually a universal phenomenon, while racism, it has been contended, has roots in mainly 14th- to 20th-century developments. Racism, based on religion, was drawn at individual level with his/her religious identity and not how an individual presents himself/herself. Unlike racial characteristics, beliefs or religious identities are viewed as normal and are alterable by a demonstration of will. It is helpful, as reminded by Horowitz, that for some class outside the West, 'religion is not a matter of faith but a given faith association/identity, a necessary piece of their personality and for around an inseparable segment of their feeling of people-hood' (Horowitz, 1985). Yet Kundnani (2009) points out another way in which the dissident Muslims, especially the young, construct somewhat differently presumed community from within of its whole.

Racism and racial bias are rising in the profundities of ultra-present-day Western social orders with various qualities from the past, however, with an astounding and stressing destructiveness. These rushes of prejudice and racism vouch for many feelings of trepidation that fill the skylines of cutting-edge social orders, undermining their inside dependability as well as simply their majority democratic settings. Critically reviewed audit of Islamophobia construct reveals it is a racial prejudice, demonstrating that two principle definitions are grinding away: Islamophobia as xenoracism or connected to the supposed conflict of clash of civilizations (Alietti & Padovan, 2013).

TYPES OF RACISM

Racism itself is a loaded and complex construct, which may not simply be used to indicate some kind of aversion to a group of people; rather, the reasons for aversion or desecration are fundamentally significant to name the behaviour. Hence, it becomes exceedingly crucial to understand as what different facets or kinds of racism the available literature highlights and how are they defined. The following text would shed some light on this.

Aversive Racism

Aversive racism is a type of racism in which a man's oblivious negative assessments of racial or ethnic minorities are acknowledged by an industrious shirking of cooperation with other racial and ethnic gatherings. The term was devised by Joel Kovel to portray the unobtrusive racial practices of any ethnic or racial group that rationalizes its aversion for a specific community by offering standards or stereotypes (Gaertner & Dovidio, 1986).

Some psychologists suggest that one may suffer from aversive racism even being unaware of it. This is more often unintentional and unconscious among the people who intentionally avoid becoming racist in their behaviour. Opposite to aversive racism would amount to blatant racism like being aversive to mixing with coloured-skinned people. This is not merely the case with people with coloured skin, but this may also occur within socially homogenous groups on the basis of some kind of clan or creed affiliation or even economic heterogeneity. Usually, such racist attitude persists at subconscious level of an individual who could hardly control its prevalence in his/her behaviour. Nonetheless, as it is at subconscious level and mostly people avoid demonstrating their racial attitudes socially and individually, hence, it is quite challenging to notice such racist feelings, except with highly structured modern gadgetry that uses better methods.

Racism in Cultural Perspective

Cultural differences are real and, at times, exist in imaginary terms; and in contemporary mediated world, they are manufactured. In this kind of racism, not biological differences, but the differences in culture between groups become the basis for divide. Modern and cosmopolitan societies deny cultural perspective of racism, more specifically in the USA, but it is quite common to observe in many European countries. Recent bans of women veiling and headscarf in many parts of Europe are indicative of the existence of cultural racism as Muslims claim women veiling as their cultural and religious trait. Huntington (1993) also counts on it as the fault line of future world conflicts, which would not be based on biological racism, but cultural differences or cultural racism. Modern societies are colour blind, but culture sensitive.

Since the Second World War, cultural differences among the groups due to high influx of immigrants crossing boundaries of the developed world have become visible, which raised serious concerns among the natives. These concerns of various nature with or without any indignation to immigrants were termed as cultural racism. It gave the world a fresh form of racism, which can be assumed with characteristic of convictions of a particular society that progresses in presumption and is a result of given certain culture in which customs and traditions of that particular society are far more superior than other societies. Cultural racism exists when there is an across-the-board acknowledgment of stereotypes concerning distinctive ethnic or populace groups (Blaut, 1992).

Othering Concept of Racism

'Othering' is one of the biggest social problems of the 21st century around the world, especially in Western societies, beset by seemingly intractable and overwhelming challenges; virtually every global, national and regional conflict is wrapped within or organized around one or more dimension of group-based difference. Othering undergirds territorial disputes, sectarian violence, military conflict, the spread of disease, hunger and food insecurity, and even climate change.

'Othering' is a term that not only encompasses the many expressions of racism and prejudice on the basis of group identities but also provides a clarifying frame that reveals a set of common processes and conditions that propagate group-based inequality and marginality. Although particular expressions of othering, such as racism or ethnocentrism, are often well recognized and richly studied, this broader phenomenon is, however, inadequately recognized.

The Haas Institute defines othering as a set of dynamics, processes and structures that engender marginality and persistent inequality across any of the full range of human differences based on group identities (Menendian, 2016). The opposite word of othering is 'belonging', which means having a meaningful voice and being afforded the opportunity to participate in the design of political, social and cultural structures (Menendian, 2016). A significant part of the procedure of othering depends on imagined distinction or the desire of difference. Spatial difference can be sufficient to reason that 'we' are 'here' and the 'others' are over 'there' (Said, 1978).

The concept of othering, as developed by Powell and Menendian, is grounded in in-group position theory, which comes from sociology. This theory posits that humans have a universal tendency to assign themselves and others to social categories and to judge members of one's own category or group as superior to others. This innate bias engenders beliefs and narratives about the inferiority of other groups that are deployed particularly when there is a conflict over symbolic or real resources. These beliefs and narratives justify the priority of the claims of one group over another. Conflict of this sort, in turn, reinforces beliefs in group differences and produces new and narrow narratives. Social scientists have long referred to this process of stereotyping other groups as 'othering'. There are wide varieties of contemporary conflicts around the world in which the dynamics of 'othering' appear to be important, including the persecution of the Rohingya people by the government of Myanmar. Recent US actions by the President Donald Trump also demonstrate that 'othering' is also a socio-cultural and political position, which shocked and alarmed millions of Americans who not only supported his intent to build a wall along the USA–Mexican border to keep out 'criminals and rapists' but also demanded a ban on Muslim immigrants, even Syrian refugees, from entering the USA. Mitt Romney, the 2012 Republican nominee, condemned Donald Trump for 'creating scapegoats of Muslims and Mexican immigrants'.[2]

Environmental Racism

A few definitions hold that exclusive purposeful discrimination against minorities on issues with respect to the earth constitutes environmental racism, while others concentrate on the nearness of hostile environment conditions for minorities, deliberate or not. Benjamin Chavis, African American civil rights leader, points out that (Melosi, 1995):

> environmental racism is racial separation in environmental racism policy making and authorization of controls and laws, the deliberate targeting of

[2] Retrieved from http://www.bbc.co.uk/news/election-us-2016-35717888.

groups of shading for harmful waste facility areas, the authority endorsing of the nearness of perilous toxic substances and contaminations for groups of shading, and the historical backdrop of barring non-white individuals from initiative of the natural development.

Racial Segregation

Racial segregation is the separation of people into racial or other ethnic communities in everyday life. It might transform into actions, for example, eating in a hotel, drinking from a water fountain, utilizing public toilet, going to school, heading off to the cinema, riding on a transport or in the rental or buy of a home. Racial segregation is mostly prohibited but may exist through social customs, notwithstanding when there is no solid individual inclination for it, as recommended by Thomas Schelling's models of segregation and further research (Schill & Wachter, 2001). Till the early 20th century, the world history is fraught with social categorization on the basis of racial profiling whole across the world. Segregating people with coloured skin does not need any reference, and during the colonization of the East, 'dogs and Indians are not allowed'[3] kind of instructions in elite clubs on Indian lands are also some of the glaring examples of racial segregation.

State Racism or Institutional Racism

In 1960, Stokely Carmichael coined the term institutional racism. This is a form of discrimination instituted by either the state, religion, business companies, educational institutes or organizations/associations capable of influencing the lives of people at large. It may also be regarded as the state racism, structural racism or systemic racism. In case of inflicted by the state, it affects the social and political fabric of the society deeply. If taken in a more sensitive manner, minority identification for political or social purposes in various countries of the world

---

[3] Retrieved from http://www.independent.co.uk/news/world/asia/gymkhana-club-delhi-private-members-club-turns-away-guests-who-looked-like-maids-a6821831.html. Other examples may include 'Foreigners Only', quite common at places even in contemporary India, which is nothing but hangover of the British colonialism.

demonstrates state racism. Declaration of minority groups in India, Pakistan, Bangladesh and others for political reasons may amount to state racism, which is constitutionally protected and practised form of racism. Moving further on its subtleties, even the identification of a group as minority, whether or not constitutionally declared, refers to state racism. Similarly, educational institutions prohibiting any cultural trait of a specific group to be practised also constitute institutional racism. Recent banning of wearing veils or headscarf at schools and colleges in France, Denmark and Switzerland is one of the conspicuous examples of institutional or state racism towards a group of people, that is, what regarded as sheer demonstration of Islamophobia in the hands of state or state institutions.

Scientific Racism

One of the most crucial form of racism is scientific racism, which says that racism towards certain groups of people in the world may be substantiated with scientific reasoning. This form of racism is also regarded as race realism and race biology. This may appear in the form of racial inferiority or racial superiority. This form of racism may make one group of people as the special creatures of God or most inferior of the God's creatures. It has long been an established notion among some races in the world; and finally after the Second World War, international organizations formally put an end to this frivolous approach. Anti-Semitism may be considered as one of such examples where Jews were considered as the worst creatures on the planet Earth. Interestingly, its reverse seems to be in practice where some Jews consider themselves to be the privileged and divinely ordained race to take over the world affairs. Zionism reflects the same.

Some examples are as follows: During his presidency, Abraham Lincoln in 1858 floated his views while opposing slavery in the USA; he said that there is no political and social balance between White and Negro race, nor he supported the Blacks to take part in voting or even as attendants. He was also against marriage with Blacks and he did not see them to hold the public office. Scottish Philosopher and Financial Analyst David Hume stated:

I am able to presume the Negroes to be normally second class compared to the Whites. There hardly ever was a civilized nation of that color, nor even any individual, famous either in real life or in hypothesis. No ingenious manufacture among them, no science, no arts. (Garrett, 2000)

German logician Immanuel Kant expressed, 'The yellow Indians do have a small ability. The Negroes are far underneath them, and at the lowest point are a part of the American people' (Eze, 1997, p. 118).

In the 19th century, the German Scholar Georg Wilhelm Friedrich Hegel proclaimed that 'Africa is no recorded piece of the world' (Graness, 2016). Hegel furthered with saying that Blacks had no 'feeling of identity; their soul dozes, stays sunk in itself, makes no progress, and accordingly parallels the compact, undifferentiated mass of the African continent' (Graness, 2016).

Animal Racism or Speciesism

Humans hardly care for respecting animal rights. Any harsh treatment to them takes space in literature and gets noticed quickly, while animals, as living organisms, do not enjoy any preferential treatment even closer to what humans enjoy. We murder them for our sustenance, keep them restricted and use them in traumatic laboratory experiments without any qualm of conscience or any feelings of disrespect to animal rights. The ethic thinkers need to ask what applicable distinction vindicate this difference in treatment (Steinbock, 1978). Singer (1987) said that non-human creatures do not have certain abilities that humans have, and this may legitimize distinctive treatment. However, it does not uphold that giving less attention to their requirements and interests is justified. A recent exhibition in China, —'a series of diptychs, each one containing a photo of an African person paired with the face of an animal', titled 'This is Africa'[4]—was criticized widely on both the fronts, as racist in general and for animal racism in particular. The exhibit was called off afterwards.

Animal racism is also named as speciesism; however, when targeted as human, it is usually referred to as human speciesism. Its connotation

[4] Retrieved from https://www.theguardian.com/world/2017/oct/14/chinese-museum-accused-of-racism-over-photos-pairing-africans-with-animals.

may well be understood when used in White supremacy over Black coloured human beings. This faulty ethical assumption of sexist or racist, whether religious, cultural or any other, does not legitimize this wrong belief that women or Negro/Blacks are way less brilliant, less truthful or trustworthy than the White race. Although there is no reliable definition whether it were authentic that women and Blacks are less determined and faithful than White race, nothing would allow anyone giving them less importance in terms of human rights, their interests and requirements. The term speciesism is somewhat not like the concepts of racism and sexism. The term itself tells the story about it, that is, the species supremacy (Singer, 1973).

Animal Holocaust

The resemblance of animal treatment (unabated slaughter/killing) and the Holocaust as of late came to public notice with PETA's[5] 'Holocaust on Your Plate' show, with extensive photographs looking at the phenomenon. How animals are dealt with in modern-day world and how Jews were treated during the Holocaust was the subject matter of the show. Pretty much point-by-point examinations can be and are made by animal liberationists between animal abuse and the Holocaust quite recently within the domain of this debate. Nonetheless, as a matter of fact, this comparison can be delineated not just for particular actions towards the animals, for example, serious repression, live experimentation, hunting, skinning and many more, but also broader highlights on the two sides, for example, the incredible quantities of casualties, mercilessness, exploitation and cruel discrimination, must be brought to surface (Sztybel, 2006). Kymlicka et al. (2014) said that neither dominant part nor minority is called upon today to legitimize how they

---

[5] PETA stands for People for the Ethical Treatment of Animals and it is a movement which intends to show the people of world as how the victimization of Jews, Gypsies, homosexuals and others who were characterized as 'life unworthy of life' during the holocaust parallels the way that modern society abuses and justifies the slaughter of animals. Please see https://www.peta.org.uk/media/news-releases/petas-holocaust-on-your-plate-exhibit-banned-in-manchester/ for more details about its objectives and activities. Lately, many of its shows in Europe were restricted.

practise power over other creatures. Some more interesting campaigns of PETA included depicting Jews in starved state during the Holocaust regime and animals in the same state, pictures showing similarity in ghettoization of Jews, etc., having shameful titles like 'To animals, all people are Nazis' displayed on the chicken cages.

Religious Racism

The appellation 'racism' is frequently employed in a loose and unreflective manner to portray the threatening or ghastly sentiments of one ethnic community or individuals, which is more often a result of negative attitudes towards them. The conative demonstration of negative racial attitudes transform into hostility towards the target group, which at times transpires in merciless actions. Such attitudes and hostility have a propensity to stay long and practising them over time make them appear normal. Usually, cogent reasons are framed to justify hostility based on racism; sometimes, it is the religion that provides the pretext, and, at some other times, these are colour, creed and credence that legitimized differential treatment with the racialized groups in the past. To legitimize the extermination of Jews in Europe, Hitler materialized the theories of racism claiming that Germans are the supreme race of the world. The USA also did not lag behind following Hitler's scheme of creating demonized group when Jim Crow law was enacted to hold the White supremacy in the South America by putting Blacks in isolation and making them unequal to the Whites (Fredrickson, 2015).

The word 'racism', in its typical sense, really assigns two different things. From one viewpoint, it involves behaviour, as a rule or a sign of contempt or hatred for people who have all-round-characterized physical qualities not quite the same as ours; then again, it involves belief system, a precept concerning human races (Back & Solomos, 2000). The two are not really connected. The common supremacist is not a theoretician; he is unequipped for legitimizing his conduct with 'logical' contentions. On the other hand, the ideologue of race is not really a 'supremacist', in the standard sense, his hypothetical perspectives may have no impact at all on his behavioural demonstrations or his hypothesis may not infer that specific races are characteristically shrewd. With a specific end goal to keep these two implications isolated, it would be apt to have refinement between occasionally acquired 'bigotry', a term assigning conduct, and 'racialism', a term saved for tenets. Moreover, the type of prejudice that is established in racialism creates especially disastrous outcomes; this is exactly the instance of Nazism. Bigotry is an old type of conduct that is most likely discovered around the world; racialism is a development of thoughts conceived in Western Europe, bloomed from the mid-18th century to the mid-20th century (Back & Solomos, 2000).

Galton's *Heredity* is the classic work that represents a milestone in the history of racialist scholarship (Galton, 1889). Like De Gobineau (1853), whose *Essai sur l'ine´galite´ des races humaines* (Essay on the Inequality of the Human Races) was published in four volumes from 1853 to 1855, Galton (1889) used 'racism' as a noteworthy system and stated that there are higher and lower races. He reviewed men on a scale of brilliance or genius from 'A' to 'G', with 'G' being the most astounding evaluation. He found the best share of people in the 'mediocre classes', indicating lump in the 'bell curve', and created a connection to intelligence testing, whereas there were just few men of awesome capacity and a similarly modest number of mental defectives. In this manner, he established that the rareness of genius and the immense wealth of average quality was no mishap yet, because of common, genetic powers. Further, those at the 'genius' level were not discovered arbitrarily among all people, but rather gathered in the higher classes of northern Europeans (Moore, 2008).

Essed (1991) debated racism in culture and power perspectives. Prejudice works through culture as well as articulation of auxiliary clash. Individuals are merely performers in a power structure. Power can create racism; however, it can likewise be used to battle the racism. Power agents, in normal circumstances, sustain racial and ethnic articulation. To be and not to be a racist may or may not be an issue, but people are always the operators of racism.

In this backdrop, discrimination based on religion amounts to religious racism. The discrimination may be verbal and non-verbal, filled with hostility or without hostility, can or cannot marginalize the people associated with the particular religion, may or may not cause ghettoization of either of the groups (discriminating or discriminated); nevertheless, every flavour of religious discrimination eventually leads to religious racism. The notable point, in this regard, is it starts in one generation or at one point in time but continues and grows with an amazing speed. Recent history testifies this notion that modernism, cosmopolitanism and multiculturalism hardly affected it to an extent of extinction.

Islamophobia, whether contemporary or old, is the classical form of religious racism. Biological exclusivism to racism faded away from the pages of history since the rise of racism based on colour, creed and religion in the 14th- and 15th-century Spain: truly known to be the home of racism (Iqbal, 2010). Sayyid and Vakil (2010) also ratify this notion when they say that racialized bodies were never exclusively biological, rather they were marked as religion, culture, history and territories to fabricate distinctions between Europeanness and non-Europeanness. Amin (2013) highlights the West's 'racialization of everything' by conjecturing bio-race and bio-political in a form that suits their objectives of controlling conversion to Islam and Muslims as a racialized group. In fact, 'the degree of alterity', what Tyrer (2013) labels, of Muslims from others, most specifically from Europeans, is one of the major causes of racialization of Muslims. It may not be out of question to point out Muslims' way of keeping themselves in isolation with lesser degree of integrity with their surroundings. Nonetheless, White supremacy, on the other hand, has often been recognized as a source of 'others' racialization in main parts of Europe. Islamophobia as a phenomenon seems to emerge from both the reasons, wherein Muslims are seen as 'indeterminate people', 'purely religious subjects' and their 'degree of alterity' to White universalism (Saeed, 2016).

The reasons and consequently manifestations of religious racism may include women wearing hijab or headscarf, mosques with huge tombs and high minarets in the Western societies, call for prayers (*Azaan*), bearded men, caps and attires usually worn by Muslims from Middle East and South Asian countries and other religious rituals. Visibility of them invokes and incites negative feelings among those who suffer from Islamophobia in religious racism perspective. This may result in hostility, negative posturing towards Muslims and Islam, and remain there even when some of the symbols are invisible to Islamophobes. It may not amount to enough validations that those in the West get strongly inclined towards their own religion and develop feelings towards others (other religions), but this form of racism may exist independent of any other factor(s). Religious racism is, in fact, a propensity of abhorrence and revulsion to religions of the minority. Nonetheless, in contemporary mass societies where media play a central role to help its audience develop pictures of others, Muslims and Islam have overwhelmed, even Jews, the media scene due to an abundance of events of extremism and terrorism in the name of religion. Every event of terrorism or extremism, if involves Muslim(s), fortifies the impressions that the global media are constantly generating. For any event of terrorism occurred anywhere in the world, the first impression of its cause leads people to Muslims' involvement. In terms of its intensity, this is the slightest form of religious racism, while its height may include attacks on people seemingly with the identities associated with Muslims or destruction of properties like Mosques. Recent attacks on mosques in the USA, Canada, Europe and Australia, and ripping off of headscarf from the Muslim women's heads are clear manifestations of religious racism and a form of Islamophobia. As compared to other forms of Islamophobia, religious racism's fatalities are high and curing it would involve long time and drastic steps such as relevant legislation, strict punitive measures and somewhat resilience on part of Muslims too in terms of their exposure highlighting their religion.

Conceptualization of Racism and Religious Racism

One of the troubles in expounding on racism is the absence of a solid definition of the construct. Major portion of writings on racism deals with faulty comprehension of what racism is all about, frequented with socio-biological meanings of race and culture (Imtoual, 2006). Racism, quite often, is a practice—the act of discrimination, at all levels, from individual to manhandle colonial abuse. Racism is a type of practice, which has been immensely critical in European culture for a few hundred years, imperative for the European capitalist economic system for its survival (Blaut, 1992; Jackson & Penrose, 1994).

Racist ideology may stem from supremacism. We, often, inherit insights and discourses on racism, as prejudices towards a group, from our parents, folks and companions or from literature and media. Our parents, peers and emblematic elites (such as instructors, columnists, writers and legislators) provide us contents to produce and reproduce feelings of prejudice and racism towards a target group. The social phenomenon that is frequently alluded to, and considerably denied, however, without much information about what precisely it will be, is racism. If there is an acknowledgement by any stretch of imagination, racism is regularly credited to others, to different nations, to other lower classes or can be considered as past (van Dijk, 2006). One reason of this unvarying and extensive refutation is that racism is frequently connected with and restricted to the extreme right, that is, with oblivious discrimination and prejudice.

Hall, Matz, and Wood (2010) described in a meta-analytic audit of past research and assessed the connection between religiosity and racism in the USA since the Civil Rights Act, 1964. Religious racism partially reflects inter-group dynamics, that is, a solid religious in-class identification is related with criticism of racial out-groups. Different races may be dealt with as out-group since religion is honed to a great extent inside race, preparing in a religious in-amass personality advances general ethnocentrism, and in the light of the fact that distinctive others have all the earmarks of being in rivalry for assets. What's more, religious racism is attached to essential life norms of social accordance and regard for custom.

Biological notion of racism does not make Muslims to qualify for becoming victims, as Muslims are those who follow Islam, while Islam is a religion being practised by almost every race, if taken in biological sense, in every nook and corner of the world. Hence, biological determinism in race perspective hardly gives space to hate or prejudice Muslims. Allport's (1954) theorization of prejudice on the basis of one's deep attachment with in-group develops indifference, prejudice or hatred towards the out-group, depending on the degree of in-group affiliation within, structure of in-group and out-group, and perceived characteristics of the out-group. Inter-group relations, arguably, are fairly dependent on many factors, contemporarily in vogue, including historic patterns. Nonetheless, much research in inter-group relations concerns the potential for mediations (e.g., inter-group contact) to lessen majority's tendency to victimize the minorities. Thus, it becomes fundamentally significant as how minority amass individuals understand such mediations, particularly as they influence their capacities to act as far as their aggregate personality to acknowledge the social change. To address this issue, the focus should be on minority's convictions and speculations concerning the inter-group progression lying behind their underestimation in the hands of larger group (which may be regarded as in-group in West's perspective).

Racism, like Islamophobia, is a complex and an umbrella construct, which brings in its ambit cynicism, prejudice, discrimination or antagonism towards someone of a different race on the basis of the belief that one's own race is superior.[6] There are competing but scholarly debates on what exactly constitutes racism. Nevertheless, hardly any explanation of racism dares excluding two important deleterious traits—prejudice and discrimination. Prejudice is generally agreed as a predisposition of a group towards others, which may turn into hostility or discrimination, while discrimination is a product or manifestation of any socio-psychological anomie and, in itself, discrimination is a social action. Hence, we may say that racism constitutes essentially two elements, that is, cause and effect, wherein prejudice is the cause and discrimination is an effect. Understandably, racism is a distinct construct from prejudice; however, broader than the latter. Prejudice may be latent and may not appear to be harmful, if seen in the light of 'harm principle' by Stauart Mills (2001), and exists as an independent variable in a given social system. But it may elicit actions or turn to be action-oriented if it operates under the influence of racism. In that, discrimination as an action may arise as an effect of prejudice, while both the cause and effect constitute racism.

---

[6] Retrieved from https://en.oxforddictionaries.com/definition/racism.

Fundamentally, racism ideology distinguishes human groups either as superior or inferior due to some innate sociocultural or biological identities. For instance, the denominations of Sepulveda and Las Casas were in use in sub-Saharan regions for the people who were made slaves and transferred to the newly discovered Americas in the early 16th century. Sepulveda referred to enslaving sub-Saharan Africans without any qualm of conscience or guilt, as if they had no soul and were not humans (but subhumans). On the other hand, Las Casas labelled them as humans, but savages, hence, culturally inferior to Christians (Grosfoguel & Mielants, 2006; Wallerstein, 2006). From now onwards, racism seems to have multiple facets such as biological racism, cultural racism, epistemic racism and religious racism. Biological form of racism is the oldest among them, while other emerged due to emergence of power play in the realm of social sciences. Dominant groups inextricably intertwine factors that can help them muster power in a social system (van Dijk, 1997); consequently, racialization or inferiorization of the subject group(s) becomes inevitable. Resultantly, racism is shaped.

Is there any difference between cultural racism and religious racism? Islamophobia is entitled to both in the literature. This makes it significant to differentiate between them and characterize both forms of racism for its better conceptualization. Although contemporary conceptualization of Islamophobia forms around cultural racist discourses where religion plays a dominant role, especially in case of Islam that is not merely a religion but also a cultural system, governing individuals' behaviour in every dos and don'ts. Hence, a culture that develops around religious lines might suffer from this obliquity, but some cultures are inferiorized beyond religious domains like the sub-Saharan African cultures. Even in cultural racism, the term racism is seldom used. Sometimes, region(s) or caste name says it all having cultural inferiority embedded with in it deeply, like the subaltern classes in parts of India and Africa.

Islamophobia, on the other side, may be an epiphenomenon emanating from racist discourses or innate hostility towards Islam and Muslims. It blends religious, regional as well as cultural racism to form a menace, which has badly entrapped the contemporary world. Literature on Islamophobia clearly demonstrates that Islam is the only identity for Muslims, which makes one entitled to be the victim or potential victim of the menace. Whether from Middle Eastern countries, Arab world, Asia or even converts from Europe, all may face racial prejudice on the pretext of being Muslims. That is why, Islamophobia is, but religious, cultural and regional racism. Association with the religion of Islam, following Islamic culture or being from Muslim world are some of the characteristics considered essential for Islamophobia to occur.

Racism to take shape of Islamophobia takes two distinct routes—cultural racism and religious racism. Religious racism, as the name reflects itself, naturally leads to Islamophobic construction, while cultural racism refers to the culture of Muslim societies only and hostility towards it. The following diagram can help us to understand as how religious or cultural racism leads to Islamophobia.

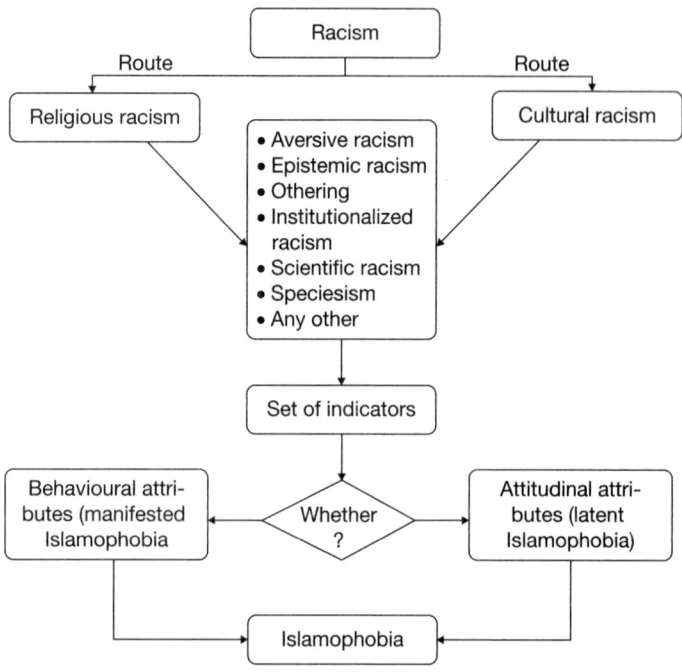

Whether religious racism or cultural racism, it essentially takes any specific form of racism—aversive racism, epistemic racism, etc., before it becomes Islamophobia. To know as what exactly the form of racism would become is all the way important if we plan to hatch out a strategy to root out Islamophobia from any society as a form of racism. Set of indicators in this connection are important to be drawn before collecting data on it. Another important aspect is to understand as what kind of Islamophobia might occur because of racist feelings towards Muslims and Islam—whether it dwells at cognitive and affective levels of attitudes without touching conative boundaries, or it has crept into behavioural propensities. Availability of Islamophobic sentiments at attitudinal level may be termed as latent Islamophobia; while it has become a behavioural attribute, it may be termed as manifested Islamophobia. Manifested Islamophobia may result in Islamophobic attacks, verbal abuses of Muslims and Islam, etc. On the other hand, latent Islamophobia may lead the perpetrators to aversive behaviour towards Muslims and some kind of non-verbal pattern of hostility and prejudice. Nonetheless, it is important to note that any untoward happening at social level may turn the attitudinal level Islamophobia into behavioural attributes. The given pattern may help collecting empirical data on Islamophobia in racism perspective.

Contemporary Religious Racism

Gada (2015) has explained that a social body reliant on colonialist barbarity to manage its lifestyle must find an ideology that can deny dependency if it is to maintain legitimacy. Different sorts of racism have played that part in the present period; Islamophobia, now, is the favoured frame. The typical protest of characterizing it along these lines is that Muslims are not a race. However, since all racisms are socially and politically developed as opposed to be dependent on the truth of any biological race, it is consummately workable for cultural markers related with Muslimness (types of dress, customs, language, traditions and so on) to be transformed into racial signifiers. He pointed out that the West has diverse courses in which Islam and Muslims experienced Islamophobic racism, for example, violence against Muslims, use of abhorrent language and assaulting the Muslim faith through legislation (for instance, veiling ban).

The horrific episode of 9/11 in New York led to the rise of radicalized and extremist version of Islam at the start of the 21st century. The strong provocative discourses, in political and media spheres, on Islam and Muslims, have recently created fear, which has caused Islamophobia's spread in the West and ambivalence towards Muslims. The net outcome was unleashed hatred that led the Westerners to attack on Muslims and Mosques. Not only individuals, the states also behaved oppressively inciting state departments, especially the police, to profile Muslims in the West. The discriminating and racist evidence against diasporic European Muslims provide measurable confirmations of Islamophobia; the USA also frequently gave blunt manifests in this discrimination about Muslims, which stirred normalcy in the Muslim world.[7] Islamophobia is said to draw upon chronicled affiliations identifying with the long-standing antagonistic vibe and military clashes that happened in wars of Crusades and that sentiment against Muslims, which developed in medieval times, still prevails in the Western world. The term crusade against radical Islam was used again in the 20th century by the US President George W. Bush, which spurred a debate in European nations such as France and Italy. These countries chastised Islam with references about oppressive treatment of women having no liberty for them and backwardness by comparing Islam with Christianity in orientalist's perspective. This discourse provokes and propagates Islamophobia in Europe. This bitter depiction of Muslims and Islam has constantly been considered as religious racism (Rattansi, 2007). The EU showed concerns about the aftershocks of 9/11 catastrophe and constituted a committee to monitor attacks on Muslims living in Europe. It was reported by the European Monitoring Centre in 2002 that hate crimes against Muslims increased in which

---

[7] For instance, when 'Innocence of Muslims' trailer was uploaded on YouTube in summer 2012, the US government and other state institutions considered it a matter that pertains to freedom of expression, and even courts did not respond to it. That caused huge loss to property and human lives in entire Muslim world due to enraged protests.

assault on hijab-wearing women and mosques were prominent (Allen & Nielsen, 2002).

RELIGIOUS RACISM AND ISLAMOPHOBIA

Robert Kilroy-Silk, the BBC morning host, had to face a backlash when he branded Arabs as 'suicide bombers, limb amputators, women repressors' and asked what they had given to the world other than oil.[8] His opinion piece appeared in *Sunday Express* on 4 January 2004. His comments were conceived as racist towards Islam and Arabs, and were considered as Islamophobic. He vehemently denied as being racist in his talks later and on social media.[9] While this illustration may appear to be excessively constrained by its unique situation, it enables an investigation of issues significant to different occasions, repeating quite often in political realm of the world. In his opinion piece, the reflection of his writing about the conflation of race and religious belief, Arabs in Europe and Islam was provocative and aimless. He furthered in his article by saying that we (European) are not indebted to Arab nations. The article happened to be a blast among the Arabs living in Europe and were working for genuine reasons and for the advancement of human lives. He wrote that Islam and Muslims have no true devotion to humanity; Arabs have only oil to sell; they are women oppressors and are providing suicide bombers to kill us. He portrayed the Arab world as cruel and vicious. Like many others, his polemics assumed plainly that not all cultures are equal at ethnic level. Because of Kilroy-Silk's racist comments, his morning show was stopped by the BBC, and the nation ended up noticeably involved in yet another debate on the significance of racism and the 'political rightness' to which he had as far as anyone knows fallen victim (Halliday, 1998).

Baber (2004) explained about this moot point in India. According to him, the right-wing political party, Bharatiya Janata Party, which is purely Hindu centric in its politics, is promoting Aryan race in cultural

---

[8] http://news.bbc.co.uk/1/hi/uk/3383589.stm.

[9] https://www.theguardian.com/media/2004/jan/16/broadcasting.race1.

perspectives through broadcast media to radicalize the masses towards Muslim. Muslims are constructed on racial grounds as Persian and Turks, who do not belong to Indian continent, and are rendered as such in media.

The literature on Islamophobia mainly focuses on Eurocentric development of distinction in Said's (1978) orientalist perspective, which gives a complex but solidified arrangement of negative stereotypes about Islam and its adherents. This viewpoint may recommend that Islamophobia-driven racism refers to a truly inferred set of rather hard stereotypes of the extreme out-group. This historical point of view, although, is itself to some degree ahistorical as it neglects to address the current sociopolitical elements that shape contemporary hostility towards Islam and Muslims (Mescher, 2008).

Sajid (2005) interestingly explained that hostility towards Muslims as religious racism has been a visible element in the European culture since crusades to present days with distinctive structures in various circumstances. For instance, in contemporary Britain, what quite observable are assaults on Muslims wearing religious dresses and on mosques; across the board hate/racists generalizations in all segments of media coupled with sensationalist eveningers; bureaucratic bottlenecks due to Muslim solicitations for more prominent social affectability in training and medicinal services; increased racial or religious judgement in employments, etc. Further, the racism monitoring associations seem disinterested in the unmistakable highlights of bigotry against Muslims, particularly Muslims' worries about social affectability. The Stephen Lawrence Inquiry report was very shocking on racism against Muslims but could hardly make any noise in media. The QNews, a Muslim magazine, asked a question 'where's the Muslims' in the White and Black Britain? The report was given enough space in pages of the magazine, but it presented the facts in a shambles as its major part covered obvious minorities, while less on how to manage racism or racist acts on grounds. Nevertheless, as casualties of Islamophobia are proliferating, a general realization is that any endeavours to handle racist attacks without additionally handling Islamophobia will be worthless. Much as Muslims need to stand up against prejudices and racism, they have turned out to be disappointed with efforts towards anti-racism developments that decline to battle Islamophobic views and which in many cases, is as abusive as the foundation itself. A publication in *The Muslim News* remarked that 'the genuine litmus trial of whether the lessons of the Lawrence catastrophe have been learnt will be if, a young Muslim killed on in an Islamophobia assault and his murder isn't dealt with similarly'. This is another extreme.

The post-9/11 circumstances could not change substantially and there are victors and losers in this procedure. Lamentably, the Muslim world is one of the principle loser in a way. Rising tide of Islamophobia in the West would not help in bringing worldwide peace and prosperity; rather it would do more damage than good. It has arguably been discussed that the worldwide media is a vital participant of educating masses informally. Yet awfully major worldwide players overwhelm it and they utilize it to impact globally by stigmatizing Islam and Muslims. Islamophobic industries seem to work day and night to worsen the already stroppy affairs of the world. The product that they make is anti-Islam and anti-Muslim sentiments, which by way could advance world peace if Islam continues to be marked as a religion of violence and Muslims are branded as terrorists (Ahsan, 2005).

Uludag and Molyneux (2014) argued that Islamophobia is clearly racism. This is a baseless argument on racial perspective that Islam is a religion, and not a race; hence, Islam may not be subject to racism. But what about Muslims, Islam's followers, whose major proportion of their culture is greatly affected by their religion? In fact, Islam is unique in many ways as it does not cover the space of being a religion for its followers but also a complete code of life essentially having enough to overwhelm their culture. Nonetheless, defining racism has more often been dependent on colour and creed of individual subjects who often consider themselves as alien race for certain reasons in a set-up where they form a minority. The Asian race, Jewish race, Black race, Indian race and White race are the labels bestowed on to people from various regions. It might be interesting to note that regions, colour of skin and religion are forming the basis for racism in these cases. Ideally, entire humanity belongs to a single species, that is, human. In Britain, quite recently, Irish were subjected to racist stereotyping and discrimination so severely; while Irish is not a race but a national identity. The question arises as why Islamophobia, as a form of religious racism, spans over people from various parts of the world with a little cognizance of their regional, colour or creed identity that had become subject of racism.

RACISM (RELIGIOUS PERSPECTIVE) IN SPAIN

Shortly after the rise of Islam during the 11th and 12th centuries, systematic demonization of Islam started posing Islam as an unorthodox variety of Christianity. Different 12th-century polemicists exhibited Prophet Muhammad (PBUH) as an enemy in the custom of Arius. While a few writers did this through gathering vivid, outrageous and, to a great extent, innovative polemics of Prophet Muhammad (PBUH). Spanish writers kept on building up the conventions of Arab Christian rational theology, giving them a keener, more hostile representation supported by the Christian success leaving apart what Muslims contributed. This Spanish historical convention, importation of north by scholars, for example, Petrus Alfonsi and Peter of Cluny, in next 100 years, educated the more learned reactionary scholarly responses to Islam. Eastern Christian hostile perspectives of Islam were foreign made to Spain, where they were modified and transferred to Northern Europe. In the meantime, different ways to portray Islam as heretic were introduced by the European writers and artists. Before the end of the 12th century, European journalists had made the fundamental depictions of Islam that would be expounded upon, modified and conveyed for various purposes for quite a long time to come (Tolan, 2002).

Islamophobia or racism against Muslims has been a characteristic of Western human advancement since the crusades and showed itself in different forms at various intervals of time. Today, it is communicated in diverse forms of discrimination while recruiting or employing Muslims: expanded assaults on Muslim religious and Islamic centres and contempt towards those appearing in typical Arab or Asian clothing; objectionable stereotyping of Muslims in the media; the bureaucratic deterrence to allowing cultural sensitivity in education as well as health care system;

treatment of Muslims as secondary citizen by the law and more specifically the ongoing assaults on Muslims and Muslim states in the name of War on Terror. Clearly, there is a political plan behind these outrages and waged war, where the only superpower, the USA, with the assistance of its Western partners, is attempting to oppress oil-rich Muslim world. Since the present war is coordinated towards deceiving the Muslims, which constitute more than 1.5 billion of total world population, the careful analysis of these deceptions and as a result thereof to recommend some remedial measures turn out to be exceptionally critical.

At a broader level, contemporary discussions on Islam in the West are prejudicial and ill-informed about Islam in a period of 750 years down to 711 AD conquest of Spain and Constantinople in 1453 AD. As for now, Muslims try to defend the non-Muslims at social level for believing in and respecting every other religion (Schwartz, 2010). The Spanish model, employing racism, created strives between Muslim and non-Muslim worlds. Although Muslims ruled Spain for a few centuries, Christian rulers recaptured it, and, instead of restoring their system and authority, they were more inclined towards labelling them as 'other' culturally and constructed the idea that Muslims worship wrong God, unlike Christians. To sustain power, their polemicists justified their criticism by stereotyping that Muslims have wrong way of worship and so have least role in Christian society than European Christian citizens have (Stephenson, 2017).

One of the most vital social phenomena in the global setting is the stream of migration from developing nations, propelled by financial and employment-related issues. Discrimination can be drawn closer to being a health hazard factor inside the migrant population's workplace, particularly for those foreigners who are at more serious hazard from social avoidance and marginalization. Experiences of discrimination can influence their emotional and mental health and are unequivocal components with respect to access to medical services or health care services. There is much need to use mix strategies in both the nations of origin and the host nation to recognize labour and social rights, and to additionally look into individual and social factors that influence the health of the migrated populations (Agudelo-Suárez et al., 2009). Gee (2002) reported that on account of racial discrimination on the grounds of having a place with a particular ethnic group, the so-called systematic racism would be a structural hazard factor, found at the base of strategies and practices that are drawn closer without thinking about the need of respecting the fundamental rights of every single ethnic group and not only of those who make up most of the general public. It would likewise be shown in the operational mechanisms set up inside political, social and financial organizations themselves.

Aversive racism has been growing remarkably against migrants in Spain: Muslims turn out to be more under the light since individuals blame them as fundamentalists, terrorists and so on. The illustration is of this state of mind that a Spanish student singles out Moroccans as the most hated immigrant group. Nevertheless, Spaniards have more negative sentiments towards Africans than Latino settlers, especially those with Muslim background. If descent or social affinity is the thing that makes the imagined community, may be a nation, then the immigration of non-White and Muslim population represents a risk to the every identity of individuals, particularly when the social and cultural difference run as an inseparable unit with increase in a given outsider group, just like the case with Moroccans in Spain. Additionally, the historical strains among Spain and North Africa still persist at subconscious level, and the Spanish media tend to connect North Africans with criminality, terrorism and Islamic fundamentalism, possibly making apprehension or doubt (Wojcieszak, 2014). After the 11 March 2004 terrorist attacks in Madrid, different politicians and analysts estimated about the likelihood of growing Islamophobia in Spain. Under this execrable vision, it was the last straw that broke the camel's back for Spaniards and their famous proverbial tolerance. Earlier, Muslim migrants in Spain, its greater part from Morocco, had shown, in specific circles, a level of worry over the social danger that *los moros* (the Moors) would once again pose to Spain (Noya, 2007).

Islamophobic representation of 'Muslim women' in Spanish and French media is another form of religious racism. The veil banning law in France, which is considered as Islamophobic 'neocolonial sexism' is the 'best asset' accessible to fuel Islamophobia (Ramírez, 2006).

Feminism in the colonial period (19th century and mid-20th century), when the state of colonized women was utilized to make colonized men primitive, affirms the fundamental thought that Muslim women were compliant and frail, and Muslim men were tyrant and forceful. Islamophobia today seems to be constructed to a great extent in light of how the women of 'other men' are viewed, and is particularly noticeable in the criticism of the circumstances of Muslim women who wear headscarves and appear to need salvation (Navarro, 2010).

López (2017) embarks to exhibit that considering Islamophobia as a type of racism stops us from grasping the complex and multifaceted nature of the phenomenon. He clarified that there are distinctive sorts of Islamophobia, keeping in mind that some are racist, others are most certainly not. To contend this point, he draws on a contention that was started inside a Spanish extraordinary right party rotating around two unique originations of the person and society, one established in the *völkisch* custom and the other in the Catholic convention. By analysing a book by a leader of that party, it may be perceived as how these two originations could cause two distinct sorts of Islamophobia: one völkisch, and the other Catholic. Both offer an indistinguishable vision of Islam from an imperative 'risk' towards the 'West', yet they contrast in their comprehension of the establishments of the Muslim and European personalities—racist versus religious points of view.

After Barcelona assaults, Muslims in Spain saw disdain spike. Numerous Islamophobic incidents occurred after attacks; however, before these assaults, Spain looked invulnerable to hostility to Muslimism or anti-Islam opinions (Jobse, 2017). The level of Islamophobia in 2014 was high; the police data on hate crime in 2015 representing Islamophobia filed at 40 per cent (Spain, 2016). One of the episodes is interesting to be put up here, wherein Fatima El Himer, 17, and her sister Haffssa, 20, had gone shopping in a mall in Granada, where they grew up. They were going to get the transport back home when Fatima saw a gathering of Spanish women discussing them. The sisters heard them saying that it was a disrespect that we were around here shopping while in Barcelona people were being killed by us (Muslims). It made them stunned as they had never heard anybody say anything like that recently.

Other incident happened to a store owner, Chafik El Boudali, 35, who owned a fruit and vegetable shop in the Madrid neighbourhood of Tetuan. He said that some of his standard clients had stopped visiting his store since the Barcelona assault. All Muslims are not militants, but what had occurred in Barcelona, where Islam had nothing to do with that, made Spaniards suspicious of every Muslim or those who looked like Muslims. The Seville Mosque Foundation's inside was targeted with anti-Muslim loathe discourse, for example, 'Executioners, you will pay', and another that used a slur for North Africans. In the meantime, a mosque in Granada was attacked with flares by a group of individuals in an awful racist assault (Nagesh, 2017).

Holland and Spain are moderate and progressive nations, cracking down the xenophobia and religious racism or racism at any level. Spanish government made an attempt to take the insight about the integration of immigration by constituting an advisory in 2006. It was March 2006 when Spain established Observatory to look into the issues of xenophobia and racism with the responsibility to report in detail about religious hate or racism and xenophobic elements in the Spanish society. This could lead to the advancement of society and empowerment of people and improvement of equity standards. In Spanish society, yet no one would deny the presence of a chronicled Islamophobia that proceeds with today in dissent to Western Saharans and lineage of Moriscos of the particular treatment granted to all others with colonial associations in Spain. Nonetheless, insofar as this ontological issue is borne as mindset, there is much to pick up from this creative way to deal with Spain's association with Islam as of today (Green, 2014).

Securitization of Islam and Muslims

In the wake of 9/11 tragic epoch, concerns about Islamophobia have increased and terrorism is now perceived to be *the key threat for international peace and security* (Rychnovska, 2014). Consequently, several groups of people have been represented as a security threat. This applies to Muslims, in general, whether a minority group or majority in a country, and the religion of Islam, in particular. Western countries generally equate Islam with the Palestinian issue, Iran and Al-Qaeda or ISIS movement; their discourses of the religion (of Islam) involve an essentialized approach to a multifaceted faith (Cesari, 2012). Therefore, anti-Muslim sentiments and Islamophobia have been generated to the extent where Western identities and values are perceived to be threatened by Islam (Krumme, 2010), particularly its fervent followers. Although the trepidation of Islam and Muslims got rampant after 9/11, Islamophobic behavioural tendencies and attitudes are not the creation of mere this incident. According to some scholars, the escalation of anti-Islam and anti-Muslim perceptions started in the late 1970s after the Iranian Revolution; however, Islamophobia as a term was in use incessantly during the whole 20th century. The term got famous after the release of the Runnymede report in 1997 and later got documented in January 2001 by the Stockholm International Forum on Combating Intolerance. The United Nations in the same year also raised concern over prejudice against anti-Islam and declared these sentiments as unwanted as that of anti-Semitism.

Runnymede Trust's report in 1997, 'Islamophobia: A Challenge for Us All', has documented the phenomenon of Islamophobia as an antagonism against Muslims and Islam. It further raises serious concerns over this hostility in the form of discrimination against Muslim communities and, more specifically, against the marginalization of the Muslims from mainstream social and political matters. In its schematization, which is binary in nature, the Runnymede report has made Muslims and Islam appear as a 'security threat' (Runnymede Trust, 1997).

Anti-Muslim and anti-Islam sentiments are on the rise in the USA and Europe. Therefore, Muslims and Islam have been securitized on different occasions across Europe and the USA. To name just a few, mosques controversies in different states of the USA, media discourses about an Islamic centre at Ground Zero, the 'minaret' issue in Switzerland and anti-niqab/veiling legislation in France and other European countries. Hence, terrorism, extremism and violence stand at the core of these discourses about Muslims and Islam. The use of this kind of trite portrayal of Muslims and Islam in academic and professional discourses has established a contradictory policy of state systems both fearing and fostering radicalization in a process 'securitization' of Islam (Cesari, 2012).

SECURITIZATION OF ISLAM AND MUSLIMS: A HISTORICAL PERSPECTIVE

Islam as a security threat is universal and has historical tracing, of which manifestations are persistently discernible despite the lapse of centuries since the colonial period and Ottoman Empire. Ever since Catholic Europeans were in a struggle with the Ottoman Empire, Islam was labelled as a security risk for Christianity (Schantz, 1993). Khadduri (1966) indicated that with the advent of Islam as a universal religion, it faced problems in dealing with Judaism and Christianity. He further adds that jihad and military discourses have affected its relationship with the non-Islamic world (Khadduri, 1966).

Author and specialist on the Middle East, Raymond Ibrahim, opines that Islam has been figuratively erasing Christianity. John Esposito, a non-Muslim scholar in his famous work *Islamic Threat: Myth or Reality?* recognized Islam as 'threat' to the West and its incapability to promote peace (Esposito, 1999). Later in *Unholy War: Terror in the Name of Islam*, he debated that underlying agenda behind American foreign policy is mapping the anger and particularly the agenda of

Muslim militants. Similarly, Kidd (2013) found that Protestants have always feared Islam as a global threat and portrayed Islam in the light of false religion and evil.

Later on, the early 17th century witnessed major challenges and hostility towards Islam. The advent of Islam was presented as a threatening other, new intellectual reason positioned against Christianity. John of Damascus further intensified the sensitivity of the issue in the 8th century; after his encounter with Islam and Muslims in the Umayyad dynasty, he viewed Islam as an 'alien' and a 'problem'. Likewise, subsequent Christian scholars were even harsher, focused to distort and malign the image of Islam. Following the crusades in 1096, prejudiced inclination towards Islam was also evident across Europe.

Following the beaten path, the Medieval Age authors also painted the image of Islam as a dreadful religion, inspired by the Antichrist ideology that posed a threat to Christianity. Similarly, Martin Luther also attacked Islam by authoring different treaties; he felt threatened by the Ottoman Turks advancing in Europe. Additionally, Luther also viewed Islam as a false religion (Kimball, 2017). It is important to note that during the Medieval Era, Islam and Muslim world were perceived as 'other' owing to cultural superiority of the Christians and not mainly as a security threat to the European Christendom (Stuchtey, 2011).

Thereafter, industrial revolution in the 18th century transformed Islamic societies, economies and European politics. This paradigm shift resulted in a new form of government with national interest based on the implementation of legislations and waging wars. Additionally, the response of the Islamic world was seen in the form of jihad (holy war) and cooperation with the Western bloc was considered a betrayal (Esposito, 1998). Hence, the perception of Islam and Muslims during tough resistance to colonization in the Muslim majority states made Islam appear as a security threat.

The same widespread hostile attitude towards Muslims and Islam prevailed even during the 19th and 20th centuries. Majority of non-European states were colonized by the European powers. Esposito (1998) writes that from Khomeini to Saddam Hussain, Islam has been portrayed as militant, threatening other, expansionist and anti-American.

Brief evidence presented here indicates that Muslims and Islam were perceived primarily as 'enemy' and 'security threat' to Christianity, Judaism and whole Western society. Our discussion also reveals that medieval discourses are occupied with hostility towards Islam and Muslims, and modern literature also seems to be adding to it (Iqbal, 2010). Hence, European securitizing actors in the Medieval Era securitized Islam with reference to Islamist extremists' expedition and convinced the individuals that the existence of European Christendom was threatened by Islam (Siddikoglu, 2015).

CONCEPTUALIZING THE SECURITIZATION

Securitization is a process that transforms a non-security issue into a security concern (Messina, 2016). According to Cesari (2012), securitization refers to extraordinary measures besides the rule of law; emergency conditions justify it as a threat to the existence of the community. Theorists further add that securitization functions outside the realm of politics, as it responds to an existential threat. It involves actors who project Islam as an existential threat to secular and political norms and, therefore, justify extraordinary measures to control it (Buzan, 1998).

Securitization Theory

Theory of securitization was proposed in the 1990s by the security studies theorists Ole Waever, Jaap de Wilde and Barry Buzan (1998) from the Copenhagen School (McDonald, 2008). This theory redefined the conceptual framework in the security studies that had dealt with the state and military. This theory deals with the way public issues appear, distribute and disappear (Rychnovska, 2014). More specifically, it is about *how* threats are securitized. According to Balzacq (2010), this theory asserts that *language is not only concerned with what is 'out there', but it is also constitutive of that very social reality.*

The Process of Securitization
Source: Krume (2010)[1].

Supposedly, this theory is comprised of two main dimensions: first, the process of securitization of an issue, as to the criteria before someone can securitize an issue. Second, successful securitization of an issue, from non-politicized to politicized and finally as the securitized one (Wæver, 1993). The speaker presents some issue as an existential threat to an audience; the said process is a securitizing move. However, a successful securitization can only occur when a securitization move is recognized by the audience (referent object) and that securitized issue is being considered as a threat. More precisely, the speaker makes a securitizing move; next, the issue has been framed as a threat and, finally, the referent object (audience) must accept that created threat to complete the process of securitization. This theory has been found to be useful, contemporarily, and has great explanatory power and is applicable to different security issues.

ANALYTICAL FRAMEWORK

The present work is focused on the discursive strategies that characterize the securitization of Islam and Muslims in academic and professional discourses. Securitization theory provides the theoretical framework which is helpful to understand how issues were linked with security and how it further justified the implementation of extraordinary measures against Muslims. Hence, this study aims to explore how

[1] The process of securitization was explained in the paper produced as requirement of a course on International Security at the University College Dublin by Tobias Krume under the supervision of Dr Ben Tonra in December 2010. The paper was retrieved from http://mhamchi.yolasite.com/resources/Islam%20-%20Religion%20or%20 Security%20Threat%20An%20Analysis%20of%20The%20Securitization%20of%20 Islam%20in%20The%20West.pdf.

the rising perception about Islam as an existential threat to Western secular norms, values and identities is able to occur and further to identify different actors involved successfully in securitizing Islam. Therefore, this study will also seek to explore the 'threat' dimension of Islamophobia and, for a complete picture, analysis of the ways in which Islam has been perceived and constructed as a 'security threat' in the academic discourses.

This work is divided into three parts. First, it gives a theoretical conceptualization of different concepts, including the background of Islamophobia. Second, it makes use of the securitization theory proposed by the Copenhagen School as an analytical framework for the later analyses. Third, it attempts to explore the dimensions and further sub-dimensions related to securitization of Islam as a 'security threat' in academic and professional discourses, and finally it concludes by evaluating literature and suggests remedies and measures on the phenomenon/construct under study.

DISCOURSES ON SECURITIZATION OF MUSLIMS AND ISLAM

Last few decades have witnessed a significant increase in academic and journalistic publications regarding Muslims and Islam and this increased attention has mainly been prompted by international developments, mainly of political and conflicting nature. These include the Rushdie Affair, the Iranian Revolution, Gulf War and Afghan War (Shadid, 2002). This section will seek to explore the way Muslims and Islam are securitized in academic discourses in the Western countries. Later on, scholarship on the topic will also analyse whether either Muslim or Islam, or both pose the 'security threat' to the Western society.

Muslims as a Threat

Uenal (2016) asserts that in German public discourses, Islam and Muslims are contextualized as symbolic threats (threats to values, culture and norms), realistic threats (threats to jobs, social welfare system, political system and safety) and terroristic threats (physical safety and well-being). With the immigration of Muslims to America,

European countries and Australia, newly developed socio-religious dynamics have consequently made Islam in the West a new field of research. The Salman Rushdie Affair, Muslim women headscarf, hijab and veil controversies across Europe, 9/11 attacks and the Danish cartoons controversies are few examples of international issues that have brought to the light the links between global Muslim community and Islam and Muslims in the West. These new circumstances necessitate conceptual and methodological challenges for the study of contemporary Islam, and it has also become crucial to avoid essentializing either Muslims or Islam and resist the symbolic construction of discourses that are preoccupied with terrorism and security.

Moreover, this study analyses Islamophobia as a multidimensional construct containing both anti-Islam sentiments and anti-Muslim prejudice while analysing the effects of symbolic, realistic and the terroristic threats. The results of this study indicate that Islamophobia constitutes a two-dimensional phenomenon that consists of anti-Muslim and anti-Islam sentiments. Furthermore, findings of this study also revealed that terroristic threats constitute a significant amount of variation in anti-Islam sentiments and is perceived as a major contributing factor for anti-Islamic sentiments (Uenal, 2016).

Similarly, Hansen (2016) while analysing the portrayal of Muslims in Swedish discourses argues that the securitization of Islam is also the securitization of Muslims. Hansen further contends that the representation of Islam as a threatening religious ideology could raise serious concerns for the local cultures and eventually a potent threat to their national cohesion; and as Muslims follow Islam, they could also pose identical threats. According to his analysis, as a consequence of perception of 'Islamic terrorism' in the political discourses of Europe, policy implementation on Muslims is on the rise (Hansen, 2016).

Furthermore, Cesari (2013) argues that in the European and American academic discourses, Islam has been a topic of interest for the last few years. There also exists a significant difference between American and European approaches to Muslims and Islam. In Europe, the debates around Muslims and Islam primarily focus on the integration of immigrants and refugees to this region and, to some extent, the scholarship on Islam in Europe has been constructed within this framework. This has also generated an interesting debate, whether the integration process for Muslims is similar to the experience of other immigrants from other parts of the world or their Islamic orientation introduces a distinctive element into this phenomenon.

Cesari further asserts that with regard to immigrants, individual religious identity dimension has been less researched in the past and other factors like position in the sociopolitical and economic marketplace are frequently highlighted over the religion. Nevertheless, the interest of scholars in processes of integration has developed to cover more aspects, not only cultural but also social and political. Therefore, scholars from diverse academic backgrounds have become more concerned to study the integration of Muslims (Cesari, 2013). Hence, in American and European debates, both Muslims and Islam have been securitized as a security threat.

With regard to symbolic threat construction of Islam, the huge body of literature has highlighted the issue of construction of mosques, legal status of mosques, surveillance of imams and minarets across the USA and Europe. The scholastic debates by Cesari (2013), Fregosi (1998) and Maussen (2007) have also shown great interest in these considerations. According to their analysis, Islamic architecture is also seen as a growing topic of research because architecture styles of mosques are seen as a sign of acceptance or rejection of the dominant environment.

Similarly, another major area of interest for scholars and symbolic securitization of Muslims and Islam is Islamic schools in the UK and the Netherlands. The greater part of the research on Islamic schools holds inquiries into the educational curriculum and the relationship between the schools and state institutions and, more specifically, the practice of Islam in these new educational settings. Another area of important consideration for research into the integration of Islam in the Western countries is the religious authorities; this includes the status of imams and focuses on religious training in Islamic institutions.

Stephenie Howard and Altaf Husain from Howard University provided significant insight into the impact of religious micro-aggressions against Muslims settled in America on social work policy, practice and education. Their study revealed that due to the racialization of religion, Muslims in America face religious micro-aggressions. This article has identified main themes religious micro-aggressions as the religious homogeneity, construction of Muslims as alien and sanctioning religious stereotypes of Muslims as terrorists (Husain, 2017).

Another important element in securitizing Muslims highlighted by Carr (2015) in his book *Experience with Islamophobia: Living with Racism in the Neoliberal Era* is that of hijab and niqab, which are used to express the supposed failure of Muslim communities to integrate into the Western nation states. He further added that across Europe, policies have been endorsed that directly impact Muslim communities and their abilities to manifest their faith, such as hijab/niqab or burqa ban in Belgium, Germany and Spain along with ban imposed on the building of minarets in Switzerland (Carr, 2015).

Whereas Madu (2015) in his doctoral dissertation 'The Burqa Ban in France and Its Potential Implications on Islamic Terrorism', while examining laws which ban wearing veil (burqa) in the public places, asserts that data on participants did not correlate between the Islamic terroristic acts and veil ban, but somehow, they feel that burqa/veil ban destabilizes Islam (Madu, 2015).

Recently, a law that has been passed in the parliaments of the Netherlands, Belgium, Spain, France and Denmark, which bans wearing of hijab/niqab in public places to de-Islamize their lands. Whereas Annelies Moors, professor of sociology and anthropology at the University of Amsterdam, declares this law as a ban on freedom of expression for women (Iqbal, 2010).

ISLAM

Securitization is the process of convincing an audience (state, individuals or society) of an issue as an existential threat by the securitizing agent/actor. This approach is largely employed by the contemporary securitizing actors in the West to securitize Islam as a threat to the Western society and its security. Such securitization discourses are mainly justified with reference to non-state actors such as Daesh and

Al-Qaeda or their affiliates, linked with terrorist attacks against the West (Cesari, 2012).

According to Jawad (2010), Islam in the Western discourses is associated with 'fundamentalism' and 'extremism'. It is also linked with terrorism and is one of the major strategic threats to the security of the West (Jawad, 2010). Interestingly, Siddiqi (2018) explored the theoretical and practical aspects of changing perceptions of Western securitization of Islam from the Middle Ages to the modern era and probed deeply into the ways in which securitizing discourses on Islam have diverged. Contrary to the Medieval Era where the securitization of Islam in the West was constructed pertinent to its hostile relations with the Islamic world, contemporary negative images of Islam as threatening others in the West have remained utterly contradictory to its political and security alignment with ISs (Siddiqi, 2018).

Furthermore, Jackson (2005), in his work *Writing the War on Terrorism: Language, Politics and Counter-Terrorism* while analysing Bush's speeches, contends that Bush's rhetoric supported the necessary mission of America to rid itself and the world of the evil they represent, more specifically, to protect good people and good Americans. This depiction in his speeches explains the way fear has given rise to discrimination and also the way some groups have formed an opposition and expressed anti-Islamic rhetoric over what American state considers a 'threat' including the 'Islamization' of America (Jackson, 2005).

Interestingly, this new perception of Islam as a threat to the European states has been more or less absent throughout the 20th century because, at that time, communism was extensively regarded as the major threat to the Western states. After the fall of the Soviet Union, Huntington stressed that as people seeking identity, enemies are somewhat essential, and the most dangerous enmities occur between the world's major civilizations (Huntington, 1996). As a result, with this line of thought, civilizational clash between the West and Islam has appeared.

Securitization of Islam is essentially a negative and multidimensional construct directed towards Muslims and Islam. Thus, on the basis of the literature, this phenomenon can further be studied under two broad categories. As the following figure indicates, two broad categories related to 'security threat' dimension of Islamophobia may be helpful in understanding the securitization process, namely ideological threat and existential threat. The ideological threat dimension may be studied and understood in further four sub-dimensions, namely totalitarianism, jihadism, Wahhabism and Sharia Law. Similarly, the existential threat dimension is further classified into threats related to immigrants and refugees.

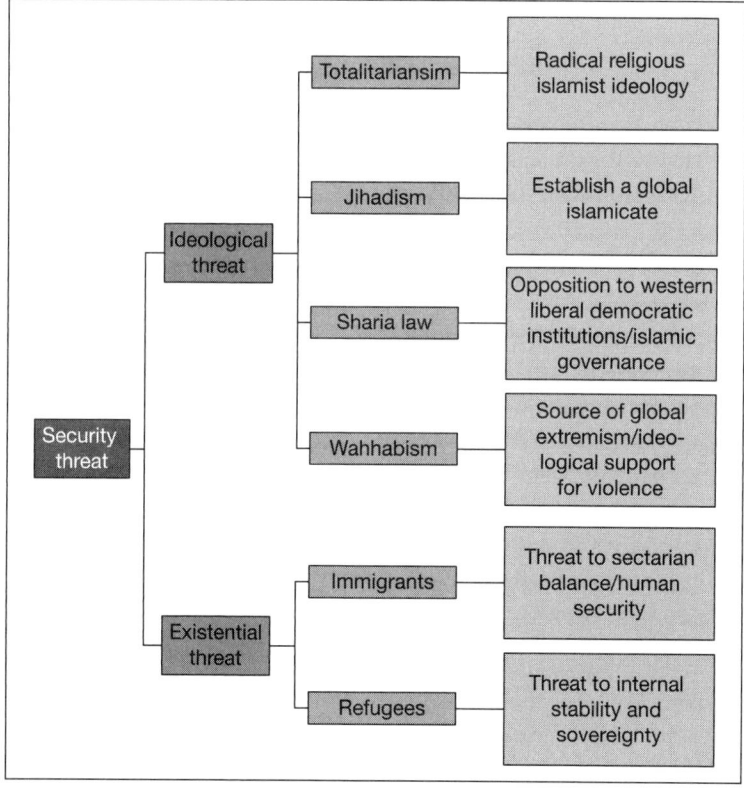

Dimensions of Islam as a Security Threat
Source: The author.

So far, this section has revealed that a growing perception of both Muslims and Islam as a threat to Western values, identities, human security and national security has a visible potential to occur. As Hansen (2016) puts it, the securitization of Muslims is in fact due to lack of Muslims' and Islam's integration into the Western societies, which has been copiously heightened by several actors such as state, politicians, policymakers and media. Discourses on Muslims and Islam have also revealed that right-wing politicians have triggered public debates and have attempted to securitize Muslims as well as Islam as a security threat to the Western civilizations (Hansen, 2016).

MAPPING THE DIMENSIONS

Based on the existing literature, the following section provides an overview of the dimensions or variables; reflections upon each dimension will also be presented.

IDEOLOGICAL THREAT

Islam is a religion that covers all the aspects of human life and influences private as well as social life. For the Westerners, it appears to be more threatening than any of the other ideologies like communism (Iqbal, 2010). The phenomenon of securitization of Islam contextualizes Islam as an ideology spreading all the way from Afghanistan and Iraq to European countries. According to this perception, Muslims are confined in their past and incapable to meet the challenges of liberal religious thinking and Western political development (Cesari, 2012).

Similarly, Bonansinga (2018) argues that Islam has acquired a level of salience in the public debate through the securitization process. Consequently, Islam is being equated with migration, extremism and terrorism, and is also framed as a security threat. In European debates, Islam is represented as fundamentalists' ideology promoting extremism and violence, thus providing the ideological grounds for terroristic acts. Additionally, Islam is also labelled as fanatical and totalizing religion and because of this universalistic tendency, Islam controls every aspect of the private, social and political life of humans (Bonansinga, 2018).

Totalitarianism

Geert Wilders, a politician from the Dutch Party, famous for his anti-Islamic sentiments, has manifested that Islam is a *totalitarian fascist ideology*,[2] and also that he has *nothing against the Muslims just something against Islam*. He considers Islam not a religion but a totalitarian ideology. In an interview, Geert Wilders furthered with his venomous approach towards Islam by saying that though Islam has many trappings of religion, it connects more with totalitarian ideologues such as fascism and communism, and needs to be treated as such (Wilders, 2013).

Following the similar lines, Bill Warner (2017) declared that Islam is a totalitarian political ideology and demands submission to Islam and the Sharia from its followers. He further documents that this totalitarian ideology is enforced by conversion of non-believers to the religion of Islam and this has been referred to as a *fundamental transformation* (Warner, 2017). Similarly, Tibi (2007) in a study argues that totalitarian Islamism carried out by minority groups could create opposition to Western liberal democratic institutions. According to Tibi, a well-organized ideological movement comprised of the multifaceted network of a transnational religion has been proliferated due to international migration (Tibi, 2007).

Richard Mitchell in his book *The Society of the Muslim Brothers* relates Muslim indoctrination and totalitarian ideologue with intellectual and extremists' terrorism and its historical roots with the totalitarian movement 'Muslim Brotherhood'. Concluding his work, he regards this as the first movement of Islamic fundamentalism and also that this ideological movement poses an existential threat to the secular norms of the Western society (Mitchell, 1993). Daniel Philpott in his study, 'The Challenge of September 11 to Secularism in International Relations' and, similarly, Mark Juergensmeyer in *The New Cold War? Religious Nationalism Confronts the Secular State* have

---

[2] Retrieved from https://www.telegraph.co.uk/news/politics/7376682/Geert-Wilders-showing-my-film-was-victory-for-freedom-of-speech.html.

discussed the religion of Islam as a political and jihadist ideology established by 'Muslim Brotherhood', which is nothing but destruction for the Western societies (Juergensmeyer, 1993). Furthermore, Daniel Philpott sees the imposition of Islamic government all across the world as the far most agenda of this movement that succeeded in its mission to a large extent. It has managed to propagate its totalitarian and radical religious Islamist ideology through madrasas in Europe. The phenomenon of religious fundamentalism is also linked with this new Islamist totalitarian ideology with the aim to restructure Western political order to the new totalitarianism (Philpott, 2002).

Sharia Law as Threat

There has been a huge volume of news media discourses on Sharia Law in Britain. Journalistic debates on Sharia in Britain consistently focused on barbarism and violence (Moore, Mason, & Lewis, 2008). Moreover, debates about Muslims and Islam in the UK have often been centred on Sharia Law. As Shah (2010) noted, since Sharia Law has been on the rise in many European countries, it gained more attention in Britain than in other countries. Moreover, fierce criticism was seen in the year 2008 after Dr William's speech at Royal Courts of Justice, in which William backed official recognition for Sharia within English Law. He further envisaged a sophisticated version of Sharia council and addressed concerns of the Muslim community like to live under Sharia Law according to their will. Later on, in response to his speech, Dr William faced immediate forceful reaction from religious scholars and academicians, who while criticizing Dr Williams' stance pictured Sharia Law as unwanted and having negative impact on the British legal system (Shah, 2010). Thereafter, Islam faced support and criticism for the integration of Muslims in European societies. Importantly, Pew Research Forum in its 2008 report noticed the rapid increase of Islamophobia in the UK and views (mostly negative) of Britain public after 2005 London bombings and subsequent terrorist attacks. On the other side, recently, Sharia Law is penetrating in the UK as over 130 Sharia Law courts are working in the UK. Interestingly, British PM Theresa May is to some extent Islam-friendly. In the wake of the recent Islamic terror attack that resulted in the murders of four people, Theresa May said that the terrorist was not Islamic and that he practised a 'perversion' of a great religion.[3]

In Europe, extensive debates about Muslims and Islam could be seen demonstrating the incompatibility of Sharia Law with human rights in the Western society and also that Muslims desire a completely separate legal system. For the European community, Sharia Law and Islam are foreign cultures. More specifically, Nicolas Sarkozy, a French politician and former president of France, has differentiated between 'good' and 'bad' Islam on the basis of European secular laws threatened by Sharia regime. Most importantly, in the perception of the European public, the Sharia legal system poses serious security concerns of terrorism. Moreover, there is a widespread negative perception in the USA about a strong sense of Islamic identity and Islamic terrorism as major concerns in debates on the implementation of Sharia Law, wherein Islam is also seen as a threat to ordinary US life.[4]

In the aftermath of 9/11, a great deal of interest in the integration of Muslims into American society has been observed. There also exists a concern that Muslims settled in America cannot be loyal and faithful to both—the USA and their religion (Islam), primarily due to the deeply engraved perception that the Western liberal democracy and Islam are incompatible with each other. Anti-Sharia measures are also advocated by different segments of the state and society to prevent the dangers of this system (Choudhury, 2013). Moreover, Sharia Law has also been declared as a national security threat by the proponents of anti-Sharia measures. In academic and professional discourses, Sharia Law has been equated with jihadist ideology and the law in itself is jihadism, which will eventually lead towards the establishment of an Islamist state.

Furthermore, Center for Security Policy in a report 'Shari'ah: The Threat to America' declares that the USA is under ideological threat, which consists of totalitarian sociopolitical doctrine known as Sharia (Islamic law) and every Muslim is obligated to wage jihad against

---

[3] Retrieved from http://www.wbdaily.com/diversity-multiculturalism/british-prime-minister-theresa-may-sharia-compliant/.

[4] Retrieved from http://www.euro-islam.info/key-issues/islamic-law/.

those who do not adhere to this totalitarian and political–military code of conduct. This report further states that this Islamist law seeks to impose a totalitarian ideology on its followers (Muslims) all over the world. Another key finding of this report includes that Sharia commands violence, Islamic terrorism and, more specifically, the civilizational jihad combined with jihadism of extremist kind may prove to be a threat for the national security of Americans and other Western societies.

In a somewhat contrasting report 'Understanding Sharia Law' by Center for American Progress, Duss and Ali (2011)[5] argue that conservative analysts have identified the Islamic religious law (Sharia) as a threat to the US security and by the imposition of its tenets extremists are intended to transform the USA into an IS. According to the conservatives, Muslims are engaged in civilization jihad to bring West under Sharia Law. The authors further assert that by adopting such misrepresented and flawed analysis would actually divert attention from actual threats that the USA is confronted with, while this misrepresentation of Islam and Muslims would alienate American Muslims who are our allies in our efforts against radicalization. Furthermore, the report has also highlighted the real face of Sharia and how misunderstanding about Sharia could prove to be harmful to the national security of America and threaten the freedoms guaranteed by the constitution. While declaring Sharia as a threat for non-believers, Warner (2010) says:

> Sharia has a lot to say about Kafirs (non-Muslims) and how they are to be treated, subjugated and ruled. Sharia claims political supremacy over the Constitution. Even though Sharia violates every principle of our Constitution, it is being implemented today, because Americans are unaware of what Sharia means. (p. 10).

Belt (2014) in his doctoral dissertation, 'Framing Islam as a Threat: The Use of Islam by Some US Conservatives as a Platform for Cultural Politics in the Decade after 9/11' discusses that after 9/11, a group of political elites and the US security experts categorize Islam as a major

---

[5] Retrieved from https://cdn.americanprogress.org/wp-content/uploads/issues/2011/03/pdf/sharia_law.pdf.

security threat and this perceived threat has resulted in measures and bills to prevent the spread of Sharia (Islamic law). He further asserts that negative sentiments about Sharia have been expressed in professional discourses on different occasions, as one of the Republican Party's presidential front runner exclaimed, 'I believe Shariah is a mortal threat to the survival of freedom in the United States and in the world as we know it' (Belt, 2014, p. 1).[6]

Jihadism

Jihadism has posed significant security challenges throughout the world. In countries such as the USA, Canada and the UK, Muslim migrated communities have been seen with traces of radicalization towards political violence (Hogan, 2014). The global jihadist ideology driven by the militant interpretation of Islam presents the persistent and significant threat to Muslim governments and Western nations alike. Al-Qaeda Movement, the driving force of the Jihad Movement globally, guides the ideological and operational agenda and its philosophy will continue to spread with the increased pace of globalization. Moreover, its extremists' philosophy urges Muslims to fight local jihad with their governments, and methodology of suicide to conduct mass fatality is gathering momentum. Additionally, through the Internet, this Global Jihadist Movement will reach out to Muslim migrants/diaspora; nevertheless, propaganda prevalent on the Internet has self-radicalized Muslims catalysing home-grown jihad; hence, a phenomenon threatening the fabric of multicultural societies (Gunaratna, 2017).

Tibi (2007) argues that Islamist Jihadism is a new movement of warfare and the new ideology of religious extremism. This new Jihadism Movement combined with Islamist ideology seeks to globalize Islam and is also a challenge to international security. Tibi further states since totalitarianism of Jihadist Islamists is a global movement, it cannot be controlled by state armies (Tibi, 2007). Hence, it is a great threat to national security across the world. As Wiktorowicz (2001) notes in his study, 'The New Global Threat', that contemporary global threat to

[6] Retrieved from https://vtechworks.lib.vt.edu/bitstream/handle/10919/51128/ Belt_DD_D_2014.pdf;sequence=1.

national security of the USA is a transnational network of radicalized Islamists, known as 'jihad'. While highlighting the menace of ideological Salafi thought, he also calls for improved security measures and policies to further prevent the 'Jihadization' in the USA. Following the same lines, Brachman (2008) discusses jihadism as a controversial phenomenon and labelled it as a violent extremist Islamic ideology. Adherents of this jihadist ideology use violence to take action against non-believers to establish Islamic governance in accordance with Sharia. Moreover, it has also been equated with Sunni Muslims who use violence to pursue their extremist political ideologies to establish a global Islamicate.

In the past few years, and especially after 9/11, jihadist structures have been discovered in European countries including Germany, the UK, France, Poland, the Netherlands and Italy. Notably, there also exists a perception in Western Europe that global jihad came to Europe with refugees; these refugees could also form coalitions with Islamist radicals and pose a serious threat to peace and normalcy in the Western states. Moreover, these jihadists are linked with Al-Qaeda's movement in plotting terroristic campaigns against Jews, America and Israel. Equally important, the Iraq War has contributed to the radicalization of Muslims in the European states, hence, providing support for jihadists to recruit youth and further finance them (Neumann, 2006). Shuck (2015) divulges that Al-Qaeda and ISIS use online recruitment strategies to spread propaganda, radicalize and recruit new members. Through online media, terrorist groups connect with each other worldwide to promote their ideologies and particularly networks across time and space. The geographical distance between terroristic networks and a potential recruit has been reduced due to swift and easy access of the Internet globally, which also helps to penetrate the growing threat of the home-grown attacks in the Western countries inspired by jihadist or extremists abroad (Shuck, 2015).[7] Supporting the same line of idea, Uuf, Reddick, and Chatfield (2015) revealed that in Iraq and Syria, IS poses serious threats to national security in the digital age. ISIS uses social media platforms such as YouTube, Twitter and Facebook for

[7] Retrieved from https://jscholarship.library.jhu.edu/bitstream/handle/1774.2/39436/SHUCK-THESIS-2015.pdf?sequence=1&isAllowed=y.

spreading propaganda, recruiting young fighters and also promotes terrorist messages of radicalization and violence through these easily accessible and free media (Uuf, Reddick, & Chatfield, 2015).[8]

Wahhabism

Wahhabism has emerged as religious fundamentalism after the break-up of the Soviet Union (Zelkina, 1999). The Pew Forum in its report 'The Global Spread of Wahhabi Islam: How Great a Threat?' states that the new threat faced by the USA is not just terrorism, rather it is 'Islamist terrorism' stimulated by an extreme intolerant stream of Islam 'Wahhabism' linked with the movement of Muslim Brotherhood and Salafi ideology. According to BBC report (2015), the Saudi government instrumentalized Wahhabism when Afghanistan was invaded by the Soviet Union in the 1970s, young Muslims were sent to Afghanistan to take part in the jihad against Russian regime under this religious ideological umbrella. After their exile from Syria, Iraq and Egypt, the Muslim Brotherhood (Al-Akhwan) also supported Wahhabi lobbyists. Strasbourg European parliament has declared Wahhabists' ideology as the key source of global terrorism. Media and intellectual discourses on Wahhabism also link it with Syrian War and Benghazi attack and consider Wahhabism as a root cause of Al-Qaeda, ISIS and violent jihadists. Wahhabism has also claimed to reach in the UK through sponsoring extremism in Islamic educational institutions, which has caused the distribution of extremist literature across the UK.

Mandaville and Hamid (2018) argued that Wahhabism is a rigid brand of Islam, which has led to the radicalization of Muslims in different parts of the world and Saudi Arabia has represented itself as the home of Wahhabism and a base ground for terrorism. Some scholars opine, though Saudis claim official friendship with the USA, simultaneously, they are funding the Islamic extremists who then attack America. Similarly, Michael (2009) analysed that Wahhabism, a religious ideology of Saudi Arabia, is a major contributing factor in

---

[8] Retrieved from https://ro.uow.edu.au/cgi/viewcontent.cgi?referer=https://scholar.google.com.pk/&httpsredir=1&article=6056&context=eispapers.

escalating the global terrorism; it has also provided the permissive environment for Al-Qaeda to spread Wahhabism. He further adds that Saudi's financing to madrasas, charities and Islamic centres throughout the world is also a contributing factor in supporting Al-Qaeda to plot attacks against the USA and other Western targets.

Importantly, concerns among the Western scholars are high on the spread of radicalism and extremism through curriculum taught in the Saudi educational institutions, which then exported to madrasas and Islamic centres worldwide. More specifically, these madrasas and centres have also been debated in academic literature as places for recruitment for Wahhabists' movement. However, recently, Saudi Arabia with the support of private donors and charities has taken measures to reform curriculum in educational institutions, but these measures have not been fully implemented and seem less successful in identifying the problems in the curriculum. Wahhabis ideology practised by Al-Qaeda is viewed as intolerant of other religious factions and, hence, poses a security threat to the West as well as the Muslim world (Dillon, 2009),[9] whereas prominent religious scholars from Saudi Arabia have at many occasions declared that radicalism and extremism do not belong to Saudi Arabia and Islam.

Furthermore, Freedom House report states that the Wahhabism, which the report regards as Islamic extremism, is the greatest dangerous ideological challenge of recent times. This report also argues that the term Wahhabism as Islamic militancy has been exaggerated; nevertheless, Wahhabism is certainly the major source of global extremism. Rakic (2012) declared the spreading of Wahhabism as the militant religious ideology in European countries. He also pointed out potential threats and suggested security measures for Europe, also to prevent further penetration of this extremist Islamic movement. Hayat Alvi in his study also claims that terrorism and Islamic violence are

---

[9] Dissertation submitted to Naval Postgraduate School, USA. Retrieved from https://www.nps.edu/documents/105988371/107571254/DillonWahhabismThesis.pdf/23fc46fb-17a6-41da-83b8-8e312191b5bb.

increasing because of extremists ideologies based on a new wave of support from Wahhabi/Salafi beliefs (Alvi, 2014).

Whereas in contrast to previous arguments, Dillon (2009) in a dissertation 'Wahhabism: Is It a Factor in the Spread of Global Terrorism?' analysed the possibility of Wahhabi ideology as a major contributing factor in the spread of violent radicalization in the Muslim world. The findings of this study revealed that though Wahhabism to some extent supports extremism ideologically, it is not the only cause of violent radicalization. Furthermore, the study also discusses that Wahhabism is not a direct contributor to violent extremism but rather a facilitator to this stream of ideology (Dillon, 2009).

EXISTENTIAL THREATS

After 9/11, Muslim minorities faced increased hostility throughout the USA and Europe. Politicians across Europe have generated negative discourses against Muslims and Islam, and presented them as a serious national security threat (Verkuyten, 2005). Moreover, major political discussions in Europe revolved around Muslim immigrants. While understanding prejudice as a major contributing factor causing negative perceptions towards Islam and Muslim immigrants and refugees, Scroggins (2005) points out that in European public debates Muslims and Islam are perceived and portrayed as an existential threat to security, national identity and culture. Zolberg and Long (1999) also revealed that Islam has now been debated with reference to diversity and immigration perspective in European political discourses, which is greatly illustrated by different events such as niqab and headscarf controversies, Danish cartoons, issues related to Islamic schools and other Islamic institutions.

Immigrants as a Threat

In the recent years, the most debated areas of concern for the new security agenda have been international migration, which has emerged at the end of the Cold War. Recent academic literature has also debated on existential threats posed by migration to human security and national sovereignty. The perception of migrants as a threat has made its way to the forefront that made the securitization process of immigrants a contributing factor in creating migration as a threat to national security all across the world. All in all, illegal and unwanted migrants are considered as threat to the stability of a state. Hence, the security agenda has been linked to many aspects of policy measures against immigrants. Moreover, transnational threats and war on terrorism have been linked to migration in the Western debates (Tallmeister, 2013; Wohlfeld, 2014).

Since 11 September 2001, the connection between terrorism and immigration has been reinforced through the discursive strategies and immigration has become prominent in the counterterrorism agenda. Thereafter, immigration in the USA became a matter of national security and discourses on the urgent implementation of counterterrorism through immigration laws dominated the political debates (Spencer, 2008). The labelling of immigrants as a security threat creates chaos and does more harm to the American society than it does to protect them, as it develops racist attitudes and the negative perceptions of the migrants as the enemy.

In the 2016 US presidential election, Donald Trumps' speeches stressed security concerns and implementation of strict policies against immigrants from specific countries living in the USA. Donald Trump declared Mexican immigrants as a security threat to the US citizens shortly after assuming the POTUS office. In his speeches and tweets, Trump both as a presidential candidate and the president declared Muslims as 'bad' and henceforth, generated narratives of evil Muslims and good Americans, the West versus Islam. Nevertheless, he and his administration have succeeded in altering immigration measures, policies and perception of the public about immigrants (Romero, 2018). During recent heated debates between the US President Donald Trump and Mayor of London Sadiq Khan on social media, Trump argued that immigration has changed the fabric of Europe and he thinks it is bad and declared Sadiq Khan as a threat to the Government of London, whereas Ibrahim Hooper, a spokesperson for CAIR called Trump's action as the 'anti-immigration hysteria'; he also reminded that Trump's political career is actually based on Islamophobia (Iqbal, 2018).

In a surprising move, US President Donald Trump put a travel ban on eight Muslim majority countries (Libya, North Korea, Iran, Chad, Somalia, Yemen, Venezuela and Syria) as a strategy to device immigration system to protect safety and security of Americans in an era of increased terrorism and worldwide crime. As Trump said, 'I must protect the security and interest of the United States and its people', whereas Carlos Guillermo Smith from Florida, Representative Democrat, declared this travel ban as senseless and more debated by personal interests and Islamophobia (Iqbal, 2018).

Through the process of securitization, immigration has been labelled as an existential threat; actors like political elites, the government along with public opinion construct migration as the security threat. Moreover, this nexus of security and immigration has resulted in negative perceptions about immigrants and creates a distinction between 'good' and 'bad' citizens, 'wanted' and 'unwanted' immigrants, and also 'bad Islam' and law-abiding 'good Islam'. In turn, these perceptions pave the way for security-driven measures and policies to secure and control borders. Political discourses such as Islamization threat of the West and Muslim invaders are on the rise. Erisen and Kentmen (2016) argue that trust on political institutions, affiliation with democratic values, tolerance and emotional reactions are perceived threats from immigrants; research also suggests that distinction between in-groups and out-groups can also influence attitude towards immigrants. The securitization of Muslims is the composite interconnected diverse category. Further, Cesari (2012) asserts that while analysing the securitization of Muslims, securitization of immigration must also be examined, as these are interrelated concepts in the Western discourses. Additionally, Cesari with regard to immigrants discusses that individual religious identity dimension has been less researched in the past and other factors, such as position in the sociopolitical and economic marketplace is frequently highlighted over religion. Nevertheless, the interest of scholars in processes of integration has developed to cover more aspects, not only cultural but also social and political. Therefore, scholars from diverse academic backgrounds have become more concerned to study the integration of Muslims (Cesari, 2013). Hence, in American and European debates, both Muslims and Islam have been securitized as a security threat.

Most importantly, different actors such as media and politicians have mainly politicized Islam and the integration of Muslims into the Western societies. Particularly, public discourses surrounding integration and multiculturalism have been on the rise in recent times. Furthermore, politicians have securitized Islam as an existential threat to the Western society (Krumme, 2010). Therefore, a vast amount of literature indicates that there are anti-immigrant/refugee and anti-Islam feelings prevalent across the globe.

Refugees as Threat

All over the globe, the refugee crisis has raised different debates and divided society in the EU. Security is one of the main issues associated with refugees in Western Europe. Refugee crimes, social conflicts, the stability of country and terrorism are the main possible security threats for the European community. Following the similar lines, a study 'Citizens' Perception of Security Threats Stemming from Syrian Refugees' conducted by Beirut Research Centre revealed that Syrian refugees were identified as the main security challenge across Lebanon. Moreover, top concerns were the fear of becoming a victim of crime and threats to sectarian balance resulting from the long stay of refugees. Moreover, in Greece, discourses on Islam are interlinked with the current refugee crisis and immigrants across Europe. Rallies against Islamization of Greece have been on the rise in Greece mentioning that Greece Islamization is progressing very quickly and that Greeks are becoming a minority in their country.

In the wake of the Syrian War, an unprecedented amount of people have crossed the European borders and there has been a securitization of Muslim refugees and asylum seekers. The securitized discourses project Muslim refugees as a security issue and a potential threat for Swedish society and its welfare system. Some scholars argue that the securitization of refugees could also have hidden risks for the host population in a way that it may lead to fear and anxiety, and the feeling of being under threat, which can potentially contribute to nationalistic policies, xenophobia and even racism (Hanson, 2016). During the 1980s and 1990s, racist attacks against Muslim refugees intensified and in the late 1990s and after 9/11, Islamophobia and anti-Muslim racism spread across the world. Discourses on refugees reached the hegemonic position. The current refugee crisis has turned out to be a crucial moment for the EU.

South-eastern European countries are the first landing shores for the refugees coming from Afghanistan, Syria and Iraq, while the majority of them continue onto Germany. In the next stage, political discourses in the USA and Europe link terrorism issue with the refugee issue. Furthermore, officials of the US House Committee on Homeland Security continue to admit concerns over Syrian refugees, fearing a terrorist could enter the USA, which led to strict screening of the Syrian refugees to pre-empt any possible terrorist attack. As quoted by Pamela Geller, refugees enter hungry saying Allah O Akbar, which she interprets as a declaration of war against the West; she also calls refugees the hostile invaders and comprised immigration jihad (Iqbal, 2018).

With the emergence of international jihadists' terrorism after 9/11 attacks in the USA and later events such as London train suicide bombings, Madrid train bombing, Islam and Muslim refugees were given the status of a rational 'security' concern for the host community. Humphery (2009) argues that perceptions about Muslims as socially and culturally incompatible in a multicultural society also existed even before 9/11, but the incident amply securitized Muslims and Islam as a social problem for the world. Hence, Islam and Muslim refugees became the object of securitization through measures and policies directed at their policing and border controls (Humphery, 2009). However, in contrast, Hammerstad (2014) asserts that refugee crises have been over-securitized and associated security threat undermines the international refugee protection regime.

In academic literature and public discourses, forced migration and refugee influx have faced an unparalleled securitization. Moreover, migrants and refugees have been framed as an existential threat to global peace and security. Refugee diaspora may contribute to threats towards internal stability and sovereignty, and refugees can also weaken their home and host states. There are two main assertions regarding the perception of refugees as a security threat. First, analysts argue that migrants and refugees carry destruction and war from violent or poor peripheral to stable and rich states, as did the refugees from Liberia to Sierra Leon in the 1990s. Second, some of the writers are concerned with state sovereignty (Hammerstad, 2014).

CONCLUSION

Discussion on securitization of Islam has revealed that the relationship between Islam and the West is somehow troubling in nature and it represents perceived security threat(s). The model presented in preceding pages might help in understanding the theoretical and empirical aspects of security threat construct about Islam as an existential and ideological one. Here, the ideological and existential threat dimensions and its sub-dimensions have been identified along with their indicators/factors that might lead to the securitization of Islam in the West. The model may further be improved and improvised by developing another set of indicators for mediated threat dimension of the security threat construct.

Moreover, by applying the Copenhagen School's securitization theory, this work has documented the security discourse within the academic, professional and public debates concerning Islam and Muslims. It has also revealed that the integration of Muslims and Islam in Western societies has been securitized by politicians and policymakers, which further triggered public discourse. Hence, professional and public discourses have securitized Islam as an existential threat to the Western countries and as a result of which extraordinary measures and policies towards Muslims and Islam have been formulated leading towards the exclusion of Islam from the West. So far, the dominating component of the securitization of Islam had been the securitization of jihad, Wahhabism and Sharia Law, but now immigrants and refugees have become an equal target and present a turning point in the security discourse.

Furthermore, the rhetoric structure of the security discourses, while planning a securitizing move, may contain a wide range of terms, statements, phrases and techniques from ambiguous and diffuse descriptions of threats and solutions to explicit descriptions of the construct. There also seem to have a change in the components emphasized in the securitization of Islam and Muslims as the academic and professional discourse has moved on from focusing on radicalization, extremism, totalitarianism to immigration and different discursive strategies, amply applied by the actors (policymakers, state systems, public and scholars) of securitization.

Nonetheless, hostile attitudes intensify the fear of the public about Islam as a security threat. Such assumptions of Muslims and Islam are grounded in the ancient times and experience of the past with colonial oppression, and not on the current conditions prevailing in the Muslim world. Additionally, in the future by studying variables scientifically, we might be able to comprehend further dimensions of security narratives on Islam and Muslims.

REMEDIAL MEASURES

Despite the aforementioned academic and professional discourses, efforts to combat deleterious perceptions against Muslims are on the move in different European countries. Different initiatives have been taken by the states to protect Muslims' rights in various domains, such as new laws against hate speech in the Netherlands, Spain and the UK. Few Muslim organizations are engaged in documenting hate incidents to push the legislators for helpful policies, the establishment of the Islamic Anti-Defamation League of Italy in 2005, an interfaith dialogue between Christians and Muslims in Germany and France with a focus to facilitate Muslim scholars/leaders and authorities to defuse conflicts are some of the examples.

This study broadly suggested a few remedies to not take Muslims and Islam as a security threat by the West. There is a need to educate the public on the inclusion of Islam in public spheres and support the implementation of alternative measures to counterterrorism, for the West by highlighting its counterproduction manifestations, and for the Muslim world to avoid perpetuating conflict between the West and Muslims. Legal measures introduced in some Western countries to distinguish between good (native) Muslims and bad (immigrant)

Muslims have created a hostile environment, which needs to be revisited to ameliorate the situation. Additionally, few other measures could also be taken, such as acceptance policy to engage Muslims in not only Islamic issues but also in mainstream social issues to separate domain of international politics from Islam, religious fanaticism should be discouraged and condemned by religious scholars and leaders across the world. Most importantly, counterterrorism and security measures should be interpreted in a restrictive way and also under the fundamental values of liberty and equality.

Islam as a Political Threat

Islamophobia popularly emerged as a concept in the late 1990s and was used by political activists to draw the attention and actions directed at Islam and Muslims in the Western liberal democracies. As discussed at length in the previous chapters, Islamophobia has evolved from political and sociological concepts for the purpose of analysing increased presence of Muslims and Islam in the West. Researchers have begun to use this term to identify the history, dimensions, causes, presence, intensity and consequences of anti-Islamic and anti-Muslims sentiments. Contemporarily, Islamophobia has developed roots in public, political and academic discourses. To a certain extent, it has become a widely competitive term in social sciences and many scholars have identified Islamophobia as a political tool to override different racial and supremacist groups generally in the West and particularly in the USA. A recent example of the political use of Islamophobia is the US elected President Donald Trump, who successfully used it in the US politics, but Geert Wilders, a notorious Islamophobe of the Netherlands, failed badly in practising this technique in his country (Bleich, 2012).

The term Islamophobia has at times seemed too imprecise and politically loaded that is why scholars ignored it, and historically, this remained the main reason for its lack of objective definition(s). It does not have any widely accepted definition; however, some scholars have made their attempts to define it. Some definitions covering the political spectrum of Western democracies are mentioned here, mainly in political terms. Gottschalk and Greenberg (2008) call it 'a social anxiety towards Islam and Muslim cultures'. Lee et al. (2009) define it as 'Fear of Muslims and the Islamic faith'. For Zúquete (2008), Islamophobia is 'a widespread mindset and fear-laden discourse in which people make blanket judgments of Islam as the enemy, as the "other", as a dangerous and unchanged, monolithic bloc that is the natural subject of well-deserved hostility from Westerners'. Semati (2010) defines it as 'a single, unified and negative conception of an essentialized Islam, which is then deemed incompatible with Euro-Americanness'. In one of the most carefully considered definitions, Stolz (2005) asserts that Islamophobia is 'a rejection of Islam, Muslim groups and Muslim individuals on the basis of prejudice and stereotypes. It may have emotional, cognitive, evaluative as well as action-oriented elements (e.g., discrimination, violence)'. Rana (2007) in his research paper 'The Story of Islamophobia' operationalized the construct labelling 'Islam as a threat to white Christian supremacy, Islam is constructed through a racial logic that crosses the cultural categories of nation, religion, ethnicity, and sexuality'.

Islamophobia according to the Runnymede Trust is 'an outlook or world-view involving an unfounded dread and dislike of Muslims, which results in practices of exclusion and discrimination' and may include the perception that Islam is inferior to the West and is a violent political ideology rather than a religion. In another report, the Trust noted that 'Islamophobia is an unfounded hostility towards Islam. It also refers to the practical consequences of such hostility in unfair discrimination against Muslim individuals and communities, and to the exclusion of Muslims from mainstream political and social affairs' (Holloway, 2016).

Islamophobia is a newly emerged term that refers to an irrational fear or bias towards Muslims and Islam as it condemns the religion of Islam and its entire history as extremist and considers Islam as a problem for the Western world (Moten, 2017). The 'Islamophobia Center' at the OIC defines Islamophobia as 'an irrational or very powerful fear or dislike of Islam'. Its manifestation includes prejudice, hostility stereotyping, discriminatory treatment, denigration of the most sacred symbols of Islam and non-recognition of Islam and Muslims by the law of the land.

POLITICAL ISLAM

Since its birth, Islam has emerged as a powerful religion and started growing briskly, the existing monopolizing powers, for instance, Judaism and Christianity, felt danger. Mainly Christianity, having centre in the West with pervasiveness over more than half of the world at that time, took Islam as endangering its existence and influence. According to Lewis (1990), Christianity was ruling over the world with its dichotomous method, religion and state; the religion was being regulated through church, whereas the state through political institutions. So the political part of the West in alliance with other political stakeholders dealt with Islam negatively. The West maligned Islam, since its inception, as a religion of terror and extremism. This attitude had become much more pronounced in the 8th century and established its identity as a cause for concern to the Muslim world.

Kumar (2012) in her book *Islamophobia and the Politics of Empire* stated that Islam had politically passive or quietest role but over time, Islamic clergy reinterpreted the definition of Islam to meet the political challenges and to enhance its identity in the political landscape. On the other side, Christianity was the political monster in the world. She wrote that Muslims broke 1,100 years of quietness by rereading the Islamic teachings and redefining the strategies. In this perspective, Ayatollah Khomeini played a significant role, adopted Shia Islam as a means to mobilize the Islamic clergy, student organizations and other religious groups and finally came up with political Islamic revolution in Iran and overthrew Shah in the name of Islam. Khomeini established the state according to Shia Islamic laws and put the Palestine conflict at the top of its foreign policy agenda.

Nonetheless, in Sunni tradition, we can take the example of Muslim Brotherhood (*Ikhwan-ul-Muslimeen*) in Palestine; it was established in 1967 with the political schema to liberate the holy land (for all three main religions of the world—Islam, Christianity and Judaism) from the clutches of Israel. However, sections of the Muslim Brotherhood broke the silence and sought to reinterpret Islam to serve the goals of national liberation. They viewed the struggle to liberate Palestine as a religious struggle (jihad), which was obligatory for Muslims to fight because it took place under defensive conditions (occupation, dispossession and colonialism). In 1987, the formation of Hamas, a group dedicated to the liberation of Palestine, contributed in political scenario of the Middle East. This is how Islamists put it by believing that why should Islam be viewed as a dead entity to what is going on in the region and just confine itself to mosques and cut itself off from social and political life.

In the meantime, many other Islamist groups emerged as political stakeholders such as Islamic Supreme Council of Iraq (ISCI), the Islamic Dawa (Call) Party and the Sadrists (followers of Muqtada al-Sadr) in Iraq; Hezbollah and Amal in Lebanon and the Islamic Republican Party in Iran. More such Islamist groups, however, emerged out of the Sunni branch of Islam, since Sunni Islam is practised by about 85 per cent of all Muslims around the world. Iranian revolution somewhat impended Western democracies, which isolated Iran geographically, politically, economically and strategically. The West accused Iran of spreading political Islam in the Middle East and around the *peace-loving* world. For the West, the fear of Islam is rational and political Islam is unacceptable. For Deepa, three major factors led to the spread of political Islam, which are: the failure of secularism, weakness of the left and onslaught by the economic crisis (Kumar, 2012).

In an article 'Will Islam Conquer Europe?' published in *The Real Truth*[1] in 2004, it was stated that for centuries, the West, mainly Europe, had a commonality that beautifully united all the people speaking different languages. That common point was their traditional Christian heritage. This religious heritage had fascinating past that, of course, cannot be denied. The history discloses that all those powers that tried to have control over the European continent faced encounter with Islam. The major Christian control over Europe was the great influence on a small city 'Vatican' which was the capital of ancient Rome and was the headquarter of the Christian Catholic Church.

---

[1] Retrieved from https://rcg.org/realtruth/articles/253-wice.html.

During those years, the Vatican's influence was the main factor that tied together the Holy Roman Empire. The Popes held ultimate power and gave their patronage and blessings to the secular political parties to carry out their certain agendas. This combination of both church and secular political parties was imposed on the public with the help of secret police and military. They compelled hundreds of thousands of Muslims to allegiance throughout Europe as well as Jews and Protestants during the Crusades. This powerful hegemony was responsible for slaughtering of immense numbers during power exercising period and for many centuries, this influence perpetuated to force millions of people to death or convert to Catholicism.

The ruling elite in Europe, throughout the history, created specific descriptions of the 'Muslim enemy' to enhance their political ambitions. They showed the image of Islam through the soda straw of their bias. In simple words, the history of 'Islam and the West', as it is generally termed, is a story not of religious conflict but of conflict born of political rivalries and competing imperial agendas. These historical facts are essential elements to understand the future of Eastern and Western relationships. Because of the European history, it has been branded as having strong Christian roots. The modern Western scholarship is depending on the Christian roots to be the new player of the puzzle in turning the West into a superstate of global supremacy, just because this great religious inspiration has been the basis of modern Western culture and stands alone with open arms across the world's leading economic system.

Some observe that the West, particularly Europe, is becoming a post-Christian civilization with an ever-diminishing understanding of its historical Christian values. Many are calling this the 'hallowing out' of traditional Christianity. In her famous book, *The Force of Reason*, a well-known Italian journalist and writer Oriana Fallaci claimed that Christianity's ancient monopoly on the European continent is swiftly giving way to the determined and assertive religion of Islam. According to British scholarship, mosques grab more religious practitioners than churches. If Muslims' growth continues at the present rate, churches will most probably appear vacant unlike their historic identity. The great Italians, French, Germans and, in general, the Western culture and many others may be swapped by a new global Muslim identity (Fallaci, 2006).

Recently, Israeli foreign ministry by referring to Pew Research Center survey report stated that Islam has become the second largest religion in Europe. According to this report, most European states perceive the presence of radical Muslims as a threat to the modern Western lifestyle. The growth of Muslims in Europe is so rapid that it is approaching almost 15 million. The report states:

> According to the demographic data, the number of Muslims will continue to gradually rise due to high birth rate and secondly, continuous mass immigrations from the Muslim countries. The rapid growth of Muslims in Europe indicates that Muslims will shape the future of Europe according to Shariah Law.

According to Pew Research Center survey report of 2015:

> Germany and France have the largest Muslim populations among European Union member countries. As of 2010, there were 4.8 million Muslims in Germany (5.8% of the country's population) and 4.7 million Muslims in France (7.5%). In Europe overall, however, Russia's population of 14 million Muslims (10%) is the largest on the continent. *The Muslim share of Europe's total population has been increasing steadily.* In recent decades, the Muslim share of the population throughout Europe grew about 1 percentage point a decade, from 4 per cent in 1990 to 6 per cent in 2010. This pattern is expected to continue through 2030, when Muslims are projected to make up 8 per cent of Europe's population.[2]

The spread of Islam has had strong influence on the globalization of culture. Islam has spread not only as a religion but has led to give birth to different languages, which are today spoken in different parts of the world by many non-Muslims than Muslims. Swahili in Africa is considered today the most important native language that was basically emerged out of Africa, while it emerged with the Islamic and African cultural interaction. This language borrowed many alphabets

---

[2] Retrieved from http://www.pewforum.org/2011/01/27/future-of-the-global-muslim-population-regional-europe/.

from languages being spoken in Islamic countries like Arabic, Farsi, Urdu, etc. Today, Quran is the most widely read book in its original language in human history. Muslims are expected to read the Quran in its original Arabic language and not a translation that may change the intended meaning. It becomes the main cause for the spread of Arabic language in the world. The Christian Bible is the most widely read book in translation. At the end of the 20th century, both migration of Muslims to the West and conversion rate to Islam within the West shaped a new Islamic presence (Sharif, 2000). Sharif (2000) further says that the manifestation of the Islamization of the Western world is presence of mosques and Islamic centres, which are now more than 1,000 in the USA alone. Furthermore, the country has many professional associations for Muslim engineers, educators and social scientists. There are almost six million Muslims in America and the number is rising remarkably. Also, Islam is the fastest growing religion in Central Asia.

Turkmenistan and Tajikistan made an official place for Islam as the dominant religion. In France, Islam has become the second most important religion statistically after Catholicism. In Britain, some Muslims have been experimenting with an Islamic parliament of their own, and many others in the UK are demanding state grants for Muslim schools with Islamic identity. In Germany, it has been realized that the decision to import Turkish Muslim technicians and workers in the 1970s was a mistake, and the bigger mistake was allowing them to build minaret and appoint muezzin in the mosques in German cities. As a result, there are new mosques, Muslim schools with their Islamic identity and Quranic centres throughout the world (Sharif, 2000).

The Western political institutions considered Muslims' globalization as a danger for their monopoly and started conspiring against Islam and Muslims. When Muslims throughout the world resisted against the vicious strategic and cultural invasion of the West, they had to pay a huge cost in the form of degradation and denigration. Such Muslim resistance is portrayed as an 'Islamic threat' by some of the Western scholars. Conflict between the Western and Islamic civilizations, Huntington in *The Clash of Civilizations* points out, has been going on for more than 1,400 years. The Gulf War, which took place in 1990, is the most recent and important example. His argument has been considered as the centre of controversy for the past many decades. At this juncture, it is crucial to ponder whether Islam is a monolithic force, whether the clash between Islam and the West is inevitable and whether the Islamic development poses a major threat to the West. Huntington depicts the Islamic countries as part of a wider pan-Islamic movement, united in their enmity to the West and the USA. He believed that the recent Gulf War was based on historic clash between Islam and the West. The representation of Islam and Islamic countries as a monolithic bloc may lead to the errors of the orientalist mindset, which refuses to take into account the diversity within Islam for suitability of a simple and surface-level explanation.

Todd H. Green authored *The Fear of Islam: An Introduction to Islamophobia in the West* and much of the book has surveyed Western fears and anxieties towards Muslims and Islam. Green (2015) explored the historical, political, economic, social and religious roots of anti-Muslim prejudice, focusing on how theologians, headlines and reports construct images and build narratives that link Muslims and Islam with violence, often arousing attitudes of fear and distrust not only towards the perpetrators of the misdeeds but also towards all Muslims and the Islamic faith. The 9/11 attacks on the USA had no doubt a profound effect on the American cultural and political landscape, leading to a tension about a powerful Muslim enemy that would stop at nothing to destroy Western values and individual freedom. The USA was not alone in yielding to fears of an 'Islamic threat', Europe also felt similar fear, stemming in part from the new paradigm of global terrorism and also arising from a series of events on European soil that heightened concerns about the internal threat to security and Western values posed by the growing number of Muslim immigrants.

Truth be told, Westerners in fact know very little about Islam. A lack of direct interactions or relationships with Muslims, combined with a little, if any, sustained study of Islamic texts and traditions, creates a vacuum of ignorance in the West concerning the world's second-largest religion. Yet plenty of Europeans and Americans hold extensively strong and clearly negative opinions about Islam and Muslims. What we know about Islam, or what we think we know, is filtered primarily through the media and the stories and images it provides to audiences and consumers. The media determines how to tell the story of Islam. What image of Islam is to be shown to the consumers. All the information regarding Islam is at the disposal of media (Belinda, 2016). In an editorial for *The Wall Street Journal*, Harvard Law Professor Alan Dershowitz asks, 'How should and can Western democracies fight against an enemy whose leaders preach a preference for death?'[3] She further argued that it is very difficult for Western democracies to fight against political Islam. Islamic leaders have many war tools to fight against the enemy of God. Similarly, *The New York Times* published a story on 15 November 2010, with the title 'Oklahoma Surprise: Islam as an Election Issue' and stated that a bill has been passed regarding the ban of Islamic Sharia Law in Oklahoma courts; the amendment's co-authors stated that the purpose of the bill was to stop the pending 'onslaught' of Sharia Law in Oklahoma.[4] Regarding this bill, the State Representative Lewis Moore stated, 'Are we not at war with this ideology? Are we not at war with them? Then why would we give in to this?' State Senator Anthony Sykes added, 'Sharia law coming to the US is a scary concept. Hopefully the passage of this constitutional amendment will prevent it in Oklahoma'. He continued, 'It's not a problem and we want to keep it that way'. Hardly 1 per cent of Oklahomans are Muslim and that Sharia has never been employed in a judicial decision within the state, over 70 per cent of voters approved the ballot measure.

While American media and political institutions have been and are doing their best to stereotype the term 'Sharia' as an anti-human law, the Western interpretation of Sharia is to meet their political agenda to target Islam and Muslims. They are trying to politicize Sharia to meet their political commitments, what they have made during certain campaigns (Louis, 2017). According to NBC News on 10 June 2017, ACT! for America initiated the 'Stop Shariah Now' campaign in 2008. The SPLC said the group's website described its mission 'to inform and educate the public about what Shariah is, how it is creeping into

---

[3] Retrieved from https://www.wsj.com/articles/SB120450617910806563.

[4] Retrieved from https://www.nytimes.com/2010/11/15/us/15oklahoma.html.

American society and compromising our constitutional freedom of speech, press, religion and equality what we can do to stop it'. More than 13 US states have introduced bills banning Sharia Law because of the campaign (Ali, 2012).

'It is absolutely impossible for any religious law to take over US law',[5] Beirich said in an NBC programme. He furthered, 'Constitutionally, there is a separation of church and state'. According to the SPLC, another main group is the 'Thin Blue Line Project', which is a 'Radicalization Map Locator' in nature that lists down the addresses of almost every Muslim Student Association (MSA) in the USA as well as a number of mosques and their addresses and Islamic institutions. The project, accessed only by preregistered law enforcement, describes itself as a 'one-stop internet resource for information regarding the perceived Muslim-threat infiltration of terrorism in the country'.

Rashid (2017) says that the way Western media is portraying Islam and Muslims is obviously Islamophobic. The Western media has historically been using value-loaded and biased language to represent Islam as a dangerous religion, deep-rooted in violence and irrationality. Media is the most approachable and undifferentiating disseminator of Islamophobic and biased ideas at local and global levels. Except some responsible media organizations, certain specific and often many predictable media sources have been attributing all Muslims as involved in violent activities. Overall, the media portrayed Islam as overwhelmingly different from and a serious threat to the West and Muslims within the West as different from and a threat to 'us' (Rashid, 2017).

Christopher Allen writes in his book *Islamophobia* that it was common in the West right after the incident of 9/11 that 'Sons of Allah' enacted 9/11, all the Muslims are sons of Allah and have ability to do so. Every single Muslim is a threat to all non-Muslims, who considered them as infidels. For Muslims, killing the infidels is a straight way to heaven (Allen, 2010). Homi K. Bhabha in his book *Location of Culture* narrates that the West is projecting the idea/concept of 'us' and 'them' to make clear distinction between the East and the West. The West is

[5] Retrieved from https://www.cnbc.com/2017/06/10/act-for-america-stages-nationwide-marches-against-sharia-law.html.

also highlighting the concept of 'native' and 'immigrants' to identify the position of 'Black skin' people living in the West. To maintain the supremacy of 'White skin' people, it is being admonished that two cultures cannot survive at the same location (Bhabha, 1994).

The US mass media, according to many researches, have been found to be posing Muslims and Islam in negative frames. Generally, the following are the dominant frames:

1. Islam is a terrorist religion: Islamophobic counterterrorism training often brands Islam as the enemy in the 'war on terror'. Private security groups and their speakers define the threat using ideological and theological terms that link Islam inextricably to terrorism. Within this frame, the problem is not simply the terrorists who are Muslim but also an 'evil' Islam itself.
2. An Islamic 'Fifth Column' or 'Stealth Jihad', is subverting the USA from within: This frame posits an existential threat to the USA even greater than that posed by Al-Qaeda. The domestic rise of political Islam aims to transform the USA into a Muslim country ruled by Sharia Law. The argument is supported by a conspiracy theory in which Muslim–American advocacy groups act as front organizations for foreign Islamists, like the Egyptian Muslim Brotherhood.
3. 'Mainstream' Muslim Americans have terrorist ties: Islamophobic counterterrorism trainers routinely categorize civil rights groups such as the Muslim Public Affairs Council (MPAC), Islamic Society of North America (ISNA) and CAIR as a support network for terrorists. For this charge, they lean heavily on guilt by association, citing a few instances of members or former members with troublesome associations as evidence of organizational complicity.
4. Muslim Americans wage 'Lawfare'—Violent Jihad by other means: The 'lawfare' frame holds that Muslim extremists use litigation, free speech and other legal means to advance a subversive agenda and silence opponents—using democracy to subvert democracy. 'Lawfare' utilizes a kind of Orwellian doublespeak in which 'terrorism' is not the use of terror, but the use of legal procedures. Law becomes warfare when used to oppose Islamophobia or assert Muslim Americans' civil rights.

5. Muslims seek to replace the US Constitution with Islamic Sharia Law: This frame raises the spectre of a repressive Islamic caliphate ruling over America and suggests that support for Sharia, rather than kinetic violent terrorism, is the 'the most dangerous threat'. Like the Islamic 'Fifth Column' conspiracy theory, this Sharia evokes cold war fears of global communism. The menace of a global Islamic dictatorship stands in for the former Soviet one. Sharia is a set of ideals that defines a properly constituted Islamic existence. Selective interpretations of Islamic jurisprudence are used by some terrorists to mobilize recruits with the ultimate goal of establishing a global Islamic government or caliphate. This frame is used to stigmatize civil rights advocates who fight religious discrimination by vilifying religious accommodation as capitulation to Islamic rule.

Edward Said in his book *Covering Islam* blames media practitioners for the misrepresentation of Islam without even knowing it and creating mistrust in the people who believe in Islamic tenets. Said says that media is the main stakeholder in the negative portrayal of Islam (Said, 1981). The US media's portrayal of Islam and Muslims has made the Westerners believe that Islam and Muslims are the threat to the Western lifestyle, threat to the Western political systems and Muslims are incompatible with the mainstream Western world. A story published in *The Washington Post* by Sam Harris says that there was an argument that we are not at war with 'terrorists', we have to admit that we are at war with Islam, Muslims and Arabs.

Since the events of 9/11, the question of political Islam has taken centre stage in world politics. The 'war on terror' has transformed the whole discussion on the relationship between Islam and the West. A massive number of books and essays have appeared on this topic since then. Predictably, conservative analysts, recycling old orientalist clichés, have advanced the idea that the West is once again at war with Islam. The underlying logic behind this argument is 'we' are secular and democratic, while 'they' are mired in the backwardness born out of an adherence to Islam. These arguments have become part of the common sense ideology in the USA and elsewhere.

Niqab, face veil and other Islamic cultural aspects are incompatible to the Western lifestyle. Mosques in East London present a symbol for the replacement of Christian European culture with the Islamic culture. Christian supremacists claim that Muslims intend to establish Islamic republic in London by 2025. It is refreshing and heartening that President Trump acknowledges the need for an ideological campaign against 'radical Islam'. This deserves to be called a paradigm shift. President Bush often referred to a 'war on terror' but terror is a tactic that can be used for a variety of ideological objectives. President Obama stated that he was opposed to violent extremism and even organized an international summit around this subject. Yet, at times, he made it seem as if he worried more about Islamophobia than about radical Islam. In a speech to the United Nations General Assembly in 2012, Obama declared, 'The future must not belong to those who slander the prophet of Islam' (Aydin, 2017).

POLITICAL DIMENSIONS OF ISLAMOPHOBIA: A TRI-NODAL APPROACH

Islam is one of the fastest growing religions in the world, particularly in Europe and the USA, contemporarily. A massive influx of workers and other migrants from the Middle East and former colonial territories in Africa, Asia and the Caribbean region led to a growing presence of Muslim residents within Europe (Buijs & Rath, 2002). According to Pintak (2014), Pew report released in 2011 estimated that the number of Muslims in the USA would be more than double by 2030, from 2.6 million to 6.2 million.

During the last two centuries, history has witnessed Muslims under dominance of the West resulting into a perpetuating conflict in the West–Muslim relationship (Seven, 2010). After the 9/11 attack on the twin towers of WTC in 2001, the relations of the West with Muslims and Islam have been presented as a fear and menace in the global mediated political discourse. The right-wing political parties across the world have described a dreadful picture of Islam and Muslims, and claimed that Islam has become a potential threat for the democracy, the traditional liberties and identity of the Western countries. They further explicated that Islam is a great menace to culture, norms and values, to the institutions plus the entire field of British politics (Allen, 2010).

While surveying literature and events related to Islam and Muslims, the following figure identifies three approaches to study political dimension of Islamophobia in a scientific and systematic fashion. This model proposes to study the construct prevailing at system, individual and epistemic levels. The assumption behind this model is that political dimensions of Islamophobia can be observed in both macro-societal terms (system level), that is, democracy, Sharia Law and political Islam, and in micro-societal terms (personal or individual level), that is, human rights and racism, and at epistemic level.

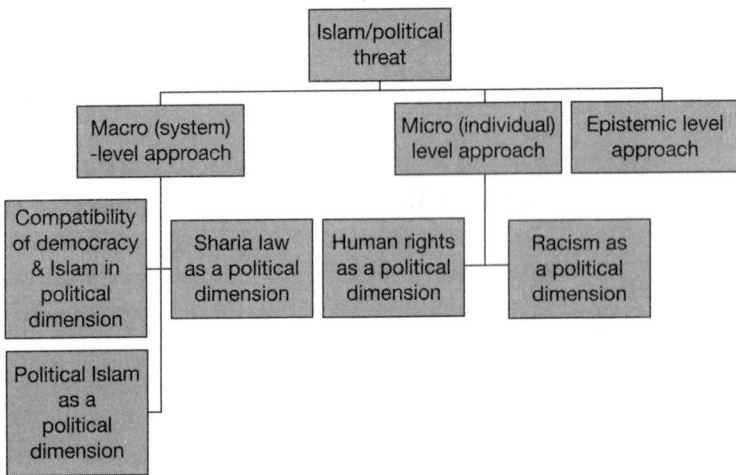

As democracy and society deal with issues on relatively larger canvas, they have been placed in the category of the system-level variables. First, democracy always depends on wisdom behind enlightenment of the people and their representatives; thus, it necessitates a system-level approach to deliberate on democracy (Mansbridge, Bohm, & Chambers, 2012). Second, political Islam has also been placed under the system-level approach due to its macro-level interference with the social system. On the other hand, political Islam is also considered a threat at system level and overturns basic suppositions regarding religion and politics entrenched in Western versions of secularism

(Hurd, 2007). Third, Sharia Law created havoc in the UK and the US politics lately and was appropriated as a system-level threat to their political systems. To avert people thinking and talking about Sharia Law in 2008 in the UK and the USA, many bills were introduced to ban accommodation of Sharia Law.

The individual or micro-level approach in political dimension of Islamophobia may well be explained under two major, but not limited to, sub-dimensions, namely (individual) human rights and racism.

MACRO (SYSTEM)-LEVEL APPROACH

Islam as a Political Threat to Democracy in the West

Dominant perception in the West concedes that Islam and democracy are not in harmony with each other and any endeavour to establish democracy following Islamic lines in the Muslim nations would create uncertainty and pose menaces to the global peace and security. The Western media and elite often demonize Islam and portray it as a religion averting democracy. Many researchers argue that Islamic tenets on political system have pessimistic view of democracy. Mishra (2005) finds that the US media coverage of Islam versus democracy has mismatch of both three times higher than the compatibility of both. The letters to editors and the editorials were emphasizing the compatibility more than it was done in the news stories, columns and opinion pieces. Researchers argue that the Christian doctrines are in line with the model of democracy, while Islamic teachings have a clear aversion from the democratic norms. It has been authenticated by Cacers (2007), who expresses that Islamic and Muslim doctrines have an overall negative view of democracy, whereas the Christian school of thought is much more at harmony with democratic values.

Practically, democracy is suitable for Islam as it refutes state of pretence of divinity. The holy book of Muslims does not identify a particular form of government that surrenders to the divine will but it demarcates the social and the political norms and values that are cardinal to the Muslim polity. It can be reasonably argued that the democracy is, among the forms of rule, the most effective system.

According to this model, democracy is a pertinent form of government advocated by the boundaries set by Islam to govern because Islam also prohibits the rulers of the state from becoming its gods and pretend to become divinely powerful (El Fadl, 2005).

Democracy is a system of government, wherein the power is concentrated in the people so as to allow them to apply and exercise that directly, and in Islamic form of governance also, the voice of the people is given preference. Naz (2016) studied the bond of Islam and democracy in practice and thus offered a new perspective. Democracy in Islam can best be defined as functioning at two levels: individual and collective. Individually, the person has the freedom to take the way of worship that he or she likes, but when it comes to the collective level, it becomes a group matter, and the voice of the people in Islam is given preference.

Modern democratization is being practised in Muslim majority countries over a century and has taken many forms. Muslims and Muslim states have always been looking for freedom in terms of politics and personal liberty to possess fair judicial systems and to have freedom of expression, which can be achieved by democracy only. The surveys of Gallup propose that Muslims do not follow any belief where Islam and democracy are at crossroads and choosing one means denying the other, rather the two systems can coexist inside one functional government. A current detailed survey in 10 populous Muslim countries with more than 80 per cent of the global population of Muslims recorded that Muslims regard the West most for its political, personal and speech freedoms as well as its judicial system; however, they repent that once ISs also had more functional and powerful judicial systems.

This sub-dimension of macro-level threat within the domain of Islam as a political threat needs to be investigated carefully to be able to counter and thwart it effectively. At political system level, Islam and modern democracy stand at binary positions in the perceptions of the Westerners. Of course, political elites, hatemongers and media have made both of them appear to confront each other, instead searching for common grounds for peaceful coexistence. In fact, Islam has more often been viewed as a political force, of which manifestations are presented in the form of ISIS, Daesh and Taliban regime in Afghanistan. Not only this, monarchs in Arab world are also depicted as the true form of Islamic governments, while they, by no way, are Islamic in their outlook and practices. This caricature of Islamic political system dreads the Westerners who took centuries to achieve the level of democracy that they are enjoying at present. There is no denying the fact that a common man is left with no other option but to refute a political system that follows ISIS and Daesh-like organizations' designs or resembles with monarchs of the Middle East.

To study this aspect of political dimension of Islamophobia, role of the agencies engaged in promoting the faulty image of Islam that is hell bound to overcome the West and establish its rule must be investigated. Who controls these agencies and what motives they have to pose Islam as a political system aiming at controlling and usurping the Western lands are some of the relevant questions. Additionally, to dispel misguided perceptions wherein Islam is supposed to take control of the Western democracies, it needs to be studied as at what level of perceptions and attitudes they exist and how deep they are engraved in the cognitions of common masses.

SHARIA LAW AS A POLITICAL DIMENSION OF ISLAMOPHOBIA

Sharia Law has been derived from Holy Quran and the practical life of Prophet of Islam (PBUH) by way of the Sunnah. Sharia Law is intertwined with morality. Sharia is an Arabic language concept with literal meaning of a spacious road that leads to a source of running water. Sharia Law is not compatible with Western values as the term 'Sharia' is widely used in the West, but it is widespread with inconsistency and confusion (Berger, 2018). In 2003, a respectable institution like the European Court of Human Rights ruled that 'sharia clearly separates from [the European] Convention [of Human Rights] values'.

The West feels threatened with Sharia. According to Reaboi (2010), Sharia is authoritarian in character, mismatched with American Constitution and a threat to freedom here and around the world. This is how Sharia is being introduced into the fabric of American society. According to 'The One Law for All Campaign', which was launched on 10 December 2008, Sharia Law is implemented in Britain through a number of Sharia Councils and Muslim Arbitration Tribunals (MATs). Both the Sharia Councils and MATs have undermined the legal rights of a large section of the population of Britain.

The anti-Sharia movement is part of larger Islamophobia. Many myths have arisen around the issue of Sharia in the USA. It has been assessed that there are over 85 Sharia Councils and MATs operating in the UK. The Sharia Council serves to facilitate Islam's compatibility with the West as well as counters the massive disagreement and propaganda over the issue. It was found through literature that the vast majority (over 90%) of people (mostly women) use Sharia Councils for an Islamic divorce (*The Independent Review*, 2018).

Westerners are of the view that the influence of Islam in their society needs to be resisted in law and politics. There is a baseless claim that Muslims in America want to incorporate Sharia into the American legal system. Americans characterize Sharia as a prejudice towards women, an institutionalized intolerance and harsh treatment to petty offences. Those who know little about Muslims and their faith often take such claims very seriously.

The scholars from the West have varying understandings, and some of them consider Sharia in a positive manner. As far as Muslims in America are concerned, Sharia is no threat to American constitutional law. Islamic law calls upon Muslims to obey the laws of the countries where they live (Pintak, 2014). Situation in the UK is not very different from the USA. Kerry Moore (2008), after extensive study on Islam, Sharia, Islamophobia and terrorism, have found that the British media have been reporting stories on a theme that 'mosques beat churches'. Further, it was noted that the UK press has been publishing articles with the headlines such as 'no more mosques', 'call to ban the building of any new mosques', 'we must stop building mosques now' and 'stop building mosques in UK'. However, it is indeed significant to examine whether there are pros or cons of Sharia Law, why Western media is reporting it a threat to the Western society and a challenge to their rules. One of the reasons as why Western media is portraying Sharia negatively might be 'war on terror' and reporting on operations against extremist and jihadi groups across the globe.

On the other side, the extremist groups such as ISIS and Taliban maintain that there is a further literal explanation of the teachings of Holy Quran and that of other sources of divine knowledge that include things such as stoning the adulterers to death and necessarily oppress women within certain boundaries. For militant jihadists, it is important to include their desire for Sharia Law in the conversation because the goal of establishing Sharia Law reveals a lot about these groups. For instance, in Nigeria, a jihadi group Boko Haram (BH) and IS, operating in Iraq and Syria, have recently produced remarkable threats. These groups have been advocates of unleashing violent operations to establish multinational empires, 'caliphate', aiming to erase national borders (Celso, 2015). This jihadi group (IS) is operating in Iraq and claims to rule according to Sharia and is portraying a violent image of Sharia.

According to Auda, the principal purposes of Islamic laws are to accomplish their original purposes of justice, freedom, rights, common good and tolerance in today's setting. Similarly, back in 1987, Souryal made a comparative study of Sharia (divine) law practised in Saudi Arabian society with six Muslim countries in the region. The study claimed that a high level of compassion in Saudi Arab is due to the application of Sharia Law. He studied crime rates in the Kingdom of Saudi Arabia and compared them with other neighbouring countries not applying Sharia Law. It was found that crime rate was intensely lower in the Kingdom of Saudi Arabia than the median rate among the group as well as considerably lower than in any individual country. However, there might be other associated reasons for low crime rate and poverty in Saudi Arabia as compared to other neighbouring countries of the Gulf.

Sharia Law is a much debated but less understood subject in the Western media, which has created massive misunderstanding of a law that has roots in the holy books and practices of the Prophet of Islam (PBUH). Has Sharia Law posed any threat to the West or has it been made an excuse to demean and denigrate a religion that has followers in billions? Whatever is the reason for confusions on Sharia Law, it has been discussed and debated in the realm of macro-level Islamophobia in the contemporary media discourses.

POLITICAL ISLAM AS A DIMENSION OF ISLAMOPHOBIA

The term 'political Islam' or Islamism first emerged in Europe in the 1940s, while defining anti-colonial movements. These anti-colonial movements described themselves as Islamic in orientation. Being a 20th-century concept, it is believed to have been expressed prominently throughout 1927 when Muslim Brotherhood of Egypt was founded (Paracha, 2014). The post-9/11 global politics massively altered the entire debate on the relationship between the West and Islam, wherein political Islam seems to have a war with the West. Political Islam resorts to original sources to demonstrate Muslim responses to perceived threat of Westernization and, notably, the development of political Islam as a reaction to the evolving sociopolitical conditions in the Middle East (Granada, 2009).

The term political Islam is defined in different contexts by the Western and Muslim scholars. Western view of political Islam follows a political agenda, which cannot be resolved with the basic principles of democracy, liberties and individual civil rights. For Muslim scholars, political Islam is an academic and political expression which is used to describe the Islamic guidance and evolution of political movements, defining Islam as a political system of controlling the affairs of the state; a belief that Islam is not merely a religion with few rituals related to worship but also a perfect and an all-inclusive system of politics, a social system, a legal system and an economic system with the potential to construct the relations of the state (Rababa'a, 2012). Threats like association of political Islam with underdevelopment, autocratic governance and disregard for human rights make it appear as Islamophobia and make America wary of supporting political Islam.

Many more factors give negative connotation to the term political Islam, as highlighted by Koningsveld and Shadid (2002), who opine that significant debate on Islam has mainly been driven by national and international expansions. These international expansions include the Islamic revolution in Iran, the hue and cry over the objectionable writings of Rushdie, the Gulf War, the war in former Yugoslavia, the upheavals of Afghanistan—all, in a nutshell, contributed to make Islam and the Muslim world a global political issue. Second noticeable factor has been the increasing trend of migration of Muslims to the countries constituting the EU.

The term political Islam has negative connotation in the West, whether it is their media or general public discourse. Pervaiz (2007) analysed that Muslims are being judged through the prism of West's own history. He found that Western press perceives the political issues related to Islam as a menace. Contrary to this, some scholars have investigated that mosque attendance and religious participation by Muslims create more positive political participation in American democratic values, as it sounds like peace-loving individuals. Dana and Oskooii (2018) conducted Muslim American Public Opinion Survey (MAPOS), which had a large sample size of American Muslim respondents ($N = 1,410$), they recorded that the mosque has risen as a sign of social and political incorporation of Muslims into American society. Their analysis further demonstrates that mosque attendance and participation, beyond creating a common identity among American Muslims, leads to more political contribution in the USA. It was concluded that religiosity promotes support for American democratic values.

Nonetheless, dominant views about political Islam are clearly negative and demonstrate active participation of Muslims holding tightly their religious beliefs to win over other religious and cultural identities in the Western lands. Such moves and motives are taken as invasion of the West by the Muslims, which get support from the history, and media and public discourses. Consequently, rise in anti-Muslim and anti-Islam sentiments forms Islamophobia.

MICRO (INDIVIDUAL) LEVEL APPROACH

Micro-level approach in political dimension of Islamophobia sheds light on individual-level relationship between Muslims and the people from other religions. Generally, threats emanate from micro-level results on isolated attacks by the bigots, seclusion of Muslim students at schools, workplace harassment of employees with Islamic identity, intolerance for veiling women or men with beard and turban, to include a few. Kaya (2015) describes anti-Muslim prejudice and racism almost completely by individual-level factors. Here, the micro-level Islamophobia approach in political dimension is categorized into two main subdivisions: racism as a political threat and human rights violations.

Racism as a Political Dimension of Islamophobia

Islamophobia is not an intractable construct, rather a highly enterprising phenomenon. In fact, it is a multifaceted bundle of multiple dimensions such as sociocultural differences, belief systems, global political economic systems and, very importantly, racism.

Every day, Muslims are targeted due to racism, and Islamophobia is considered as an anti-Muslim racism affecting people when they are applying for a job or visiting doctors. There is a kind of a structural form of Islamophobia impacting people in their everyday lives. *The Politics of Islamophobia* by Tyrer (2013) is an important contribution to the expanding literature on the social phenomena of Islamophobia. The author seeks to describe the situation through real-life stories and proposes conceptual account of Islamophobia as a political appearance of racism, while Islam does not discriminate on the pretext of race, colour, group of people, tribes or classes. Rather, it distinguishes individuals on the basis of piety and piety only (Andrabi, 2016).

British media often highlight Islam against a background of cultural difference between British Muslims and other Brits. Similarly, Moore, Mason, and Lewis (2008) analysed one of the approaches of racism, wherein British media regularly report on women veils, the peculiar dress, the arranged marriage against the will of the brides by constructing the Muslim minority as a distinct cultural and political group. Media covered the caricature dispute of Denmark in sarcastic fashion creating the cultural chasm and separating Muslims of Britain from the rest of the population.

Islamophobia, as a phenomenon, has been equated with racism by some scholars. For instance, Saeed (2008) while investigating British media reporting on Islam and Muslims declared racism as the primary reason for the misrepresentation of British Muslims. Many scholars are of the viewpoint that anti-Muslim racism was primarily due to recent increase of xenophobia and then Islamophobia in the aftermath of 9/11 catastrophe. Racism and Islamophobia have always been linked with inequality, mental illness and hopelessness. West (2016) in her book stated several complete approaches of racism caused by psychosocial analysis, racism, Islamophobia and fundamentalism which are understood with respect to growing inequality, mental illness and hopelessness, all within a context of broken economies, malfunctioning democracies and the reduction of education's purpose.

One of the aspects of Islamophobia is the colour consciousness. This aspect is seeing Muslims as of a particular colour and from a particular descent with a known and vilified cultural and religious background, making them citizens of not the first but deserving to be treated as second-class citizens. Islamophobia is one of the root causes of racial prejudice in America. The unfortunate attacks of 9/11, the crisis of refuges and the urges from the prominent public figures for strict actions like the US President Donald Trump, etc., are adding fuel to it. This has resulted in an enormous increase in the crimes based on hatred against the Americans of the Middle East origin. The advocates of the rights of civilians are striving to solve this issue, however. Placing Islamophobia into the well-worn context of racism provides clear illustrations to study and understand the multidimensional manifestations of the phenomenon in the social and political spheres, and makes it less anomalous and less mysterious, while racism has always been present in the history of human being, especially after the 14th century, and Islamophobia has been playing an important role in the social construction of racism.

Most of the Western world's offending unreal and disfigured narratives have been manufactured against Muslims and their religion.

This includes the establishment of an overall mindset, deeply rooted among masses, and has the potential to invoke in the wake of communal clashes, resulting in the involvement of Muslims therein. The political reasons of Islamophobia are represented by many right-wing extremist movements, which employ Islamophobia as a means to gain popularity by intimidating Muslims and promising their electorates, if elected, to enact strict laws against Muslims. Based on these realities, including racial profiling of Muslims, Islamophobia has become a form of racism mixed with cultural intolerance as a whole, rather than simply intolerance of Muslims and Islam.

HUMAN RIGHTS AS POLITICAL DIMENSION

Religions have often been separated from human rights in the US press. Mishra (2008) analysed that the dialogues and narratives in the mainstream press of the USA oft-times suppose the prominence of the religious exhibition publicly and politically, which automatically hints at the non-presence of any regards to human rights. The USA and Muslim countries have a shared history of awkward relationships with the UN Human Rights system. The mistaken impression that the USA is a strong backer of international human rights law has been encouraged because it has often vigorously promoted human rights overseas as part of its foreign policy, for example, the US invasion in Iraq (Mayer, 2006).

Women's status in Islam has always been misunderstood and misrepresented. Laura Navarro (2017) argues that woman has been one of the most misinterpreted and deformed topic in discussions and discourses on Islam. The manufactured records of women hailing from Islam shown on media amid asking for ways to get rid of the veil (hijab) and sometimes going to the extent to give up the religion of Islam being too narrow not only run through the veins of the media of Britain but also filter into national and foreign policy measures. Studies have analysed that Muslims want to replace worldly Western model with Islamic public law but are facing the challenge of basic universal human rights.

Religions have often been detached from human rights. Sharia is restricted by minimum standards of universal human rights

(An-Na'im, 1987). Said (1979) argues that like other civilizations, Islam also has the human rights centred on the self-respect of the individual, the protection of self-esteem and personal identity, and it supports human community. The religion of Islam, with an intention to enhance freedom, ensure justice and increase opportunities, has laid down foundations of an order in the society for ensuring human rights perfectly. Mayor (2007) maintains that the Islamic concept of the basic rights of man is very often seen as a static nexus between the two. The fact is this relationship is complicated and alterable. In an age, when the status quo is facing changes that are unsettled, the understandings about Islam and the rights of human beings have a decided sensitivity towards the shift of political diversities. In the present scenario, the perception that the human rights and Islam are contradicting inherently, that assumes two settled commodities in a strong relationship, has become hard nut to sustain, as is the position that human rights are indispensable part of the civilization of the West. Contrarily, Muslims argue to prove that Islam promises more human rights than any other religion and political system of the world. Human rights are those principles which are of utmost concern in Islam.

There are issues which are working alternatively, in quite opposite directions of the aforementioned perceptions. The US policies of demonizing Islam as hostile towards human rights and portraying that Muslims are looking towards the Western set of rights of men are nefarious plotting. This is quite obvious and should be taken without any qualm that Islam, according to all definitions, is in harmony with the human rights and it has the elasticity to adjust and readjust with the changing times and spaces.

EPISTEMIC APPROACH

There have been endeavours on part of scholars studying Islam vis-à-vis its epistemology. They have done so with an intention to look for possibilities of any Islamic epistemology, whether or not the Islamic body of knowledge is of any use for epistemologies. The Quran and the Sunnah are at the heart of Islamic epistemology.

Tawhid for Salam and Shaikh (2014) is at the heart of Islamic epistemology with the main sources of knowledge, namely al-Quran and al-Sunnah, and *Ijma* (consensus) as the tertiary source gathered from social consensus but not contradicting Quran and Sunnah. Hurd (2007) investigated the epistemological skeleton of the foreign policy of America and Europe regarding the political facet of Islam. He found that the approaches of both towards political face of Islam are in accordance with the common possession of a set of secular propositions about religiosity and towards the politics. These hallmarks decide major effects of it on the foreign policy of America and Europe. This secular epistemic consideration evolves a comprehensive set of normal politics, which look with a certain coloured lens towards the politics of societies with Muslims in majority. The wisdom dominated by secularism influences foreign policy doubly. At the first place, political facet of Islam is demonized and equated with a system devoid of tolerance and predominated with fundamentalism. Second, the degree or extent of gap between Islam and politics whether or not existing in the current societies having Muslims in majority may appear manifested as a mismatch to the so-called European secular model or may not appear at all.

Islam cannot possibly be adapted with democracy due to the epistemological and ontological gaps. Sardarnia and Bahrampour (2017), amid using a research technique of comparison and analysis, while investigating the possible ways of acclimatization of Islam with democracy and the compatibility of the two, or even the contrasting factors of the two, reached the hypothetical argument that the differences between Islam and democracy are epistemic and ontological, hindering the adaptability of the one with the other. A critical insight into the matter noted that domestication is not unreasonable. Seeking the divides between the two is not reasonable enough due to various reasons such as the basic Islamic foundations are same as those practised through Islamic history, the rule of despotic rulers and radical Islamists and the universal secular narrative of democracy combining with the ethnic chauvinism.

Othering as Islamophobia

Othering is a process in which an individual or a group is vilified and denied the characteristics of nobility, pride, love, dignity, heroism, reason and so on. It is not only denigration, vilification and scapegoating but also denying the 'other' entitlement to any human rights. It is a phenomenon of defining and establishing one's own identity by vilifying and opposing the other. The other based on religion, ethnicity, race, gender or nationality is a minority group which is denied its essential and basic humanity. They are denied their own voice and the opportunity to speak for themselves, and are exploited and oppressed. Greeks' use of 'barbarian' to describe non-Greeks, Rwandan genocide and ethnic cleansing of Bosnia are some examples of *othering*.

The concept of 'other' has a lot of complexity, and it is difficult to explain what it means. We all are others for someone; similarly, everyone is other to us. We cannot understand the whole concept of 'other' as it is changeable and dynamic. When we indicate someone as other, concurrently, we are also other to them and they think the same about us (Engelund, 2012). Contemporarily, the notion of 'other' stems from Edward Said's concept of orientalism, wherein the West perceives Islam as 'inferior', 'strange' and 'threatening' *other* (Said, 2003, p. 3). Said argues that orientalism has its roots in the polarization of the Occident West and the Orient other (Said, 1997). He argues that the Western media, by misrepresenting the East, has made the Orient as its 'other' (Said, 1978, 2003). He further stresses that 'orientalism' is a doctrine used by the West with political intentions where the Orient is not understood and represented in its true nature but on the basis of Western European experience about the Orient, while the Westerners believe it as the objective representation. Such representations turn into stereotypes, and the latest media technology has solidified and accelerated the process (Said, 1978, 2003). Said claims that it is the representation of Islam by the Western media which creates problems, rather than Islam itself.

In general terms, anyone 'separate' from one's self is considered as the 'other', and the existence of the 'other' is essential and fundamental for one's own identity (Ashcroft, 2013). Gayatri Spivak coined the term *othering* for the process in which the imperial discourse creates its 'other' (Ashcroft, 2013; Spivak, 1985). The term refers to the psychological and/or social methods by one group (imperial/powerful) to 'marginalize', 'exclude' and 'master' the 'other' (Ashcroft, 2013). The 'other' people/groups are to be 'homogenized' and 'collectivized' into iconic 'they' (Pratt, 1985).

Lévi-Strauss (1955), Levinas (1969) and Lacan (1988) are the theorists whose extensive works have helped theorizing the concept of other. All these scholars seem to be inspired by one another. Levi-Strauss (1955, 1992) suggests that throughout the history, people have used two strategies to deal with the other, stranger, deviant, foreigner, etc. The first one is to incorporate them into their own society or even into their own identity by elimination of boundaries. However, this phenomenon of absorbing strangers has been less practised throughout the history. The second one is to exclude or leave them out from one's own society, to make boundaries for them and to keep them under control of stronger institutions (Levi-Strauss, 1955, 1992).

Philosopher Levinas (1969) has based his moral philosophy on the face-to-face encounter of individuals, that is, with another man or woman, viewing the moment of this come upon as the one irreducible and urban way of setting up a relation with the opposite, as in opposition to counting on summary and impersonal rules of ethics to accomplish that. Psychoanalyst Lacan (1988) examines how the ego is formed through the initial years of infancy as a child sees his/her own face in the mirror. A child being really young first comes across himself/herself as 'other' and misunderstands himself/herself as somebody else, after that maintaining this recognition in the eyes of 'other'.

This, therefore, creates quite an interesting connection between the idea of the other and isolation. Othering is a manner that can be carried out to oneself, wherein one sees oneself as a stranger. So Lacan's (1988) concept sees this 'self-othering' as a process where the symbolic order is set up—the unaware stranger within ourselves. A man, for instance, has no desire but to stay calm or perhaps kill the 'female in him'. It can be observed through the work of Lacan (1988) that *othering* is just a process, a natural procedure of differentiation, as different individuals cannot be expected to act in similar ways, for instance, males and females, Christians and Muslims, etc. Therefore, *othering* is a phenomenon where various individuals or groups are distinguished on the basis of their characteristics. Further on, Strauss' (1955) work on *othering* explains a negative connotation linked with it, as it distinguishes, expels and eliminates the 'other' from the main focus or majority. Levinas' (1969) work further explores face-to-face *othering*, where individuals are others on the basis of any characteristic, which is not part of mainstream. Thus, *othering* is to expel them from the majority on the basis of religion, belief, gender or any other element.

First, theoretical and systematic explanation of the notion *othering* was coined by Spivak in 1985 (mainly through her explanation of subaltern class). According to her, the concept of othering draws on several theoretical and philosophical traditions. Significantly, the notion of othering draws on the 'understanding of self', which is based on the generalization of Hegal's concept. Hegal explained the theory of self and other in which a combination of self and other towards the other constitutes the self (Jensen, 2011).

Othering can also occur in any region among various groups that recognize each 'other' distinctly, and they might have lived in close proximity for hundreds of years but still *othering* can lead to genocide. The genocide of Rwanda and the ethnic cleansing of Bosnia are glaring examples. In those conditions, othering is precipitated by means of what Freud (1921) called 'narcissism of minute variations'—the individual or group of people that 'othered' is the one in closest bodily and figurative proximity, as it is far visible to present a major chance to anyone's identification and conceit precisely what befell to Freud and masses of thousands of Jews in Europe, especially Germany.

The concept of 'otherness' has the most centralized status in sociological analysis that how minority and majority identities are built. This is because the most powerful political group within the society has control over representation of different groups/identities. Sociologists/social scientists are needed to put a serious spotlight on methods and techniques in which social identities are constructed to understand the idea of other. We often think that identities are innate and natural, and everyone has his/her identity by birth, but it is surprising that many sociologists considered this view as not a truth but an erroneous and inaccurate understanding of social identities (Zevallos, 2011).

According to Farouk (2016), the *othering* of Muslims dates back to the fight between Spanish Christian monarch and the Islamic side of Spain (Al-Andalus) in 1492. Since then, the expulsion of Muslims from Christian Spain was based on religious discrimination and was a 'proto-racist process' (Farouk, 2016). After that, with the beginning of colonial enterprise, the imperial powers started characterizing Muslims as 'uncivilized' and 'violent' in 'full racist perspective' (Farouk, 2016). Farouk (2016) argues that 'religion' is a key in the latest cultural racist discourses. Today's inferior 'other' depictions as 'savage', 'barbarian', 'primitive', 'uncivilized', 'authoritarian', 'underdeveloped' and 'terrorist' are concentrated in 'their' religious beliefs and practices (Farouk, 2016).

Othering is a strategic process where the emphasis is on 'differences rather than similarities', where the 'distribution of power' between the 'known' and 'unknown' is stressed, and where the 'other' is always 'judged', 'repressed' and 'mediated' in an 'unequal' and 'biased' way (Mertens, 2016; Nurullah, 2010; Tsagarousianou, 2016). The distinction between 'us' and 'them' is stressed through differing religious, ethnic and racial attributes and characters (Nurullah, 2010). During the *othering* process, the Western media 'misrepresent' the Orient to create its 'other' (Said, 1978, 2003). Media 'include some and exclude others' on the basis of various 'criteria', 'characteristics' and 'differences' (Ottosen, 1995). The process includes the 'individualizing' of the perpetrator to appease any 'racial accusations', and then 'othering' the individual by linking him/her to 'radicals' outside 'our' territory who 'brainwashed' the perpetrator with the 'extreme religious and murderous ideology' (Poole, 2016). Thus, the perpetrator is linked to 'Islamic ideology' (Ibid., p. 29).

Othering is a discursive process in which the 'other' is represented, labelled and constructed as strange and different to 'us' (Wadumestri, 2010). It serves as a discourse wherein the differences within unequal relations are articulated and naturalized. There are various forms of *othering* identified by different scholars. For instance, the representation of different ethnicity and race under the impact of imperialism and colonialism occurs through the *othering* discourses (Roy, 2009).

Summarily, *othering* can be:

- → Textual
- → Discursive
- → Socio-psychological
- → Intentional
- → Unintentional

Adams (1994) argues that *othering* is the common pattern followed by the West. Basically, it is considered as a system in which their binary categorization is on the basis of an object and a subject. The subject is a notorious, recognized individual of the society having control over mind and body, whereas the other, which is the object, may be any individual or group, who/which is the ultimate receiver of ideas or insights of the subject. This procedure can lead to the exploitation of objects according to the desires of the subject. This structure of *othering* takes place in culture, gender and species.

The 'us' versus 'them' strategy assumes the exotic culture as inferior, ancient, partial and belated, and incomplete as compared to the Western culture. The binary relationship between 'us' and 'them' is stressed by emphasizing on 'our' tolerance being abused by 'those' who want to impose 'their' lifestyle on 'us' (Poole, 2016). The binary positions are highlighted by concentrating on 'censorious nature of Islam' as compared to 'our' liberal and freedom of speech (p. 31). Muslims are 'collectivized' and constructed as being at odds to 'our' values such as democracy, rule of law, liberty and freedom of speech (p. 35). The 'marginalization' and 'demarcation' of 'them' illustrate 'social categorization', that is, the division of society into two proto-types: in-group and out-group. In-group (we) and out-group (them) members are compared on the basis of various characters. Numerous attributes and drawbacks are associated with the out-group members such as collectivism, backwardness, laziness, religiousness, violence, low education, being economic burden, crime, poverty, high fertility and hard to be integrated.

Usually, individuals keep distance between them and others, considering them as someone finer or better and keep apart from the estranged other group taken as 'different'. A hidden reason behind this *othering* is the presumption about the other culture or beliefs, due to which they alienate them. History reveals that this *othering* remained unavoidable as the world's devastating challenges are based on global, national and regional divergence and is inclusive of group-based aspects. People are evaluated on the basis of their cultural beliefs and norms. This *othering* is propagated by those people who are against diversity in culture and do not accept individuals from other societies. A major example in this regard is that of ideology of orientalism (Said, 1978), which illustrates how the Western world defines the Eastern world. Although the East has its own defined norms and beliefs, the Western world has a presumed view about it and considers the Eastern world as subordinate and inferior.

MacKenzie (1995) illustrates that Western people's understanding about the East is that they are alien, suspicious and uncultured. They define the Eastern world as a place for slave market and exposed women. Not only their cultural norms are taken as degraded ones but also their cultural beliefs are considered inferior. People consider their religious beliefs as superior and evaluate other religions within their own frames. Islamophobia is the obvious example to illustrate the *othering* ideology. According to Allen (2010), as there is diversity of predispositions regarding Islam and Muslims, Islamophobia cannot be defined properly. As people have certain defined sets of stereotypes about their own faith, they take themselves as authority and alienate

Muslims and consider them 'outside' the group. Muslims are thus judged on the ideology of 'none of us'.

Abdullah (2014) describes the term 'othering' as the process of reducing the dominance of people or groups which are present in the periphery to assist subordination. It substantiates the moral obligation of the powerful or strong self to inform, educate, change and improve the weaker self. This term identifies the difference from recognized normal social groups, which makes one oneself and 'others', especially in terms of gender, ethnic, racial and relational aspects.

From the earlier explanation, it is quite obvious that *othering* can be on the basis of:

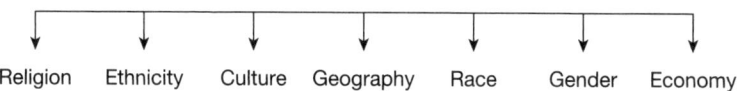

Religion   Ethnicity   Culture   Geography   Race   Gender   Economy

The idea of other is relevant to Said's (2003) *Orientalism*. The other is the Orient, an individual who lives in the East and who's socially and historically built as both different and exclusive, as opposed to the relationship with the people of the Occident. Thus, they are considered as different to the Europeans in the dynamic and enlightened Western world.

Said's (1978) work explores the cultural representations, which are primarily based on orientalism. He explains orientalism as West's pretentious representations of the East—the societies and people who inhabit the locations of Asia, Africa and the Middle East. Said further explains that orientalism denotes Western scholarship about the Eastern part of the world, which is inevitably linked to the imperialist societies who created it. While referring to the contemporary role of media and USA's handling of the others, he says:

> America through its media always mentions Moslems and Arabs as either oil providers or terrorists. Little or have none of the element, the human density, the passion of Arab–Moslem existence has entered the attention of even those people whose profession it's far to file the Arab world. What they've, as a substitute, is a chain of crude, indispensable caricatures of the Islamic world, offered in this kind of manner as to make Islam or Muslims susceptible to military violence.

Said's (1981) explanation of orientalism suggests that the West has held biased view of Arabs and Islam. According to Said, orientalism can mean different things as he places it:

> The most with no trouble suited designation for Orientalism is an academic one…each person who teaches, writes, informs or researches the Orient…is known as Orientalist, and what she or he does is Orientalism…. A more well known explanation for Orientalism…is a pattern of thought primarily based on an ontological and epistemological difference made among 'the Orient' and (majority of the time) 'the Occident'.

Scholarly work by Christina (2010) deals with the question as to what extent thoughts of others and thoughts of one's own society play a role in decision-making, and whose cultural, social and anthropological considerations weigh more. It is generally presumed that often a critical mindset towards one's own societal contemplations in comparison to other's inclines towards cogitation, but not an average individual who accepts his own values without challenging them. The theoretical part of her work specializes in how categories of 'us' and 'others' are built. In major portion of her work, ethnocentrism, Eurocentrism, orientalism and exoticism, othering and the concept of stereotyping in addition to postmodern and feminist processes are discussed. Furthermore, the topic of strangeness is taken into account, and diverse opportunities of the belief of the stranger are provided.

Furthering with Christina (2010), within the theoretical debate, it is far from approximate thinking, seriously examining the development of crucial classes of self and other. Against this historical past, exceptional ideas are also found to be difficult to answer the question; qualitative interviews had been performed with beginners of cultural and social anthropology in Vienna. It turned into all approximately making subconscious ideas in relation to the others seen. This painting seeks to demonstrate the need for a critical method to one's own thoughts and assumptions that affect the illustration of others. Based on the empirical investigation, exceptional conceptions of own society and the opposite can be provided, in addition to uncommon depiction and the need for admiration and appreciation for others, and the preference to enhance the state of affairs of others will be decisive for the choice of examining sociocultural and anthropological recognition.

SUBTLE OTHERING

Afua Hirsch (2018), a staffer of Sky News and the *Guardian*, experienced a different kind of racism, and later on some scholastic pieces on *othering* revealed that it is not just all about violent racism but, as she described them, 'micro-aggressions' and 'subtle prejudice'. This describes the idea of subtle *othering* where it is not that obvious, and rather concealed, under some manifested and latent patterns and systems. This actually crystallizes the religious ideologies of individuals. It also includes the examples of *othering* among sects within the same religion.

Othering is a term that no longer simply focuses on various expressions of prejudice on the basis of group identifications; however, it is argued that it offers an illustrative body that mentions hard and fast rules of not unusual processes and conditions that promote institutionalized inequality and marginality (Thomas, 2016). Despite the fact that particular expressions of othering, along with racism or ethnocentrism, are frequently well identified and richly studied, this broader phenomenon is inadequately recognized as such. In literature, 13 dimensions of othering are identified and discussed that are varyingly based on, but not exceptionally restrained to, religion, sex, race, ethnicity, socioeconomic reputation (elegance), disability, sexual orientation, and pores and skin tone. Even though the axes of difference that undergird those expressions of othering vary significantly and are deeply contextual, they incorporate a similar set of underlying dynamics.

Thus, on the basis of Hirsch's (2018) and Thomas' (2016) explanation of group-based *othering*, it can be argued that there is a subtle form of *othering* which is present within various groups. These can be religious or racial groups. For instance, in the religion of Islam, Muslims, who are a part of different sects, consider individuals from other sect(s) as different or inferior. In a way, this is also *othering* but does not essentially include extreme elements in it. However, contemporarily in many parts of Muslim-majority countries, sectarian strives are on the rise.

Example:

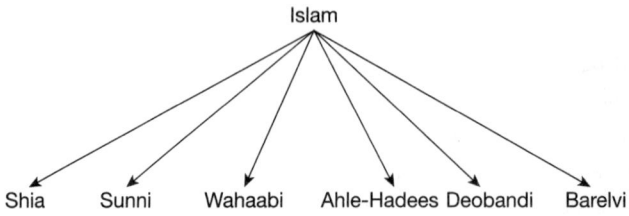

According to Menendian (2017), othering does not only focus on the bigotry patterns of discrimination, but it also actually clarifies the framework which exposes the common procedures that disseminate group-based discrimination or inequality. Although certain aspects, such as racism or ethnocentric ideologies, are studied deeply, this dimension of *othering* is insufficiently recognized. While further elaborating the idea of group-based *othering*, Menendian (2017) discusses that it is not just all about religion, socio-economic status, disability, race, sex, ethnicity, skin colour or sexual orientation. Nonetheless, the dimensions of these expressions of *othering* are deeply contextual, and they have same patterns of underlying motives. Also, *othering* or alienation can be individual as well as at group level. Most individuals have experiences of being at a place where they were exposed to an awkward situation when entering into a place or conversation with which they feel either not related or uncomfortable; and the people around make them somewhat irrelevant even in general social talks. This nature of feeling might be temporary but is felt by the individual, and hence he/she suffers being *othered*.

Scholars also explored the subtle othering, which may be understood as a hierarchization of society. A majority separates itself from a minority through attributions and affords itself as being privileged or distinct, thereby sending an elusive message to others as being different and somewhat irrelevant. The minorized others are thus denied getting the right of entry to social resources. Othering occurs via attributions of countrywide linguistic, spiritual, cultural, ethnic and also sexual nature.

OTHERING AS ISLAMOPHOBIA

According to Mahamdallie (2015), Islamophobia is one of the major forms of racism in Europe in today's era. It has established to be compelling, persuasive and comprehensive at not only political level but also at state level evidently. It immensely signifies a disruptive force as 'Muslim question' has been the major factor of 'war on terror', wherein they are portrayed as being the people who pose serious challenges to the Western civilization, modern norms and values. This has eventually disposed Muslims to their luck, making them face strict security measures, and military intrusions are imposed on them by the West in a bid to eliminate 'Islamist terrorism' at all levels. This form of racism or Islamophobia is similar to prejudice where the other is victimized, marginalized and considered as a threat to peaceful societies. Said (1978) observed that hatred against Islam in the West has increased with time, and prejudice has evolved over time.

Creutz-Kämppi (2008) analysed the polarizing discourses in Swedish language dailies in Finland. Depiction of Islam in the Finnish media is generally related to happenings all across the globe. These representations serve as a prelude to cumulative arrangements with influence on groupings for self-identifications in certain cases. The discussions on media portrayal of cartoons of Prophet Muhammad (PBUH) in the Swedish language dailies are analysed to see the 'othering discourses'. The representation of Islam, which is being built upon the immense custom of othering, is quite similar to primitive representations. The advancement in technology has revolutionized the idea of local media, which is now part of global public's sphere. This leads to not only a concern about happenings all around the world but also one's own placement in the expanded community. The media representation develops pictures of the 'outside world' and simultaneously creates the grouping for self-identification, particularly on globally controversial issues like 'war on terror'. This eventually raises the query as 'whom do I represent'. Although there is an understanding of propaganda tactics at the rear of this type of political conversation, it still creates an impact of individual and religion worldwide. Europe is the major or prominent figure for this phenomenon of othering of Islam. Discourses of violence, colonialist secularization and clash of civilizations are commonly observed when it comes to representation of Islam in the European media. Thus, media increase the chance to develop more diversified 'reality'—all through the history, providing ground or basis to the argument, which eventually leads to shared future.

Riggins (1997) describes that discourses of other are presented through major majority and subsidiary minorities. Others are not just agencies that can be devaluated, demeaned or silenced via dominant majorities, but for apparent political motives, generally research specializes in the discourses of *othering* present in the conventional populations. Similarly, Silva (2016) through his work employs Said's orientalism and various aspects in othering context to explore the evolution and conversion of discourses of radicalization in media, specifically news media. It is explored using the discourse analysis method of enquiry; various news articles that discourse on radicalization are not new; rather, they are the consequence of complicated socio-linguistic and evolutions in history, which cannot be compressed to assertive modern understanding of the idea and associated to single happening or crisis. Later on, a comparison was made among these news items, documents and speeches of government and various communications at official level. This scrutiny reveals that conceptualization of media regarding radicalization, which once bespeaks about economic and political differences, has now deviated mindboggling focus on Islam. In essence, the discourse of radicalization has invoked the construction of radicalization as a signified indicator between the East and the West. Therefore, it is argued through this study that conscious decisive effort is made by the media to conceptualize differences, which are used to construe Muslims as 'aliens' and 'others' to the West. Silva's study reveals that radicalization discourses are comparatively simple and are general portrayal of interposed form to political violence. More investigation is required to see the impact on society, diverse institutions in creating and recreating our knowledge, and approach of terrorism-related aspects. Perpetual issues and problems are linked with radicalization and very less focus is given to the organizations or institutions that are developing them in general manner. Media has developed a prominent understanding of radicalization by linking it with Islamic regulations, thus narrowing the definition of Islam for the general audiences. This has aroused and created the concept of 'us' and 'them', presenting different representations of East and West, providing ingredients for strong perceptions against the Islamic culture. Thus, media is the source for this radicalization, and these discourses of radicalization have implications on other dimensions of society as well.

MEDIA AS A CATALYST

According to Kamenova (2014), media has this capability of creating powerful images, which sink into not only the minds but also the subconscious minds of the people. It has great significance as the mind is a very fragile and important part of human body, particularly when it is related to the behaviour of 'other'. Researches on the role of media in creating that otherness are very limited. Trattner (2016) through his work describes that although media has this power of unlimited number of representations, even then various mediums, especially video games, still opt for condensed, simple, eulogized and typical depiction of characters and also implied environment. Othering on the basis of religion, gender, culture or race is a commonly observed approach in any category. It is illustrated further in this study that at many instances, the element of religion is just the depreciating factor and is explicit only when examined deeply and that too in comparison to some other category. This study reveals the presence of othering on the basis of religion in video games in comparison to other categories. Games like Medal of Honor: Warfighter (released in 2012) proved to be a clear example of representation of Islam and the Middle East as existing modern military shooters. A deep analysis of the comments on YouTube uncovers that the same about the religion of Islam is perceived by the gamers as well. Not all the cultural commodities are created in vacuum; rather, they inhibit the biasness of their creators. Having an equal relationship with the societal discourse, video games not only have the perceptions and inclination in the sense that they replicate them, but they also publicize and merge them. This article has further taken into account the phenomenon of othering on the basis of religion present in different layers of video games and also how it is re-arbitrated by the gamers. Representation of Islam in this particular case study of Medal of Honor: Warfighter is a prominent example in this regard, where religion is a marginalizing factor and linked directly with delimiting identity makers. This game has prominent images of war on terror, which is also present in other media in the form of textual contents, visuals or images on radio, TV or newspapers. These famous imaginations are perceived as innately connected to Islam, Muslims, the Middle East and jihadism. This consummated analysis of discourses of gamers has divulged that the creators of these games also to some extent believe in othering of Islam. The representation of othering discourses on the basis of religion, especially Islam, through video games is endorsed by majority of gamers but at the same time disapproved and undermined by others.

Thus, it is obvious that the stance of media in electronic, social or print platform has strong impact on the thinking patterns of people. The depiction of Muslims as terrorists in video games or dramas or movies further exasperates the views of people against Muslims and Islam. Thus, media is playing the role of catalyst in this regard. Stephans (2013) in his work argues that human nature can be seen in a manner that humans will always prepare themselves into categories such as in-organizations and out-organizations. This is generally conceived in racial terms, wherein race of people is perceived as a part of human identity. This (racial) categorization has led human beings to view those who are not inside the identical institution as distinct or different, and eventually 'the others'. In this manner, they assign nice characteristics to themselves and bad qualities to people who they regard as others while considering it to be natural. This examination could be carried out by figuring out the main variations of inferiority, incompetence and violence of respondents discourse; *othering* then appears to be central to most of them due to the fact that they understand themselves to be better than their racial different.

Conclusively, media at various occasions is acting as a catalyst in creating othering discourse. It can incite and infuriate the thought process of individuals who already have negative feelings about others, which may be any individual or group, or any community.

Clash of Civilization or Islam versus West

It is interesting to note that, on the one hand, social media is creating a unified culture across the world by bridging the sociocultural and political gaps, whereas, on the other hand, the emergence of Daesh, ISIS, Al-Qaeda and ongoing wars in Afghanistan, Syria and Iraq is pushing the world into a clash of civilization like situation. The state of engagement between Islam and the West, as competing partners, is the most visible account of the ongoing state of conflicts in the contemporary world. Islam is often regarded as misanthropy and its followers as misanthropists and anti-democratic entities, whereas the West is evinced as the democracy lover and torchbearer of human rights. There is no denying the fact that Europe achieved the status of a democratic continent, which demonstrates its long struggle to take lessons from its history fraught with miseries and wars, enabling it to establish democracy, human rights and religious and cultural diversity as its inviolable and inalienable rights for its inhabitants. Nonetheless, Muslims also have a strong and shining past, and Islam has been advocating all those sociocultural and political traits that are hallmarks of the West today.

Both worlds, Islam and the West, are grossly perceived incorrectly, especially by each other. Talking about Islam in the West is unpleasant, and the West is criticized in the Muslim world, mostly in the context of US policies towards them. Islam versus the West is not essentially Islam versus Christianity. In other words, Islam versus America is different from Islam versus Europe. The West is not all about America. In the case of Europe, many countries have a history with relation to Islam and Muslims. There is an extremely important distinction to be made between American and European awareness of Islam. France and England recently left Muslim countries as their colonial masters. Italy and Holland had colonies with Muslim majority populations. Many have close territories with Muslim countries or once had Muslim states. As Said (1997) puts it, there is a different orientalism discipline in the USA and Europe for understanding Muslims within the orient or beyond the orient.

It is an anxiety of our time and the most confusing discussion: the Islam and the West. Either this is the discussion between the Muslim and non-Muslim countries or the discussion between the Western countries and Muslims who are living in the West. Both sides are speedily increasing the Gulf; Muslims are unwilling for diversity and the West is misrepresenting the Muslims. The Western modernization model should not be the ultimate for the whole world, especially for Muslims living in more than 50 states. On the other side, the unitary approach of Muslims cannot be followed by many diverse ethnicities of the world. The degree of aggressiveness in Muslim countries is an alarming threat for the non-Muslim states (Halliday, 2005).

The protection of Western civilization through 'war on terror' was important, but the dark side also emerged gradually. It lacks the sociological assistance. The impact of such jingoistic policies on Muslims has been problematic. Although it is articulated that counterterrorism was for the sake of protection, the underlying truth is missing. It draws attention towards civilized and de-civilized concepts that helped misconceptualize the Islamic civilization, the result of which is Islamophobia. It includes cultural, historic, political and geographical misconceptions, and tags Middle East problems with Islam. This imaginary conception is incompatible with Euro-Americanness, wherein a brown cultural identity is considered exotic in Western cultures (Semati, 2010). This identity crisis has been symbolized as threat and terror.

CLASH OF CIVILIZATIONS

Dichotomies between Islam and the West can better be explained in the light of Huntington's clash of civilization theory. He argued that the clash is not just the problem of religion or civilization but it includes politics in it, and 'the fault lines between civilization will be the battle lines of the future'. According to Huntington, cultural identities are civilizational identities capable of reshaping everything from religion to politics (Seib, 2005). At certain places in his seminal work, he has been found criticizing the USA in terms of creating enemies to test its friends and constructing real and virtual monsters to justify its arsenal hordes.

The West adopted Huntington's clash of civilization thesis again in defending civilization immediately after 9/11. The sociopolitical connection of Western Muslims with diehard radicalized Muslim groups was explored under the state policies of Western governments. Muslims everywhere in the West were viewed as potential terrorists regardless of their allegiance, affiliation with their states and decade-long spotless past in the West. For instance, the UK government's strategies for counterterrorism provided enough evidence to demonstrate hatred towards Muslims within the state. Nobert Elias' concepts of 'civilizing' and 'de-civilizing' help understand the targeted process against the Muslim community. The majority of non-Muslim Britain wants such restriction on Muslims for their security (Vertigans, 2010); however, it is nothing but an overt disregard towards Muslims' contribution in the economic development of the British society. But some luminous personalities like Sadiq Khan, the mayor of London, refuted the negative construction of Muslims in the UK.

Islamophobia, to some scholars, is racism as well as the fear of civilizational invasion of the West. This fear mainly emerged just after 9/11, mostly cited as security threat perception in literature. Although numerous laws were enacted to prevent anti-terrorist acts that are visibly anti-Muslims, the Westerners do not seem inclined to accept this despite being victims of these freedom-flinching laws. Muslims and Islam are seen as alien under post-9/11 discriminatory laws, which have been made even more discriminatory, punitive and stringent after Trump came into power. Most Europeans also want Muslims to be a part of the European culture, terming them as 'European Muslims'—a kind of their denial as Europeans and obviously pejorative. With the rise in Muslim population in the West is attached the fear of demolishment of Judo-Christian culture (Merranci, 2006). Islam locates itself in the centre of debates concerning politics and relations between religions all over the world. The West talks about the fight against the so-called 'evil' and implemented their means of good laws. Jürgen Habermas said during a conference that 9/11 has led to problematizing the relations between the East and the West; nonetheless, without any solution till today, rather a new debate on secular and religious society has started, which was actually a debate of clash of civilization and culture. More than Islam, the threat is from Sharia law that has resulted in increased anti-Muslim sentiments across the West, wherein mass media greatly influence the public debates.

World Values Survey (WVS) and European Values Study (EVS) provided the evidence to examine Huntington's *Clash of Civilization*. According to the WVS and EVS, more than 75 per cent people from Muslim and non-Muslim societies support Huntington's primary argument of cultural existence and religions' impact on it. But his assumption regarding democracy that it is the epicentre of clash between Muslim and non-Muslim societies is not approved. Yes, the Muslims' stance on society's leadership is different from the Western one, but many non-Islamic societies also differ from the West on the point of political structure of a society. Huntington also did not succeed to identify the fault lines of culture between the West and Islam, which includes the equality of gender and liberation of sex. The cultural gulf involves more Eros than Demos.

The following fundamental questions are needed to be answered for a better understanding of clash of civilization theorem and in turn Islamophobia as its one of the facets. Does civilizational clash emanate from social identities and do social identities glue the individuals in some kind of unbreakable social bonds reducing the chances of social bridging with 'other' social groups? And if strong social identities of long time create social clashes and set the climate of social and cultural conflicts, which over a period of time shape into clash of civilization? To answer these, we need to have ken of SIT. SIT is an integrationist social psychological theory. It was introduced in the 1970s and developed in the 1980s, helpful in recognizing the processes of social identity and inter-group relationship. Sub-theories under SIT deindividualize identities and analyse the group norms and leadership within the group and also between the groups of different identities

(Hogg, 2002). Majorities' discrimination against minorities' social identities can be evaluated through the tools developed in the light of SIT. Minorities' collective identities can be affected by the majorities' social collectivism. In the name of Islamophobia, British Muslims' positive identity had been damaged over the past few decades. The marginalization of Muslims in Britain has the consequences of the social identity problem as a group identity. It also influences the contact between the inter-groups (Hopkins, 2006). A religious identity directly or indirectly affects the national identities. Islamic identities of Muslims in Germany and Norway affect the national identity of Muslims in both the countries. Using the structural equation model, research findings have made the effects of Muslims national affiliation evident on the West as a result of Islamophobia (Kunst et al., 2011).

Identity process theory (IPT) states that identity undergoes a process of continuous change. Three main components of this theory are identity, social action and social change. The theory examines how in social change the construction and protection of identities (individual or group) take place. Three prominent questions are: How we see ourselves? How others see us? How we are seeing others (Jaspal & Breakwell, 2014)? The identity of ethnic minorities is a question in the principles of identity relationship among different groups in every society. Ethnic identities in the domain of social psychology can be judged with the help of IPT as a threat to ethnic identities. Definition of ethnic boundaries is important for diverse ethnic societies in social psychology.

When *The Civilizing Process* (La civilization des moeurs) by Nobert, published in 1939 but popularized in 1973, was translated in English, it hit the debate on civilization. The International Sociological Association listed it among seven milestone works of sociology of the 20th century. Nobert in its first volume discussed the human habits, behavioural formulations, psychic structures and social attitudes. In the second volume, the centralization of modernism and interconnections of civilization was discussed, especially in the context of Europeans (Aya, 1978). The debate addressed the question as how European societies considered themselves more civilized than their neighbouring societies. Nobert observed shame and embarrassment with respect to bodily property and violence. The connection between the state monopolies, economics and people is important as societies (of a state) being the organs of a civilization are interconnected. The division of Europe into sovereign states and the power struggle greatly influenced the process of civilization in modern nations because of social and structural changes. These changes move the domestic and international social structures and emotions of modern people (Linklater & Mennell, 2010). Norbert Elias' application of civilized and de-civilized concepts help to understand how Muslims communities in the UK were targeted by the security forces. Nobert explains as how the process of identity development was interrupted by the British security forces after attacks on the Twin Towers in the name of civilization protection. The majority of population thinks that the forces are protecting them from Muslims (Vertigans, 2010).

ANOTHER PERSPECTIVE ON CLASH OF CIVILIZATION

The idea of clash of civilization is a war-like idea that stems from ancient Greece and Rome, transmitted by the Catholic Church right after the collapse of the Roman Empire. Since that day, the West, led by the Christians, claimed to be the centre of Christian civilization. Later on, orchestrated Christians' Western civilization spread around the American and Australian regions. The essence of the idea of clash of civilizations was that the Islamic and Western civilizations are at war and not compatible to each other, which is not based on any kind of reality; rather, it is a bunkum speculation.

Huntington presented Western civilization as true, natural and purely representative of whole humanity. On the other hand, Islamic civilization has been portrayed as alien to 'true' civilization having fashions of the classical age and all-time anti to the modernity (Western civilization). Arabs who conquered almost more than half of the world and gave this world unmatchable scientists, such as Jabir Ibn Hayyan, Ibn-e-Khaldun and Muhammad Ibn Musa al-Khwarizmi, who significantly contributed to the landscape of knowledge, more specifically yielded many disciplines of science and technology, and have been portrayed as ignorant, illiterate nomads, conservatives living outside the civilized scientific world. Islam in the clash of civilization perspective has been introduced as having no relation with the advance scientific world and the biggest threat to the world's peace (Bambery, 2012).

By the obscure distinction of civilizations, Huntington yielded new discussions; much of the things were not on ground as presented in the book, but intensely required for the new world order as he mentioned in the title *The Remaking of World Order*. The clash created by Huntington has become the manifesto of the US government. Many critiques are of the view that after the release of the book, every strategic movement of the USA is according to it (Adib-Moghaddam, 2008).

Indeed, the concept of civilizational identity like the West is elusive. Most of the people would say that East Germany has become a part of what we generally name as the Western countries, whereas the Estonia, for example, would be considered as different. Similarly, Japan does not resemble with the identity of the West, although it is a liberal secular democratic country. The Turkey, former Czechoslovakia or Albania, even if are liberal, secular democracies would have a much tougher time being regarded as Western. Although Turkey has invested a considerable amount of effort into establishing its identity as a Western country, more people would tend to think of Israel as ideologically and strategically closer to being a member of Western civilization than Turkey (Fadl, 2011).

Huntington's vulgarization of Islam is objectionable, because he judged Islam by the standards that are not genuine and even alien to Islam. He made his arguments without making distinction between primitive cultures, customs and traditions with those originally revealed as Islam. The major problem with Huntington's *Clash of Civilizations* is that it is fundamentally ahistorical, not purely based on history. It treats 'civilizations' as discrete cultural units that developed on their own without any overlap with universal values, and notably it ignores the extent to which individual nations and cultures have been developed in relation to others in specific historical contexts; in other words, he refuses the interconnectedness of the world.

For Huntington, Afghanistan and the US war can be seen as a clash between the West and an Islamic civilization. But, unfortunately, an unbiased investigation would make it obvious that the rise of Taliban cannot be separated somehow from the West.

It is indeed undeniable that the world is full of clashes and many significant conflicts. But the nature of conflicts sometimes becomes problematic. Although tensions among nations, states and regions exist, it does not mean that these are the clashes between civilizations. If the significant clashes in the world are not accurately identified at this point, obviously such misdiagnosis can lead to the misconception about their nature. The conflicts that occurred in the beginning of the 21st century mentioned by Samuel Huntington should be conceptualized in the context of globalized realities of the time, rather than being viewed through a narrow soda straw (Voll, 2009).

'Civilization' as defined by Samuel Huntington in *Clash of Civilizations* does not meet the criteria of any dictionary; it is rather an imaginary civilization. Huntington identified the outdated definition of civilization described as 'large cultural units of identity that were distinct from one another'. But in this post-positivist world, there are lot many differences even in the eight 'civilizational blocs'. Civilization cannot be identified only on the basis of 'religion'; there are many other factors involved in it. If it is so, then why, according to Bernard Lewis, the Christians separated the state from the religion, which might sound like contaminating their civilization. Such clearly distinct units of identity no longer exist anywhere in the world.

The diversity of identity is more often due to the violent territorial conflicts of the time, for example, the Kashmir conflict, Kurdish–Iraqi conflict, Turkey and Iran conflict, Sri Lanka–Tamil Tiger's conflict and so on; these conflicts were and are not because of the 'civilizational' differences. The most violent conflicts in Iraq have their origin in sectarian, regional, ethnic and political differences, and not utterly based on the differences in civilizations. The Muslim–Christian conflicts in Sudan and Nigeria are clearly misunderstood and will never be resolved, if they are specifically viewed in the context of Muslim–Christian conflicts between two civilizations: 'Islamic civilization' and 'Western civilization' (Yusuf, 2007). Many analysts have rejected the 'clash of civilization' and they named major conflicts as conflict between the 'modernity' and forces against the 'modernity'. The identity of civilizations is nowhere to be seen in the contemporary clashes. They claim that the major conflicts of our time are not originally the clashes of civilizations, they are clashes and competitions between different modes of modernity, and it could be named as 'a clash of modernities', not 'a clash of civilizations' (Chiozza, 2002).

In the profound global conflicts, the concept of 'clash of civilizations' is not only invisible, but is a dangerously misleading concept. If the battle against extremist organizations working on the name of Islam and terrorists is considered as a part of 'clash of civilizations' between 'Islam' and 'the West', it means that a notable majority of Muslims that is the part of the many movements working for democratic modernity are flatly ignored and alienated. It shows that the supporters of democratic movements towards modernity are weakened by self-imposed fake conceptualizations of clashing identities (Voll, 2009).

Noam Chomsky once said, 'The concept of Clash of Civilization is a new justification for any atrocities that they wanted to carry out, which was required after the cold war as the Soviet Union was no longer a viable threat.' Huntington created his own boundaries of civilizations ignoring the previously evolved cultural identities and drew zigzag cultural units. Ancient Egyptian, ancient Greek, Persian and Roman civilizations are nowhere in the civilizational map drawn by Huntington.

Alina Mungiu-Pippidi conducted a survey in 2005 to test the civilizational boarder between Central Europe and the Balkans, which Huntington highlighted as culturally, politically and religiously different. For this purpose, she selected three states: Romania, Bulgaria and Slovakia; two of them are Balkan and one Central European states. What she found was entirely different from Huntington's predictions. She found no differences in political culture and could not find even a single indicator which can cause cultural conflict (Mungiu-Pippidi, 2002). Similarly, Jonathan Fox also conducted a study 'Paradigm Lost:

Huntington's Unfulfilled Clash of Civilizations Prediction into the 21st Century' in 2005 to find out the civilizational clashes claimed by Huntington. He tested domestic conflicts using the minorities at risk and did not find sufficient evidence in Huntington's support. There were less civilizational conflicts and more non-civilizational conflicts in his selected sample areas (Fox & Szilassy, 2012). The findings of this study show that Huntington's proposed paradigm is incorrect. Moreover, the post-9/11 trends are to conform and legitimate Huntington's theory.

Huntington defines civilization as 'the highest cultural grouping of people and the broadest level of cultural identity people have short of that which distinguishes them from other species'. In his article of 1993, he identifies seven or eight major civilizations based on history, language, custom and religion. His eight identified civilizations are: Western, Confucian, Japanese, Islamic, Hindu, Slavic-Orthodox, Latin American and possibly African.

Civilizations will be at conflict with each other because the differences among them are of very basic nature, fundamental and are irreconcilable, such as views on the relations between God and man, individual and state, parents and children, man and wife, rights and responsibilities, liberty and authority, equality and hierarchy. For Huntington, these are the ingredients of a civilization, and the views differ from one civilization to another. He distinguished eight civilizations on the basis of the differences in views on given indicators. For Huntington, civilizations share no common views regarding these questions.

The following figure shows that every civilization has some common features in practical life, but they perform them with a different point of view. The ingredients of civilization in the following figure were originally proposed by Samuel Phillips Huntington, which have been further operationalized keeping in view grass-roots level realities. It is a kind of checklist to see how one civilization differs from others. If any civilization has some commonalities given in the figure, they are compatible with each other. The more they differ, the more they are at conflict with each other.

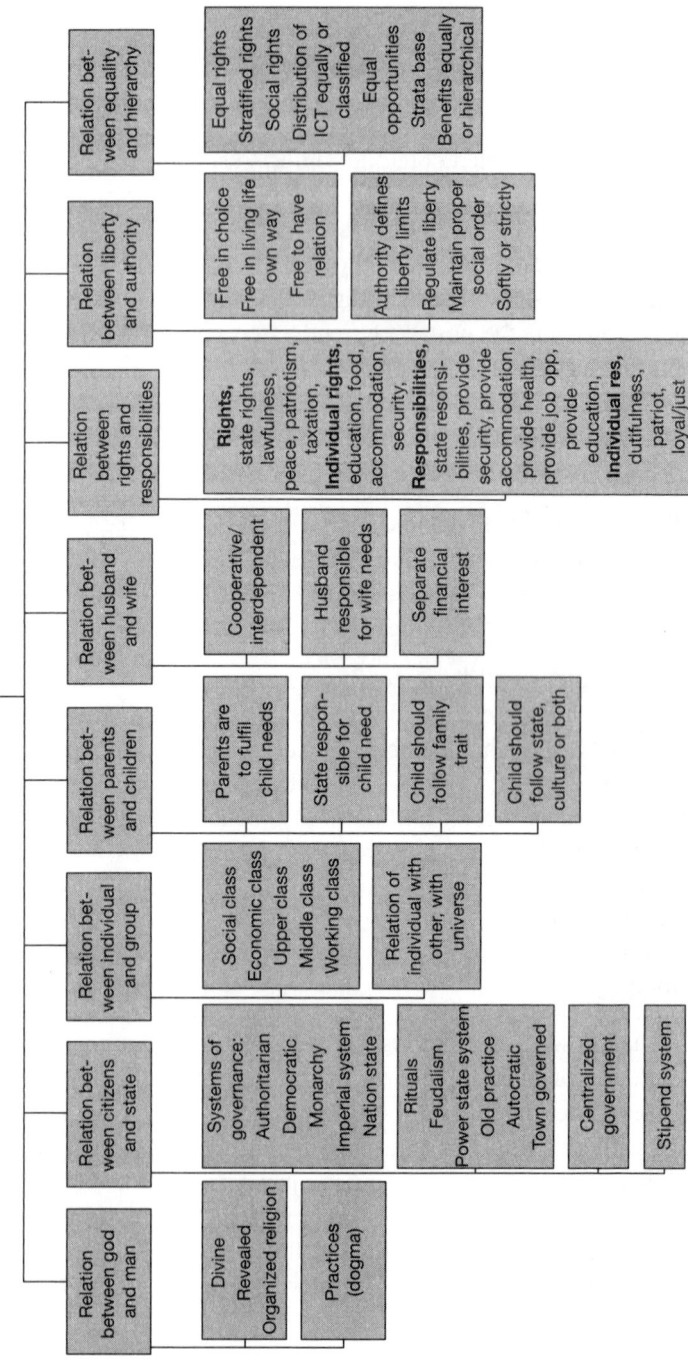

Huntington seems, at many places in his thesis, to be negating globalization. The observers of globalization are of the view that the increase in interaction among the people of different states and civilization would minimize the differences. The world is becoming alike and globalization has emerged as a significant cause of promoting cooperation among nations. Nonetheless, Huntington is standing 180° opposite to these views. He says that an increase in interaction among people of various civilizations heightens the awareness of their fundamental values. More they are exposed to differences, more they are at conflict with each other. According to Huntington, these differences will not disappear soon because they have their roots in the history of their social systems. Hence, exposure to civilizational differences may make people define themselves in ethnic and religious terms, which is the solid justification of clash with other civilizational entities. Huntington further suggests that the clash will occur on both at the macro level—interstate clash, mainly between the countries sharing their boarder with a difference of the civilizational approach—and at the micro level—intra-state conflict, within the state, between the state and minorities.

A number of scholars are of the view that Huntington's idea does not have its implications in the future. Huntington assumes that the post-Cold War world was divided in two major power blocs: the Western (Europe and the USA) and the Islamic blocs. He sees the Chinese civilization very closer to the Islamic civilization and it would be at war with the West mainly with the USA. According to the civilizational judgemental system proposed by Huntington, Latin America is not the part of the West, Japanese do not fall in any civilizational bloc, Sunnite Muslims and Shiite Muslims do not fall in one civilization, and conservatives and liberals in spite of living in the same bloc do not make up any single unit. In general, Huntington's thinking in terms of blocs is clearly obtuse and incompatible with the digitally interconnected world in which even the rival nations, for instance, the USA and China, are heavily dependent on each other (Shirazi, 2002).

The most compelling evidence of the failure of Huntington's definition of civilization is provided by the fact that the clash between rival cultural blocs has failed to materialize. The bloodiest battles were fought and are still being fought within the civilizations, not between the civilizations. Africans killed Africans in Congo, Muslims are killing Muslims in Egypt, the civil war of Syria claimed more carnage than the USA killed in Iraq, a long-standing battle was fought between Iran and Iraq, Iraq and Kuwait. There is a long list of clashes within the civilizations. And let us not forget that back in the 1990s, the West waged a war in Yugoslavia to help out Muslims. Huntington's *Clash of Civilizations* seemed refuted in 2001. It is obvious that Al-Qaeda terrorists have never been the representatives of mainstream Islam, rather the rootless adherents of an Islamic-marked Western nihilism. Al-Qaeda killed more Muslims than the natives of other religions in the world (Richter, 2013).

IS INDIA–PAKISTAN CONFLICT A CLASH BETWEEN CIVILIZATIONS?

For Huntington, the India–Pakistan conflict is a clash between two civilizations: Hindu civilization and Islamic civilization. Both of these civilizations have different manifestations of life and the social system. They are culturally, politically, religiously and ethnically not inextricable. Both civilizations have a different philosophy of life, they have different views on the relation between man and God, they have different perspectives on the relation between a state and its citizens, they deal their citizens differently, the relation between a husband and a wife is dissimilar in both the countries, they deal hierarchy and equality differently, they have different social systems, the classification of their people is of different nature, and their views on the relation between parents and children are entirely different. Indians deal their kids differently than Pakistani parents do. According to Huntington's formula, both India and Pakistan were and are at conflict with each other because of the civilizational differences.

Truly, this is not a yardstick to measure the differences between nations. Neither these measures are the cause of separation from each other nor do they become the reasons for conflict among nations. Conflicts do not occur on these bases, rather it is ideology and religion that compel nations to fight for. Pakistan was not separated from

India on such measures. If Pakistan was separated from India on the so-called civilizational basis, then why today more Muslim population than Pakistan is still living in India? According to Giridharan Velamore, the separation was the result of colonial failure and a move against the colonial system. The colonial system had badly failed in controlling the subcontinent, the British were pulling their governing elements back from the subcontinent. With the British evacuation, there were two major entities in the subcontinent—the Hindus and the Muslims. The Muslim League was established in 1906, and within a short span of time (41 years), they were separated. In 1857, both Hindus and Muslims fought together against the British monopoly in the subcontinent. If there was a conflict between Hindu and Muslim civilizations, then why both the nations had been living together for many centuries? Islam came in the subcontinent around the beginning of the 8th century. For a long time, no clash occurred between Hindu and Muslim nations in this region. Some scholars are of the view that the lack of good governance and good administration led Muslims to the independence movement. So during the confrontation, both sides used religious slogans and demanded separation and made it reality in a short span of time. Newly independent state of Pakistan did not form any separate civilization nor did it jump into the Islamic civilization from the Hindu silo. This was not a jump of Indian Muslims from the Hindu pool into the Islamic pool, that is, civilization.

There are more than 300,000 active mosques in today's India and more than 428 Hindu temples were in Pakistan in 1990 when Huntington was writing his book *Clash of Civilizations*. On the other hand, Indian movies are being equally watched in Pakistan, some Indian heroes belong to Pakistani; on the other hand, Pakistani dramas have substantial consumption in India. The showbiz industry of both countries is mutually operational, many Indian actors are working in Pakistani movies and Pakistani actors are contributing to India entertainment programmes. So there is no clash and causes of clash that exist which lead to separate civilizations.

It is evident that Pakistan was not separated from India on a civilizational basis. If it is so, then why the eastern Pakistan separated from the western Pakistan in 1971 with a new name Bangladesh, although both were sharing the same heritage, culture and religion and contributed equally in India's Independence movement. Sheikh Mujeeb did not mention in his six-point formula that we have different culture or civilization that is why our separation is inevitable. Neither Pakistan separated from India on a civilizational basis nor did Bangladesh separated from Pakistan. There were many other reasons that led to the separation of both countries. The point to be noted here is that Huntington's formulation of civilization by the views on different relations did not lead the nations to the conflict.

RESPONSES TO HUNTINGTON'S CLASH OF CIVILIZATION

The strongest response to Huntington's *Clash of Civilization* came from Edward Said, who wrote an article in 2001 titled 'The Clash of Ignorance' to refute Huntington's thesis. Said argues that Huntington ignored the dynamics, interdependency and interaction of culture while defining the boundaries of world civilizations. The boundaries of civilizations set up by Huntington are illogical, irrational and chaotic in nature. It is not the original face of the civilization what Huntington showed to the world through his thesis. He further says that the *Clash of Civilizations* is an example of the pure discriminatory racism; it looks like the parody of Hitlerian science has been directed against Arabs and Muslims (Said, 2001).

Noam Chomsky also criticized Huntington's concept of 'clash of civilization'. Chomsky said that clash of civilization is just a new justification for the USA for any kind of atrocities and outlawed invasion that they wanted to carry out. It was required after the Cold War to legitimate new enemy, as the Soviet Union was no longer a viable threat (Chomsky, 2001). Berman (2003) argued that in the present world there do not exist distinct cultural boundaries—no Islamic civilization, no Western civilization. So the evidence of clash of civilization is not appealing when examining the relationship between the USA and Saudi Arabia. In spite of declaring both of them worst enemies by Huntington, they are establishing good relations with each other. For some states, ideology, culture, religion and ethnicity do not matter; they base their relations on financial and political benefits. The Belt and Road Initiative (BRI) by China speaks volumes on this.

Fethullah Gülen rejected Huntington's *Clash of Civilizations* by saying that it is not more than a technique to create a new enemy. After the collapse of the Soviet Union, Americans needed a new enemy, so they came up with this conspiracy theory. Gülen believes that when there is a need of interfaith dialogue, the USA drags the nations into a new conflict. Huntington's developed civilizations revolve around the West and present Western civilization as central civilization and rest of the civilizations at war with it. He revived the two major polls and replaced communism with Islam. By this message, masses are being prepared for a new war with a new enemy—more dangerous than the former one (Penaskovic, 2007).

Patrick (2005) in response to Huntington's *Clash of Civilizations* said that the categorization of world civilizations by Huntington is not appropriate, weak and based on minor differences, which might lead the world towards disharmony and disintegration. Sen (1999) in an article, explicitly referring to Huntington (1999), states that cultural diversity is known as a valuable feature across the world. For Edward T. Hall and many other anthropologists, cultural diversity is the real beauty of the world. Different cultures in the world are like different colours of flowers in the garden, which enhance the beauty of the nature, whereas Huntington presents the cultural diversity as combating factors.

In a nutshell, scholarship around the world, whether representing the West or Islamic world, is of the view that this is the time for the reconciliation and integration of the world.

MUSLIMS IN THE WEST: ISLAM AND WESTERN CIVILIZATION

Islamophobia is not just the disliking of Muslims, but it involves much other negativity associated with Muslims and Islam, such as violence and terrorism. The recent Pew Global Attitudes Survey suggests that perceived realistic and symbolic threats are among the main sources of Islamophobic attitudes in the Western countries (such as Britain, USA, France, Spain and Germany). Perceptions of educated individuals are however slightly different than general public, who think that Muslims are violent and associate with terrorism because of their physical and cultural affiliations (Ciftci, 2012). About half of the Muslims living in the West were born there; their ancestors immigrated to the West in the 1950s and 1960s. The generation brought up in the West opposes the values of their migrated parents and are acculturated with Western values. When Dr Kalim Siddiqui called for a parliament of Muslim in the UK, the majority of UK-based Muslims rejected this demand. The message like the call of Siddiqui gives a perception about Muslims that they are not willing to be a part of mainstream Western civilization. According to him, Europeans found it difficult to make a natural balance in relation to their Muslim countrymen. Not only this, but they are also otherized, persecuted and molested; for instance, a Turkish labourer was killed in Germany after a racial attack, and the French media negatively portrayed hijab-wearing schoolgirls and, as a result, many were rejected to be enrolled in schools. Evidence indicates that in the 1990s Muslims were living a better life in the USA than their Europe an counterpart until the freedom movements of the Blacks were associated with Muslims, and 9/11 was the watershed. Muslims from different regions have different cultural values and physical features, but whether they are Arabs, Asians or Indians, the West considers them the same (Armstrong, 2001).

Several Muslims in the West do not adapt to secular values. France and Britain have their freedom to practise their customs and religious festivities. But the demand of Muslims for declaring Rushdie as a blasphemous or Siddiqui's protest and declaration not to obey the British law changed the situation. Also, in France, when a Turkish imam claimed publicly that Sharia is important to French Muslim and a better law than the French law, the West seriousness about democracy may face serious challenges in such cases. The West seriousness about democracy however, the law has to take its course if it is challenged in practice.

The Western civilization feels threatened from Islam and the need of the hour is to know what factors are intensifying this fear. The elite political discourse on media, of course, is one of the reasons involved in deepening the fear of Muslim cultural invasion of the Western civilization. To understand its nuances well, we essentially need to focus on cultural distinction within Muslims and for that social movement theory might help. After 9/11, media and political parties started presenting Al-Qaeda as the whole Islam. The conservatives from the West vehemently rejected the implementation of Sharia law by creating huge storms in the cup and presented bills in the assemblies to erect bulwark against the Islamic law. Muslims for most of the Westerners are the one with beard and turbans, and savage looks. Common masses were made to think that by implementing Sharia law, women will no longer be free and the domestic violence will be legal and normal. Political actors highlighted extremist aspects of Islam and Muslim societies, and then the situation was aggravated post-9/11 episode to create fear among the Westerners, which crystalized and galvanized Islamophobia (Belt, 2014).

One Dutch adult out of two has negative feelings and prejudice in favour of Muslim minorities. The comparison between realistic and symbolic threat from Muslims with the help of the structural equation model and integrated threat theory shows that there exists only symbolic threat in the Netherlands. Prejudice and stereotypes affect the inter-group contact and multiculturalism in the case of Muslim minorities owing to predicted symbolic threats (Gonzales et al., 2008). It has been a matter of debate since the 1970s that how the liberal democracies of the West manage their diverse ethnic and religious minorities despite such a state of affairs. The space for unity and diversity in the Western countries and for creating equality among different religious and ethnic groups is not sufficient (Abbas, 2004). If not timely and properly addressed, the wave of negative feelings like the case of the Netherlands would continue to become unabated. Similarly, hate against Muslim women in the West is actually related to the fear of loss of freedom leading to Islamophobia against Muslim women in the West. The relationship between the scarf ban in France and the fear of losing freedom for Muslim women and others has been found to be quite evident in various studies. According to most of the people, the concept of wearing scarf/burqa or veiling is a sign of suppressing women freedom. The fear of losing freedom is making it difficult for Muslim women to wear scarf and burqa, which is equally true for non-Muslims, of which primary justification could be taken from feminism (Carland, 2011).

Contemporarily, negativity towards Muslims and Islam is deeply engraved in the 'Grand Narrative', which started in the first war and reached its climax during 'war on terror', and then the narratives found from Huntington's *Clash of Civilizations* to Bernard Lewis' 'The Roots of Muslim Rage'. In the shadow of Bush's grand narrative, Muslims not only faced problems in Afghanistan and Iraq, but they were also tortured in the USA. Many left America with broken dreams because of rising brutality aimed at Muslims. Bush's policies made it a war between Islam and Christianity and between Muslim and Non-Muslim worlds in cultural and civilizational perspective (Ahmed, 2004). The counterterrorism started post 9/11 by the US government developed a binary distinction between individuals, groups and states that either they are with 'civilized' world or with terrorists. Any government who chose to be ally of terrorists was considered as the enemy of 'civilization'. This civilization is based on freedom, pluralism and progress, which are against the barbarian cultures.

A general misconception about Muslims is that all Muslims are one nation and have one political aim, but practically they are from different worlds and have different cultural and national identities. In the post-9/11 climate, the wearing of scarf by Muslim women is considered as a branding, which separates them from 'civilized' societies. Also, the concept of *Umma* (the people of Islam) is a religious identity worldwide; nonetheless, Muslims have ethnic, geographic, national and linguistic identities that create within them multiple complexities like superiorities of some over the others. Critics criticize Muslims for their reluctance to adapt to hosting cultures and synthesizing or cultural synergizing process. The Muslim women identities are criticized more in this regard. Re-Islamization increased rapidly in post-9/11 America; increasing the number of young daughters of immigrant Muslims who considered veiling as the identity of Muslim girls, but some, as explained earlier, took it as an anti-women emancipation move. The study of two decades on American Muslims communities and Muslims youth reveals that headscarf has become Muslim identity in the USA—a public advocate positively posturing that the American system allows the freedom of speech and religion. But at the same time, it has also become a symbol of opposition to effort to root out Islam from America, which views Islam as a religious or ideological enemy (Haddad, 2007).

After 9/11 attacks, the ratio of hate crime increased rapidly in first nine weeks against American Muslims. There are probably four variables which caused surge in hate crime; first, the intervention of the US president claiming 9/11 to be an attack by the Islamists; second, anti-Muslim law enforcement interventions including profiling of Muslims; third, the local-level tensed situation created by religious, civic and educational groups; fourth, the lack of clarity about 'war on terror'—whether it was against the terrorists or Muslims. The Internet and the rise of Al Jazeera as alternative sources of information to the government and American media outlets represented the situation for alternative opinion beyond embedded journalistic practices. Hate crime statistics by the FBI and anti-discrimination groups examined the total number of violent hate crimes against American Muslims during 2000–2002 and declared them higher than anytime (Kaplan, 2007). Muslims, immediately after the 9/11 catastrophe, were considered the most violent and uncivilized nation (Ciftci, 2012), which resulted in the highest ever wave of Islamophobia in the USA in particular and across the West in general.

IN BETWEEN CULTURES

Today, humans are living in a transit moment where time and space create complex differences of figures and identities, past and present, and inner and outer space. Theoretically, it is the need of the hour to think beyond narratives' subjectivities and focus on the process of articulation of cultural differences. These differences provide space for new selfhood strategies to individuals and to communities for the idea of new societies and cultures. The cultural comparativism is in the process of redefining. The national boundaries are relatively different in the modern culture. There is more sense of hybridity of communities' social identities. The new in internationalism is moving from specific to general (Bhabha, 1994). The 'hybrid culture' concept of Bhabha developed in the discourse of cultural aesthetics and political minorities. Hybridity does not come from the outside but it is developed within the cultural boundaries to reshape the thinking on social psyche (Werbner & Modood, 1997).

Terrorism committed by Muslims tagged as 'Islamic terrorism' or 'Islamic fascism' means the West is claiming more than 1.2 billion Muslims of the world as terrorist or fascist. This is what Global War on Terrorism (GWOT) called a war against Islam. The use of word *jihad* as terrorism means to label Islam as terrorism. Jihad has its specific explanation in specific conditions. The alternative vocabulary is needed because the mainstream Muslims are blamed by such contents. Suicide bombing is not the result of Islamic ideology, but it is due to the sociopolitical situation of Muslim countries (Afghanistan, Iraq, Palestine, Chechnya, etc.). Muslims want peace process. Arabs are not only Muslims at all. America itself is a hurdle in the peace process. The mass media portrayal of Muslims as terrorists or fascists is damaging the religious and cultural identity of Muslims in international communities (Ahmed & Matthes, 2017). The threat of Islamic militant is exaggerated by the videos produced by right-wing organizations in the USA. In these videos, the conspiratorial fantasies are projected to specifically target Muslims to safeguard political interests of the elites. Stein and Salime term these documentaries as 'pseudo documentaries'. The producers use footages, news facts and other materials to construct Islamophobia among the ordinary citizens of the USA (Stein & Salime, 2015).

Pew Global Attitudes Survey has been used to test three perspectives while gauging the public opinion about Muslims and Islam—perceived threats from Muslims and Islam, social identity and cognitive capabilities of individuals in the USA. Resultantly, it has been seen that Islamophobia is a symbolic threat to the West. As per Pew Global Attitudes Survey, majority of the West thinks that Muslims are the supporters of Al-Qaeda. People associate Muslims with terrorism and feel threatened by the Muslims' physical and cultural existence

(Ciftci, 2012). Rising Islamophobia has created anti-Islam discussions in the USA, which more often results in discrimination and hatred towards Muslims. Roots of Islamophobia in terms of discriminatory state action and hate crimes in the USA increased manifold in the last decade. This has led to anti-Muslim and Islamophobic civil rights activism having historical context and backing.

In Europe, the real reason of political mobilization against Islam is the identity of Western Europe. Almost all political parties are against the increased Muslim population in Western Europe. It is threatening for the people if they see mosques or minarets increasing in number and visibility all across Europe. The political parties are not in the favour to consider Islam as a religion with equal status of other religions in Europe. Parties like Schweizerische Volkspartei raised question on Islam regarding individualism, secularism and gender equality on the basis of culture, values and identities. They develop the frame of liberal fundamental values and evaluate Islam in Europe (Betz & Meret, 2009).

Intercultural confrontation and compatibility are the reasons of conflict between the West and Islam. The most obvious problem is the unsettled relation between America and the Middle East political conflicts, which influence the cultural context. Another element is the Islamic revivalism. Politicization of identities establishes conflicts among the beliefs and develops distrust between the parties. It is a barrier for intellectuals to overcome the cultural conflicts. A 'new story of intercultural complementarity' can help the mediators of conflict transformation and minimize the difference to build peace (Funk & Said, 2004). Whether it is news or entertainment chunk, British media represents Muslims other than the normal. The 'hypervisibility' of Muslims spreads more negative social representation in the society overall. In the light of IPT and inter-group threat theory, British media hybridized the threat of Muslim as inter-group and national ethnic group identities. The projection of Islamophobic threat through media causes the Islamophobic prejudice. These hybridized messages by media transmit Islamophobia to dominant social representation (Jaspal & Cinnirela, 2010).

MULTICULTURALISM
OF THE WEST AND ISLAMOPHOBIA

Multiculturalism and bilingualism were fashioned in the 1970s when every immigrant wanted their children to speak English in British accent, but it is now considered chauvinism, racism, cultural imperialism and cultural genocide if English prevails. The fundamental values of multiculturalism have deep senses of different values of different cultures and same weightage and respect for all. While in the realm of relativism, multiculturalism fails to make cross-cultural judgements. The notion of Western secularism itself is 200 years old and it is claiming respect for the cultures of centuries. If the country law is giving freedom to all regardless of their religion or ethnic belongings, then why it is needed to give the freedom to religious institutions in the territory of that country (Ibn & Warraq, 1995). The West perceives that Islam can challenge the Judo-Christianity being the part of transcultural process. The West considered Islam as real threat to their multicultural perspective because of the differences between Islamic values and European transculturation (Marranci, 2004). British multiculturalism got affected owing to 9/11 political upheavals. Some experts commented that British multiculturalism is returning to its assimilationism. The increase in religious and cultural racism in Britain affects the immigrant from different parts of the world, especially from North Africa and the Middle East. The changing concept of multiculturalism in the context of Muslims' identity in Britain raised the question on its diverse society (Abbas, 2004). Saeed (2007) claimed that the British media represent the British Muslims as the aliens. This representation of Muslims is linked with racism, which has deep roots in history and cultural context. The British Muslims belong to heterogonous ethnicities but the media (British) treat them as a single ethnic minority.

Muslims who got asylum in Western countries are another cause of Islamophobia. The persons who seek the asylum make the difference within the group of Muslim community, which increases the disliking against Islam and Muslims. The negative perception within the group is because of conflicting beliefs and ideologies. The countering strategy of Islamophobia is to clarify the conflicts among the group and to reshape the media and foreign policy of the West (Moten & Rashid, 2012). Islamophobia has created a tendency to conflate all Muslims as belonging to a single nation of Islam that does not recognize and respect boundaries imposed by the Western geopolitics. This has been done by some to create and by some others to generate a sense of exclusive unity. It concludes that the multiplicity of Muslim's identities sits more easily within the permeable unbounded *Umma* applicable to the global as well as local without necessarily always privileging one or other identity (Afsher, 2013).

ISLAMOPHOBIA: THE CIVILIZATION DIMENSION

Islam is the name of negativity as it is being cultivated through cultural commodification of mainstream news and entertainment channels of the Western world. It has been described by numerous scholars as such and explained the dominant discourse(s) of orientalists instrumental in constructing Muslims as 'others' and this particular rhetoric has occupied significant space and time on broadsheets, broadcast gadgets, silver and TV screens. The tone of this anti-Islam rhetoric has been accelerated rapidly and tremendously due to penetration of computer-mediated communication (CMCs) through social media websites, chat groups, web pages and blogs, etc. Such Islamophobic rhetoric packed with negative connotation towards Islam and Muslims are more often the product of racism, xenophobia and stereotyping images (Karim, 2002, Poole, 2002; Sardar, 1999).

Weedon (2004) argued that Islamophobia is unjustified hostility against Islam and Muslims. It's a strong discrimination towards Muslims around the globe, in general, and the communities living in Western world as immigrants, in particular. In order to further strengthen and prolong hegemony of the West and ideology of White supremacy, lethal weapon of Islamophobia has been deliberately and systematically used to isolate and segregate Muslims. Consequently, it portrayed and posed Islam and Muslims as threat against Western culture and civilization. In the view of Sardar (1999), Islam has proved to be a stumbling block in the way of Western universal agenda of globalization. He further argued that Muslims declined to subsume to adopt and even showed reluctance to follow Western philosophies and ideals of politics and culture (Sardar, 1999). One of the outcomes of Islamophobia resulted in shape of racism as Allen (2005) has rightly remarked that manifestation of this latest type of racism predominantly depends on the ideals of cultural and religious factors instead of colour. Similarly, such argument has been profoundly observed in the discourse of Huntington's *Clash of Civilizations*. Huntington argued that the ideals of contemporary cold and cold-blooded inside war are centred not on the pillars of economics and politics but on culture.

Classical research work on orientalism and Islam also presented and endorsed the similar views as Said (1985) built up his argument that Western domination does not merely rest on political and economic, but it is also based on cultural form, which fundamentally provided foundation to the orientalist discourse, while its structure projected the difference between West as 'us' and the other side was defined as the orient—the East or 'them'. Apart from different activities by anti-Islam groups and organizations, mainstream news media and entertainment moguls of the West are the key players engaged in constructing and cultivating negative representation of the religion of Islam and its followers and are also responsible for the rampant rise of Islamophobia across the European world in general and the USA in particular. For instance, mainstream news channels such as Fox News, NBC and CBS portrayed Islam as a major violence and militancy triggering ideology in their news coverage during 2007 and 2013 (Considine, 2017).

Western scholarship overwhelmingly links Muslims and Islam with terrorism and extremism; consequently, media caricatured them negatively and then researches carried them so, which developed a circular motion of negative construction of Muslims and Islam in scholarship and media alike. According to Karim (2002), contemporary negative connotation of Islam and damaged image of Muslims have extensively reigned the US media ever since Iranian revolution in 1979.

Rafique (2010) argues that during colonization in the 15th century, the Europeans took great interest in Arabic, science, literature and language particularly in Islamic philosophy and through this learning they gained control over the orients. In the West (the Occident), it was believed that Muslims were irrational, uncivilized and backward, which made it draw their lines to lead Muslims to follow the path of welfare. Blemished understanding of Muslims and Islam had roots in history fraught with inimical relations eclipsed by long wars (crusades) between the binary religious forces fortified the notion of orientalism—'us' and 'them'. Predominantly, such a flawed understanding of issues between Islam and the West had deep links with the academia and religious scholarship who were engaged in selective readings with their predisposed positioning where Islam was a godly threat to them and their religion. This biased inclination helped them in highlighting the cultural differences. Consequently, foundation of every research framework were these inherited biases. It happened to be so when European scholars generally and academically defined Islamic philosophy, their deeply engraved biases overwhelmed their scholarship. Some researchers rightly pointed out Duncan McDonald who is a considered expert on Islam but clearly declared Muslim minds as feeble and unable to comprehend the complexity of global affairs. Like McDonald, other celebrated scholars also construct Islam and Muslims under this approach and don't seem interested in approaching the problem in scientific manner with more realistic understanding of its historic roots.

Unlike other religions, writing and debating Islam in negative fashion is considered as an inalienable right to freedom of expression. Rather, some quarters name Islamophobia as a restriction to right of freedom of expression when it comes to Islam and Muslims. Nafisa (2016) noted this religious sensitivity while highlighting the political and religious effects of venomous expression on religious affairs, particularly in the context of Islamic civilization and its clash with freedom of expression. She explained religious freedom with the freedom of expression and suggests freedom of expression is not to insult any religion and it is not absolute but there should be some ways to care about religious defamation. Danish cartoons episode is one of the examples, which demands careful handling of religious affairs and sacred personalities associated with any religion. Blasphemous depiction through cartoons created a wave of violence whole across the world, especially in the Muslim societies. Nonetheless, it is significant to note that hatemongers insist on utilizing such tools to propagandize against Islam and prove Muslims as irrational, violence-loving and extremists that resist freedom of expression.

Huntington described in his classical work *Clash of Civilizations* that as a child learns language, beliefs and values, and composes his actions according to his culture and innate learning, it would be hard to change his beliefs and adaptation to his value system. While, on the other hand, if someone from somewhat contrary beliefs and value system interludes with him, then it would certainly result in a relationship strain. This, when takes place at a social level, develops social conflicts and when perpetuates for long with historical reasons becomes a good case of clash of civilization. But interestingly, liberals who criticized Huntington's approach said that individuals cannot change their skin colour or tone but can change their beliefs. They are found to be suggesting that uniform implementation of law in a diverse society might mitigate severity of the problem having roots in conflicting social values. A critique by Ashraf (2012) on Huntington's futuristic approach regarding international politics and role of America in the context of clash of civilization stresses that the approach is not only the interpretation of future world politics, but it is more concerned about the world conflicts due to Western liberal policies. Interestingly, Huntington's way of resolving world problems in the context of clash of civilization shoulders more responsibility on the Muslims scholars to integrate with the Western value system in order to create intercultural and interfaith harmony with the world. Though events like Danish cartoon controversy and New Zealand bloody saga took place much later than his time, otherwise he might have advised scholars and politicians of the West to accept Islam as a distinct reality and ideology, which does not pose any threat to the West ways of life and its value system.

Saeed (2015) studied the media representation of Muslims, particularly its reflections after 9/11. He explained that in the post-war terror scenario, Muslims were portrayed as a dominant threat to the West. Like other racial groups, global media represented Muslims as uncivilized, extremist or Islamic terrorists. Saeed (2015) concluded that media posed them as a symbol of bigotry in an extremely bigot manner. According to him, media revel negativity and then generalize it to the whole world. Although multiculturalism is the best way to challenge social bigotry against Muslims and a way forward to the integration of the European Muslims in the European culture of music, film, sports and even fashion, it would not pay much as does the confrontation. Religious issues create a confrontational environment that leads to the clash of civilization and long wars. War economy since the beginning of the 20th century has tremendously contributed to develop some portions of the world, leaving many to ashes, however. Peace journalism scholars, on the other hand, argue to blur the division between Islam and the West by bridging the sociocultural gaps. They claim that Islamic science and Western science are similar in nature; rather, the Western science is an advanced step of Islamic science.

Generally perceived notion indicates that policies towards the Muslim world, intellectual thoughts and media editorialization are shaped under the influence of West's biases. These biases are nurtured and maintained in the perspective of clash of civilization. Muslim circles name it Westophobia, whereby ideas are constructed on the grounds of limited and faulty information. For instance, Huntington's approach identifies social and economic indicators as the primary reasons for the clash and separating the nations; but this clash seems to have only been existing between Christianity and Islam, and not between Christians and Jews or Hindus. Moving deep back to history, it is linked with crusades. Norris and Inglehart (2002) while exploring Islamic and non-Islamic societies around the globe and their beliefs and values have confirmed Huntington's approach that culture matters. Yes, culture matters and matters a lot, but Huntington's fundamental concern rested on democracy or on politics, which he said was one among the prime reasons of clash between nations; nonetheless, according to available evidence, there are visible differences in Islamic and non-Islamic societies in terms of gender equality and sexual liberties. Also, the West separated the church from politics, but religious leaders in Muslim-dominated states have a great influence on all spheres of polity.

It sounds pretty irrational to compare Islam with geographical boundaries instead of a religion as several researchers have tried to analyse Islam and similarly Muslims with the West, which is generally perceived as geography and not with Christianity and Judaism.

Islamophobia, as explained earlier, has multiple dimensionalities. Confining discussion to a narrowly designed structure on such a subtle and complex phenomenon would do more harm than presenting a way out towards its diagnosis and prognosis. Moreover, enough has been said and done in dealing with it in qualitative terms, though with a little focus, but less is available on its quantitative understanding and measurements, including the identification of its possible dimensions and then illustrative modelling on its various facets/dimensions. This state of affairs furthered the convolutions about the construct, lest providing means and ways to cure the epidemic of which traces are found all across the globe. Quite recent example is New Zealand, which has always been considered to be a migrant-friendly land and a symbol of peaceful coexistence in a contemporary multicultural and multiethnic world.

Foregoing in view, the civilizational dimension of Islamophobic threats may be deconstructed in some viable and related concepts for its better understanding and paving a way for its quantitative assessment. Following deconstruction or modelling may make us understand it in some scholastic and methodical fashion:

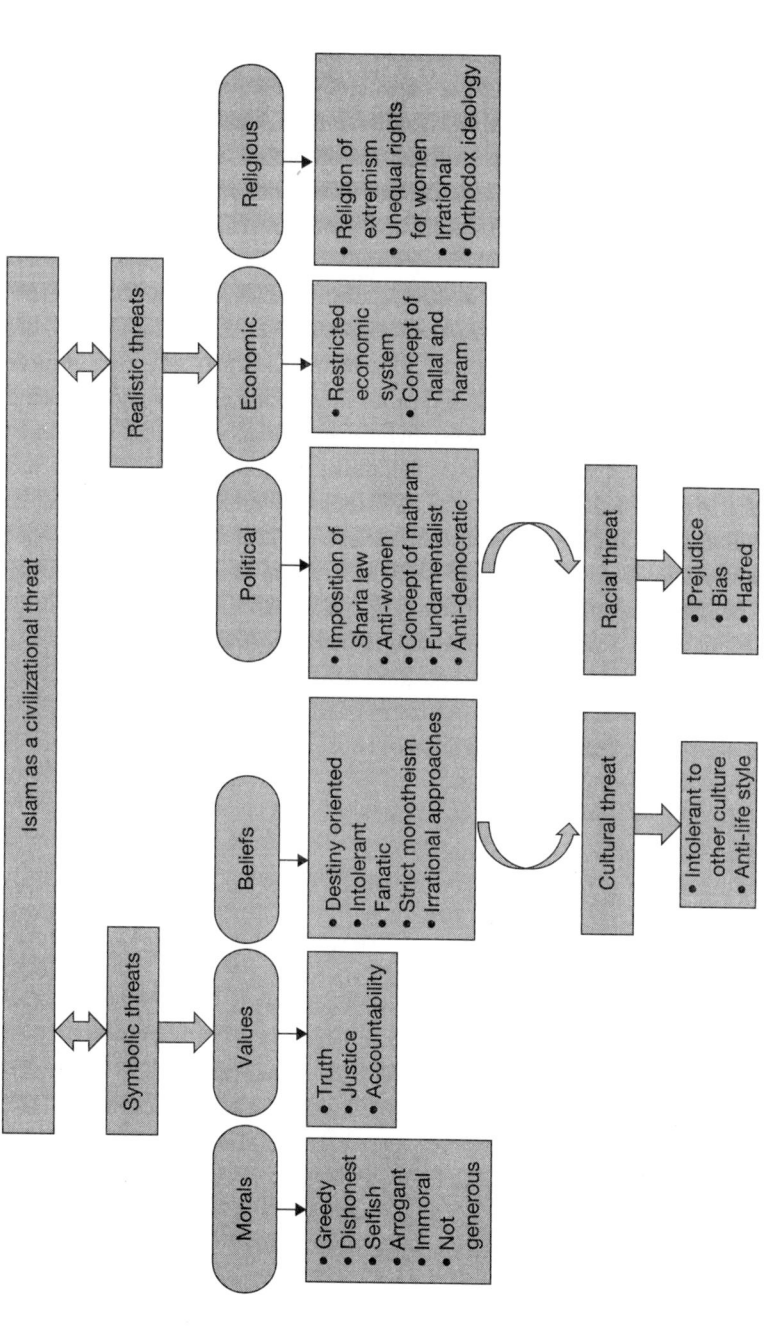

CONCLUSION

The West's fear of Islam in civilizational perspective has many causes. The Islamic invasion as cultural and civilizational commodities is the basic threat to the West because Islamic values can challenge the Western civilization. The Muslim civilization is less based on their cultures and more on Islamic values. The Islamic code of conduct provides an alternative to Western cultures. The other problem is the politicization of the clash of civilization. The Arab culture and the Islamic culture considered as the same in the West, and the political conflicts between the West and Arabs are misperceived as the conflicts between Islam and the West, which is either political or cultural; nonetheless, it is not religious at all. It is important to reiterate that the West is not only the USA, and also there is a huge cultural difference between the native Muslims of the West and immigrant Muslims. The terrorism or extremism associated with Islam is also a cause for the identity crisis among Muslims in the West. There is need to identify the cultural values, which Muslims have, on the basis of ethnicity, regionalism, nationality and cultural belongings. The identification of Muslims should be as the followers of Islam, which is much broader than their association with any country, region, ethnicity or race.

References

Abbas, T. (2004). After 9/11: British South Asian Muslims, Islamophobia, multiculturalism and the state. *The American Journal of Islamic Social Sciences, 21*(3), 26–38.

Abdullah, A. S. (2014). Ethnic othering in true lies. *The Criterion: An International Journal in English, 5.*

Adams, C. J. (1994). *Neither man nor beast: Feminism and the defense of animals.* New York, NY: Continuum.

Adhikari, S. (2018, 14 May). *10 oldest ancient civilizations ever existed.* Retrieved from www.ancienthistorylists.com and https://www.ancienthistorylists.com/ancient-civilizations/10-oldest-ancient-civilizations-ever-existed/

Adib-Moghaddam, A. (2008). *Iran in world politics: the question of the Islamic Republic.* New York: Columbia University Press.

Agudelo-Suárez, A., Gil-Gonzalez, D., Ronda-Pérez, E., Porthe, V., Paramio-Perez, G., García, A. M., & Garí, A. (2009). Discrimination, work and health in immigrant populations in Spain. *Social Science & Medicine, 68*(10), 1866–1874.

Afshar, H. (2013). The politics of fear: What does it mean to those who are otherized and feared? *Ethnic and Racial Studies, 36*(1), 9–27.

Ahmed, A. (1992). *Postmodernism and Islam: Predicament and promise.* London: Routledge.

Ahmed, A. S. (1999). *Islam today: A short introduction to the Muslim world.* London: I.B. Tauris.

Ahmed, N. (2004). Islamophobia and antisemitism. *European Judaism, 37*(1), 124–127.

Ahmed, S., & Matthes, J. (2017). Media representation of Muslims and Islam from 2000 to 2015: A meta-analysis. *International Communication Gazette, 79*(3), 219–244.

Ahsan, M. (2005). Post-9/11 Islamophobia: Promoting interfaith harmony and global peace. *IPRI Journal, 5*(1), 1–26.

Ajami, R. A., & Goddard, G. J. (2018). *Global business: Competitiveness and sustainability.* Oxford: Routledge.

Akbarzadeh, S. (2016). The Muslim question in Australia: Islamophobia and Muslim alienation. *Journal of Muslim Minority Affairs, 36*(3), 323–333.

Ali, A. H. (2017, 16 August). Burka debate: What's at stake is equality of women. *The Australian.* Retrieved from https://www.theaustralian.com.au/nation/inquirer/burka-debate-whats-at-stake-is-equality-of-women/news-story/2b7f315275d158719f13cc84edda9c1c

Ali, S. A. (1949). *The spirit of Islam* (5th ed.) London: Christophers.

Ali, T. (2002). *The clash of fundamentalisms: Crusades, Jihads and modernity.* London: Verso.

Ali, Y. (2012). *Shariah and citizenship.*: How Islamophobia is creating a second-class citizenry in America *California Law Review, 100,* 1027–1068.

Alietti, A., & Padovan, D. (2013). Religious racism. Islamophobia and antisemitism in Italian society. *Religions, 4*(4), 584–602.

Allen, C. (2005). *Islamophobia: Contested concept in the public space.* Birmingham: University of Birmingham.

Allen, C. (2007). Islamophobia and its consequences. In Amghar, S.; Boulbekeur, A. & Emerson, M (Eds.), *European Islam: Challenges for public policy and society* (pp. 144–168). Brussels: Centre for European Policy Studies.

Allen, C. (2010). *Islamophobia.* Berlington, Surrey, Farnham, UK: Ashgate Publishing Limited.

Allen, C., & Nielsen, J. S. (2002). *Summary report on Islamophobia in the EU after 11 September 2001.* Vienna: European Monitoring Centre on Racism and Xenophobia.

Allievi, S. (2010). Mosques in Europe: Real problems and false solutions. In S. Allievi (Ed.), *Mosques in Europe: Why a solution has become a problem* (pp. 13–52). London: Alliance Publishing Trust.

Allport, G. W. (1954). *Nature of prejudice.* Cambridge, MA: Addison-Wesley.

Allport, G. W., & Ross, J. M. (1967). Personal religious orientation and prejudice. *Journal of Personality and Social Psychology, 5*(4), 432.

Al-Olaqi, F. M. (2010, Summer). Image of the messenger Muhammad (peace be upon him) in the English literature from early middle ages to present. *Insights, 4*(2), 29–100.

Al-Olaqi, F. M. (2017). The distorted image of Prophet Muhammad in Percy's Mahomet and his heaven (1601). *Advances in Social Sciences Research Journal, 4*(14), 137–157.

Alvi, H. (2014). The diffusion of intra-Islamic violence and terrorism: The impact of the proliferation of Salafi/Wahhabi ideologies. *Middle East Review of International Affairs (Online), 18*(2), 38.

Aly, W. (2011). Monoculturalism, Muslims and myth making. In R. Gaita (Ed.), *Essays on Muslims and multiculturalism* (pp. 47–92). Melbourne: The Text Publishing Company.

Amin, M. (2013, 31 March). *Review of 'The Clash of Civilizations and the Remaking of World Order' by Samuel P. Huntington.* Retrieved from https://www.mohammedamin.com/Reviews/The-clash-of-civilizations.html

An-Na'im, A. A. (1987). Religious minorities under Islamic Law and the limits of cultural relativism. *Human Rights Quarterly*, *9*(1), 1–18.

Anawati, G. C. (1976). Dialogue with Gustave E. von Grunebaum. *International Journal of Middle East Studies*, *7*(1), 123–128.

Andrabi, A. A. (2016). Human rights in Islamic perspective. *International Journal of Humanities and Social Science Research*, *2*(5), 21–26.

Anthony, E. (2016). *Effects of conflict news on intercultural othering an international comparative study.* Retrieved from https://pdfs.semanticscholar.org/1930/ff04fdaa80ee259ba64565f27c63fc65455d.pdf?_ga=2.6725874.1924001319.1569317443-1954964792.1569317443

Armstrong, K. (2001). *The battle for God: Fundamentalism in Judaism, Christianity and Islam.* New York, NY: HarperCollins.

Arnold, T. W., & Alfred, G. (1997). *The legacy of Islam.* New Delhi: Kitab Bhavan.

Ashcroft, B. G. (2013). *Post colonial studies, the key concepts* (3rd Ed.). New York, NY: Routledge.

Ashraf, M. M. T. (2015). The clash of civilizations? A critique. *Pakistan Journal of Social Sciences*, *32*(2), 521–527.

American Medical Association. (2000). *Physician masterfile: Physician statistics now-graph.* Retrieved from www.ama-assn.org: www.ama-assn.org/ama/pub/category/2687.html

Aya, R. (1978). Norbert Elias and 'the civilizing process'. *Theory and Society*, *5*(2), 219–228.

Aydin, C. (2017). *The idea of the Muslim world.* New York, NY: Harvard University Press.

Baber, Z. (2004). Race, religion and riots: The radicalization of communal identity and conflict in India. *Sociology*, *34*(4), 701–718.

Back, L., & Solomos, J. (2000). *Theories of race and racism: A reader.* Oxford: Routledge.

Balzacq, T. (2010). *Securitization theory: How security problems emerge and dissolve* (p. 56). Abingdon: Routledge.

Bambery, C. (2012, 11 February). *Counter fire.* Retrieved from www.couterfire.org: http://www.counterfire.org/history/17682-islamophobia-debunking-the-clash-of-civilisations

Banton, M. (1983). *Racial and ethnic competition.* Cambridge: Cambridge University Press.

Barker, M. (1981). *The new racism: Conservatives and the ideology of the tribe.* London: Junction Books.

Barry Buzan, O. W. (1998). *Security: A new framework for analysis.* Boulder, CO: Lynne Rienner Publishers.

Batson, C. D., & Schoenrade, P. (1993). *Religion and the individual: A social-psychological perspective.* New York, NY: Oxford University Press.

Bayrakli, E., & Hafez, F. (2016). *European Islamophobia report 2015.* Ankara: Foundation for Political, Economic and Social Research.

BBC Report (2015, 19 December). *Is Suadi Arabia to blame for Islamic State?* Retrieved from https://www.bbc.com/news/world-middle-east-35101612

Belinda, D. F. (2016). *Negative media portrayal of Muslims.* Toronto: Global Research Centre, Canada.

Belt, D. (2014). Framing Islam as a Threat: The use of Islam by Some US conservatives as a platform for cultural politics in the decade after 9/11 (Doctoral dissertation). Virginia Tech, Blacksburg, VA.

Berger, M. S. (2018). Understanding Shariah in the West. *Journal of Law, Religion and State, 6*(2), 236–273.

Berman, P. (2003). *Terror and liberalism.* New York, NY: W. W. Norton & Company.

Bernard, A. (1927). L'islam et l'Afrique du nord Paris: Félix Alcan (Islam and North Africa Paris: Felix Alcan), pp. 103–22. *Conference Proceedings: L'islam et la politique contemporaine. Conférences organisées par la Société des anciens élèves et élèves de l'Ecole libre des sciences politiques (Conference Proceedings: Islam and Contemporary Politics. Conference organized by the Society of Alumni and Students of the Free School of Political Science)*, 103–122.

Betz, H. G., & Meret, S. (2009). Revisiting Lepanto: The political mobilization against Islam in contemporary Western Europe. *Patterns of Prejudice, 43*(3–4), 313–334.

Bhabha, H. K. (1994). *The location of culture.* New York, NY: Routledge.

Blair, I. (2002). The malleability of automatic stereotypes and prejudice. *Personality and Social Psychology Review, 6*(3), 242–261.

Blaut, J. M. (1992). The theory of cultural racism. *Antipode, 24*(2), 289–299.

Bleich, E. (2012, Winter). Defining and researching islamophobia. *Middle East Studies Association of North America, 46*(2), 180–189.

Blitt, R. C. (2011). The bottom up journey of 'defamation of religion' from Muslim states to the United Nations: A case study of the migration of anti-constitutional ideas. *Studies in Law, Politics and Society (Special Issue Human Rights: New Possibilities/New Problems), 56*, 121–212.

Blumer, H. (1969). *Symbolic interactionism: Perspective and method.* Berkeley: University of California Press.

Bolt, A. (2017, 23 March). Andrew Bolt: Bloody links between Islam and political violence. *Herald Sun.* Retrieved from https://www.herald-sun.com.au/subscribe/news/1/?sourceCode=HSWEB_WRE170_a_GGL&dest=https%3A%2F%2Fwww.heraldsun.com.au%2Fnews%2Fopinion%2Fandrew-bolt%2Fandrew-bolt-bloody-links-between-islam-and-political-violence%2Fnews-story%2F63f4250c1013af1b33c85e20b54e2485&memtype=anonymous&mode=premium&v21suffix=57-a

Bonansinga, D. (2018). Emotionality in right-wing populism security discourse and its impacts on information processing. Retrieved from https://www.psa.ac.uk/sites/default/files/conference/papers/2018/DB_Paper%20PSA.pdf

Bowering, G. (2015). *Islamic political thought* (pp. 1–24). Princeton, NJ: Princeton University Press.

Boyle, J. S., & Henderson, G. (2017, 22 March). Attack on parliament march 22: The Westminster rampage at the heart of Britain's democracy. *The Telegraph*. Retrieved from http://www.telegraph.co.uk/news/2017/03/22/man-shot-police-outside-parliament-officer-reportedly-shoots/

Brachman, J. M. (2008). *Global Jihadism: Theory and practice*. Abingdon: Routledge.

Bray, J. (1984). The Mahometan and idolatry. *Studies in Church History*, 21, 89–98.

Brewer, M. (1999). The psychology of prejudice. *Journal of Social Issues*, 55, 429.

Brown, R. (1995). *Prejudice: Its social psychology*. Cambridge, MA: Blackwell Publishers.

Buijs, F.J., & Rath, J. (2002). *Muslims in Europe: The state of research*. IMISCOE Working Paper. Retrieved from http://citeseerx.ist.psu.edu/viewdoc/download?doi=10.1.1.597.4161&rep=rep1&type=pdf

Burns, R. I. (1960). Journey from Islam: Incipient cultural transition in the conquered kingdom of Valencia (1240–1280). *Speculum*, 35(3), 337–356.

Burns, R. (1984). *Muslims, Christians, and Jews in the crusader kingdom of Valencia*. Cambridge, MA: Cambridge University Press.

Burton, J. L. (1918). *The Christian approach to Islam*. Boston, MA: The Pilgrim Press.

Cainkar, L. (2004). The impact of the September 11 attacks and their aftermath on Arab and Muslim communities in the United States. In John Tirman (Ed.), *The maze of fear: Security and migration after 9/11*. New York, NY: The New Press.

Carland, S. (2011). Islamophobia, fear of loss of freedom, and the Muslim woman. *Islam and Christian—Muslim relations*, 22(4), 469–473.

Carment, D. & James, P. (1995). Internal constraints and interstate ethnic conflict: Toward a crisis-based assessment of irredentism. *Journal of Conflict Resolution*, 39(1), 82–109.

Carr, J. (2015). *Experiences of Islamophobia: Living with racism in the neoliberal era*. Abingdon: Routledge.

Catherine, S. (1988). Chambers English Dictionary. Cambridge: Chambers.

Cell, J. W. (1982). *The highest stage of White supremacy: The origin of segregation in South Africa and the American South*. New York, NY: Cambridge University Press.

Celso, A. N. (2015). Zarqawi's legacy: Al Qaeda's ISIS 'Renegade'. *Mediteranian Quarterly*, 26(2), 21–41.

Cesari, J. (2012). Securitization of Islam in Europe. *Die Welt des Islams*, 52(3–4), 430–449.

Cesari, J. (2013). *Why the West fears Islam: An exploration of Muslims in liberal democracies*. Berlin: Springer.

Chadia, L. (2016). The clash of thoughts within the Arab discourse. Unpublished MA Thesis submitted to Department of Political Science, University of Florida, Orlando, USA. Retrieved from http://etd.fcla.edu/CF/CFE0002949/Louai_Chadia_200912_MA1.pdf

Chatfield, A. T. (2015). Tweeting propaganda, radicalization and recruitment: Islamic state supporters multi-sided twitter networks. *16th Annual International Conference on Digital Government, ACM*, 239–249.

Chatfield, A. T., Reddick, C. G., & Uuf, B. (2015). Tweeting propaganda, radicalization and recruitment: Islamic State supporters multi-sided Twitter networks. *Proceedings of the 16th Annual International Conference on Digital Government Research*, 239–249. Retrieved from http://dl.acm.org/citation.cfm?doid=2757401.2757408

Chazan, R. (1989). *Daggers of faith: Thirteenth-century Christian missionizing and Jewish response*. Berkeley, CA: University of California Press.

Chesterton, G. (1925). *The everlasting man*. London: Hodder & Stoughton.

Chiozza, G. (2002). Is there clash of civilization? Evidence from patterns of international conflict involvement, 1946–97. *Journal of Peace Research*, *39*(6), 711–734.

Chomsky, N. (2001). *Militarism, democracy and people's right to information*. Retrieved from www.india-seminar.com and http://www.india-seminar.com/2002/509/509%20noam%20chomsky.htm

Choudhury, C. A. (2013). Shari'ah law as national security threat? *Akron Law Review*, *46*(1), 46–49.

Churchill, W. S. (1899). *The river war* (1st Ed., Vol. II). London: Longmans, Green.

Ciftci, S. (2012). Islamophobia and threat perceptions: Explaining anti-Muslim sentiment in the West. *Journal of Muslim Minority Affairs*, *32*(3), 293–309.

Clark, A. (2017, 10 March). Pauline Hanson warns Malcolm Turnbull government on knife's edge in WA vote. *Financial Review*. Retrieved from https://www.afr.com/politics/federal/pauline-hanson-warns-malcolm-turnbull-government-on-knifes-edge-in-wa-vote-20170310-guvb0p

Cobain, I. (2016, 24 November). Britain's far right in 2016: Fractured, unpredictable, dispirited … and violent. *The Guardian*. Retrieved from https://www.theguardian.com/world/2016/nov/24/britains-far-right-in-2016-fractured-unpredictable-dispirited-and-violent

Cole, P. J. (1993). O God, the heathen have come into your inheritance (PS 78.1): The theme of religious pollution in crusade documents (1095–1188). In M. Shatzmiller (Ed.) *Crusaders and Muslims in twelfth century Syria* (pp. 84–111). Leiden: Brill.

Considine, C. (2017). The racialization of Islam in the United States: Islamophobia, hate crimes, and 'flying while brown'. *Religions*, *8*(9), 165.

Constable, O. R. (2010). Regulating religious noise: The council of Vienne, the mosque call and Muslim pilgrimage in the late medieval Mediterranean world. *Medieval Encounters*, *16*, 64–95.

Conway, G., & Richardson, R. (1997). *Islamophobia: A challenge for us all*. London: Runnymede Trust.

Cook, S. A. (1923). The history of religions. *The Journal of Theological Studies*, *25*(97), 101–109.

Cox, C. (2017, 17 July). The moment a Manchester mosque went up in flames after a possible arson attack. *Manchester Evening News*. Retrieved from http://www.manchestereveningnews.co.uk/news/greater-manchester-news/moment-manchester-mosque-went-up-13342585

Creutz-Kämppi, K. (2008). The othering of Islam in European context, *Nordicom Review, 29*(2), 295–308.

Crone, P., & Cook, M. (1980). *Hagarism: The making of the Islamic world.* Cambridge, MA: Cambridge University Press.

Daniel, N. (1960). *Islam and the West: The making of an image.* Edinburgh: Edinburgh University Press.

Dearden, L. (2017, 22 June). Muslim woman suing estate agent 'after being told black hijab made her look like a terrorist'. *Independent.* Retrieved from http://www.independent.co.uk/news/uk/home-news/muslim-woman-black-hijab-terrorist-employment-tribunal-discrimination-suing-bury-manchester-a7803666.html

Delafosse, M. (1910). Létat actuel de lafrique occidentale francaise [the current state of French West Africa]. *Revue Du Monde Musualman (Review of the Muslim World), 11*(5), 32–53.

Dewick, E. (1953). *The Christian attitude to other religions.* New York, NY: Cambridge University Press.

Dewey, J. (1981). *Experience and nature, the later works, 1925–1953 (Vol. 1).* Carbondale: Southern Illinois University Press.

Diekman, A. B., & Eagly, A. H. (2000). Stereotypes as dynamic constructs: Women and men of the past, present, and future. *Personality and Social Psychology Bulletin, 26*(10), 1171–1188.

Diekman, E., & Eagly, A. H. (2005). What is the problem? Prejudice as an attitude-in-context. In J. F. Dovidio, P. Glick, & L. A. Rudman (Eds.), *On the nature of prejudice: Fifty years after Allport* (pp. 19–35). Malden: Blackwell Publishing.

Dillon, M. R. (2009). *Wahhabism: is it a factor in the spread of global terrorism?* (Masters Dissertation). Retrieved from https://www.nps.edu/documents/105988371/107571254/DillonWahhabismThesis.pdf/23fc46fb-17a6-41da-83b8-8e312191b5bb

Dinet, E., & Ibrahim, S. (1925). *L'orient vu de l'occident.* Paris: Piazza-Geuthner.

D'Souza, D. (1995). *The end of racism.* New York, NY: Free Press.

Dunn, E. W., Moore, & Nosek, B. A. (2005). The war of the words: How linguistic differences in reporting shape perceptions of terrorism. *Analyses of Social Issues and Public Policy, 5*(1), 67–86.

Duss, M., & Ali, W. (2011). *Understanding Sharia Law: Conservatives' skewed interpretation needs debunking.* Washington: Center for American Progress, March. Retrieved from https://www.americanprogress.org/issues/religion/reports/2011/03/31/9175/understanding-sharia-law/

DW. (2015). *Publisher abandons Turkish-born Pirincci over Pegida speech.* Retrieved from http://www.dw.com/en/publisher-abandons-turkish-born-pirincci-over-pegida-speech/a-18794193

Edward, H., & Chomsky, N. (1988). *Manufacturing consent: The political economy of the mass media.* New York, NY: Pantheon Books.

Edwards, V. (2017, 8 April). Peak Islamic council 'needs a female mufti'. *The Australian.* Retrieved from https://www.theaustralian.com.au/subscribe/news/1/?sourceCode=TAWEB_WRE170_a_GGL&dest=https%3A%2F%

2Fwww.theaustralian.com.au%2Fnation%2Fnation%2Fpeak-islamic-council-needs-a-female-mufti-says-south-australian-imam%2Fnews-story%2F9d73 7c12f2ec059f4b601164d7547c96&memtype=anonymous&mode=premiu m&v21suffix=58-a

El Fadl, K. A., & Brown, L. C. (2005). The great theft: Wrestling Islam from the extremists. New York, NY: HarperOne.

Engelund, S. R. (2012, 16 February). 'The other' and 'othering'. Retrieved from https://newnarratives.wordpress.com/issue-2-the-other/other-and-othering-2/

Erisen, C., & Kentmen-Cin, C. (2016). Tolerance and perceived threat toward Muslim immigrants in Germany and the Netherlands. *European Union Politics*, 1–25.

Esposito, J. L. (1992). *The Islamic threat: Myth or reality*. Oxford: Oxford University Press.

Esposito, J. L. (1998). *Islam and politics* (4th Ed.). Syracuse, NY: Syracuse University Press.

Essed, P. (1991). *Understanding everyday racism: An interdisciplinary theory*. SAGE series on race and ethnic relations (Vol. 2). Thousand Oaks, CA: SAGE Publications.

Eze, E. C. (1997). Race and the enlightenment: A reader. New York, NY: Wiley-Blackwell.

Fadl, K. A. (2011, 16 May). *ABC religion and ethics*. Retrieved from www.abc.net. au and http://www.abc.net.au/religion/articles/2011/05/16/3218247.htm

Fahlbusch, E., Lochman, J. M., Mbiti, J., Pelikan, J., Vischer, L., Bromiley, G. W., & Barret, D. B. (2001). *Encyclopaedia of Christianity* (pp, 758–762). Brill: William B. Eerdmans Publishing Company.

Fallaci, O. (2006). *The force of reason*. New York, NY: Rizzoli International Publications.

Farouk, A. F. 2016. Deciphering the othering of Muslims. Retrieved from https:// www.nst.com.my/news/2016/11/192292/deciphering-othering-muslims

Farhat-Holzman, L. (2016). The Myth of the Andalusian Paradise: Muslims, Christians, and Jews under Islamic rule in medieval Spain. *Comparative Civilizations Review*, 74(74), 11.

Field, C. (2012). Revisiting Islamophobia in contemporary Britain, 2007–10. In M. Helbling (Ed.), *Islamophobia in the West: Measuring and explaining individual attitudes*. London: Routledge.

Foner. C. N. (2015). Is Islam in Western Europe like race in the United States? *Sociological Forum*, 30, 885–899.

Fox, J. E., Moroşanu, L., & Szilassy, E. (2012). The racialization of the New European migration to the UK. *Sociology*, 46(4), 680–695.

Foxe, J. (1838). *The acts and monuments of the Church containing the history and sufferings of martyrs (Part I)*. London: Printed for Scott, Webster and Geary.

Fredrickson, B. L. (1998). What good are positive emotions? *Review of General Psychology*, 2(3), 300–319.

Fredrickson, G. M. (1987). *The black image in the white mind: The debate on Afro-American character and destiny, 1817–1914*. Middletown, CT: Wesleyan University Press.

Fredrickson, G. M. (2015). *Racism: A short history*. Princeton, NJ: Princeton University Press.

Fregosi, P. (1998). *Jihad in the West: Muslim conquests from the 7th to the 21st centuries*. New York, NY: Prometheus Books.

Freud, S. (1921). *Group psychology and the analysis of the ego* (Standard ed.). London: Hogarth Press.

Funk, N. C., & Said, A. A. (2004). Islam and the West: Narratives of conflict and conflict transformation. *International Journal of Peace Studies, 9*(1), 1–28.

Gaertner, S. L., & Dovidio, J. F. (1986). The aversive form of racism. In J. F. Dovidio, & S. L. Gaertner (Eds.), *Prejudice, discrimination, and racism* (pp. 61–89). San Diego, CA: Academic Press.

Gada, M. Y. (2015). The Muslims are coming! Islamophobia, extremism, and the domestic war on terror. *Arab Studies Quarterly, 37*(2), 205–208.

Galton, F. (1889). *Natural inheritance*. London: Macmillan.

Garrett, A. (2000, April). Hume's revised racism revisited. *Hume Studies, 26*(1), 171–178.

Garth, T. R. (1925). A review of racial psychology. *Psychological Bulletin, 22*(6), 343–354.

Gartrell, A. (2017, 5 March). Pauline Hanson blasts Muslims, praises Putin, questions vaccines in ABC interview. *The Sydney Morning Herald*.

Gee, G. C. (2002). A multilevel analysis of the relationship between institutional and individual racial discrimination and health status. *American Journal of Public Health, 92*(4), 615–623.

Geisser, V. (2003). *The new Islamophobia*. Paris: La Decouverte.

Goertz, G. (2005). *Social science concepts a user's guide*. Princeton, NJ: Princeton University Press.

González, K. V., Verkuyten, M., Weesie, J., & Poppe, E. (2008). Prejudice towards Muslims in the Netherlands: Testing integrated threat theory. *British Journal of Social Psychology, 47*(4), 667–685.

Gorsuch, R. L. (1972). Single vs multiple-item scales for measuring religious values. *Journal for the Scientific Study of Religion, 11*(1), 53–64.

Gottschalk, P., & Greenberg, G. (2008). *Islamophobia: Making Muslims the enemy*. Lanham, MD: Rowman & Littlefield.

Graness, A. (2016). Writing the history of philosophy in Africa: Where to begin? *Journal of African Cultural Studies, 28*(2), 132–146.

Grant, C. (2007). *Uncertainty and communication*. Hampshire: Palgrave MacMillan.

Grautoff, G. G. (2000). Vidal Mayor: A visualisation of the juridical miniature. *Medieval History Journal, 3*, 67–89.

Green, S. (2014). The Muslim struggle for civil rights in Spain: Promoting democracy through migrant engagement. *Journal of Contemporary European Studies, 22*(4), 1985–2010.

Green, T. H. (2015). *The fear of Islam: An introduction to Islamophobia in the West.* Minneapolis, MN: Augsburg Fortress Publishers. Retrieved from Project MUSE database.

Grosfoguel, R., & Mielants, E. (2006). The long-duree entanglement between Islamophobia and racism in the modern/colonial capitalist/patriarchal world-system. *Human Architecture: Journal of the Sociological of Self-Knowledge, 1,* 1–12.

Grunebaume, G. E. (1955). *Islam: Essays in the nature and growth of a cultural tradition* (p. 80). London: Routledge & Kegan Paul.

Gunaratna, R. (2017). Fighting terrorism with smart power: The role of community engagement and terrorist rehabilitation. In *Talking to the enemy* (pp. 67–90). Nomos Verlagsgesellschaft mbH & Co. KG. Henning Glaser (Hrsg.).

Habermas, J., & Luhmann, N. (1971). Theory of society or social technology. Frankfurt: Suhrkamp.

Haddad, Y. Y. (2007). The post-9/11 hijab as icon. *Sociology of Religion, 68*(3), 253–267.

Hall, D. L., Matz, D. C., & Wood, W. (2010). Why don't we practice what we preach? A meta-analytic view of religious racism. *Personality and Social Philosophy Review, 14*(1), 126–139.

Hall, J. A., & Carter, J. D. (1999). Gender-stereotype accuracy as an individual difference. *Journal of Personality and Social Psychology, 77*(2), 350.

Hall, S. (1992). New ethnicities. In A. Rattansi and J. Donald (Eds.), *Race, culture and difference* (p. 298). London: SAGE Publications.

Halliday, F. (1996). *Islam and the myth of confrontation: Religion and politics in the Middle East.* London: I.B. Tauris.

Halliday, F. (1999a). 'Islamophobia' reconsidered. *Ethnic and Racial Studies, 22*(5), 892–902.

Halliday, F. (1999b). *Revolution and World politics: The rise and fall of the sixth great power.* New York, NY: Palgrave.

Halliday, F. (2001). *Two hours that shook the world: September 11, 2001: Causes and consequences.* London: Saqi Books.

Halliday, F. (2003). *Islam and the myth of confrontation. Religion and politics in the Middle East.* London: I.B. Tauris.

Halliday, F. (2005). *The Middle East in international relations: Power, politics and ideology.* New York, NY: Cambridge University Press.

Halverson, J. R. (2011). *The Tariq Ibn Ziyad master narrative* (Vol. 1101). Tempe, AZ: Arizona State University.

Hamilton, A. (1985). *William Bedwell, the Arabist* (p. 67). Leiden: Brill.

Hammerstad, A. (2014). *The rise and decline of a global security actor: UNHCR, refugee protection, and security.* Oxford: Oxford University Press.

Hansen, L. (2011). The politics of securitization and the Muhammad cartoon crisis: A post-structuralist perspective. *Security Dialogue, 42*(4–5), 357–369.

Hansen, M. (2016). *To securitize or not to securitize, that is the question.* Lund: Lund University.

Hanson, R. E. (2016). *Mass communication: Living in a media world*. New York, NY: SAGE Publications.

Harding, E. (2017, 28 September). Students invite radical Islamic speakers to over 110 events in a year despite the government's terror crackdown. *The Daily Mail*.

Harrison, C. (1988). *France and Islam in West Africa, 1860–1960*. Cambridge, MA: Cambridge University Press.

Harvey, L. (2005). *Muslims in Spain, 1500–1614*. Chicago, IL: University of Chicago Press.

Heilman, M. E. (1983). Sex biases in work setting: The lack of fit model. *Research in Organizational Behavior, 5*.

Henderson, & Tucker. (2001). Clear and present strangers: The clash of civilizations and international conflict. *International Studies Quarterly, 45*(2), 317–338.

Herek, G. M. (1987). Religious orientation and prejudice: A comparison of racial and sexual attitudes. *Personality and Social Psychology Bulletin, 13*(1), 34–44.

Heylyn, P. (1682). *Cosmographie (historical cultures & geography, 1600–1750)* (reprinted). New York, NY: Thoemmes Continuum.

Hirsch, A. (2018, 18 February). Othering, micro-aggressions and subtle prejudice: Growing up Black and British. *News Statement America*. Retrieved from https://www.newstatesman.com/culture/books/2018/02/othering-micro-aggressions-and-subtle-prejudice-growing-black-and-british.

Hobson, J. M. (2004). *The Eastern origins of western civilization*. Cambridge, NY: Cambridge University Press.

Hogan, H. (2014). The importance of family: The key to understanding the evolution of Jihadism in Australia. *Security Challenges, 10*(1), 31–50.

Hogg, M. (2002). *Social psychology* (3rd Ed.). London: Prentice Hall.

Hollander, R. (2004). *Dictionary of the middle ages* (Vol. 4). London: Charles Scribner's Sons.

Hollar, J., & Naureckas, J. (2008). *Smearcasting: How Islamophobes spread fear, bigotry and misinformation*. New York, NY: FAIR.

Holloway, L. (2016). *Islamophobia is still a challenge for us all*. London: Runnymede Trust.

Hopkins, N., & Kahani-Hopkins, V. (2006). Minority group members' theories of intergroup contact: A case study of British Muslims' conceptualizations of 'Islamophobia' and social change. *British Journal of Social Psychology, 45*(2), 245–264.

Horowitz, D. (1985). *Ethnic groups in conflict*. Berkeley, CA: University of California.

Howell, S. (2014). *Old Islam in Detroit: Rediscovering the American Muslims past*. New York, NY: Oxford University Press.

Humphery. (2009). Securitisation and domestication of diaspora Muslims and Islam: Turkish immigrants in Germany and Australia. *International Journal on Multicultural Societies, 11*(2).

Huntington, S. (1993, Summer). The clash of civilizations? *Foreign Affairs*, 72(3), 22–49.

Huntington, S. P. (1996). *The clash of civilizations and the remaking of World order.* New York: Simon & Schuster.

Huntington, S. P. (1999). The lonely superpower. *Foreign Affairs*, 78(2), 35.

Huntington, S. P. (2004, Spring). Dead souls: The denationalization of American elite. *The National Interest.*

Hurd, S. (2007). Anxiety and non-anxiety in a distance language learning environment: The distance factor as a modifying influence. *System*, 35(4), 487–508.

Husain, A. (2017). Religious microaggressions: A case study of Muslim Americans. *Journal of Ethnic & Cultural Diversity in Social Work*, 26(1–2), 139–152.

Ibn, W., & Warraq, I. (1995). *Why I am not a Muslim.* New York, NY: Prometheus Books.

Imhoff, R., & Recker, J. (2012). Differentiating Islamophobia: Introducing a new scale to measure Islamoprejudice and secular Islam critique. *Political Psychology*, 33(6), 811–824.

Imtoual, A. (2006). Young Muslim women's experiences of religious racism in Australia. *Australian Religion Studies Review*, 19(2), 189–206.

Iqbal, Z. (2010a). Islamophobia or Islamophobias: Towards developing a process model. *Islamic Studies*, 49(1), 81–101.

Iqbal, Z. (2010b). Understanding Islamophobia: Conceptualizing and measuring the construct. *European Journal of Social Sciences*, 13(4), 574–590.

Iqbal, Z. (2018). Media discourse. YouTube Video. Retrieved from https://www.youtube.com/channel/UCz6f4Nr2zeWN_AQi6S75M_w/videos

Jackman, M. R. (1994). *The velvet glove: Paternalism and conflict in gender class and race relations.* Berkeley, CA: University of California Press.

Jackson, R. (2005). *Writing the war on terrorism: Language, politics and counter-terrorism.* Manchester: Manchester University Press.

Jackson, P., & Penrose, J. (Eds.). (1994). *Constructions of race, place, and nation.* Minneapolis, MN: University of Minnesota Press.

Jahanbegloo, R. (2013). *The Gandhian moment.* Cambridge, MA: Harvard University Press.

Jaspal, R., & Breakwell, G. M. (2014). *Identity process theory: Identity, social action and social change.* New York, NY: Cambridge University Press.

Jaspal, R., & Cinnirella, M. (2010). Coping with potentially incompatible identities: Accounts of religious, ethnic, and sexual identities from British Pakistani men who identify as Muslim and Gay. *British Journal of Social Psychology*, 49(4), 849–870.

Jawad, H. (2010). Islam and democracy in the twenty-first century. In *Muslim societies and the challenge of secularization: An interdisciplinary approach* (pp. 65–81). Dordrecht: Springer.

Jensen, S. Q. (2011). *Othering, Identity Formation and Agency. Qualitative Studies*, 2(2).

Jobse, H. (2017). Spain's Muslims see hatred spike since Barcelona attacks. *Deutsche Welle*. Retrieved from https://www.dw.com/en/spains-muslims-see-hatred-spike-since-barcelona-attacks/a-40294207

Jones, J. M. (1972). *Prejudice and racism*. Reading, MA: Addison-Wesley.

Jones, P. O. (2008). *Counter extremism organization*. Retrieved from www.counterextremism.org/resources/details/id/99/muslims-under-siege-alienating-vulnerable-communities.

Juergensmeyer, M. (1993). *The new cold war? Religious nationalism confronts the secular state* (Vol. 5). Berkeley, CA: University of California Press.

Kaplan, J. (2006). Islamophobia in America? September 11 and Islamophobic hate crime. *Terrorism and Political Violence, 18*(1), 1–33.

Kamenova. (2014). Media and othering: How media discourse on migrants reflects and affects society's tolerance. *Politické vedy, 17*(2), 170–184.

Karen, C. (2018, 13 May). *What is a city state? Definition*. Retrieved from www.quartr.us: https://quatr.us/government/city-state-definition.htm

Karim, K. H. (2002). Making sense of the 'Islamic peril': Journalism as cultural practice. In B. Zelizer, & S. Allan (Eds.), *Journalism after September 11* (Vol. 101–116). London: Routledge.

Kaya, S. (2015). Outgroup prejudice from an evolutionary perspective: Survey evidence from Europe. *Journal of International and Global Studies, 7*(1), 16–31.

Kazmi, Z. (2016, 2 August). Islamophobia and the new Britishness. *Foreign Affairs*. Retrieved from https://www.foreignaffairs.com/articles/united-kingdom/2016-08-02/islamophobia-and-new-britishness

Kedar, B. (1984). *Crusade and mission: European approaches toward the Muslims*. Princeton, NJ: Princeton University Press.

Kelle, K. J. (2007). *The UN secretary general and moral authority: Ethics and religion in international leadership*. Washington, DC: Georgetown University Press.

Khadduri, M. (1955). *War and peace in the law of Islam*. Baltimore, MD: Johns Hopkins University Press.

Khadduri, M. (1966). *The Islamic law of nations: Shaybani's siyar*. Baltimore, MD: The John Hopkins Press.

Kidd, T. S. (2013). *American Christians and Islam: Evangelical Christians and Muslims from the colonial period to the age of terrorism*. New Jersey, NJ: Princeton University Press.

Kimball, C. A. (2017). Muslim-Christian dialogue. In *The Oxford Encyclopedia of the Islamic world*. Oxford Islamic Studies Online. Retrieved from http://www.oxfordislamicstudies.com/article/opr/t236/e0567

Kirbassov, G. (2006). Has 'the clash of civilizations' found empirical support? *The Fountain*. Retrieved from https://fountainmagazine.com/2006/issue-56-october-december-2006/has-the-clash-of-civilizations-found-empirical-support

Kostiner, J. (2018). *Monarchy government*. Retrieved from www.britannica.com and https://www.britannica.com/topic/monarchy

Kousser, J. M., & McPherson, J. M. (Eds.). (1982). *Region, race, and reconstruction: Essays in honor of C. Vann Woodward*. New York, NY: Oxford University Press.

Kritzeck, J., & Daniel, N. (1961, Apr–Jun). Islam and the West: The making of an image. *Journal of the American Oriental Society, 81*(2), 139–140.

Krumme, B. (2010). Explaining family cohesion in an immigration context: Patterns of intergenerational relationship quality among young adult Turks and their parents. Open access paper. Retrieved from https://www.ssoar.info/ssoar/bitstream/handle/document/36947/ssoar-2010-baykara-krumme-Explaining_family_cohesion_in_an.pdf?sequence=1&isAllowed=y&lnkname=ssoar-2010-baykara-krumme-Explaining_family_cohesion_in_an.pdf

Kumar, D. (2012). *Islamophobia and the politics of empire*. Chicago, IL: Haymarket Books.

Kundnani, A. (2009). *Spooked! How not to prevent violent extremism*. London: Institute of Race Relations.

Kunst, J. R., Tajamal, H., Sam, D. L., & Ulleberg, P. (2011). Coping with Islamophobia: The effects of religious stigma on Muslim minorities' identity formation. *International Journal of Intercultural Relations, 36*(4), 518–532.

Kymlicka, W., & Donaldson, S. (2014). Animal rights, multiculturalism and the Left. *Journal of Social Philosophy, 45*(1), 116–135.

Lacan, J. (1988). *The seminar of Jacques Lacan, the ego in Freud's theory and in the technique of psychoanalysis, 1954–1955*. New York, NY: Norton.

Laffin, J. (1988). *Holy war: Islam fights*. London: Collins Publishing Group.

Lean, N. (2012). *Islamophobia industry*. New York, NY: Pluto Press.

Levinas, E. (1969). *Totality and infinity: An essay on exteriority*. Pittsburgh, PA: Duquesne University Press.

Lévi-Strauss, C. (1992). *The view from afar*. Chicago, IL: University of Chicago Press.

Lévi-Strauss, C. (1955). *Tristes tropiques (Sad Tropics)*. Harmondsworth: Penguin.

Lewis, B. (1990, September). The roots of Muslim rage. *The Atlantic Monthly, 226*(3), 47–60.

Lewis, B. (2014). *The Jews of Islam*. Princeton, NJ: Princeton University Press.

Lichter, I. (2017, 19 August). Veiled agents of political Islam: Burka, hijab have new meanings. *The Australian*. Retrieved from https://www.theaustralian.com.au/nation/inquirer/veiled-agents-of-political-islam-burka-hijab-have-new-meanings/news-story/80ca102fc455b568c6d09e2309699cf8

Linklater, A., & Mennell, S. (2010). Norbert Elias, the civilizing process: Sociogenetic and psychogenetic investigations: An overview and assessment. *History and Theory, 49*(3), 384–411.

Lopez, F. B. (2011). Towards a definition of Islamophobia: Approximation of the early twentieth century. *Ethnic and Racial Studies, 34*(4), 556–573.

Lopez, F. B. (2017). Völkisch vs. Catholic Islamophobia in Spain: The conflict between racial and religious understandings of Muslim identity. *Magazine of Mediterranean International Studies, 22*, 141–164.

Louis, J. (2017, 14 August). *PolitiFact*. Retrieved from www.politifact.com and http://www.politifact.com/truth-o-meter/statements/2017/aug/16/roy-moore/alabamas-roy-moore-says-whole-communities-midwest-/

Love, R. (2013–2014). *The representation of Muslims in the UK national press after the Woolwich murder*. Retrieved from www.academia.edu/.../Love_R._2014_._Representations_of_Muslim_people_and_Isl...

MacKenzie, J. M. (1995). *Orientalism: History, theory and the arts*. Manchester: Manchester University Press.

Madu, I. V. (2015). The Burqa ban in France and its potential implications on Islamic terrorism. Unpublished PhD thesis submitted to College of Social and Behavioural Sciences, Walden University, Minnesota, USA. Retrieved from https://pdfs.semanticscholar.org/2fe8/933472acd02a3797e9222b668f2d7 5b8d5d0.pdf?_ga=2.262057037.1924001319.1569317443-1954964792. 1569317443

Mahamdallie, H. (2015, 11 April). Islamophobia: The othering of Europe's Muslims. *International Socialism Journal, 146*.

Malik, M. (2012). *Anti-Muslim prejudice: Past and present*. New York, NY: Routledge.

Mandaville, P., & Hamid, A. (2018). *Islam as statecraft: How governments use religion in foreign policy*. Foreign Policy at Brookings. Retrieved from https://www.brookings.edu/wp-content/uploads/2018/11/FP_20181116_islam_as_state-craft.pdf

Mansbridge, J., Bohman, J., Chambers, S., Christiano, T., Fung, A., Parkinson, J., & Warren, M. E. (2012). A systemic approach to deliberative democracy. In J. Parkinson, J. Mansbridge (Eds.), *Deliberative Systems: Deliberative Democracy at the Large Scale*. Cambridge: Cambridge University Press.

Marcus, C. (2017, 6 June). Denial is deadly. *The Daily Telegraph*. Retrieved from http://www.mediadiscourse.pk/media/CRIGM_-_Monthly_Edition_-_June_17.pdf

Marr, W. (1879). *The victory of Judaism over Germanism* (8th Ed., translation). Bern: Rudolph Costenoble.

Marranci, G. (2004). Multiculturalism, Islam and the clash of civilizations theory: Rethinking Islamophobia. *Culture and Religion, 5*(1), 105–117.

Marsh, H. (1663). *A new survey of the Turkish Empire and the government*. London: Printed for Henry Marsh at the Sign of the Princes Arms in Chancery Lane.

Marty, P. (1921). *L'islam en guinée fouta-diallon (Islam in Guinea Fouta-Diallon)*. Paris: E. Leroux.

Massari, M. (2006). *Islamophobia: Fear and Islam*. Rome: Laterza.

Matar, N. (2004). *Islam in Britain (1558–1685)*. Cambridge, MA: Cambridge University Press.

Matar, N. (2009). Britons and Muslims in the early modern period: From prejudice to (a theory of) toleration. *Patterns of Prejudice, 43*(3–4), 213–231.

Maussen, M. (2007). *The governance of Islam in Western Europe: A state of the art report* (IMISCOE Working Paper). Amsterdam: University of Amsterdam.

Mayer, A. E. (2006). Clashing human rights priorities: How the United States and Muslim countries selectively use provisions of international human rights. *Chennai Journal of Intercultural Philosophy, 44*, 44–77.

McAuley, J. (2017, 20 August). In Barcelona, a heartening rejection of Islamophobia. *The Washington Post Europe*. Retrieved from https://www.washingtonpost.com/world/europe/in-barcelona-a-heartening-rejection-of-islamophobia/2017/08/20/dbee8954-852f-11e7-9e7a-20fa8d7a0db6_story.html?utm_term=.d80854474260

McDonald, M. (2008). Securitization and the construction of security. *European Journal of International Relations, 14*(4), 563–587.

McDonough, S. (1994). *Gandhi's responses to Islam*. New Delhi: D.K. Printworld.

McIlroy, T. (2017, 5 April). Australia needs programs to 'assimilate' Muslim migrants: Ayaan Hirsi Ali. *The Age (Melbourne, Australia)*.

McMichael, J.R. & Taft, B. (1989). *The writings of William Walwyn* (p. 528). London: Oxford University Press.

McQuail, D. (1994). *Mass communication theory: An introduction*. Thousand Oaks, CA: SAGE Publications.

Meer, N. (2014). Islamophobia and postcolonialism: Contunity, orientalism and Muslim consciousness. *Patterns of Prejudice, 48*(5), 500–515.

Melosi, M. V. (1995, Autumn). Equity, eco-racism and environmental history. *Environmental History Review, 19*(3), 1–16.

Menendian, J. A. (2017, Summer). The problem of othering: Towards inclusiveness and belonging. *Othering and Belonging, 1*.

Menendian, J. A. (2016, Summer). The problem of othering: Towards inclusiveness and belonging. *Othering and Belonging: Expanding the Circle of Human Concern, 1*(1), 14–40.

Mertens, S. (2016). European media coverage of Islam in a globalizing world. *Representations of Islam in the News: A Cross-Cultural Analysis*, 59–73.

Mescher, H. (2008). Policing and Islamophobia in Germany: The role of workplace experience. *International Journal of Conflict and Violence, 2*(1), 138–156.

Messina, A. M. (2016). Securitizing' immigration in Europe: Sending them the same (old) message, getting the same (old) reply? *Handbook on Migration and Social Policy*, 239.

Miah, S. (2017). The Muslim problematic: Muslims, state schools and security. *International Studies in Sociology of Education, 26*(2), 138–150.

Mignolo, W. D. (2006, Fall). Islamophobia/Hispanophobia: The (re)configuration of the racial imperial/colonial matrix. *Human Architecture: Journal of the Sociology of Self-Knowledge, 1*(19).

Milani, M. (2015, 20 July). Islam: The 'open civilisation' confounds closed minds. *The Conversation*. Retrieved from http://theconversation.com/islam-the-open-civilisation-confounds-closed-minds-44416

Miller, W. M. (1976). *A Christian's response to Islam*. Phillipsburg, NJ: Presbyterian and Reformed Publishing Co.

Mills, T. (1685). *The history of the holy war, began anno 1095, by the chiftian prices of Europe against the Turks for the recovery of holy land, and continued to the year 1294.* London: Thomas Malthus.

Mishra, V. (2005). What was multiculturalism? *Journal of Multidisciplinary International Studies, 2*(2), 1–47.

Mishra, V. (2008). Multiculturalism. *The Year's Work in Critical and Cultural Theory, 16*(1), 132–165.

Mitchell, C. (2017, 10 April). Lifting the veil: Hirsi Ali's awkward truths about Islam. *The Australian.*

Mitchell, R. P. (1993). *The society of the Muslim brothers.* Cary, NC: Oxford University Press.

Modood, T. (1997). Difference, cultural racism and anti-racism. In P. Werbner and T. Modood (Ed.), *Debating cultural hybridity: Multi-cultural identities of anti-racism* (pp. 154–172). London: Zed Books.

Monk, P. (2017, 13 March). Islam shouldn't be an exception. *The Australian.*

Moore, K., Mason, P., & Lewis, J. M. W. (2008). Images of Islam in the UK: The representation of British Muslims in the national print news media 2000–2008. 1–41. Retrieved from http://orca.cf.ac.uk/53005/1/08channel4-dispatches.pdf

Moore, K., Mason, P., & Lewis, J. M. W. (2008). Images of Islam in the UK: The representation of British Muslims in the national print news media 2000–2008. Working paper, Cardiff: Cardiff University. Retrieved from http://jppsg.ac.uk/jomec/resources/08channel4-dispatches.pdf

Morgan, G., & Poynting, S. (2012). *Global Islamophobia: Muslims and moral panic in the West.* Surrey: Ashgate Publishing Limited.

Moten, A. R. (2012). Understanding and ameliorating Islamophobia. *Cultural International Journal of Philosophy of Culture and Axiology, 9*(1), 155–178.

Moten, A. R. (2017). *The West, Islam and the Muslims, Islamophobia and extremism.* Kuala Lumpur: South East Asia Regional Centre for Counter Terrorism.

Muir, W. (1861). *The life of Muhammad.* Edinburgh: Oliver and Boyd.

Muir, W. (1884). *The rise and decline of Islam.* London: The Religious Tract Society.

Mummendey, A., Simen, B., Dietze, C., Grünert, M., Haeger, G., Kessler, S., & Schäferhoff, S. (1992). Categorization in not enough: Intergroup discrimination in negative outcome allocation. *Journal of Experimental Social Psychology, 28*(2), 125–144.

Mungiu-Pippidi, A. (2002). *Was Huntington right? Testing cultural legacies.* New York, NY: Stony Brook University.

Nafisa, S. (2016). *Honour and violence: Gender, power and law in Southern Pakistan.* New York, NY: Berghahn Books.

Nasrin, T. (1993). *Lajja* [shame]. London: Penguin.

Navarro, L. (2010). Islamophobia and sexism: Muslim women in the western mass media. *Human Architecture: Journal of the Sociology of Self-knowledge, 8*(2), 95–114.

Nawaz, M. (2017, 1 July). *Eerie poster alleged acid attacker published on Facebook before hate crime on Muslims.* Retrieved from http://www.lbc.co.uk: http://www.lbc.co.uk/radio/presenters/maajid-nawaz/eerie-facebook-post-of-alleged-acid-attacker/

Naz, F. (2016). Is Islam compatible with democracy? *Research Journal of Political Science, 5*(5), 63–73.

Neale, J. M. (1847). *A history of the holy Eastern Church: The patriarchate of Alexandria.* London: Joseph Masters.

Neilsen, J. S. (2009). *Yearbook of Muslims in Europe* (Vol. I). Leiden: Brill.

Neumann, P. (2006). Europe's Jihadist dilemma. *Taylor & Francis Survival Global Politics and Strategy, 48*(2), 71–84.

Newton, C. (2017, 6 June). *US politician says 'Kill them all' after London attack.* Retrieved from http://www.aljazeera.com/news/2017/06/politician-kill-london-attack-170606013304292.html

Nieuwkerk, K. V. (2004). Veils and wooden clogs don't go together. *Ethnos, 69*(2), 229–246.

Nonneman, G. (1996). Muslim communities in the new Europe: Themes and puzzles. In Gerd Nonneman, Tim Niblock and Bogan Szajkowski (Ed.), *Muslim communities in the new Europe* (pp. 3–24). Reading: Ithaca Press.

Norris, P., & Inglehart, R. (2002). Islamic culture and democracy: Testing the 'clash of civilizations' thesis. *Comparative Sociology, 1*(3–4), 235–263.

Noya, J. (2007). Spaniards and Islam. *Analysis of the Elcano Royal Institute (ARI), 105.*

Nurullah, A. S. (2010). Portrayal of Muslims in the media: '24' and the othering process. *International Journal of Human Sciences, 7*(1), 1020–1046.

OECD. (1976). *Measuring Social Well-Being: A Progress Report on the Development of Social Indicators.* Paris: OECD.

O'Leary, D. L. (1923). *Islam at crossroads: A brief survey of the present position and problems of the world of Islam.* London: Kegan Paul, Trench, Trubner.

Omi, M., & Winant, H. (1994). *Racial formation in the United States: From the 1960s to the 1990s.* New York, NY: Routledge.

Oskooii, K. A. R., & Dana, K. (2018). Muslims in Great Britain: the impact of mosque attendance on political behaviour and civic engagement. *Journal of Ethnic and Migration Studies, 44*(9), 1479–1505.

Ottosen, R. (1995). Enemy images and the journalistic process. *Journal of Peace Research, 32*(1), 97–112.

Patrick, L. (2005). *A response to Huntington's clash of civilization.* Manchester: Manchester University Press.

Payne, R. (1990). *The history of Islam.* New York, NY: Dorsey Press.

Pears, E. (1886). *The fall of Constantinople* (pp. 239–240). Manhattan, NY: Harper & Brothers.

Penaskovic, R. (2007). *Muslim world in transition: Contributions of the Gulen movement* (M. Fethullah Gülen's Response to the Clash of Civilizations Thesis, pp. 407–418). Leeds: Leeds Metropolitan University Press.

Perry, S. (1997). *Aspects of contemporary France.* London: Routledge.

Peters, I., & Wemheuer-Vogelaar, W. (2016). *Globalizing international politics: Scholarship amid divide and diversity.* London: Palgrave MacMillan.

Pettigrew, T. F. (1999). Gordon Willard Allport: A tribute. *Journal of Social Issues, 55*(3), 415–427.

Pettigrew, T. F., Tropp, L. R., Wagner, U., & Christ, O. (2011). Recent advances in intergroup contact theory. *International Journal for Intercultural Relations, 35*(3), 271–280.

Philpott, D. (2002). The challenge of September 11 to secularism in international relations. *World Politics, 55*(1), 66–95.

Pintak, L. (2014). Islam, identity and professional values: A study of journalists in three Muslim-majority regions. *Journalism, 15*(4), 482–503.

Poole, E. (2006). *Muslims and the news media.* London: I.B. Tauris.

Poole, E. (2002). *Reporting Islam: Media representations of British Muslims.* London: I.B. Tauris.

Poole, E. (2011). Three phases of representation 1994–2008: The reporting of British Islam. In S. Hutchings, C. Flood, G. Miazhevich & Henri Nickels (Eds.), *Islam in its international context: Comparative perspective.* Cambridge: Cambridge Scholars Publishing.

Poole, E. (2016). The United Kingdom's reporting of Islam and Muslims; Reviewing the field. In S. Mertens & H. de Smaele (Eds.), *Representations of Islam in the news: A cross-cultural analysis* (pp. 21–36). Lanhum, Maryland: Lexington.

Poole, E., & John, R. (2006). *Muslims and the news media.* London: I. B. Tauris.

Powell, A. A. (2010). *Scottish orientalists and India: The Muir brothers, religion, education and empire.* Suffolk: Boydell & Brewer.

Powell, J. M. (1990). *Muslims under Latin rule* (pp. 175–203). Princeton, NJ: Princeton University Press.

Pratt, M. L. (1985). Scratches on the face of the country; or what Mr Barrow saw in the land of the Bushmen. *Critical Inquiry, 12*(1).

Prideaux, H. (1697). *The true nature of imposture fully displayed in the life of Mahomet with a discourse annexed, for the vindicating of Christianity from this charge: Offered to the consideration of the deists of the present age.* London: W. Rogers.

Prideaux, H. (1808). *The true nature of imposter, fully displayed in the life of Mahomet* (10 Ed.). London: W. Nicholson.

Quellien, A. (1910). *The Moslem Policy in French West Africa* (p. 133). Paris: Emile Larose.

Rababa'a, G. (2012). Political Islam: Discussions of civilization. *British Journal of Humanities and Social Sciences, 7*(1), 40–54.

Rafique, Z. (2010). An exploration of the presence and content of metacognitive beliefs about depressive rumination in Pakistani women. *British Journal of Clinical Psychology, 49*(3), 387–411.

Rakic, M. (2012). Wahhabism as a militant form of Islam on Europe's doorstep. *Studies in Conflict & Terrorism, 35*(9), 650–663.

Ramírez, Á. (2006, 8 October). Neocolonial sexim. *El País.* Retrieved from https://elpais.com/diario/2006/10/08/opinion/1160258412_850215.html

Rana, J. (2007). The story of Islamophobia. *Souls, 9*(2), 148–161.

Rashid, Q. (2017, 2 December). Shariah Law: The five things every non-Muslim (and Muslim) should know. *HuffPost*. Retrieved from https://www.huffingtonpost.com/qasim-rashid/shariah-law-the-five-things-every-non-muslim_b_1068569.html

Rattansi, A. (2007). *Racism: A very short introduction*. Oxford: Oxford University Press.

Reaboi, D. (2010) (edited). *Shariah: The threat to America (an exercise in competitive analysis—report of team 'B' II)*. Washington, DC: The Centre for Security Policy.

Reilly, A. (2016, 16 September). Australia is in danger of being swamped by Muslims? The numbers tell a different story. *The Conversation*. Retrieved from: https://theconversation.com/australia-is-in-danger-of-being-swamped-by-muslims-the-numbers-tell-a-different-story-65477, retrieved on April 23, 2019.

Reporter, S. (2017, 28 March). One nation supporter tells TV show of 'Muslim domination plan'. *9News*.

Richter, N. (2013). *Where Huntington got it wrong*. Retrieved from https://en.qantara.de/node/17072

Riggins, S. H. (1997). The rhetoric of othering. In S. H. Riggins (Ed.), *The language and politics of exclusion: Others in discourse*. London, New Delhi and Thousand Oaks (CA): SAGE Publications.

Robinson, H. (1643). *Liberty of conscience: Or the sole means to obtain peace and truth*. London.

Roland, I, & Recker, J. (2012). Differentiating Islamophobia: Introducing a new scale to measure Islamoprejudice and secular Islam critique. *Political Psychology, 33*(6), 811–824.

Romero, M. (2018). The inclusion of citizenship status in intersectionality: What immigration raids tells us about mixed-status families, the state and assimilation. *International Journal of Sociology of the Family, 34*(2), 131–152.

Ross, A. (1688). *The Alcoran of Mahomet*. London: Randal Taylor.

Roth, N. (1976, Spring). The Jews and the Muslim conquest of Spain. *Jewish Social Studies, 38*(2), 145–158.

Roy, S. (2009). Media representations and othering of the UN in US media in times of conflict post 9/11. Unpublished PhD thesis submitted to Washington State University, USA. Retrieved from http://www.dissertations.wsu.edu/Dissertations/Spring2009/s_roy_042509.pdf

Runnymede Trust (1997). Islamophobia: A challenge for us all. *Commission on British Muslims and Islamophobia*. London: Runnymede Trust.

Rushdie, S. (1988). *Satanic verses: A novel*. New York, NY: Viking Press.

Russett, B. M., Oneal, J. R., & Cox, M. (2000). Clash of civilizations, or realism and liberalism Deja Vu? Some evidence. *Journal of Peace Research, 37*(5), 583–608.

Rychnovska, D. (2014). Securitization and the power of threat framing. *Perspectives: Central European Review of International Affairs, 22*(2), 9–32.

Saeed, A. (2007). *Media, racism and Islamophobia: The representation of Islam and Muslims in the media*. Newcastle: Cambridge Scholars.

Saeed, A. (2015). Racism and Islamophobia: A personal perspective. *Identity Papers: A Journal of British and Irish Studies, 1*(1), 15–31.

Saeed, T. (2016). *Islamophobia and securitization: Religion, ethnicity and the female voice* (eBook). London: Palgrave Macmillan.

Said, E. (1978). *Orientalism*. London: Routledge & Kegan Paul; New York, NY: Penguin.

Said, E. W. (1979). Zionism from the standpoint of its victims. *Social Text, 1,* 7–58.

Said, E. W. (1997). *Covering Islam* (rev. ed). New York, NY: Vintage.

Said, E. (1981). *Covering Islam: Challenges & opportunities for media in the global village. New York Times Book Review*, New York, NY.

Said, E. (1985, Autumn). Orientalism reconsidered. *Race and Class, 27*(2), 1–15.

Said, E. (2001, October 4). Clash of ignorance. *The Nation*. Retrieved from https://www.thenation.com/article/clash-ignorance/

Said, E. (2003). *Orientalism*. New York, NY: Penguin.

Sajis, A. (2006). Islamophobia: A new word for an old fear. In H. Schenker and Z. Abu-Zayyad (Eds.). *Islamophobia and anti-Semitism* (pp. 1–12). Princeton, NJ: Markus Wiener Publishing.

Sajid, A. (2005). A new word for an old fear. *Palestine-Israel Journal, 12*(2). Retrieved from https://pij.org/articles/344/islamophobia-a-new-word-for-an-old-fear

Sale, G. (1734). *The Koran, Commonly Called the Alcoran of Mohammed: Translated into English Immediately from the Original Arabic; with Explanatory Notes, Taken from the Most Approved Commentators, to which is Prefixed a Preliminary Discourse*. London: C. Ackers.

Sardar, Z. (1999). *Orientalism*. Buckingham: Open University Press.

Sardarnia, K., & Bahrampour, Y. (2017). Islam and democracy: A critical reappraisal of adaptation and contrast theories. *Journal of Politics and Law, 10,* 1–12.

Sayyid, S. (2010). Out of the devil's dictionary. In S. Sayyid & A. Vakil (Eds.), *Thinking through islamophobia: Global perspectives* (pp. 5–18). London: Hurst and Co. Publishers.

Sayyid, S. (2014). A measure of Islamophobia. *Islamophobia Studies Journal, 2*(1), 10–25.

Sayyid, S., & Vakil, A. K. (2010). Who's afraid of Islamophobia. In S. Sayyid & A. K. Vakil (Eds.) *Thinking through Islamophobia* (pp. 271–278). Oxford: Oxford University Press.

Scally, D. (2017, 27 February). Police take on Islamophobic trolls after car attack in Heidelberg. *The Irish Times*. Retrieved from https://www.irishtimes.com/news/world/europe/police-take-on-islamophobic-trolls-after-car-attack-in-heidelberg-1.2991342

Schaff, P. (1960). *History of Christian church* (3rd Ed., Vol. 8). Edinburgh: Hendrickson.

Schantz, B. (1993). Islam in Europe: Threat or challenge to Christianity? *Missiology, 21*(4), 443–454.

Schiffer, S. A. (2011). Anti-Semitism and Islamophobia: New enemies, old patterns. *Race and Class, 52*(3), 77–84.

Seib, P. (2005). The news media and 'the clash of civilizations'. In P. Seib (Ed.), *Media and conflict in the twenty-first century* (pp. 217–234). New York, NY: Springer.

Schill, M. H., & Wachter, S. M. (1993). A tale of two cities: Racial and ethnic geographic disparities in home mortgage lending in Boston and Philadelphia. *Journal of Housing Research, 4*(2), 245–276.

Schwartz, S. (2010). Islamophobia: America's new fear industry. *Phi Kappa Phi Forum, 90,* 19–21.

Scroggins, D. (2005). The Dutch–Muslim culture war. *Nation, 280*(25), 21–25.

Semati, M. (2010). Islamophobia, culture and race in the age of empire. *Cultural Studies, 24*(2), 256–275.

Sen, A. K. (1999). Democracy as a universal value. *Journal of Democracy, 10*(3), 3–17.

Servier, A. (1924). *Islam and the psychology of the Musulman.* London: Chapman Hall Ltd.

Seven, S. (2010). Attachment and social behaviors in the period of transition from preschool to first grade. *Social Behavior and Personality, 38*(3), 347–356.

Shadid, P. S. (2002). *Religious freedom and the neutrality of the state: The position of Islam in the European Union* (Vol. 1). Leuven: Peeters Publishers.

Shah, P. (2010). A reflection on the Shari'a debate in Britain. *Studia z Prawa Wyznaniowego (Studies of Ecclesiastical Law). 13,* 71–98.

Shaheer, M. (2010). Concept of clash of civilizations: A comparative analysis between IBN Khaldun and Samuel P. Huntington. *Research Proposal, 12.*

Shadid, W., & Koningsveld, P. S. van (Eds.). (2002). Religious freedom and the neutrality of the state: The position of Islam in the European Union. *Archives de Sciences Sociales des Religions, 136*(4), 214–283.

Sharif, M. S. (2000). Islamic culture and globalization. *Journal for East–West Cultural and Economic Studies,* 12–15.

Sherman, A., Lee, J. M., Gibbons, J., Thomson, J., & Timani, H. (2009). The Islamophobia scale: Instrument development and initial validation. *International Journal for the Psychology of Religion, 19*(2), 92–105.

Shirazi, S. (2002). *Your new enemy.* Retrieved from http://dissidentvoice.org/Articles/Shirazi_Huntington.htm

Shryock, A. (2010). *Islamophobia/Islamophilia: Beyond the politics of enemy and friend.* Bloomington, IN: Indiana University Press.

Shuck, G. (2015). *Online Jihadism: Propaganda, recruitment and homegrown radicalization* (Doctoral Dissertation). Johns Hopkins University. Retrieved from https://jscholarship.library.jhu.edu/handle/1774.2/39436.

Shumack, R. (2017, 21 June). The real factors behind extremist acts. *The Age.*

Siddikoglu, H. (2015). Global economic crisis and insecurity in Afghanistan, Pakistan and Tajikistan. In J. L. Leon-Manriquez & T. Moyo (Eds.), *The global financial and economic crisis in the South: Impact and responses.* (pp. 261–287). Dakar, Senegal: CODESRIA.

Siddiqi, H. (2018). Securitisation of Islam in the West: Analysing Western political and security relations with the Islamic states. *Hiroshima Journal of Peace*, 1, 32–54.

Silva, D. M. D. (2016, March). The othering of Muslims: Discourses of radicalization in the New York Times, 1969–2014. *Sociological Forum, 32*(1), 138–161.

Simon, L. J. (1987). Jews in the legal corpus of Alfonso El Sabio. *Comitatus: A Journal of Medieval and Renaissance Studies, 18*(1), 80–97.

Skanda, S. (2017, 22 June). A new, new right rises in Germany. Retrieved from *The Atlantic*. Retrieved from https://www.theatlantic.com/international/archive/2017/06/a-new-right-rises-in-germany/529971/

Smith, R. B. (1874). *Mohammed and Mohammedanism* (pp.75–85). London: John Murray.

Smedley, A., & Smedley, B. D. (2012). *Race in North America: Origin and evaluation of a world view*. New York, NY: Routlege.

Southern, R. W. (1962). *Western views of Islam in the middle ages*. Cambridge, MA: Harvard University Press.

Soyer, F. (2007). *The persecution of the Jews and Muslims of Portugal. King Manuel I and the end of religious tolerance (1496–7) [The medieval Mediterranean. Peoples, economies and cultures, 400–1500. Volume 69]*. Leiden: Brill.

Spain, Country Coordinator. (2016). Spain: Islamophobia has become the main hate crime. Retrieved from https://ec.europa.eu/migrant-integration/news/spain-islamophobia-has-become-the-main-hate-crime

Spencer, A. (2008). Linking immigrants and terrorists: The use of immigration as an anti-terror policy. *The Online Journal of Peace and Conflict Resolution, 8*(1), 1–24.

Spivak, G. C. (1985). The rani of Sirmur: An essay in reading the archives. *History and Theory, 24*(3), 247–272.

Srivastava, M. (2004). *Narrative construction of India: Forster, Nehru and Rushdie*. New Delhi: Rawat Publications.

Stein, A., & Salime, Z. (2015). Manufacturing Islamophobia: Right wing pseudo-documentaries and the paranoid style. *Journal of Communication Inquiry, 39*(4), 378–396.

Steinbock, B. (1978). Speciesism and the idea of equality. *Philosophy, 53*(204), 247–256.

Stephans. S. (2013). Categorization based on race and 'othering' discourse. Retrieved from https://www.academia.edu/10941489/Categorization_based_on_Race_and_Othering_Discourse

Stephenson, C. (2017). *Orientalism: The constructed, violent Muslim 'race'*. Retrieved from https://digitalcommons.augustana.edu/cgi/viewcontent.cgi?article=1012&context=mabryaward

Stolz, J. (2005). Explaining Islamophobia. A test of four theories based on the case of a Swiss city. *Swiss Journal of Sociology, 31,* 547–566.

Stuchtey, B. (2011). Colonisation and imperialism, 1450–1950. Mainz: Institute of European History.

Sunar, L. (2017). The long history of Islam as a collective 'other' of the West and the rise of islamophobia in the US after Trump. *Insight Turkey, 19*(3), 35–51.

Sztybel, D. (2006). A living will clause for supporters of animal experimentation. *Journal of Applied Philosophy, 23*(2), 173–189.

Tajfel, H., & Turner, C. (1986). The social identity theory of intergroup behavior. In S. W. Austin (Ed.), *Psychology of intergroup relations*. Austin, Chicago, IL: Nelson-Hall Publishers.

Tallmeister, J. (2013). Is immigration a threat to security. Retrieved from https://www.e-ir.info/2013/08/24/is-immigration-a-threat-to-security/

Tamdgidi, M. H. (2006). Editor's note: Probing Islamophobia. *Human Architecture: Journal of the Sociology of Self-Knowledge 5*(1), 7–9.

The Independent Review (2018, February). *An independent review into the application of Shariah Law in England and Wales*. A report submitted to the Command of Her Majesty. Retrieved from https://assets.publishing.service.gov.uk/government/uploads/system/uploads/attachment_data/file/678478/6.4152_HO_CPFG_Report_into_Sharia_Law_in_the_UK_WEB.pdf

Thiara, R. K., Condon, S. A., & Schrottle, M. (2011). *Violence against women and ethnicity: Commonalities and differences across Europe*. Berlin: Barbara Budrich Publishers.

Thomas, G. (2016). *Othering and belonging*. Berkeley, CA: University of California.

Thompson, D., & Mallett, A. (2013). *Christian-Muslim relations. A bibliographical history. Volume 5 (1350–1500)*. Boston, MA: Brill.

Tibi, B. (2007). The totalitarianism of Jihadist Islamism and its challenge to Europe and to Islam. *Totalitarian Movements and Political Religions, 8*(1), 35–54.

Mitchell, R. P. (1993). *The society of the Muslim brothers*. New York, NY: Oxford University Press.

Tolan, J. V. (2002). *Saracens: Islam in the medieval European imagination*. New York, NY: Columbia University Press.

Townsend, P. (2014). *Questioning Islam: Tough questions & honest answers about the Muslim religion*. North Charleston, SC: Createspace Independent Publishing Platform.

Trattner, K. (2016). Religion, games, and othering: An intersectional approach. *Gamevironment, 4*, 24–60.

Tsagarousianou, R. (2016). Muslims in public and media discourse in Western Europe: The reproduction of aporia and exclusion. In S. Mertens & H. de Smaele (Eds.), *Representations of Islam in the news: A cross-cultural analysis* (pp. 3–20). Lanham: Lexington Books.

Turner, B. S. (1989). From orientalism to global sociology. *Sociology, 23*(4), 629–638.

Turner, R. B. (2003). *Islam in the African-American experience* (2nd Ed.). Bloomington, IN: Indiana University Press.

Tyrer, D. (2010). Flooding the embankments: Race, bio-politics and sovereignty. In S. Sayyid & A. Vakil (Eds.). *Thinking through Islamophobia: Global perspectives* (pp. 93–110). London: Hurst and Co.

Tyrer, D. (2013). *The politics of Islamophobia: Race, power and fantasy*. London: Pluto Press.

Uenal, F. (2016). Disentangling Islamophobia: The differential effects of symbolic, realistic, and terroristic threat perceptions as mediators between social dominance orientation and Islamophobia. *Journal of Social and Political Psychology*, 4(1), 66–90.

Ulger, I. K., & Benitez, M. (2017). Islamophobia in France: From racism to 'neo populism.' *LAU Sosyal Bilimler Dergisi*, 8(1), 50–66.

Uludag, M., & Molyneux, J. (2014). Racism and Islamophobia. *Irish Marxist Review*, 3(10), 64–69.

van Dijk, T. A. (1997). Discourse as interaction in society. In T. A. van Dijk (Ed.) *Discourse as social* (pp. 1–37). London: SAGE Publications.

Vascoselos, J. (1948). *La Raza cosmica*. Mexico City: D.F. Espasa Calpe.

Verkuyten, M. (2005). International relations in a changing political context. *Social Psychology Quarterly*, 68(4), 375–386.

Vertigans, S. (2010). British Muslims and the UK government's 'war on terror' within: Evidence of a clash of civilizations or emergent de-civilizing processes? *The British Journal of Sociology*, 61(1), 26–44.

Voll, J. O. (2009). *Impossibilities of the clash of civilization*. Washington, DC: Prince Alwaleed Bin Talal Center for Muslim-Christian Understanding.

Voltaire. (1792). *Recueil des lettres de voltaire (1739–41) [Collection of Voltaire Letters (1739–41)]*. Ohio: Sanson and Company.

Wadumestri, K. (2010). *Being other: The experiences of young Australian-Lebanese-Muslims*. Unpublished PhD thesis from School of Global Studies, Social Science and Planning, RIMT University. Retrieved from https://researchbank. rmit.edu.au/view/rmit:160955/Wadumestri.pdf

Wæver, O. (1993). *Securitization and desecuritization* (p. 48). Copenhagen: Centre for Peace and Conflict Research.

Wallace-Hadrill, J. M. (1981). *The fourth book of the chronicle of Fredegar and its continuators*. London: Praeger.

Wallerstein, I. (2006). The curve of American power. *New Left Review*, 40(6), 77–94.

Wansbrough, J. (2004). *Quranic studies: Sources and methods of scriptural interpretation*. New York, NY: Prometheus Books.

Warner, B. (2017). *Totalitarian Islam*. Video by Bill Warner. Retrieved from https://islamandwesterncivilisation.com/posts/islamic-supremacism/totalitarian-islam-dr-bill-warner/

Warner, B. (2010). *Sharia law for the non-Muslim*. Brno: Center for Study of Political Islam.

Watt, M. (2004). *The influence of Islam on medieval Europe*. Edinburgh: Edinburgh University Press.

Weedon, C. (2004). *Identity and culture: Narratives of difference and belonging*. Berkshire: McGraw-Hill Education.

Weiten, W. (2017). *Psychology: Themes and variations* (10th Ed.). Boston, MA: Cengage Learning.

Werbner, P. (2005). Islamophobia: Incitement to religious hatred—legislating for a new fear? *Anthropology Today, 21*(1), 5–9.

West, C. (2016). *Breaking bread: Insurgent black intellectual life.* Boston, MA: Routledge.

Wiktorowicz, Q. (2001). The new global threat: Transnational Salafis and Jihad. *Middle East Policy, 8*(4), 18–38.

Wilders, G. (2013, February 19). Islam a dangerous and totalitarian ideology. *The Sydney Morning Herald.* Retrieved from https://www.smh.com.au/national/islam-a-dangerous-and-totalitarian-ideology-wilders-20130219-2epx5.html

Willie, C. V. (1975). *Oreo: A perspective on race and marginal men and women.* Cambridge, MA: Parameter Press.

Winant, H. (2001). *The world is a Ghetto: Race and democracy since World War II.* New York, NY: Basic Books.

Wistrich, R. S. (2005). *European anti-Semitism reinvents itself.* New York, NY: The American Jewish Committee.

Wodak, D. R. (2014). Right wing populist parties on the rise. *Cyprus Mail Online.* Retrieved from http://cyprus-mail.com/2014/03/04/right-wing-populist-parties-on-the-rise/

Wohlfeld, M. (2014). Is migration a security issue. Migration in the Mediterranean: Human rights, security and development perspectives. *University of Malta,* 61–77.

Wojcieszak, M. (2014). Aversive racism in Spain—testing the theory. *International Journal of Public Opinion Research, 27*(1), 22–45.

Worchel, S., & Cooper, J. (1988). *Understanding social psychology.* Chicago, IL: Doresay.

Yallop, D. (2007). *The power and the glory: Inside the dark heart of John Paul II'S Vatican.* London: Constable and Robinson Ltd.

Yusuf, H. B. (2007). Managing Muslim–Christian conflicts in Northern Nigeria: A case study of Kaduna state. *Islam and Christian-Muslim Relations, 18*(2), 237–256.

Zafar, I. (2010, January). *Islamophobia, Islamophobes: Towards building a process model.* Retrieved from http://www.researchgate.net

Zelkina, A. (1999). Islam and security in the new states of central Asia: How genuine is the Islamic threat? *Religion, State & Society, 27*(3–4), 355–372.

Zevallos, Z. (2011, 6 October). What is otherness. Retrieved from https://othersociologist.com/otherness-resources/

Zick, A. (2014). *The fragile middle–hostile situations: Right-wing extremist attitudes in Germany.* Bonn: Verlag J.H.W. Dietz.

Zick, A., Pettigrew, T. F., & Wagner, U. (2008). Ethnic prejudice and discrimination in Europe. *Journal of Social Issues, 64*(2), 233–251.

Zolberg, A. R., & Woon, L. L. (1999). Why Islam is like Spanish: Cultural incorporation in Europe and the United States. *Politics & Society, 27*(1), 5–38.

Zúquete, J. P. (2008). The European extreme-right and Islam: New directions? *Journal of Political Ideologies, 13*(3), 321–344.

Index

About the Author

Zafar Iqbal, PhD, has more than 23 years of teaching and research experience. He received doctorate in mass communication in 2003. He serves at International Islamic University, Islamabad, and has published in the reputed national and international journals. During the last 10 years, he remained a post-doctoral scholar at the University of Surrey, UK, University of Southern California, LA, USA, and a Chevening Fellow at the University of Oxford, UK. His work aims at exploring the negative sentiments that historically exist between Muslims and non-Muslims, and attempts to figure out the present state of hostility towards Muslims/Islam in the contemporary media-dominated world. His basic assumption explains that Islamophobia as a phenomenon is historic in nature, and contemporary construction is mainly mediated and its epistemic/symbolic dimension has different connotations. As such, its construction is rendered in a pluralistic manner; hence, it appears as a corpus constituted of Islamophobias. He tested an instrument for measuring Islamophobia in the epistemological spheres by finding its nexus with media and other social antecedents.